LACLAU

Over the last thirty years, the work of the political theorist Ernesto Laclau has reinvigorated radical political and social theory. Taking concepts previously ignored or unused within mainstream political theory, such as the political, hegemony, discourse and identity, he has made them fundamental to thinking about politics and social theory. Resisting the dead end of postmodern politics, his work has drawn in stimulating ways on Gramscian, poststructuralist and psychoanalytic theory.

Laclau: A Critical Reader is the first full-length critical appraisal of Laclau's work and includes contributions from several leading philosophers and theorists. The first section examines Laclau's theory that the contest between universalism and particularism provides much of the philosophical background to political and social struggle, taking up the important place accorded to, amongst others, Hegel and Lacan in Laclau's work. The second section of the book considers what Laclau's 'radical democracy' might look like and reflects on its ethical implications, particularly in relation to Laclau's post-Marxism and thinkers such as Jürgen Habermas. The final section investigates the place of hegemony in Laclau's work, the idea for which he is perhaps best known.

This stimulating collection also includes replies to his critics by Laclau and the important exchange between Laclau and Judith Butler on equality, making it an excellent companion to Laclau's work and essential reading for students of political and social theory.

Contributors: Judith Butler, William E. Connolly, Simon Critchley, Fred Dallmayr, Mark Devenney, Torben Dyrberg, Rodolphe Gasché, Jason Glynos, David Howarth, Ernesto Laclau, Oliver Marchart, J. Hillis Miller, Aletta Norval, Rado Riha, Urs Stäheli, Jelica Šumič, Yannis Stavrakakis, Linda Zerilli.

Simon Critchley is Professor of Philosophy at the New School for Social Research, New York and at the University of Essex. **Oliver Marchart** is a lecturer in Cultural and Media Theory at the University of Basel and in Political Theory at the University of Vienna.

LACLAU

A critical reader

Edited by
Simon Critchley and Oliver Marchart

LONDON AND NEW YORK

First published 2004
by Routledge
2 Park Square, Milton Park, Abingdon, Oxon OX14 4RN

Simultaneously published in the USA and Canada
by Routledge
270 Madison Ave, New York, NY 10016

Reprinted 2006, 2008

Routledge is an imprint of the Taylor & Francis Group, an informa business

Typeset in Goudy by
HWA Text and Data Management Ltd, Tunbridge Wells
Printed and bound in Great Britain by
MPG Books Ltd, Bodmin

British Library Cataloguing in Publication Data
A catalogue record for this book is available from the British Library

Library of Congress Cataloging in Publication Data
A catalog record for this book has been requested
Laclau : a critical reader / edited by Simon Critchley and
Oliver Marchart.
p. cm
Includes bibliographical references.
1. Laclau, Ernesto. 2. Political science–Philosophy.
I. Critchley, Simon, 1960– II. Marchart, Oliver.
JC255.L33L33 2004
320'.01'1–dc22

ISBN 978–0–415–23843–4 (hardcover)
ISBN 978–0–415–23844–1 (pbk)

CONTENTS

List of contributors vii
Acknowledgements x
List of abbreviations x

Introduction 1
SIMON CRITCHLEY AND OLIVER MARCHART

PART I
Philosophy: universality, singularity, difference 15

1 How empty can empty be? On the place of the universal 17
RODOLPHE GASCHÉ

2 Laclau and hegemony: some (post) Hegelian caveats 35
FRED DALLMAYR

3 Politics and the ontological difference: on the 'strictly philosophical' in Laclau's work 54
OLIVER MARCHART

4 Politics as the real of philosophy 73
RADO RIHA

5 This universalism which is not one 88
LINDA M. G. ZERILLI

PART II
Democracy: politics, ethics, normativity 111

6 Is there a normative deficit in the theory of hegemony? 113
SIMON CRITCHLEY

7 **Ethics and politics in discourse theory** 123
MARK DEVENNEY

8 **Democratic decisions and the question of universality: rethinking recent approaches** 140
ALETTA NORVAL

9 **The ethos of democratization** 167
WILLIAM E. CONNOLLY

10 **Anachronism of emancipation or fidelity to politics** 182
JELICA ŠUMIČ

PART III
Hegemony: discourse, rhetorics, antagonism 199

11 **Encounters of the real kind: sussing out the limits of Laclau's embrace of Lacan** 201
JASON GLYNOS AND YANNIS STAVRAKAKIS

12 **'Taking up a task': moments of decision in Ernesto Laclau's thought** 217
J. HILLIS MILLER

13 **Competing figures of the limit: dispersion, transgression, antagonism, and indifference** 226
URS STÄHELI

14 **The political and politics in discourse analysis** 241
TORBEN BECH DYRBERG

15 **Hegemony, political subjectivity, and radical democracy** 256
DAVID HOWARTH

PART IV
A reply 277

16 **Glimpsing the future** 279
ERNESTO LACLAU

Appendix I: the uses of equality 329
JUDITH BUTLER AND ERNESTO LACLAU

Appendix II: bibliography of Ernesto Laclau's work 345

Index 348

CONTRIBUTORS

Judith Butler is the Maxine Elliot Professor in the Department of Rhetorics and Comparative Literature at the University of California, Berkeley. Her books include *Antigone's Claim: Kinship Between Life and Death* (Columbia University Press, 2000), *Contingency, Hegemony, Universality*, with Ernesto Laclau and Slavoj Žižek, (Verso, 2000), *The Psychic Life of Power: Theories of Subjection* (Stanford University Press, 1997), and *Gender Trouble: Feminism and the Subversion of Identity* (Routledge, 1990).

William E. Connolly is Professor of Political Science at Johns Hopkins University. His books include *Why I am Not a Secularist* (University of Minnesota Press, 1999), *The Ethos of Pluralization* (University of Minnesota Press 1995), *Identity\Difference: Democratic Negotiations of Political Paradox* (Cornell University Press, 1991) and *The Terms of Political Discourse* (Princeton University Press, 1983).

Simon Critchley is Professor of Philosophy at the New School for Social Research, New York and at the University of Essex. His authored books include *The Ethics of Deconstruction: Derrida and Levinas* (Blackwell, 1992), *Very Little ... Almost Nothing. Death, Philosophy, Literature* (Routledge, 1997), *Ethics–Politics–Subjectivity. Essays on Derrida, Levinas and Contemporary French Thought* (Verso, 1999), and *On Humour* (Routledge, 2002).

Fred Dallmayr holds the Dee Chair of Political Theory at the University of Notre Dame. He is the author of, among other books, *Dialogue Among Civilizations* (Palgrave Macmillan, 2002), *Alternative Visions. Paths in the Global Village* (Rowman & Littlefield, 1998), *The Other Heidegger* (Cornell University Press, 1993), *Polis and Praxis. Exercises in Contemporary Political Theory* (MIT Press, 1984).

Mark Devenney teaches philosophy, politics and critical theory at the University of Brighton. He is the author of *Ethics and Politics in Contemporary Critical Theory* (Routledge 2004).

Torben Bech Dyrberg lectures at the Department of Social Sciences, Roskilde University. He is the author of *The Circular Structure of Power: Politics, Identity, Community* (Verso, 1997).

Rodolphe Gasché is Eugenio Donato Professor of Comparative Literature at the University of New York at Buffalo. His books include *The Idea of Form: Rethinking Kant's Aesthetics* (Stanford University Press, 2002), *Of Minimal Things: Essays on the Notion of Relation* (Stanford University Press, 2000), *The Wild Card of Reading: On Paul De Man* (Harvard University Press, 1998), and *The Tain of the Mirror: Derrida and the Philosophy of Reflection* (Harvard University Press, 1988).

Jason Glynos is Lecturer at the Department of Government, University of Essex, and co-editor of *Lacan and Science* (Karnac Books, 2002).

David Howarth lectures at the Department of Government, University of Essex. He is the author of *Discourse* (Open University Press, 2000) and co-editor of *Discourse Theory and Political Analysis: Identities, Hegemonies and Social Change* (Edinburgh University Press 2000).

Oliver Marchart lectures in Cultural and Media Studies at the University of Basel and Political Philosophy at the University of Vienna. His most recent books are *Techno-Colonialism. Theory and Imaginary Cartography of Culture and the Media* (Löcker, 2004), and *Starting the World Anew. Hannah Arendt and the Revolution of the Political* (Turia + Kant, forthcoming), both in German. He is the editor of *Das Undarstellbare der Politik: Zur Hegemonietheorie Ernesto Laclaus* (Turia + Kant, 1998).

J. Hillis Miller is Distinguished Professor at the University of California at Irvine. His many books include *Others* (Princeton University Press, 2001), *Speech Acts in Literature* (Stanford University Press, 2001), *Black Holes: Cultural Memory in the Present* (Stanford University Press, 1999), and *Topographies* (Stanford University Press, 1994).

Aletta Norval is Director of the Doctoral Programme in Ideology and Discourse Analysis at the University of Essex. She is author of *Deconstructing Apartheid Discourse* (Verso, 1996) and co-editor of *Discourse Theory and Political Analysis: Identities, Hegemonies and Social Change* (Edinburgh University Press 2000).

Rado Riha is Head of the Institute for Philosophy of the Slovenian Academy of Science and the Arts. He is co-author of *Law and Judgement* (Ljubljana 1993), and co-editor of *Politics of Truth* (Turia + Kant 1993) and *'Singularité' dans la psychanalyse, singularité de la psychanalyse* (CIPh, PUF, 1998).

Urs Stäheli is Professor of Sociology at the University of Berne. He is author of *Potstructuralist Sociologies* (Transcript, 2000, in German) and *Signifying Failure: A Deconstructive Reading of Niklas Luhmann's Systems Theory* (Velbrück, 1999, in German).

Yannis Stavrakakis is currently Fellow at the Princeton University Program in Hellenic Studies. He is the author of *Lacan and the Political* (Routledge 1999) and co-editor of *Lacan and Science* (Karnac Books, 2002) and *Discourse Theory and Political Analysis: Identities, Hegemonies and Social Change* (Edinburgh University Press, 2000).

Jelica Šumič is a Senior Research Fellow at the Institute for Philosophy of the Slovenian Academy of Science and the Arts. She is the author of *The Totemic Masks of Democracy* (Ljubljana 1996), *Mutations of Ethics: From the Utopia of Happiness to the Incurable Truth* (Ljubljana 2002), and co-editor *'Singularité' dans la psychanalyse, singularité de la psychanalyse* (CIPh, PUF, 1998).

Linda M. G. Zerilli is Professor of Political Science, Northwestern University. She is author of *Signifying Woman: Culture and Chaos in Rousseau, Burke, and Mill* (Cornell University Press, 1994) and the forthcoming *Feminism without Solace* (University of Chicago Press).

ACKNOWLEDGEMENTS

An earlier version of Fred Dallmayr's chapter was published as 'Hegemony and Democracy: On Laclau and Mouffe', in *Strategies* 30 (Fall 1988), pp. 29–49. Linda Zerilli's chapter, 'This universalism which is not one', was first published in *Diacritics* 28.2 (1998), pp. 3–20. The exchange between Judith Butler and Ernesto Laclau was previously published in *Diacritics* 27.1 (1997), pp. 3–15. We are grateful to the authors and publishers for their permission to reprint the essays.

LIST OF ABBREVIATIONS

PIM	*Politics and Ideology in Marxist Theory*, London: New Left Books, 1977.
HSS	*Hegemony and Socialist Strategy*, London: Verso, 1985, with Chantal Mouffe.
NR	*New Reflections on the Revolution of Our Time*, London: Verso, 1990.
E	*Emancipation(s)*, London: Verso, 1996.

INTRODUCTION

Simon Critchley and Oliver Marchart

A life in politics

Ernesto Laclau's work is one of the most innovative and influential contemporary efforts at reviving and rearticulating political thought at a time when the latter's grounds have become increasingly uncertain. Traditional concepts in political theory are more and more conceived as 'essentially contestable'. The meanings of the traditional categories of political thought can no longer be taken for granted. Without being able to appeal to secure foundations, we are obliged to raise fundamental questions: what is the nature of 'politics' and 'the political'? To what extent is something like 'society' possible? How might we conceive of the 'subject'? How is social and cultural 'identity' constructed? How might we draw the borders of 'community'? How can the relation between 'power' and the social world be conceptualized? What is the nature, if there is one, of 'order', of 'representation', of 'ideology'? How can we rethink the notions of 'freedom' and 'equality'? And can we revive our ideas of 'democracy' and of 'emancipation'?

Laclau's work has attempted to provide answers to these questions and to reformulate the basic concepts of political theory in a time of their disintegration.[1] Yet he is keen to stress that the reasons for this disintegration are not to be found *within* theory alone. For Laclau, there are historical factors which led to the collapse of the formerly stable categories of political theory: the general retreat of the very idea of an ultimate ground or basis of society; the proliferation of new social and political struggles from the 1960s onwards; the multiplication of power centres in an epoch of increasingly disorganized capitalism; the relative decline of the nation state and post-colonial conflicts between the developing and developed world; the demise of the hegemony of the Fordist compromise; and the end of the totalizing ideologies that sustained the Cold War. Vice versa, theory is far from being disconnected from other social domains as there are many examples where intellectual developments produced a series of historical effects. Therefore, for Laclau, the separation between political theory and political practice is 'largely an artificial operation' (1994: 2).

This reciprocal contamination of the political and the theoretical domains can be witnessed in Laclau's own intellectual biography. Growing up in Buenos Aires in the 1940s, he was deeply influenced by the experience of Peronist populism. In 1958 he joined the Argentinian Socialist Party and was active in the student movement. In 1963, he joined ranks with the Socialist Party of the National Left, a splinter group of the Argentinian Socialist Party, becoming a member of its political leadership until 1968 as well as the editor of the party's weekly journal *Lucha Obrera*. In later interviews he dates his 'first lesson in hegemony' to this decade. Argentina in the 1960s was witnessing rapid social dislocation and the *coup d'état* of 1966 led to the proliferation of new antagonisms. Simultaneously, Peronism sought to provide an alternative horizon for anti-establishment symbols and to hegemonize more and more social demands. 'All I tried to think theoretically later', Laclau recounts, 'the dispersal of subject positions, the hegemonic recomposition of fragmented identities, the reconstitution of social identities through the political imaginary – all that is something I learnt in those years in the course of practical activism' (*NR* 180). Already as the editor of *Lucha Obrera*, that is, twenty years before the appearance of his and Chantal Mouffe's *Hegemony and Socialist Strategy*, he would write leader articles in which he argued for the hegemonization of democratic tasks by the socialists' struggle for working class interests. So, while there was an obvious element of class reductionism in the party's ideology, encapsulated in the assumption that there were 'natural' interests of the working class, the experience of Argentinian populism taught Laclau exactly the opposite: political alliances had to be constructed not along class lines but *beyond* class lines in a constant effort to hegemonize a larger universal task.

This led him increasingly to abandon all forms of class reductionism. In the articles written in 1969 after he came to England, and later collected in his first book *Politics and Ideology in Marxist Theory* of 1977, he had, for instance, criticized Poulantzas's reduction of the populist ideology of the 'national-popular' to the level of classes. In his later work, Laclau extended and radicalized his critique of Althusserian-style determinism 'in the last instance'. So, if we follow Laclau's trajectory as a theorist it would be difficult to discover a radical break in his thinking. What we find instead is an enlargement or theoretical elucidation of intuitions born out of political activism. When he started to read Gramsci and Althusser in the mid-1960s, his 'interpretation was essentially political and non-dogmatic because', as he says, 'I could relate it directly to my own Argentinian experience' (*NR* 199). Even his later reading of post-structuralism was always informed by the experience of political practice:

> [W]hen today I read *Of Grammatology*, *S/Z*, or the *Écrits* of Lacan, the examples which always spring to mind are not from philosophical or literary texts; they are from a discussion in an Argentinian trade union, a clash of opposing slogans at a demonstration, or a debate during a party congress. Throughout his life Joyce returned to his native experience in Dublin; for me it is those years of political struggle in Argentina of the 1960s that come to mind as a point of reference and comparison (*NR* 200).

Four shifts in political thinking: the novelty of *Hegemony and Socialist Strategy*

When Ernesto Laclau and Chantal Mouffe's *Hegemony and Socialist Strategy* was published in 1985, it triggered a series of significant transformations of both political and theoretical debates on the left. Although it initially inflamed a whole series of sometimes polemical debates about the 'true nature' of Marxism, it turned out to be immensely influential for many other areas, among them, democracy theory, social movement theory, discourse analysis, cultural studies, or regulation theory. Looking back after twenty years, and trying to delineate the trajectory of the book's influence, we detect at least four reasons for its impact.

First of all, *Hegemony and Socialist Strategy* transformed the very presuppositions of the Marxist problematic. But what was attempted by Laclau and Mouffe was not so much a complete refusal of everything which goes under the name of Marxism as a strengthening of a particular trait within Marxism: the Gramscian tradition. By putting Antonio Gramsci's category of hegemony centre stage, Laclau and Mouffe were able to undermine the deterministic assumptions of more traditional versions of Marxism, for instance the Marxism of the Second International. The category of hegemony allowed them to dismantle the Marxist dichotomy between economic 'base' and politico-ideological 'superstructure', with which Marx briefly flirted in the 'Preface' to *A Contribution to the Critique of Political Economy*, and which was so important for Engels, where the 'superstructure' would always be determined by the 'base' (albeit in the 'last instance'). So, the first of Laclau and Mouffe's interventions consisted both in the weakening of Marxist economism and in the radicalization of the Gramscian concept of hegemony.[2] In *Hegemony and Socialist Strategy*, and in particular in Laclau's later work, 'hegemony' has become a name for the general logic of the political institution of the social. As a consequence of this move, the realm of politics was significantly extended to the institution of the social as such, where political identities are articulated on a terrain which is primary and not derivable from any underlying 'reality', such as the economic 'laws of motion' that govern the relations of production.

This brings us to the second shift initiated by *Hegemony and Socialist Strategy*. For if the political is primary and constitutive of the social and not derivable from any other instance, then no social actor is able to lay claim to a privileged position in society. Hence, 'class' as a political actor loses its ontological privilege. Instead, we have to confront the phenomenon of a potentially endless chain of social actors forming their identities around notions other than class – such as gender, race, ethnicity, or sexual orientation. While Laclau and Mouffe were not alone in 'discovering' what came to be known as the New Social Movements, they certainly were most consistent in spelling out the consequences of their appearance for a general political project of the left. For what emerged with these diverse struggles, from an emancipatory perspective, was the need for their common articulation without however assigning a new form of ontological privilege to one group or another. Laclau and Mouffe responded to this problem by proposing, in the last chapter of their book, the project of a *radical and plural democracy*. If this project is called 'radical', it is because one of its goals is to expand egalitarian effects into more and more areas of the social. If, on the other hand, it is called 'plural', it is because the relative autonomy of the demands of different groups has to be accepted and articulated into a larger common movement, what is called 'a chain of equivalence'. From this point, Chantal Mouffe went on, in many books and articles (see Mouffe 1989, 1992, 1993, 1996, 2000), to develop the project of a radical and plural democracy with respect to and in contradistinction to political liberalism as well as in relation to political thinkers like Carl Schmitt. For his part, Ernesto Laclau, as we will see presently, advanced the debate on radical democracy by reflecting on the emancipatory tradition and specifically on the relation between particularism and universalism.

Third, *Hegemony and Socialist Strategy* decisively contributed to the 'discursive turn' within the social sciences. Insofar as social identity loses all points of anchorage in an allegedly deeper reality, identity is the outcome of a discursive construction or, to use their technical term, a discursive *articulation*.[3] In this way, the social as such is entirely reconceptualized by Laclau and Mouffe in terms of discursivity: it is simply another name for the 'discursive'.[4] What developed from here was a specific form of social and political inquiry sometimes called the 'Essex school' of political discourse analysis.[5] In *Hegemony and Socialist Strategy* the groundwork for this sort of discourse analysis was laid to the extent that Laclau and Mouffe introduced some of its key concepts and tools. For instance, they described the mechanism of identity formation by introducing a highly original concept of antagonism. The latter is supposed to account for the process by which the social, that is the realm of discursive differences, becomes homogenized into a chain of equivalence *vis-à-vis* a purely negative outside. For example, in a state of oppression, different social sectors may establish amongst themselves a relation of equivalence *vis-à-vis* their constitutive outside, the oppressor, yet the differences between these sectors will remain forgotten as long as their antagonistic relation towards the oppressor stays intact. In a situation of *decreasing* antagonism, the equivalential relation will be transformed step by step back into an array of differences. Hegemony then, from this point of view, is to be understood as the effort to discursively construct out of a terrain of differences the 'historical block' of a specific hegemonic formation. Laclau and Mouffe's strategy to reconceptualize 'the social' in terms of discursive articulation has led them to perhaps one of the most controversial claims in *Hegemony and Socialist Strategy*, namely the *impossibility of society*: 'The social *is* articulation insofar as "society" is impossible' (*HSS* 114). One should not overlook the fact that this claim neatly follows from the paradigm shift initiated by Laclau and Mouffe, for if the discursive is considered as primary with respect to all social identities, then we will never be in a situation where society has found its ultimate ground or achieved totality, where antagonism disappears and politics ends. The impossibility of society is a necessary implication of Laclau and Mouffe's constructivism: 'If the social does not manage to fix itself in the intelligible and instituted forms of a *society*,' they write, 'the social only exists, however, as an effort to construct that impossible object' (*HSS* 112).[6]

This brings us to the fourth important shift initiated by *Hegemony and Socialist Strategy*, what one could call a decisive displacement of post-structuralist thought. Obviously, Laclau's scepticism about whether such a thing as a 'closed totality' can exist is shared with many strands of post-structuralism. But with *Hegemony and Socialist Strategy* post-structuralist thought was, for the first time, extensively employed as a 'tool' for political analysis in the strict sense. For instance, the Lacanian theory of 'nodal points' was employed in order to account for processes of the hegemonic fixing of discourse. Laclau and Mouffe's overall strategy though was 'deconstructive' in many respects. This strategy would lead Laclau in his later works to the deconstruction of many classical notions of political and social thought: power, order, representation, universality/particularity, community, ideology, emancipation, and, of course, the very categories of politics, the political, society, and the social.[7] Yet, as Laclau made clear, deconstruction is in need of being complemented by a theory of hegemony. If the deconstructive operation consists in laying open the moment of ultimate undecidability inherent to any structure, hegemony provides us with a theory of the *decision* taken on such undecidable terrain (1996; *E* 66–83). Hence, post-structuralism encountered a political turn initiated in *Hegemony and Socialist Strategy* and further developed by Laclau in his later work.

Elusive universality: *New Reflections on the Revolution of our Time* and *Emancipation(s)*

In his publications after *Hegemony and Socialist Strategy*, in particular in *New Reflections on the Revolution of Our Time* from 1990, Laclau went on to spell out in an even more coherent fashion the framework of his political post-structuralism. While in *Hegemony* the argument was partly presented in the form of a genealogy and deconstruction of the history of Marxism, *New Reflections* attempts what he calls the 'impossible task' of presenting the argument 'as a logical sequence of its categories' (*NR* 4). It would not be an exaggeration to claim that *New Reflections* constitutes Laclau's *discours de la méthode*. Apart from a systematic deepening of the argument delivered in *Hegemony*, *New Reflections* includes two major reformulations of the earlier position. While remaining within the larger horizon of deconstruction, Laclau pushes further the Lacanian aspects of his previous arguments. An influential critique by Slavoj Žižek (1990, see also Laclau and Zac 1994) brought Laclau to supplement the rather structuralist idea of 'subject positions', central to the framework of *Hegemony*, with a notion of the subject as *lack* within the structure. This move allowed Laclau to avoid the impasse of an entirely passive notion of subjectivity – where the subject's position is allocated by the constructive movement of the structure – without however having to resort to the equally unfeasible idea of the classical Cartesian or voluntarist notion of the subject. As a consequence, identity is no longer conceived as a mere effect of structural construction, but is the outcome of processes of *identification* triggered by an originary 'lack of identity' named 'the subject'. Secondly, Laclau decided to radicalize his and Mouffe's notion of antagonism as the limit of the social by, again, introducing a more primary category: *dislocation*. The latter is now supposed to account for the fact that the social, or society as a purported totality, *is always already* 'dislocated' by an outside which, however, must not always or necessarily be discursively constructed in the form of antagonism.[8]

However, Laclau's work after *Hegemony* made it increasingly clear that it would be a mistake to reduce it to just another variant of post-structuralism. Laclau himself refers us to other sources of inspiration: phenomenology and post-analytic philosophy, in particular Husserl and Wittgenstein (*NR* 212). There is a strong philosophical character to many of Laclau's arguments. Large parts of his exchange with Judith Butler and Slavoj Žižek entitled *Contingency, Hegemony, Universality. Contemporary Dialogues on the Left* from 2000 turn around their respective approaches towards Hegel, whilst Heidegger's work is also a significant influence on Laclau's arguments. Laclau's work is clearly part of the anti-foundationalist philosophical tendency that can be found in Nietzsche, phenomenology, post-analytic philosophy, and post-structuralism. Given the philosophical affiliations of Laclau's thought, it should not come as a surprise that, in his 1996 book *Emancipation(s)*, a collection of some of his most important essays, Laclau chose to intervene in the debates around identity politics and multiculturalism by reformulating the very philosophical grounds of those debates.

Basically, the matter turns around the question of how new (and not quite so new) identities and cultural differences can be politically empowered in an emancipatory way. The spectrum of possible answers ranges from the strict segregationism of certain sectarian versions of identity politics to the more celebratory and anarchist affirmation of multiple, fluid, schizoid, liminal, nomadic, or hybrid identities. Laclau's view is certainly not compatible with either end of the scale. Yet, for Laclau, such theories answer to a common problem whose categorial roots lie in philosophy: the problem of the relation between universalism and particularism. Laclau's decisive contribution to this politico-theoretical debate in *Emancipation(s)* consists precisely in a radical reformulation of the relation between the universal and the particular. The tension between these terms, he warns us, must not be dissolved in favour of one or the other side. On the one hand, purely particularistic strategies – enclosing themselves within their own cultural or social identity – would not be able to enter or form a broader coalition with other forces. Instead, they would be in constant danger of ending up in some sort of self-imposed apartheid. On the other hand, a purely universalistic stance, as is the case with the Habermasian inheritors of Enlightenment rationalism, is in danger of transcending all particularism in the name of universal and rational consensus. Laclau provides us with a different and distinctive answer: Granting the necessity of some version of universalism and refusing the idea of pure particularism, Laclau in effect *inverts* the very status of the universal. It is no longer a name for the ultimate ground of the social, such as the category of 'reason' for the Enlightenment, but it is emptied of any concrete content, turning into the name of the impossible foundation of the social, another name for the absence of any ultimate ground.

Thus, the universal does not simply disappear but is retained as a necessary dimension of all social and political action. Since an extreme particularism would constitute a Leibnizian world of unconnected monads or a Hobbesian war of all against all, universality must remain there as the empty horizon of the social – a horizon, however, which will never be entirely filled up by a given particularism even though particular forces and actors will strive to incarnate it. So, the concept of *hegemony* is now understood and reformulated by Laclau as the relation between the dimensions of the universal and the particular. Within a hegemonic relation, a particular demand, group or identity takes on the task of incarnating an absent and empty universality. Obviously, the particular group will always to a certain degree play the role of an impostor. However, while no particularism will ever manage to fulfil this task, some orientation towards the universal dimension remains indispensable as long as a political project is intended to generate some hegemonic effects.

This also has obvious consequences for a political project of *radical and plural democracy*. If a politics of pure particularism or sheer multiplicity is a recipe for political failure and defeat, then a radical form of postmodernism is simply not a feasible option. As a consequence, the emancipatory tradition in politics and theory cannot simply be thrown into the dustbin of history. Of course, the demise of the classical totalizing discourses on emancipation and the simultaneous multiplication of social identities is a historical fact. But although the pure universalism of the Enlightenment project can be put to rest, figures and elements from the emancipatory tradition are set free and can be rhetorically recombined and rearticulated in a fresh way. So the deconstruction of the classical grand narrative of emancipation in the singular becomes a precondition for emancipatory movements in the plural: hence, *Emancipation(s)*. Conceived in this way, a radical democratic project would be one in which the ineliminable tension between universalism and particularism is consciously retained, the contingent nature of the political enterprise is fully accepted, and the dimension of universality remains as an empty horizon not to be turned into another positive ground.

A contemporary polylogue on the left

All of which brings us to the book that you now have in your hands. Many contributions to the volume engage, in one way or another, with Laclau's influential reformulation of the concept of universalism. While the latter reappears elsewhere in the book, there is a special focus on universality in Part I of the volume, 'Philosophy: universality, singularity, difference'. The contributors to this section are concerned with the philosophical implications or 'groundwork' of Laclau's theory. The role Hegel and Heidegger play for the latter is dealt with, with particular attention to the question of difference. Rodolphe Gasché investigates the philosophical status of an empty universality. Philosophy's role today, Gasché claims, should be to inquire into the consequences of the dislocation of the metaphysical concept of ground as it is implicated by Laclau's post-foundational theory of the empty universal. By referring to Husserl's idea of 'Europe' – understood as a task critically transcending all particularities – he also proposes to seriously consider a universality 'less' empty than Laclau's. Linda Zerilli, in her contribution, delineates the historical and philosophical contours of universality as well as discussing the current debates raging around the term. In particular she spells out the implications of Laclau's 'universalism which is not One' for feminist practice. Fred Dallmayr, concentrating on *Hegemony and Socialist Strategy*, investigates the relation of the latter to Hegel's philosophy and the questions of negativity, contingency, and necessity. For Dallmayr, *Hegemony* has to be understood as an important contribution to what he calls post-Hegelian political theory. Yet Dallmayr also discerns a Heideggerian note in Laclau and Mouffe's proposal to conceive of necessity and contingency, ground and abyss, in terms of their mutual implication. The point is taken up in the contribution by Oliver Marchart who brings our attention to the role played by ontological difference in Laclau's work. He sees the frequent employment of the ontological difference as an intervention of the 'strictly philosophical' into Laclau's work and as a basis for his differentiation between universalism and particularism. Nevertheless, the latter would have to be supplemented by the categories of the singular and the absolute as their ontological 'limit cases'. Rado Riha, from a Lacanian perspective, also points out the intrinsic relation between the universal and the singular, holding that both coincide in the place of a 'singular universal' which is nothing else than the place of the subject. Riha claims that the introduction of the idea of a singular universal amounts to both a philosophical and political intervention, thus subverting philosophy's traditional approach to politics.

Part II – 'Democracy: politics, ethics, normativity' – is devoted to Laclau's idea of radical democracy and its ethical and normative implications. Simon Critchley, in his chapter, makes the claim that if Laclau's theory is not to collapse into decisionism or voluntarism, an ethical dimension – understood best in Levinasian terms as infinite responsibility – is required. Critchley takes issue with Laclau's recent distinction between the ethical and the normative and asks what a specifically *democratic* form of hegemony would imply. Mark Devenney too is concerned with the normative implications of Laclau's theory from the standpoint of Frankfurt School critical theory. He holds that every ontology of the social rests on hidden normative presuppositions. For Devenney, Laclau's post-Marxism constitutes, in various ways, a critique comparable to the critique of instrumental rationality. Aletta Norval's contribution focuses on the relation between radical democracy and Habermasian-inspired variants of deliberative democracy. While Norval argues that the idea of a rational consensus is overstressed by deliberative models and that actual processes of decision-making are better accounted for by a post-structuralist approach, she argues for an alternative account that comes to terms with the fuzzy borders between deliberation on the one hand and the force of rhetoric and persuasion on the other. William E. Connolly proposes a different way to fold an ethical dimension into political engagement. What he calls an 'ethos of democratization' is not reducible to liberal values but, rather, combines the virtues of 'agonistic respect' and critical generosity into what he calls a 'politics of becoming'. While Connolly's points of reference can be found on the trajectory from Nietzsche to Deleuze, Jelica Šumič takes as her starting points the work of Lacan and Alain Badiou. Šumič argues that it is the 'fidelity to emancipation' which distinguishes radical democracy from other hegemonic projects and, thus, introduces an ethical moment into Laclau's theory.

In Part III – 'Hegemony: discourse, rhetoric, antagonism' – the reader will find articles assembled that seek to interrogate and develop further certain key concepts of Laclau's theory of hegemony. A dialogue is established between the latter and other disciplines such as psychoanalysis, rhetorics, systems theory, or Anglo-American political science. Jason Glynos and Yannis Stavrakakis make a case for the complementary articulation of Lacanian categories such as fantasy or *jouissance* with Laclau's discourse theory. Only by integrating a psychoanalytic dimension, they claim, will the theory of hegemony be in a position to thoroughly explicate the working of ideology. J. Hillis Miller's contribution is occupied mainly with Laclau's recent turn towards rhetoric. Miller welcomes Laclau's articulation of the theory of hegemony with rhetoric and presents us with a discussion of Laclau's engagement with Paul de Man's work. However, Miller holds, if we take the classical trivium of grammar, rhetoric, and logic as a yardstick, then Laclau's work is dominated by logic rather than rhetoric. Urs Stäheli's contribution puts the focus on competing figures of the limit, comparing the Laclauian concept of antagonism with, on the one hand, the Foucauldian figure of transgression and, on the other, the Luhmannian notion of the limit. Stäheli contends that while Foucault leaves us with more questions than answers, Laclau's concept of antagonism seems to be over-politicized if we compare it to the one by Luhmann, that is, with a non-antagonistic account of systemic closure. Torben Dyrberg is concerned with the concept of the political in the theory of hegemony. He observes that the logic of hegemony is located on two levels, which is why he proposes to differentiate the concept of the political from the concept of politics. While politics can be understood as the actual process of filling the empty place of identity, the political constitutes something like a primary terrain or condition of any hegemonic relationship. Starting from this distinction Dyrberg proceeds to systematize the conceptual framework of discourse analysis. David Howarth, after having discussed the different stages through which the notion of hegemony evolved in Laclau's work, turns toward a comparison of the latter with Anglo-American political science. In particular he points out the way in which Laclau's theory could contribute to reconfiguring the structure/agency debate. Howarth also suggests some future research tasks for discourse analysis and then closes the series of contributions by taking up once again the question of normativity and radical democracy.

Thinking of the subtitle of the recent exchange between Ernesto Laclau, Judith Butler and Slavoj Žižek, 'contemporary dialogues on the left', it would perhaps not be too exaggerated to claim that our volume constitutes an even more complex *polylogue* on the left. Not only because the articles in different ways 'communicate' with each other about many concepts and arguments in an effort to extend the horizon of the theory of hegemony and radical democracy, but also because Ernesto Laclau, in a most generous way, has made every effort to answer every single article in the volume. Laclau's contribution is more than a simple reply, as he takes the opportunity to engage with this 'polylogue' in order to specify and elaborate on different aspects of his theory.

This book has been several years in the making and a number of debts have been incurred. First, Simon Critchley would like to acknowledge an asymmetrical division of labour, particularly in the final stages of the preparation of the manuscript, and would like to thank Oliver Marchart. Second, Noreen Harburt of the Centre for Theoretical Studies at Essex has helped with this project at every turn and at every stage and we are both very much in her debt for all her hard work. Third, at Routledge, we would like to thank Tony Bruce for commissioning this book and for his encouragement along the way, Muna Khogali for her work at the beginning of the project, and Julia Rebaudo for her work seeing the manuscript through to production. Fourthly, we would like to thank all our contributors for their intelligence and patience. Finally, we would like to thank Ernesto for his enthusiasm and care for this project, his intellectual comradeship, his judgement and humour, and his uncanny ability to sing the *Internationale* in so many different languages.

Notes

1 It is clearly beyond the scope of this introduction to provide a complete overview on Ernesto Laclau's works and ideas. For this we would like to refer the reader to Torfing (1999), Smith (1998), Howarth (2000) and Howarth *et al.* (2000).

2 The development of Laclau's notion of 'hegemony' is more extensively treated in David Howarth's contribution to the volume. For a valuable and clear introduction to the main themes and topics of *Hegemony and Socialist Strategy* we would like to refer the reader to Fred Dallmayr's contribution.

3 *Articulation* is one of Laclau and Mouffe's key concepts. It is defined as 'any practice establishing a relation among elements such that their identity is modified as a result of the articulatory practice'. The 'structured totality' resulting from an articulatory practice they call *discourse* (*HSS* 105). For a discussion of the impact Laclau's concept of articulation had on cultural studies see Slack (1996). Interestingly, among the practitioners of Cultural Studies it is Stuart Hall who comes closest to Laclau, be it with respect to the discursive turn of hegemony theory, questions of democracy (see Hall 2002) or 'epistemology' (for the latter see Hall's article (1997) on 'the cultural revolutions of our time', which bears the source of its inspiration already in the title). Some aspects of the relation between Laclauian hegemony theory and cultural studies are also tackled in Marchart (2002, 2003). For an integration of Laclau's concept of articulation into the 'rival' approach of *Critical Discourse Analysis* see Chouliaraki and Fairclough (1999).

4 It is important to note that the discursive for Laclau and Mouffe encompasses both the 'linguistic' and the 'pragmatic' plane of signification. Far from being purely a matter of 'words', a discourse is always constituted *as a practice* (see their 'Post-Marxism without Apologies' in *NR* 97–134).

5 Many empirical case studies have been undertaken from an 'Essex school' perspective. They include, to name only a few, the study of apartheid discourse (Norval 1996), of British new

right discourse on race and sexuality (Smith 1994), of Peronist populism (Barros and Castagnola 2000), of European ultra-right populism (Marchart 2001, 2002), of green ideology (Stavrakakis 1997), of gay discourse in colonial Hong Kong (Ho and Tsang 2000), of Taiwanese democratization discourse (Lin 2003), and of the Kemalist imaginary in Turkey (Celik 2000).

6 Ernesto Laclau introduced the claim as to the impossibility of society in an article preceding *Hegemony and Socialist Strategy* and reprinted in *NR* (89–92). There, against essentialist and foundationalist visions of the social, he holds, 'that any structural system is limited, that it is always surrounded by an "excess of meaning" which it is unable to master and that, consequently, "society" as a unitary and intelligible object which grounds its own partial processes is an impossibility' (*NR* 90). Yet this does not imply that we can simply discard *any* notion of totality. Society, and this is what makes it an impossible object, remains there as something which is present in its very *absence*:

> Thus, the problem of the social totality is posed in new terms: the 'totality' does not establish the limits of 'the social' by transforming the latter into a *determinate* object (i.e. 'society'). Rather, the social always exceeds the limits of the attempts to constitute society. At the same time, however, that 'totality' does not disappear: if the suture it attempts is ultimately impossible, it is nevertheless possible to proceed to a relative fixation of the social through the institution of nodal points (ibid. 91).

7 Laclau's deconstructive 'inclination' is based on the conviction, in his words,

> that some of the stark oppositions that have dominated social and political theory for a long while are simply the result of making a choice for one extreme of opposition and presenting the other as its strict antithesis. We have maintained, on the contrary, that in most cases the two extreme opposites, far from rejecting each other, contaminate each other, so that it is only by focusing on their processes of mutual subversion that new language games can be designed which take into account the historical possibilities for democratic theory and practice that those *apparent* blind alleys actually open (2002: 386).

8 Laclau explains this shift in a later interview:

> When Chantal Mouffe and I wrote *Hegemony and Socialist Strategy*, we were still arguing that the moment of the dislocation of the social relations, the moment which constitutes the limit of the objectivity of social relations, is given by antagonism. Later on I came to think that this was not enough because constructing a social dislocation – an antagonism – is already a discursive response. You construct the Other who dislocates your identity as an enemy, but there are alternative forms. For instance, people can say that this is the expression of the wrath of God, that this is an expression of our sins and that we have to prepare for the day of atonement. So, there is already a discursive organization in constructing somebody as an enemy which involves a whole technology of power in the mobilization of the oppressed. That is why in *New Reflections* I have insisted on the primary character of dislocation rather than antagonism (Laclau 1999: 137).

References

Barros, S. and Castagnola, G. (2000) 'The political frontiers of the social: Argentine politics after Peronist populism (1955–1973)', in D. Howarth *et al.* (eds) *Discourse Theory and Political Analysis: Identities, Hegemonies and Social Change*, Manchester: Manchester University Press.

Butler, J., Laclau, E. and Žižek, S. (2000) *Contingency, Hegemony, Universality: Contemporary Dialogues on the Left*, London: Verso.

Celik, N. B. (2000) 'The constitution and dissolution of the Kemalist imaginary', in D. Howarth *et al.* (eds) *Discourse Theory and Political Analysis: Identities, Hegemonies and Social Change*, Manchester: Manchester University Press.

Chouliaraki, L. and Fairclough, N. (1999) *Discourse in Late Modernity. Rethinking Critical Discourse Analysis*, Edinburgh: Edinburgh University Press.

Critchley, S. (1992) *The Ethics of Deconstruction: Derrida and Levinas*, Oxford: Blackwell.

—— (1999) *Ethics–Politics–Subjectivity* London, Verso.

Hall, S. (1997) 'The centrality of culture: Notes on the cultural revolution of our time', in K. Thompson (ed.) *Media and Cultural Regulation*, London: Sage.

—— (2002) 'Democracy, globalization, and difference', in O. Enwezor, C. Basualdo, Ute Meta Bauer, S. Ghez, S. Maharaj, M. Nash, and O. Zaya (eds) *Democracy Unrealized*, Ostfildern: Hatje Cantz.

Ho, P. S. Y. and Tsang, A. K. T. (2000) 'Beyond being gay: The proliferation of political identities in colonial Hong Kong', in D. Howarth *et al.* (eds) *Discourse Theory and Political Analysis: Identities, Hegemonies and Social Change*, Manchester: Manchester University Press.

Howarth, D. (2000) *Discourse*, Buckingham: Open University Press.

Howarth, D., Norval, A. J. and Stavrakakis, Y. (eds) (2000) *Discourse Theory and Political Analysis: Identities, Hegemonies and Social Change*, Manchester: Manchester University Press.

Laclau, E. (1994) 'Introduction', in *The Making of Political Identities*, London and New York: Verso.

—— (1996) 'Deconstruction, Pragmatism, Hegemony', in C. Mouffe (ed.) *Deconstruction and Pragmatism*, London and New York: Routledge.

—— (1999) 'Hegemony and the future of democracy: Ernesto Laclau's political philosophy', interview, in L. Worsham and G. A. Olson (eds) *Race, Rhetoric, and the Postcolonial*, Albany: State University of New York Press.

—— (2002) 'Democracy between autonomy and heteronomy', in O. Enwezor *et al.* (eds) *Democracy Unrealized*, Ostfildern: Hatje Cantz.

Laclau, E. and Zac, L. (1994) 'Minding the gap: The subject of politics', in E. Laclau (ed.) *The Making of Political Identities*, London and New York: Routledge.

Lin, S.-F. (2003) '"Democratization" in Taiwan and its discontents: Transnational activism as a critique', in N. Piper and A. Uhlin (eds) *Transnational Activism in Asia: Problems of Power and Democracy*, London and New York: Routledge.

Marchart, O. (2001) 'The "Fourth Way" of the ultra-right: Austria, Europe, and the end of neo-corporatism', *Capital and Class*, 73: 7–14.

—— (2002) '*Austrifying* Europa: ultra-right populism and the new culture of resistance', *Cultural Studies*, 16(6): 809–19.

—— (2003) 'Bridging the micro-macro-gap: Is there such thing as post-subcultural politics?', in D. Muggleton and R. Weinzierl (eds) *The Post-Subcultures Reader*, New York and Oxford: Berg.

Mouffe, C. (1979) 'Hegemony and ideology in Gramsci', in C. Mouffe (ed.) *Gramsci and Political Theory*, London: Routledge.

—— (1989) 'Radical democracy: Modern or postmodern?', in A. Ross (ed.) *Universal Abandon? The Politics of Postmodernism*, London: Routledge.

—— (ed.) (1992) *Dimensions of Radical Democracy: Pluralism, Citizenship, Community*, London: Verso.

—— (1993) *The Return of the Political*, London: Verso.

—— (1996) 'Deconstruction, pragmatism and the politics of democracy', in C. Mouffe (ed.) *Deconstruction and Pragmatism*, London: Routledge.

—— (2000) *The Democratic Paradox*, London: Verso.

Norval, A. J. (1996) *Deconstructing Apartheid Discourse*, London: Verso.

Slack, J. D. (1996) 'The theory and method of articulation in cultural studies', in D. Morley and K.-H. Chen (eds) *Stuart Hall. Critical Dialogues in Cultural Studies*, London and New York: Routledge.

Smith, A. M. (1994) *New Right Discourse on Race and Sexuality: Britain 1968–1990*, Cambridge: Cambridge University Press.

—— (1998) *Laclau and Mouffe: The Radical Democratic Imaginary*, London: Routledge.

Stavrakakis, Y. (1997) 'Green ideology: A discursive reading', *Journal of Political Ideologies*, 2(3): 259–79.

Torfing, J. (1998) *Politics, Regulation and the Modern Welfare State*, London: Macmillan.

—— (1999) *New Theories of Discourse*, Oxford: Blackwell.

Žižek, S. (1990) 'Beyond discourse-analysis', in E. Laclau, *New Reflections on the Revolution of our Time*, London: Verso.

Part I

PHILOSOPHY
Universality, singularity, difference

1

HOW EMPTY CAN EMPTY BE?

On the place of the universal

Rodolphe Gasché

One of the many merits of Ernesto Laclau's political and theoretical work has been to forcefully reintroduce the problematic of universality into political philosophy at a time, precisely, when such a project would seem the least welcome, that is, at a time when this subject has become forbidden territory within the prevailing discourses. With the left hopelessly divided, trends like multiculturalism dominate, and various intellectual discourses from neopragmatism to a certain interpretation of deconstruction seem to consider any reflection on universality as inherently Eurocentric. Needless to say, this reintroduction of the question of universality into political philosophy does not amount to bringing back the spurious notion of universality which has been abandoned for historical and theoretical reasons. The criticism that has been leveled against received conceptions of universality remains in vigor, but the insight that there can be no politics, no society, and no democracy, without reference to universality, has led Laclau to rethink this concept. The problem of universality reemerges in Laclau's thought precisely in the context of the attempt to reconceive of political thought itself in the wake of the failure of the Enlightenment project, and above all, of its Marxist version, that is, in the wake of a project that amounted to a disappearance of the political. Laclau's thinking is thus a thought in process, still in the making. In the same way as the political is reinvented, so too does the concept of universality undergo a radical reformulation. Even though Laclau does not put it this way, his reference to universality as an empty space also suggests that this is a space still to be thought, or differently worded, a space that coincides with a task – the task to think the universal.

Yet, in the final pages of *Hegemony and Socialist Strategy*, Laclau and Mouffe conclude their analysis of hegemonic articulation as a condition of possibility of a radical democracy by making what they claim to be a decisive point, namely, that 'there is no radical and plural democracy without renouncing the discourse of the universal' (*HSS* 191–2). However, this seemingly intransigent declaration, which is justified by the very need to liberate the thought of hegemony from the constraints within which it remains caught in Marxism, concerns only one form of universality (though this work gives no hint as to other possible notions of universality). Laclau and Mouffe identify the target of their criticism when they write:

> The classic discourse of socialism [...] was a discourse of the universal, which transformed certain social categories into depositories of political and epistemological privileges; it was an *a priori* discourse concerning differential levels of effectiveness within the social – and as such it reduced the field of the discursive surfaces on which it considered that it was possible and legitimate to operate (*HSS* 57).

The critical debate with the Marxist discourse of universality 'in which a limited actor – the working class – [is] raised to the status of "universal class"' (ibid.), seeks to break the classical bond between socialist practice and a working class whose ontological status is tied to the centrality of economism. This Marxist discourse of universality, however, not only represents the precise historical formulation of the universal to be rejected in the name of a democratic practice of hegemony, it also provides the framework within which Laclau's subsequent elaborations on universality have taken place, and in which some of his more provocative statements – for example, that the universal is an empty place – gain their significance.

I have qualified the socialist conception of universality as one discursive form of universality among others. However, as Laclau's attempt to sketch out the genealogy of this precise form of universality demonstrates, the socialist formulation of the universal is not just one such formulation among many. Its dialectical genealogy shows that it is rather the formulation *par excellence* of the spurious form of universality. *Emancipation(s)* distinguishes three historical forms in which the relationship between universality and particularity has been discussed, that is, the classical, Christian, and rationalist conceptions of universality. Because of the very way in which this genealogy is construed, the rationalist conception of universality, the one to which Marxism subscribes, appears to be the dialectical sublation of both the classical and Christian paradigm. While the inaugural distinction between universality and particularity in ancient philosophy conceives of the universal as a pole entirely graspable by reason, and which is separated from the particular through an uncontaminated dividing line, in Christianity, a universal which is accessible to us only through revelation incarnates itself in finite and contingent reality without having any intrinsic rational connection to the latter, and according to reasons that remain opaque to human comprehension. Yet, the new paradigm that comes into being with the Enlightenment unites the classical conception of the intelligibility of the universal with the Christian conception of incarnation, now radically transformed so as to make possible a rational connection of total transparency between the incarnating body and the incarnated universal. The Hegelian conception of the rationality of the real, and the Marxist idea of a universal class, are prime examples of this novel way in which the relation between universality and particularity is shaped. Yet, even though the new notion of a 'privileged agent of history' whose particular body becomes the transparent expression of a universality transcending it, tends to 'interrupt the [Christian] logic of incarnation', 'the modern idea of a "universal class" and the various forms of Eurocentrism are [according to Laclau] nothing but the distant historical effects of the logic of incarnation'. He writes:

> the body of the proletariat is no longer a particular body in which a universality external to it has to be incarnated: it is instead a body in which the distinction between particularity and universality is canceled and, as a result, the need for any incarnation is definitely eradicated (*E* 23–4).

However complex the relation to its antecedents in ancient philosophy and Christianity may be, the new paradigm to which the Marxist discourse of universality belongs is unique in that it overcomes the difficulties that haunted the previous formulations. The theoretical superiority of the new conception of the relation between the universal and the particular, one that is due to the postulation of 'a body which is, in and of itself, the universal', lies in its ability to raise particularity to the level of universality. This conception of universalistic rationalism is, therefore, also the blueprint for Eurocentrism. The universal having found *its own* body, there is, as Laclau remarks,

> no intellectual means of distinguishing between European particularism and the universal functions that it was supposed to incarnate, given that European universalism had constructed its identity precisely through the cancellation of the logic of incarnation and, as a result, through the universalization of its own particularism (*E* 23–4).

The Enlightenment conception of the relation between the universal and the particular is admittedly a secular one. But precisely as a secular conception, the Enlightenment remains indebted to what it overcomes. No surprise, therefore, if the logic of incarnation is reintroduced into rationalist universalism, at the very moment when Europe faces resistance to its imperialist expansion and its self-proclaimed civilizing mission, by other cultures, thus effectively establishing 'an *essential* inequality between the objective positions of social agents' (*E* 25). The logic of incarnation is reintroduced as well and with the same result as soon as the Party declares itself to be the representative of the working class.

As the criticism of spurious universality demonstrates, the foil against which Laclau critically develops his own notion of universality is universalistic rationalism embodied in exemplary fashion by socialism. Indeed, as was already clear in *Hegemony and Socialist Strategy*, the rejection of socialist universalism was based primarily on its positing of the working class as the one, and sole, universal social agent. As a function of its economic position, the universal character of the working class was seen to follow with necessity. The prime target of Laclau's critique is the very restriction of the universal to one historical or social agent. This restriction is, for Laclau, always based upon the assumption that this agent occupies an essential position within the relations of capitalist production, or – more generally – because this agent is believed to embody some transcultural human essence, norms, values, or unconditioned a priori principles, from which its privilege as an agent derives with absolute necessity. The moment of necessity, he holds, is an inheritance of the rationalist tradition of the Enlightenment (Laclau 2000a: 75). Furthermore, the theological ramifications of this secular concept of universality form an essential part of the background against which Laclau reworks his notion of universality. To bring into relief the implicit theological underpinnings of the secular conception of the universal, I refer to the essay he co-authored with Lilian Zac, 'Minding the gap' (1994). There, they conclude with an assessment of the role of Hobbes for the constitution of the political discourse of modernity. Modern political theory, they argue, either deepens or develops the split that characterizes the secular conception of the political order, that is, the split between, on the one hand, the ruling function of the Leviathan and, on the other, the particular and plural contents that can possibly actualize the former. At stake in democracy, in the modern sense, 'is the institution of signifiers of a social lack resulting from the absence of God as fullness of Being' (Laclau and Zac 1994: 36). Since these signifiers are the floating and empty signifiers that assume a universalizing function, the conception of the universal as an empty space must not only be thought in opposition to the spurious formulations of the universal in which the latter is identified with a transcultural essence, or value, it must also be thought from, and with respect to, the withdrawal of God that gives birth to the secular vision of the Enlightenment, and to which it thus remains indebted (Laclau 2000c: 305).

One must not lose sight of these two aspects which configure Laclau's answer to the problem of universality – the debate with rationalist universalism, primarily in its Marxist form, and with the theological heritage of this secular form of universality. But there is a further, and equally important, aspect of his reconception of the universal that needs to be mentioned here. For Laclau, the universal is primarily a social and political category. Even though the style of the discussion of the question of universality is largely one of formal analyses, analyses that, therefore, are not necessarily formalistic, the notion of universality in question is, far from being an abstract or merely formal concept, intimately linked to other issues such as hegemonic articulation, the question of representation, democratic society, and indeed the very possibility of the social and the political. Together with particularization, universalization is a concrete move constitutive of social and political life. As we have seen, in *Hegemony and Socialist Strategy*, the very need to radically question the socialist universal discourse in order to secure democratic hegemonic practice called for the abandonment of the notion of universality. But in this work, Laclau and Mouffe also recognize:

> the symmetrically opposite danger of a lack of all reference to [...] unity. For, even though impossible, this remains a horizon which, given the absence of articulation between social relations, is necessary in order to prevent an implosion of the social and an absence of any common point

> of reference. This unraveling of the social fabric caused by the destruction of the symbolic framework is another form of the disappearance of the political. In contrast to the danger of totalitarianism, which imposes immutable articulations in an authoritarian manner, the problem here is the absence of those articulations which allow the establishment of meanings common to the different social subjects (*HSS* 188).

This important passage not only sets the stage for the criticism of multiculturalism and radical particularism in Laclau's later works, it also clearly highlights the decisive fact that a certain notion of universality is indispensable for any constitution of the social and the political. *Emancipation(s)* makes this point with all the required force: 'the abandonment of universalism undermines the foundation of a democratic society [...] Without a universalism of sorts [...] a truly democratic society is impossible' (*E* 122). Indeed, the universal:

> is absolutely essential for any kind of *political* interaction, for if the latter took place without universal reference, there would be no political interaction at all: we would only have either a complementarity of differences which would be totally non-antagonistic, or a totally antagonistic one, one where differences entirely lack any commensurability, and whose only possible resolution is the mutual destruction of the adversaries (*E* 61).

Furthermore, the claim made in *Contingency, Hegemony, Universality*, that 'the moment of the universality of the community, the moment in which, beyond any particularism, the universal speaks by itself', coincides with 'the ethical substance of the community', shows to what extent the very possibility of the social hinges on a sense of universality which concerns the social unity, or community, of individuals, or particular groups (2000a: 80, 84). As understood by Laclau, universality could be called a social or political a priori. Its concretely substantive texture is the very fabric within which the formal analyses are made concerning a relation of universality and particularity, a fabric that is distinct from the one found in socialist universal discourse, and in the history of the relation that preceded the latter. The following analyses will seek to highlight to what extent Laclau's recasting of the relation of the particular and the universal – in particular his thesis that the universal is an empty place – is a function of this social and political understanding of universality. Although the central notion of hegemony overlaps in several regards with more philosophical, or quasi-philosophical, concepts, for example, with *différance*, it is above all a socio-political category. The specific reformulation that the universal undergoes in Laclau's thought is tied to this socio-political concept which describes the political articulation of the particular and the universal. The questions that I intend to raise with respect to the definition of the universal as an empty signifier or place later in this essay are questions that presuppose this highly tangible nature of the universal. While, in her dialogue with Laclau, Judith Butler has sought to criticize what she deems to be a formalist conception of the universal on the basis of the concrete social and cultural plurality of competing universals, I would like to address some questions to Laclau's reformulation of the universal from what may be considered, in this particular context, an ultra-formalist stance. They are not questions that spring from any specific or definite philosophical concept of universality that I would hold, but rather from certain implications stemming from the concept of universality itself.

In the current socio-political configuration, Laclau's insistence on the need not only to reformulate, but to salvage the concept of universality in the first place, is targeted primarily against the particularism that threatens multiculturalism, and the 'politics of difference' advanced by it. Under the general heading of the 'logic of difference', a series of arguments serves to demonstrate that the assertion of difference insofar as it constitutes the social, is not possible without a negative reference to others, and, hence, without also a positive appeal to a unity, or totality that transcends both self and other. Against the belief that one could do away with all universality, Laclau argues that 'the assertion of pure particularism, independently of any content and of the appeal to universality transcending it, is a self-defeating enterprise' (*E* 26). Only by failing to fully constitute identity, particularity, and difference, can specific groups hope to achieve social reality and leverage. From the numerous analyses Laclau has devoted to the question of difference, particularity, identity, it is also made clear that the demands associated with the latter cannot be made in terms of difference, particularity, or identity, but only in terms of some universal principles that are shared by the particular groups. Laclau writes in *Emancipation(s)* that 'the particular can only fully realize itself if it constantly keeps open, and constantly redefines, its relation to the universal' (*E* 65). But this universal, without which no particularity or identity could assert itself, is not some abstract or exsanguine notion of the essence of what it is to be considered human. Rather, an ethnic minority, for instance, cannot but invoke, in the very process of its self-assertion, universal rights as concrete as 'the right of everybody to have access to good schools, or live a decent life, or participate in the public space of citizenship, and so on' (*E* 28).

From the stinging critique in *Hegemony and Socialist Strategy* of the modern form of universality, especially of the socialist discourse of universalism, it follows that the universal to which Laclau appeals, as well as the relation between this universal and the particular, must be of an altogether different order. This universal can no longer consist in 'some principle underlying and explaining the particular' (*E* 28), some pure human essence, such as reason, to which all particularity must necessarily submit, and which could be incarnated in one privileged social actor. Compared to the modern, that is also Western or Eurocentric, concept of the universal, the very idea of universality undergoes a radical mutation in Laclau's work – in his own words, 'a radical mutation that – while maintaining the double reference to the universal and the particular – entirely transforms the logic of their articulation' (*E* 51). Although this recast relation between the universal and the particular does not involve simply doing away with the values of modernity, particularly of the Enlightenment, it does involve opening 'the way to a movement away from Western Eurocentrism, through the operation that we could call a systematic decentering of the West' (*E* 34, see also 103). Questioning the relation of necessity according to which a given particular such as the West laid claim to the universal, this reformulation of the universal undercuts the assumption in today's socio-political climate that 'universal values [in themselves are inevitably] a strong assertion of the "ethnia of the West" (as in the later Husserl)' (*E* 47). The rethought universal would thus be one that cuts the modern bonds of necessity either to a class within society, or to a determined ethnia within humanity itself.

Distinct from the logic of difference, is the 'logic of equivalence and equality'. While the former reveals the particular's dependence on some notion of universality to assert itself, the latter articulates the operation through which such a notion is constructed. Insofar as the logic of equivalence is, like the logic of difference, a foundation of the social, the very construction of the universal is a social operation, and the constructed universal a social universal. To the extent that this logic of equivalence is constitutive of the social, it is not only a construction without which there would be no society or community, but also one that must be constantly actualized and renegotiated. The hegemonic construction of the social excludes all repetition of the immutable essence of a supposedly common substratum. Rather than a function of an ideality and its identical repetition, the social, for Laclau, is constituted through the pragmatic (understood in a non-empiricist way) operations by which one group becomes the representative of the whole, and thus acquires the power associated with creating order.[1] As Laclau writes, the universal in question is 'a pragmatic social construction', and not the 'expression of a necessary requirement of reason' (*E* 103–4). Rather than an ahistorical a priori of the social, the universal is the effect of a pragmatic construction in the concrete fabric of social and political life, notwithstanding that the analyses devoted to this universal are largely of a formal nature. As a result, the universal, instead of bearing the stamp of necessity, is contingent upon this pragmatic construction, and hence 'is a contingent historical product' (*E* 122). It is contaminated by particularity, and is thus a 'relative' universal. Its pragmatic nature explains its relative and historical character. If it is justified to speak of it as a social a priori, it is in reference to the actual and factual social and political life in which, despite antagonistic struggle and disruption, order is achieved, and/or maintained.

Laclau writes:

> The only status I am prepared to grant to universality is that of being the precipitate of an equivalential operation, which means that the 'universal' is never an independent entity, but only the set of 'names' corresponding to an always finite and reversible relation between particularities (2000b: 194).

If 'the only possible universality is the one constructed through an equivalential chain' (2000c: 304), universality, rather than preceding or regulating them, is clearly an 'effect' produced by the equivalential operations. Even though, in their co-authored work, Laclau and Mouffe already invoke the notion of equivalence, the essays in *Emancipation(s)* truly elaborate this concept, and it is to them, therefore, that I turn in order to clarify this notion which is central to Laclau's political philosophy.

As in the case of the 'logic of difference', the 'logic of equivalence' is discussed in formal and structural terms. Indeed, like the 'logic of difference', the 'logic of equivalence' is derived from the structural features inherent to a system as a system of differences, or differential identities. Furthermore, the 'logic of equivalence' is, in spite of its difference from the 'logic of difference', intimately tied to it and its constitutive failure. This co-implication is what, first, we need to make manifest. In 'Why do empty signifiers matter to politics', a reflection on system and its limits forms the context for the discussion of both logics, their difference and interrelatedness. Laclau takes his cues from structural linguistics and its analyses of the system of signification, according to which signification is possible only on condition that the linguistic identities form a system of differences, and, consequently, on the condition that 'the totality of language is involved in each single act of signification'. Laclau argues that this very possibility of signification raises the question of the possibility of the system; in short, it raises the question of the system's constituting limits, and by extension that of the system's beyond, or outside. Now, as the limits of the signifying system, these limits cannot themselves be signified. Furthermore, these limits must be exclusionary. 'The actualization of what is beyond the limit of exclusion … involve[s] the impossibility of what is this side of the limit', and hence, they can manifest themselves only in 'the *interruption* or *breakdown* of the process of signification' (*E* 37). If the system of differences hinges on an exclusionary operation, it follows that the differential elements that make up the system are inherently affected by this exclusion. They are, as Laclau, remarks, constitutively split. While its difference from other elements founds the identity of each element in the system, all difference between the elements is canceled out to the extent that all the elements are equivalent, if not identical, insofar as they belong to one system formed on the basis of a radical exclusion. Laclau writes:

> The identity of each element is constitutively split: on the one hand, each difference expresses itself *as* difference; on the other hand, each of them *cancels* itself as such by entering into a relation of equivalence with all the other differences of the system (*E* 38).

The differential nature of identity thus also causes all identities to be equivalent insofar as they belong to one and the same system, and have a common share in the system-founding exclusion. Difference and equivalence do not only co-imply one another, the latter also 'cancels' the former. The excluded outside of the system levels all difference within the system. As Laclau remarks, 'the logic of difference [is] interrupted by a logic of equivalence and equality' (*E* 49). But this excluded outside of the system which at once enables the identities to form differentially, and makes them equal, is not a substantial ground which could be signified in positive terms. Compared to the (apparent fullness of) the system, its beyond, without which there can be no objective order (with its limits), is a mere negativity. On it hinges, as we have seen, not only the possibility of a system, but, within the latter, the very possibility of differential identities. However, if this is the case, signification of this excluded outside within the system and its elements is essential lest its frontiers collapse, and cease to exist. Within the system this outside can only be signified through a collapse of the differences into equivalential chains, and the subsequent self-representation of the system as a totality. These equivalential chains engendered by the subversion of the differential nature of the system's signifying elements – a subversion rooted in the constitutive split of the elements of the system – thus come to represent the system itself, the whole in which all the elements partake, and that therefore renders them equal. Laclau writes: 'It is only by privileging the dimension of equivalence to the point that its differential nature is almost entirely obliterated – that is emptying it of its differential nature – that the system can signify itself as a totality' (*E* 39). The logic of equivalence thus leads to the formation of signifieds that imply the system as a whole, and that, paradoxically, signify (indirectly, negatively) the excluded outside, or the beyond of the system. With this, and for essential reasons, the 'value' of the universal becomes inscribed into the very logic of difference. If differential identity is only conceivable within a system, the outside of the system that levels the differences that it embraces must at all times be marked within it, and this marking is achieved by the universal. Or, differently put, difference is possible only on condition that there is an appeal to the universal, to the system as a whole, to something common even if, as is the case here, this common substrate is the mere negativity of the outside, or beyond, of the system. Yet precisely because the unifying ground of the system is the excluded outside – a negativity that cannot be signified as such – the universal is not something that can be presupposed (as an immutable essence), but must at all times be constructed through contingent and historical acts. This construction takes place according to the logic of equivalence.

Insofar as differential particularism is only conceivable in the light of the system that it forms, and, hence, also with respect to the excluded other without which this system would not come into being, that which is shared by these particularities cannot be of the order of a positive and self-identical content. Differently put, that which will come to signify the system in its totality will not be fully congruent with it since this system cannot close itself upon itself in full presence. Laclau writes that since,

> the community as such is not a purely differential space of an objective identity but an absent fullness, it cannot have any form of representation

> of its own, and has to borrow the latter from some entity constituted within the equivalential space – in the same way as gold is a particular use value which assumes, as well, the function of representing value in general (*E* 42).

'The relative universalization through equivalential logics', which combines with the logic of difference, is, as Laclau remarks, 'very different from the universality which results from an underlying essence or an unconditioned a priori principle' (*E* 53–4). The universal engendered by the logics of equivalence amounts to the unified set of equivalential demands, that (at one historical moment) are shared by the different particularities that make up the community, such as the right to general education, a decent life, and a place in public life. The universal here does not amount to a fixed content, it is an open series of demands. It also follows from this that, however intimate the connection between this universal and the particularities is, the chasm between them is not bridged, precisely because this 'universal is no more than a particular that at some moment has become dominant' (*E* 26). Still, in order to occupy the place of the absent fullness of the social system, it is not qua particularity that a specific particular can become dominant as a universal. To be able to inhabit this absent fullness – the empty place of the universal – any particularity competing for that role must void itself of its very particularity. It must approximate, without ever being able to coincide with, what Laclau calls 'the absent fullness of society'.

The operation of the equivalential logic is not yet exhausted by the operation of relative universalization. 'There is no universality which operates as pure universality', in and by itself, Laclau remarks (2000b: 208). Qua universal, that which is shared by the particularities within a societal totality must find expression, representation, or incarnation. It needs 'to be incarnated in something essentially incommensurable with it: a particularity' (*E* 57). The second moment of the operation 'is to give a particular demand a function of universal representation – that is to give it the value of a horizon giving coherence to the chain of equivalence and, at the same time, keeping it indefinitely open' (*E* 57–8). The second function of the logic of equivalence operation consists therefore in '"universaliz[ing]" a certain particularity on the basis of its substitutability with an indefinite number of particularities' (2000b: 193). At this juncture, the precise relation of Laclau's conception of the universal to his theory of hegemony becomes manifest. The system-theoretical background with which the particular and the universal are shown to be inextricably interlinked also makes the relation between the universal and the particular a hegemonic one.[2] If society is never without a constitutive outside, and hence lacks fullness and presence, one particular group with its symbols is inevitably required to take on the function of universal representation within the system of differences as a whole. As Laclau writes, 'there is no universality which is not a hegemonic universality' (ibid.). But to say that universality is at all times hegemonically articulated also means that, as in the case of the hegemonic power, such a universal will necessarily be 'precarious and threatened'

(*E* 55). Although such universals are the only socially attainable ones, without them the fabric of society would unravel.

From what we have seen so far, the universal is an inevitable, that is, necessary, dimension of the self-assertion of any social particularity. Its possibility and necessity are rooted in the constitutive split characteristic of particular identities which also opens the space for the operation of equivalence between particularities within the social system. In the same way as in the case of the logic of difference, structural and formal reasons compel a totality of particularities to enter into a relation with something that transcends them. But although the reference to a universality transcending particularities imposes itself with necessity, the structural and formal reasons for this necessity do not therefore legislate over the content of universality. Although the reference to the universal is inevitable, which particular content will symbolize the latter remains undetermined. The logic of equivalence clearly posits that such a content is the effect of a hegemonic construction at any historical moment. Laclau, therefore, speaks of 'the universal – taken by itself – [as] an empty signifier' (*E* 15). Considered by itself, the universal is an empty place whose occupant is the result of a contingent historical articulation. Since hereafter I will discuss in some detail the asserted emptiness of the universal 'taken by itself', let me try to describe as precisely as possible the reasons that Laclau advances for this qualification of the universal, and what such emptiness implies.

Whether the concern is with singular particularities or with the system of differential identities, self-identity of the particular or the totality of the system can only be achieved through reference to other particularities or to the system's other, or outside. The universal that transcends particularities, as well as the particularities aggregated into a social whole, is thus essentially, and necessarily, something exterior, other, or alien with respect to particularities or their community. Without this dimension of exteriority, the particularities or their community could not possibly achieve intimacy, or proximity to themselves. What this means is, of course, that particularities and their communities lack fullness, or self-presence, and it thus follows that 'universality is the symbol of a missing fullness' (*E* 28). Since both the logics of difference and equivalence open up onto the dimension of universality, universality taken by itself is only for formal and structural reasons negatively defined. The very notion of universality is testimony to the constitutive gap that pertains to all identity or to any communitarian order. Laclau speaks, therefore, of the universal not only as an empty signifier, but as 'an empty place'. This emptiness is constitutive of universality insofar as it is a category that is essential to the social. In *Contingency, Hegemony, Universality* Laclau remarks that 'empty signifiers represent, in my view, the limit of socially attainable universalization' (2000b: 211). Considered by itself, the universal does therefore 'not have a concrete content of its own which would close it on itself' (*E* 34). It is, as Laclau writes, 'an empty place, a void which can be filled only by the particular' (2000a: 58). Needless to say, this emptiness of the universal precludes that any content that comes to fill in its space could be logically deduced from it. Although the empty place 'has to be incarnated in *some* concrete content', this place is 'indifferent to the content of the filling' (Laclau and Zac 1994: 15). Nor is there, Laclau contends, any 'a priori reason for it not to be filled by *any* content' (*E* 60). Any force can occupy it, which is to say that 'the relation between the concrete content and its role as a filler of the gap within the structure is purely external' (*E* 92–3).

In the dialogues of *Contingency, Hegemony, Universality*, Judith Butler has questioned Laclau as to 'why [one should] conceive of universality as an empty "place" which awaits its content in an anterior and subsequent event' (Butler 2000a: 34). She asks, whether

> such a notion of universality [is] ever as empty as it is posited to be? Or is there a specific form of universality which lays claim to being 'empty'? [...] And is it truly empty, or does it carry the trace of the excluded in spectral form as an internal disruption of its own formalism? (2000b: 167)

The formulation of Butler's questions shows that she interprets 'emptiness' from a Hegelian perspective as synonymous with 'abstract' and merely formal. Her suspicion is not simply that such emptiness is the result of an operation of abstraction, and thus wrought by an exclusion of concrete social and cultural contents, but that such an act of abstraction has its genealogy in equally concrete social practices. Her further expression of doubt as to whether 'given social sectors or, indeed, given social movements are necessarily particularistic prior to the movement in which they articulate their own aims as the aims of the general community' (2000b: 163), and her assertion that, indeed, the hegemonic success of one such articulation is the result of already competing notions of universalities, not only reveals that she takes Laclau's distinction between the particular and the universal to be formalistic, but also that the bases of her criticism of formalism in the name of concrete social and cultural practices are socio-political. In his response to Butler's intervention, Laclau objected to her accusation of formalism. He also pointed out, however, that although universality must be conceived as an empty signifier, it is not, therefore, 'an *absolutely* empty signifier' (Laclau 2000c: 304).[3] As he recalls, universality as a signifier is empty because 'the only possible universality is the one constructed through an equivalential chain' (2000c: 305).[4] Yet,

> the condition of the tendentially empty character of the general equivalent is the increasing extension of a claim of equivalences between particularities. Emptiness, as a result, presupposes the concrete [...] the universality attainable through equivalential logics will always be a universality contaminated by particularity. There is not, strictly speaking, a signifier which is truly empty, but one which is only tendentially so (2000c: 304).

While fending off the accusation of formalism, Laclau, furthermore, has recourse to the Hegelian notion of the 'concrete abstract or universal'. He writes, 'what we have called the logic of empty signifiers belongs to this type of concrete abstract or universal' (2000b: 191). Rather than suggesting abstractness and formalism, the (relative, or tendential) emptiness of the signifier 'universality' is thus clearly, and I would add, paradoxically, a function of Laclau's 'pragmatic' approach to the social and political. In what is further testimony to the fact that Laclau's universal is a social universal, this, as it were, 'concrete' emptiness is construed to result from concrete movements inherent to societies – the movements of universalizing and particularizing – which actually and factually shape a hegemonic totality or system as it articulates itself.

Yet, Butler's question of how to think this emptiness of the signifier 'universality' remains. Because the empty place of the universal is a social category and the place of hegemonic articulation or construction, is, admittedly, contaminated by particularity, it is, therefore, not absolutely empty; yet precisely for this reason several other questions concerning this tendential emptiness need to be asked. To begin with, let me recall that 'emptiness' implies the complete exteriority of what comes to fill the space of the universal. Since no content is a priori predestined to occupy the empty place, by right, any content, as Laclau holds, can suture that place. But does this mean that all contents are equivalent? Given that the critique of the secularized socialist concept of the universal sought to displace the political privilege attributed to one social agent in order to secure a *democratic* plurality of voices, does this goal not come with some criterion as to which content meets this demand. Even though Laclau's radically secular position on universality excludes the assumption of any teleological essence of democracy which would be progressively attained, and even though his conception of democracy is a pragmatic one, the very notion of a *radical* democracy would seem to suggest some kind of norm. But then 'radical' means here the absence of any ultimate telos, of any 'good' content that once and for all would make democracy identical to itself. Because Laclau's theory of the empty signifier is a pragmatic theory, he can, of course, write that 'precisely because the universal place is empty, it can be occupied by any force, not necessarily democratic' (*E* 65). Furthermore, for Laclau, 'a democratic society is not one in which the "best" content dominates unchallenged but, rather, one in which nothing is definitely acquired and there is always the possibility of challenge' (*E* 100). To hold that any content can come to fill the space of the universal is also to say that no content can ever be adequate to that space. This, in turn, means

> that the 'good' articulation, the one that would finally suture the link between universal task and concrete historical forces will never be found, and that all partial victory will always take place against the background of an ultimate, an unsurpassable impossibility (*E* 63).

However plausible this radically secular conception of universality may be, I wish to point out that, even though the space of the universal is empty, it is still the space of the *universal*. Does this not imply, in spite of the fact that undemocratic contents can occupy that space, that any content that vies to fill the space in question must necessarily be one *capable* of filling that space? But if this is the case, the space of the universal is not altogether empty, and not every content is capable of filling it.

After formulating the problematic of hegemonic articulation as an intervention practised on an undecidable terrain, Laclau asserts, in *Emancipation(s)*, that the deconstruction of the metaphysical and philosophical discourse of the West has widened the field of structural undecidability, and that such a widening 'opens the way to an enlargement of the field of political decision' (*E* 88). He writes:

> Once undecidability has reached the ground itself, once the organization of a certain camp is governed by a hegemonic decision – hegemonic because it is not objectively determined, because different decisions were also possible – the realm of philosophy comes to an end and the realm of politics begins (*E* 123).

Undoubtedly, the deconstruction of the metaphysical concept of the ground shows the thought of the ground to be inseparably tied to ethico-theoretical and ethico-political decisions. But can one infer from this that philosophy has come to an end, and is replaced by the realm of politics? As Laclau's consistent attempt to salvage the notion of universality demonstrates, he is fully aware that the deconstruction of the ground does not therefore make it superfluous; by deconstructing it, a non-foundation is acknowledged as being present in the foundation, a non-presence without which the ground could not itself lay a claim to presence. Thereby the idea of a ground, which remains as unavoidable as ever, has 'only' been complexified in an unheard-of way. Even though 'no universality exists other than that which is built in a pragmatic and precarious way by that process of circulation which establishes an equivalence between an increasingly wide range of demands', Laclau ascertains that the ground 'universality' 'does not disappear but has lost [only] the transparency of a positive and closed world' (*NR* 80). The deconstruction of the metaphysics of presence does not make philosophy superfluous. Notwithstanding the ethical and political dimension that opens in philosophy with the recognition that the notion of the ground is aporetic, and hence the terrain of an undecidability that calls for decision, this opening up of the philosophical to these dimensions does not turn philosophy into politics. Philosophy remains 'philosophical' by inquiring into the structural or formal reasons that cause the notion of the ground to necessarily include a non-ground, and the consequences thereof. The questions that I will formulate, hereafter, with respect to the asserted (relative) emptiness of universality, are formal and structural questions of the order of a philosophy that has undergone deconstruction, but that, therefore, still remains 'philosophy'.

The radically secularized and socially viable universals are the result of hegemonic affirmations of particularistic demands. They are, as Laclau contends, inevitably particularistic, relative, and contingent. Yet the function of these universals is not only to fill or occupy the empty place of the universal, as the product of operations of the equivalential logic, they themselves have to be progressively voided of all content in order to be capable of occupying the place of the absent fullness of society. But if, indeed, this is so, can one, strictly speaking, still call the universals in question particularistic, relative, and contingent? Let me first recall the following generality, one on which, I presume, Laclau and I can agree: even though it is conceivable that all universals can possibly be shown to be reducible to empirical, factual, and particularistic contents, the very *concept* of the universal cannot be derived empirically. Even if one admits that empiricism might possibly succeed in explaining all concepts of universality as historically particular formations, empiricism remains incapable of explaining why a particular content has been conceived *as* universal. Said another way, empiricist reductionism lacks the means to account for the irreducible fact that some content has been *thought* as a universal. It thus fails to account for the difference that thinking makes – the difference of the concept, that is, what gives salience to something in the first place, and allows recognition of it in all its particularity – and that empiricism itself cannot but presuppose. In spite of Laclau's statement that universals are always contingent, it is, I believe, fair to say that he does not – to speak in Hobbesian terms – sensualize all concepts, and least of all the concept of the universal. He even speaks of the 'incommensurability' of the universal and the particular, that is, of the impossibility of one particular content ever being adequate to fill the empty place of the universal. It seems to me that this acknowledgment that the concept of the universal as a philosophical concept is irreducible – 'that it determines itself only according to [the logic of] "all or nothing"', to quote Derrida (1988: 116–17) – underlies also Laclau's pragmatic theory of universality. The very emptiness of the space of the universal would seem to stress the difference with the particular, as does the tendential emptying of any particularistic content that is hegemonically raised to the status of an occupant of the empty place. But if this is true, it seems to me appropriate to consider a number of questions.

What motivates these questions is that, notwithstanding his acceptance on philosophical grounds of the radical difference between the universal and the particular, Laclau rethinks this difference. The very gesture of conceiving of the universal as a place, one that furthermore is empty, is testimony to the effort to reshape the conception of the irreducibility of the universal. As has become evident, formal reasons owing to the system-theoretical assumptions concerning particularities and their aggregates explain this need to define the universal as an empty place that can only be filled by tendentially empty signifiers. If, however, these formal analyses have not only a pragmatic, but also a philosophical, charge, the now reformulated difference between the universal and the particular will also affect the concept of universality underlying the pragmatic pertinence of the theory of the empty place of the universal. The following philosophical and 'ultra-formalist' questions impose themselves. First and foremost is the question of how empty the empty place of the universal can be if it is to be the place of the *universal*. What is it that makes it possible for all particularities to relate to this empty place as the place of the universal, a place with respect to which they themselves come to understand themselves? And conversely, what permits this empty space to make the claim of universality, and to claim the particularities? Once the empty place is thought of *as* the place of the universal, does it not, as this very place, betoken a content of sorts distinct from whatever contents subsequently come to fill that place? Indeed, how is one to determine that the product of an operation of equivalence is in the position of filling the empty space of the universal, if something, in addition to its tendentional emptiness, does not render it recognizable as a contender for this task? Even if no specific content is a priori predestined to serve as a universal, something identifiable as capable of the function of universalization must inhere in it to hegemonically assume that role. In spite of the pragmatic plausibility of the conception of the universal as an empty signifier or place, the idea of the universal as a concept suggests that this empty place has, if not a content, a form or structure that makes it the unmistakable place of the universal.

Needless to say, I do not wish to allot the universal a fixed content – for instance, some immutable essence of humanity given in advance of all actual ethical and political practice. The point on which Laclau and I decidedly concur is the need to liberate the universal from its association with one *eidos*, and to open it to the possibility of plural articulations. It is not clear to me, however, whether its determination as an empty space meets this requirement without a formal and structural clarification of that space as that of the universal. At this point I wish to take up briefly the case of Husserl's conception of universality in an attempt to sketch out, however schematically, a possible direction that such a clarification could take. Laclau's description of the universal as a horizon clearly refers to Husserl's understanding of universality. And Husserl is also a frequent reference point in much of his work (see for instance *NR* 34). Even though universal values can be seen to foster 'an attitude of respect and tolerance *vis-à-vis* cultural diversity', they have also, as Laclau recalls, 'be[en] seen as a strong assertion of the "ethnia of the West"', since, for Husserl, the idea of universality is said to emerge for the first time in Greece, and subsequently to constitute Europe's legacy and telos (*E* 47). Undoubtedly, the Husserlian conception of universality is intimately linked with the West; at the same time, it is the idea of humanity itself, that is, an idea that transcends the 'ethnia of the West'. As Laclau has argued, any universal is unavoidably tied to the particular. But for a particularity to be raised to the status of the universal it must also (at least tendentially) be emptied of its particular content. Only on this condition is it possible that other particularities can recognize themselves in it, and identify with it. Yet if this is the case, the universal cannot, in principle, be of the order of a fixed, and determinable particular content. Now, the idea of 'Europe' as the idea of universal mankind, that is, of something that, first and foremost, transcends Europe as a geographical and ethnic region, is, at its deepest level, nothing but the idea of a task: the infinite task, precisely, of transcending any particularity (ethnic, racial, cultural, and so forth), and which coincides with the idea of humanity itself.[5] Thus understood, and even though it remains linked to Europe as a particular region of the world, this conception of universality is not based on an a priori given essence of any sort. But is it, therefore, simply empty? Laclau would certainly concur that, since no universal comes without a particular, this conception too is inherently contaminated by the particularity that incarnates it. Still, the question that remains concerns this conception's identification of the universal with the infinite task of the critical overcoming of all particularity, in short, the task of achieving nothing less than universality itself. Does this conception of the universal not reveal the universal to have a form of sorts, one that structures universality – a form without which the signifier, and the place called 'universal', could not be identified? As an empty signifier, the universal is certainly divested of all signified; as an empty place, the universal is free of all a priori occupants. In the quality of the former, the universal is capable of relating to all possible signifieds; in the quality of the latter, it signifies locus itself. Differently said, it signifies that in which all particularities dwell. However empty, the signifier and the place have the structure or form of 'signifying' or of 'opening the space in which to dwell'. Is it not this structure or form that makes the empty signifier and empty place the place of the universal, the signifier or the space that concerns every one and everything? Is it not thanks to this form or structure that the empty signifier or place can become the surface of inscription for a diversity of universals? Finally, considering what I have said about Husserl's concept of universality as the infinite task of critically transcending all particularities, is the form or structure of the task to transcend one's particularity not precisely that which endows the universal with the necessary exteriority, and even foreign quality, without which the claim, demand, injunction, associated with universality, could not possibly arise, and be recognized as universal? As an empty signifier or space, the universal signifies the dislocation of all particular signifiers and signifieds as well as that of all particular places. Its universality thus derives from the injunction of its form or structure to go against the grain of one's nature, and this is an injunction that, consequently, comes from the outside.

Notes

1 That the social does not rest on a repeatable identical substratum is posited in the following passage:

> In a closed system of relational identities, in which the meaning of each moment is absolutely fixed, there is no place whatsoever for a hegemonic practice. A fully successful system of differences, which excluded any floating signifier, would not make possible any articulation; the principle of repetition would dominate every practice within this system and there would be nothing to hegemonize. It is because hegemony supposes the incomplete and open character of the social, that it can take place only in a field dominated by articulatory practices.
>
> (*HSS* 134; see also Laclau 2000a: 71)

2 With the term 'system-theoretical', I refer to Ferdinand de Saussure's reflections concerning the systematic nature of language, rather than to Niklas Luhmann's theory of systems.

3 See also Laclau 1996, where the argument is made that the empty signifiers are not absolutely empty.

4 Giving as an example the symbols that in Italy, during the war of liberation from Nazi occupation, functioned as general equivalents, Laclau remarks:

> The larger the number of social demands that they inscribed within their field of representation, the more they became empty, because they became less and less able exclusively to represent *particular* interests within society. In the end, they became the signifiers of the absent fullness of society (2000b: 191–2).

5 In a work to be entitled *The Infinite Task: On the Philosophical Concept of Europe*, this interpretation of Husserl's notion of universality will be developed in detail.

References

Butler, J. (2000a) 'Restaging the universal: Hegemony and the limits of formalism', in J. Butler, E. Laclau and S. Žižek, *Contingency, Hegemony, Universality: Contemporary Dialogues on the Left*, London: Verso.

—— (2000b) 'Competing universalities', in J. Butler, E. Laclau and S. Žižek, *Contingency, Hegemony, Universality: Contemporary Dialogues on the Left*, London: Verso.

Derrida, J. (1988) *Limited Inc*, Evanston, IL: Northwestern University Press.

Laclau, E. (1996) 'The death and resurrection of the theory of ideology', *Journal of Political Ideologies*, 1(3): 201–20.

—— (2000a) 'Identity and hegemony: the role of universality in the constitution of political logics', in J. Butler, E. Laclau and S. Žižek, *Contingency, Hegemony, Universality: Contemporary Dialogues on the Left*, London: Verso.

—— (2000b) 'Structure, history and the political', in J. Butler, E. Laclau and S. Žižek, *Contingency, Hegemony, Universality: Contemporary Dialogues on the Left*, London: Verso.

—— (2000c) 'Constructing universality', in J. Butler, E. Laclau and S. Žižek, *Contingency, Hegemony, Universality: Contemporary Dialogues on the Left*, London: Verso.

Laclau, E. and Zac, L. (1994) 'Minding the gap: the subject of politics', in E. Laclau (ed.), *The Making of Political Identities*, London: Verso.

2

LACLAU AND HEGEMONY

Some (post) Hegelian caveats

Fred Dallmayr

Post-structuralism and deconstruction are frequently seen as mere academic trends, soon to be replaced or outdated by newer fashions. This view is reinforced by their prominent role in literary criticism and aesthetics – fields notoriously prone to quick fluctuations of taste. In application to politics and political theory, deconstruction often appears as little more than a mode of escapism, an attempt at verbal obfuscation oblivious of concrete social contexts and power constellations. Against this background, the work of Ernesto Laclau and Chantal Mouffe offers an invigorating breath of fresh air: brushing aside academic cobwebs; their writings – most notably *Hegemony and Socialist Strategy: Towards a Radical Democratic Politics*[1] – relentlessly and almost passionately probe the implications of deconstruction and anti-foundationalism for political life. Unpretentiously stated (and thus shunning notoriety), their arguments touch at the core of contemporary political and philosophical concerns. Countering any association with escapism or a simple-minded anarchism, the book demonstrates the relevance of post-structural or deconstructive themes for the theoretical grasp of liberalism and socialism, and particularly for the future of democratic politics.

From the vantage of Laclau and Mouffe, the relevance of deconstruction manifests itself prominently or with special virulence in the context of socialist thought (as part and parcel of the so-called crisis of Marxism). As they observe in their Introduction: 'Left-wing thought today stands at a crossroads. The "evident truths" of the past [...] have been seriously challenged by an avalanche of historical mutations which have riven the ground on which those truths were constituted' (*HSS* 2). Apart from a host of social and political changes, the authors appeal to more subtle intellectual dislocations, especially the effects of post-metaphysics with its attack on stable foundations:

> What is now in crisis is a whole conception of socialism which rests upon the ontological centrality of the working class, upon the role of the Revolution (with a capital 'r'), as the founding moment in the transition from one type of society to another, and upon the illusory prospect of a perfectly unitary and homogeneous collective will that will render pointless the moment of politics (2).

In turning to the concept of hegemony, the study seeks to do more than add a further refinement or 'complementary' twist to traditional essentialism: instead, the aim is to initiate a paradigmatic shift reverberating through the entire set of categories and providing a new 'anchorage' from which contemporary social struggles are '*thinkable* in their specificity' (3).[2] In the following I shall first recapitulate briefly some of the main themes presented in *Hegemony and Socialist Strategy*. Subsequently, I shall pick out for closer scrutiny several of the chief theoretical innovations of the study in order to conclude finally with some critical observations or afterthoughts.

I

Congruent with its paradigmatic ambition, *Hegemony and Socialist Strategy* opens with a backward glance at the history of Marxist or socialist discourse and, more specifically, with a detailed genealogy of the concept of hegemony. As the authors emphasize, the concept entered Marxist discourse initially as a stop-gap measure or as a mere supplement designed to patch up evolutionary anomalies. To illustrate the context of the concept's emergence, the opening chapter points to the dilemmas of Rosa Luxemburg as they are revealed in her book on the mass strike (Luxemburg 1906). In that work, Luxemburg recognized the fragmentation of the working class as a necessary structural effect of advancing capitalism; at the same time, however, the prospect of revolutionary struggle was ascribed not to the operation of economic laws but to the spontaneous constitution of class unity through the medium of symbolic action. It was the fissure implicit in this argument which called and made room for a supplementary category curbing the reign of economic necessity.

Initially, to be sure, this opening collided head-on with the dominant Marxist model of the time, a framework spelled out and summarized in Karl Kautsky's commentary on the Erfurt Program (of 1892). According to the Kautskian text, Marxism was an essentialist doctrine predicated on the indissoluble 'unity of theory, history and strategy'. The latter unity or totality, in turn, was based on a number of related features or assumptions – among them, that the structure of industrial society was increasingly simplified in the direction of class conflict; that the two chief classes were differentiated in their essence or by nature due to their diverse status in the mode of production; and that the *dénouement* of class struggle was intelligible as resolution of prior contradictions. It was only at the end of the Bismarck era, with the rise of organized capitalism, that the flaws of the essentialist model began to surface. What made itself felt at this point, we read, was a 'new awareness of the opacity of the social, of the complexities and resistances of an increasingly organized capitalism; and the fragmentation of the different positions of social agents which, according to the classical paradigm, should have been united' (*HSS* 18; see also Kautsky 1910).

Reactions to these changes were halting and only slowly affected the structure of traditional premises. Laclau and Mouffe discuss three immediate responses to the perceived crisis of Marxism: the establishment of 'Marxist orthodoxy', the formulation of a 'revisionist' approach by Eduard Bernstein, and Georges Sorel's 'revolutionary syndicalism'. Marxist orthodoxy, in their presentation, involves the ascendancy or privileging of abstract theory over concrete social struggles and also over the political practice of social-democratic parties. Divergences from theoretical postulates were treated either as deceptive appearances or surface phenomena or else as marginal contingencies unable to alter the predicted course of events: namely, the ascendancy of a unified proletariat under the leadership of the workers' party. Only occasionally – especially in the cases of Antonio Labriola and Austro-Marxism – did orthodoxy grant some space to autonomous political initiatives but without proceeding to integrate such initiatives within the overall theoretical framework.

The issue of the relation of politics and economics, or of superstructure and base, was the central motif underlying Bernstein's revisionist approach – a position which insisted that the fragmentation or division of the working class in advanced capitalism could be remedied only through concrete political intervention. While introducing a breach between politics and economics, however, revisionism never questioned the class-based character of political action or of the workers' party; moreover, Bernstein's Kantian leanings fostered a dualism between the realm of freedom (anchored in the autonomy of ethical subjects) and the determinism of economic laws – a gulf only precariously bridged by the notion of social 'evolution' (*Entwicklung*). Moving beyond a simple juxtaposition of domains, revolutionary syndicalism as advocated by Sorel attempted for the first time to conceptualize social autonomy, that is, to 'think the specificity of that "logic of contingency"' on which 'a field of totalizing effects is reconstituted' (*HSS* 37). Pursuing this path, Sorel was led to replace economic class unity with more amorphous social 'blocs' held together by ideological devices.[3]

A corollary of these reactions to social fragmentation was the emergence of the concept of hegemony as the site of a new or ascending political logic. In orthodox discourse the concept occupied only a marginal place, as a marker for theoretically undigested events. In the writings of Georgii Plekhanov and Pavel Axelrod, for example, hegemony designated the multiple (economic and political) tasks imposed on the Russian proletariat as a result of economic backwardness. According to Laclau and Mouffe, hegemonic relations at this point merely '*supplement* class relations. Using a distinction of Saussure's, we could say that hegemonic relations are always facts of *parole*, while class relations are facts of *langue*' (51). The reduction to supplementary status was still operative in Leninism, and especially in the Leninist formula of a 'class alliance' cemented under the leadership of a proletarian 'vanguard' party. Due to the 'ontological centrality' assigned to the proletariat, class alliance in this case did not modify essential class identities in the direction of fusing them with the democratic demands implicit in hegemonic practices. The same centrality was reinforced in the immediate aftermath of the Russian revolution – as is evident in Zinoviev's slogan of the 'bolshevization' of communist parties, where 'bolshevization' means 'a firm will to struggle for the hegemony of the proletariat' (quoted at *HSS* 61).

In terms of the study, the crucial break with Marxist essentialism was initiated by Antonio Gramsci whose work is portrayed as the decisive 'watershed' offering a formulation of the hegemonic link 'which clearly went beyond the Leninist category of "class alliance" ' (66). Extricating himself from the legacy of fixed class identities, Gramsci focused on broader social groupings called 'historical blocs' whose unity of purpose or 'collective will' was fostered by intellectual and moral leadership in a context of cultural and political hegemony. As a corollary, moving beyond simple base-superstructure formulas, his approach perceived ideology not as an abstract system of ideas but as an organic ensemble of beliefs and concrete practices partially embodied in institutions and social structures. Yet, despite these important theoretical advances, Laclau and Mouffe note a persistent ambivalence in Gramsci's work curtailing his pioneering role: namely, a tendency to return to an 'ontological' conception of class identity or to ascribe the ultimately unifying power in hegemonic formations to an economically defined class. To the extent that the Gramscian 'war of position' still paid tribute to a zero-sum construal of class struggle – they write – it revealed an 'inner essentialist core' in his thought 'setting a limit to the deconstructive logic of hegemony' (69). The same ambivalence, in their view, was reflected in social-democratic policies of the period, especially in the 'planism' of the post-Depression era and also in later technocratic models of state intervention (see Gramsci 1957).

Against the backdrop of this historical scenario, the study embarks on its central and most ambitious task: the theoretical elaboration of a non-essentialist concept of hegemony as cornerstone of a 'radically democratic' political theory. On non-foundational premises, hegemony has the character of a creative 'articulation', that is, of the 'political construction' of a social formation out of dissimilar elements. Such a creative articulation is radically at odds with a closed 'totality' or a view of society as a completely intelligible and homogeneous structure – a view partially operative in Hegelian philosophy and in versions of Marxism. To clarify their conception of hegemony, Laclau and Mouffe proceed through a detour: a confrontation with Louis Althusser's structuralist theory and its aftermath. The most promising feature of Althusser's approach, they note, was the principle of 'overdetermination' – the thesis that social formations or phenomena are not causally fixed but the result of a symbolic fusion of plural meetings. As it happened, however, overdetermination remained vague in Althusser's work and was progressively overshadowed by other structuralist ingredients, especially the claim of determination by the economy 'in the last instance'; as a result of this claim, symbolic construction functioned merely as a contingent margin of causal necessity.

The theoretical critique of Althusser's model – as inaugurated by Etienne Balibar and continued by spokesmen of British Marxism (like Barry Hindess and Paul Hirst) – focused on the logical connections among ingredients of the model and ultimately on the role and status of 'structural causality'. While promising in many respects, this critique, according to the authors, has so far resulted only in logical disaggregation and not in a radical reformulation of basic categories. Moving in the latter direction, the study advances these definitional propositions: 'We will call *articulation* any practice establishing a relation among elements such that their identity is modified as a result of the articulatory practice. The structured totality resulting from the articulatory practice, we will call *discourse*' (*HSS* 105). While differential positions articulated within a discourse are termed 'moments', the label *elements* is reserved for differences not discursively structured. Discursive formations are said to be unified neither logically nor empirically nor transcendentally but only through an ambivalent symbolic coherence (akin to Foucault's 'regularity in dispersion'). Most importantly, as articulatory enterprises, discourses only selectively structure the social domain without reaching definitive closure; due to their inherent finitude and multivocity, they never exhaust the broader 'field of discursivity' with its available surplus of meaning. Hegemony here denotes the selective structuring of the social field around distinct 'nodal points' seen as privileged discursive accents.[4]

Fleshing out the notion of discursive practices, Laclau and Mouffe comment in some detail on the role of the subject (or subjectivity) in such practices; on the contest or antagonism prevailing between discursive formations; and on the relation between hegemony and democracy. In line with the unfixity of social identities, subjects in their view cannot function as the constitutive origin of social formations – which does not entail the elimination of human agents but rather their construal as 'subject positions' within a discursive structure (possibly as nodal points in such a structure). On the level of Marxist analysis, economic classes likewise are only articulated ingredients (possibly nodal ingredients) within a selectively structured social field. Due to their finite and selective character, discursive formations are inevitably in tension with alternative possibilities. In a critical review of Marxist literature, the study sharply demarcates antagonism from such notions as 'logical contradiction' and 'real opposition' (*Realrepugnanz*): while the latter are objectively given relations, the former derives precisely from ambiguity and the contestation of givenness.

Seen as limit of social formations, antagonism results not merely from the confrontation between different empirical structures, but rather operates as an intrinsic negative potency in every formation challenging its presumed positivity or its objective givenness. According to the authors, this negative potency manifests itself chiefly through a system of equivalence which subverts all positive differences, reducing them to an underlying sameness. 'The *ultimate* character of this unfixity (of the social)', they write,

> the *ultimate* precariousness of all difference, will show itself in a relation of total equivalence, where the differential positivity of all its terms is dissolved. This is precisely the formula of antagonism, which thus establishes itself as the limit of the social (128).

Yet, just as social positivity can never fully be stabilized, negativity or negative equivalence cannot become a total or all-embracing enterprise (without canceling the very possibility of social articulation). Instead, social formations are predicated on a precarious blend of the 'opposed logics of equivalence and difference' – with full integration and total rupture only signaling the extreme ends of a spectrum.

This aspect brings into view the relation between hegemony and democracy. Viewed as a social formation, democracy cannot be reduced to total equivalence or a bipolar conflict between self-enclosed camps – despite the possible presence of deep fissures. Differentiating between 'popular struggles' (in a Jacobin sense) and 'democratic struggles', the study presents the former only as extreme variants within the broader framework of hegemonic democratic relations:

> The existence of two camps may in some cases be an *effect* of the hegemonic articulation but not its a priori condition. [...] We will therefore speak of *democratic* struggles where these imply a plurality of political spaces, and of *popular* struggles where certain discourses *tendentially* construct the division of a single political space in two opposed fields. But it is clear that the fundamental concept is that of 'democratic struggle' (137).

The theme of hegemony and democracy is further explored in the concluding chapter of the study. In the authors' view, the relation between socialism and democratic politics has involved a difficult process of adjustment: namely, the move from an essentialist doctrine – treating the bipolar division of society as '*an original and immutable datum*, prior to all hegemonic construction' – toward a more diversified democratic conception acknowledging the basic 'instability of political spaces' and the fact that 'the very identity of the forces in struggle is submitted to constant shifts' (151). The last approximation of a factual bipolarity occurred during the French Revolution, with the pervasive opposition between 'people' and '*ancien régime*'. Since that time, however, the dividing line between social antagonisms has become increasingly 'fragile and ambiguous' and its formulation has emerged as the 'crucial problem of politics'. As discussed in previous chapters, Marxism sought to reconstitute an essential polarity on economic grounds – but without succeeding in translating the distinction of classes into an automatic social-political conflict.

According to Laclau and Mouffe, the development of radical democracy has put in question the 'continuity between the Jacobin and the Marxist political imaginary', and more generally the assumption of a privileged point of rupture and the 'confluence of struggles into a unified political space' (152). Returning to the period of the French Revolution, the study portrays the insurgent 'logic of equivalence' as the basic instrument of social change and as the beginning of a long-term 'democratic revolution'. This process of democratization has gained added momentum in recent decades, due to antagonisms triggered by the so-called new social movements. The targets of insurgency in this case are chiefly the bureaucratization, commodification, and growing homogenization of life in advanced industrial societies. In theoretical terms, what these movements bring into view is the specificity of contemporary struggles constituted on the basis of 'different subject positions' (in lieu of a fixed or foundational polarity); more generally, they highlight the emergence of a 'radical and plural democracy' with a close intermeshing of radicalism and pluralism.

As the authors recognize, the shift from essentialism to plural struggles does not by itself guarantee a progressive democratic outcome. Pointing to the rise of the 'new right' and of neo-conservatism in Western countries, the study detects in our time a new valorization of positive social differences and also of individual autonomy seen as a counterpoint to mass democracy. What this counter-insurgency accentuates – Laclau and Mouffe argue – is the importance of political hegemony and the need to intensify broad-based political struggles in line with the modern process of democratization. Such struggles, they write, should locate themselves fully 'in the field of the democratic revolution' and its expanding chains of equivalence; their task, in any case, '*cannot be to renounce liberal-democratic ideology, but on the contrary, to deepen and expand it in the direction of a radical and plural democracy*' (176). Socialist strategy in the past was ill equipped to shoulder this task, mainly due to its hankering for an 'essentialist apriorism' – a hankering manifest in its reliance on privileged subjects ('classism'), on a privileged social basis ('economism'), and on a privileged policy instrument ('statism').

In a condensed form, these preferences surfaced in the attachment to the foundational role of 'revolution' (in the Jacobin mould). Overcoming this legacy means to acknowledge the differentiation of contemporary antagonisms and the multiplication of political spaces and avenues: 'There is not *one* politics of the Left whose contents can be determined in isolation from all contextual reference. It is for this reason that all attempts to proceed to such determination *a priori* have necessarily been unilateral and arbitrary' (179). Once apriorism is abandoned, socialist strategy has to insert itself into the precarious web of hegemonic democratic relations, particularly into the interplay of positivity and negativity or of the logic of difference and the logic of equivalence – an interplay which is now also phrased as the tension between equality and liberty or autonomy. Disrupting this tension in favor of one constitutive dimension conjures up the peril of a closed society (in the form of either a leftist or a rightist totalitarianism). As the authors conclude:

> Between the logic of complete identity and that of pure difference, the experience of democracy should consist of the recognition of the multiplicity of social logics along with the necessity of their [hegemonic] articulation – an articulation which needs to be 'constantly re-created and renegotiated' (188).[5]

II

As should be clear from the preceding synopsis, *Hegemony and Socialist Strategy* is a richly textured, insightful, and often provocative work; it is also tightly argued and intellectually uncompromising – in a manner barring easy access. In terms of contemporary labels, the study inserts itself in the broad movement of post-structuralism and postmodernism – but without facile trendiness (and without entirely abandoning structuralist themes, from Ferdinand de Saussure to Althusser).[6] Contrary to aestheticizing tendencies or construals, the work clearly demonstrates the relevance of post-essentialism or deconstruction for political theory; in fact, *Hegemony and Socialist Strategy* can and should be viewed as a major contribution to a present-day understanding of democracy. Most importantly, the study counteracts the widespread association of deconstruction with anarchism or with complete social and political randomness. Although devoid of essentialist moorings or ontological fixity, post-structuralist politics – as presented by Laclau and Mouffe – operates in a complex relational web endowed with distinct parameters or constraints, parameters shielding radical democracy from the perils of despotism, totalitarianism, and unmitigated violence.

Although amenable to diverse interpretations, the study (in my view) is basically a political text, offering a splendid example of innovative political theorizing. Apart from its historical resonances, the accent on hegemony involves centrally a revalorization of politics against all forms of reductionism (subordinating politics to other domains). A crucial assault launched in the study is directed at sociologism as well as economism. In a bold formulation – challenging prominent portrayals of sociology as 'master social science' – Laclau and Mouffe speak of the 'impossibility of society', that is, the inability of the social domain to provide a firm grounding of analysis. They write, pinpointing a 'decisive point' in their argument: 'The incomplete character of every totality leads us to abandon, as a terrain of analysis, the premise of "*society*" as a sutured and self-defined totality. "Society" is not a valid object of discourse' since there is 'no single underlying principle fixing – and hence constituting – the whole field of differences' (111).

What society needs to gain contours is some kind of political articulation, that is, the formulation and establishment of a hegemonic political relationship. Reminiscent vaguely of Arendtian arguments, the study defines politics as 'a practice of creation, reproduction and transformation of social relations', a practice that cannot be located at a 'determinate level of the social' since the problem of the political is 'the problem of the institution of the social, that is, of the definition and articulation of social relations in a field criss-crossed with antagonisms' (153). Moving beyond Arendt, however, the authors do not accord to politics a stable space or a completely autonomous sphere. In effect, radical democracy in their text is presented as a form of politics which is founded

> not upon dogmatic postulation of any 'essence of the social', but, on the contrary, on affirmation of the contingency and ambiguity of every 'essence', and on the constitutive character of social division and antagonism. Affirmation of a 'ground' which lives only by negating its fundamental character; of an 'order' which exists only as a partial limiting of 'disorder' (193).

The attack on the constitutive character of the social domain applies with particular force to economism as it has operated in traditional Marxism. Challenging the presumed determination of the labor process and of class struggle by an abstract 'logic of capital', Laclau and Mouffe assert the dependence of the latter on antagonisms linked with a pervasive 'politics of production'. A number of recent studies, they write, 'have analyzed the evolution of the labor process from the point of view of the relation of forces between workers and capitalists, and of the workers' resistance. These reveal the presence of a "politics of production"' at odds with the notion that capitalist development is the effect 'solely of the laws of competition and the exigencies of accumulation' (79). To be sure, attacking economism is not the same as postulating a rigid separation between economics and politics or ascribing a foundational status to the latter. According to the authors, such a view could only be maintained 'if political practice was a perfectly delimited field whose frontiers with the economy could be drawn *more geometrico* – that is, if we excluded as a matter of principle any overdetermination of the political by the economic or vice versa' (120). Given that politics is a matter of hegemonic articulation, the relationship between politics and economics cannot be permanently fixed or stabilized and depends on circumstances and prevailing articulatory practices.

The dismantling of univocal fixity and the accent on complex relationships lends to the study a quasi-Hegelian or (more properly) post-Hegelian flavor – a circumstance readily acknowledged by the authors. In terms of *Hegemony and Socialist Strategy*, Hegel's philosophy is precariously and ambiguously lodged at the intersection between metaphysics and post-metaphysics – more specifically between a theory of totality and a theory of hegemony (or else between total mediation and hegemonic articulation). In the authors' words, Hegel's work is at once the 'highest moment' of German rationalism and idealism and simultaneously 'the first modern – that is to say, post-Enlightenment – reflection on society' (94). The ambiguity has to do chiefly with the ability of reason to grasp reality as a whole; differently phrased: with the respective weights assigned to absolute logic and a more opaque and contingent 'cunning of reason'. Occupying a watershed between two epochs, Hegel is said to represent on the one hand the culmination of rationalism: namely, 'the moment when it attempts to embrace within the field of reason, without dualisms, the totality of the universe of differences' (95). On the other hand, however, Hegel's totality or synthesis contains 'all the seeds of its dissolution', as the rationality of history can be affirmed 'only at the price of introducing contradiction into the field of reason itself' (95). The continued significance of Hegel's thought resides basically in the second dimension: namely, in its role as mdiwife for a theory of hegemony, opening reflection up to the flux of contingent and not purely logical (or essential) relationships.[7]

The post-Hegelian quality of the study – or its Hegelianism with a deconstructive twist – surfaces at numerous points and most prominently in the discussion of hegemony and its relation to antagonism. As previously indicated, antagonism denotes not simply a juxtaposition of objective entities (either on a logical or a factual level), but rather involves a process of mutual contestation and struggle. In general philosophical terms, antagonism arises from hegemony's inability to effect social and political closure – that is, from the polysemy and 'surplus of meaning' constantly overreaching and destabilizing discursive practices. In language reminiscent of Hegel, the study situates social formations at the crossroads of positivity and negativity, where negativity designates not simply a lack but a 'nihilating' potency.

The tensional relation between presence and absence resurfaces or is rearticulated as the interplay of two social logics, namely, the logics of equivalence and difference. Here again it is important to notice that, although the two point in opposite directions, neither logic is able to achieve foundational status or complete self-enclosure. In the authors' words: 'if negativity and positivity exist only "through their reciprocal subversion", this means that "neither the conditions of total equivalence nor those of total differential objectivity are ever fully achieved" ' (129). Translating the interplay of logics into the more traditional correlation of liberty and equality, another passage asserts:

> The precariousness of every equivalence demands that it be complemented/limited by the logic of autonomy. It is for this reason that the demand for *equality* is not sufficient, but needs to be balanced by the demand for *liberty*, which leads us to speak of a radical and *plural* democracy (184).[8]

The notion of the correlation and interpenetration of social logics presents politics – particularly democratic politics – as an arena of contestation and interrogation, but not as a field of total domination or else mutual destruction. The accent on the relational character of antagonism injects into politics a moral or qualitative dimension, an aspect hostile to the reduction of politics to a simple organism (or mechanism) or else to a naturalistic state of war. If social identities are acquired only through agonal interaction, then it is impossible or illicit either to impose stable identity through a model of integral totality or to foreclose interaction through a system of radical equivalence. Integral closure – the lure of complete social positivity – is chiefly the temptation of the logic of difference. As the authors point out, however, due to its negative potency, antagonism signifies the 'limit' of any given social order 'and not the moment of a broader totality in relation to which the two poles of the antagonism would constitute differential – i.e., objective – partial instances' (126). The opposite temptation arises from the logic of equivalence: radically pursued, equivalence either totally negates discursive formations and social identities or else polarizes society into two hostile forces of which each operates as the negation of the other. An example of the latter alternative – Laclau and Mouffe observe – can be found in millenarian movements where 'the world divides, through a system of paratactical equivalences, into two camps' (129) related only in the mode of negative reversal. More recent instances are terrorism or totalitarian absolutism.[9]

The implications of this relational conception are multiple and significant: only a few can be highlighted here. Although the study's post-Hegelian thrust is directed chiefly against all forms of integral closure or sutured totality, the proposed remedy or antidote is not random fragmentation. While critical of the pretense of universal principles or discourses, the authors do not simply opt for particularism – which would only entail a new kind of self-enclosure or a 'monadic' essentialism. As they indicate, a mere dismantling of totality readily conjures up the peril of 'a new form of fixity', namely, on the level of 'decentered subject positions'. For this reason, a 'logic of detotalization' cannot simply affirm 'the *separation* of different struggles and demands', just as 'articulation' cannot purely be conceived as 'the linkage of dissimilar and fully constituted elements' (87). Through a strategy of disaggregation we are in danger of moving 'from an essentialism of the totality to an essentialism of the elements' or of replacing 'Spinoza with Leibniz'. The means for overcoming this danger is provided by the logic of 'overdetermination'. For, we read, if the sense of every identity is overdetermined, then

> far from there being an essentialist *totalization*, or a no less essentialist *separation* among objects, the presence of some objects in the others prevents any of their identities from being fixed. Objects appear articulated not like pieces in a clockwork mechanism, but because the presence of some in the others hinders the suturing of the identity of any of them (104).

Similar considerations apply to the issue of pluralism. Although endorsing a 'radical and plural democracy', the study holds no brief for group egotism. In the authors' words, either an absolute pluralism or a 'total diffusion of power within the social' (*HSS* 142) would blind us to the operation of overdetermination and to the presence of 'nodal points' in every social formation. With slight modifications, relationism or the interpenetration of identities also affects the status of individual autonomy or liberty. Segregated from equality or equivalence, such autonomy only fosters new modes of totalization – which points up the need to reformulate 'bourgeois individualism':

> What is involved is the production of *another* individual, an individual who is no longer constructed out of the matrix of possessive individualism. [...] It is never possible for individual rights to be defined in isolation, but only in the context of social relations which define determinate subject positions (184).[10]

Among the most significant contributions of the study are its caveats against total antagonism or against the polarization and militarization of politics. In our violence-prone age when many flirt with theories of radical discord – as an antidote to co-optation – *Hegemony and Socialist Strategy* offers a welcome corrective. In the presentation of Laclau and Mouffe, polarization was the trademark of both Jacobinism and essentialist Marxism; from Lenin's 'What is to be Done' to Zinoviev's motto of bolshevization, a military conception of politics dominated the range of strategic calculations. In this conception political struggle is basically a zero-sum game, a game producing a segregation effect in the sense that the hostile camps tend to retreat into the shells of their separate identities.

Polar vocabulary was still present – though ambiguously and in modified form – in the Gramscian notion of war of position. For Gramsci, war of position involved the progressive disaggregation of a social formation and the construction of a new hegemony of forces – but along a path which left the identity of the opponents malleable and subject to a continuous process of transformation. Thus, the military imagery was in this case 'metaphorized' in a direction colliding with its literal sense: 'If in Leninism there was a militarization of politics, in Gramsci there is a demilitarization of war' (70) – although the reformulation reached its limit in the assumption of an ultimate class core of every hegemony. Once the latter assumption is dropped, Gramsci's notion can be metaphorized further in a manner compatible with radical democracy. At this point, the distinction between popular struggles and democratic struggles becomes relevant. While Gramsci still presupposed the division of political space along the lines of popular identities (though granting their constructed character), relinquishing this premise opens the way to a fluid and non-dichotomous concept of hegemony:

> We will thus retain from the Gramscian view the logic of articulation and the political centrality of the frontier effects, but we will eliminate the assumption of a single political space as the necessary framework for those phenomena to arise (137).

Democratic struggles are precisely those that involve a plurality of political spaces.[11]

III

While greatly appreciating the depth and rigor of Laclau and Mouffe's work, I cannot refrain from voicing some reservations or critical afterthoughts. These comments are not meant to deprecate the cogency and overall direction of its arguments, but rather to amplify and strengthen the same direction – which is basically that of a viable post-Hegelian political theory. Precisely from a Hegelian vantage point, some of the accents of the study appear to me lopsided or skewed. In tracing the genealogy of hegemony, the opening chapter places a heavy – and probably excessive – emphasis on autonomous action and initiative. Thus, in the discussion of Luxemburg, the 'logic of spontaneism' is singled out as an important counterpoint to class-based essentialism and the literal fixation of social meanings. Similarly, Sorel's myth of the great strike is held up for its focus on 'contingency' and 'freedom', in contradistinction to the chain of social and economic necessity.

Influenced by Nietzsche and Henri Bergson, Sorel's philosophy is said to be 'one of action and will, in which the future is unforeseeable, and hinges on will' (36). Formulations of this kind are liable to inject into the study a flavor of voluntarism which is not entirely congruent with the authors' broader perspective. The impression is reinforced in the central portion of the study, namely, in the equation of hegemony with articulation and of the latter with a mode of 'political construction from dissimilar elements' (85). The term *construction* seems to place hegemony in the rubric of a 'purposive' and voluntaristic type of action (in the Weberian sense) – in a manner obfuscating the distinction between praxis (or practical conduct) and technical-instrumental behavior. Although perhaps inadvertent, the confluence of meanings needs in my view to be sorted out in order to differentiate hegemony more clearly from forms of instrumentalism.[12]

Once voluntarism is eschewed as a remedy for essentialist fixation, the study embarks on hazardous terrain. In fact, its theory of hegemony is lodged at one of the most difficult junctures of Hegelian thought (and of traditional metaphysics in general): the juncture marked by the categories of 'freedom' and 'necessity', of 'determinism' and 'contingency'. Occasionally, hegemony is portrayed almost as an exit route from necessity and all modes of social determinism. Thus, while Marxist essentialism is said to have banished contingency to the margins of necessity, the relationship is claimed to be reversed in hegemonic articulation – in the sense that necessity now 'only exists as a partial limitation of the field of contingency' (111). As the authors somewhat exuberantly add:

> If we accept that a discursive totality never exists in the form of a simply *given and delimited* positivity, the relational logic will be incomplete and pierced by contingency. [...] A no-man's-land thus emerges making the articulatory practice possible (110–11).

Elsewhere, however, this simple reversal is called into question – which opens the road to a complex and fascinating conceptualization of hegemony in terms of an intertwining and mutual subversion of necessity and contingency. Once the goal of final fixation recedes, Laclau and Mouffe observe, a profound ambivalence emerges: at this point not only does the very category of necessity fall, but it is no longer possible to account for the hegemonic relation in terms of pure contingency, as the space which made intelligible the necessary/contingent opposition has dissolved. What emerges at this point is no longer a simple external delimitation of two contiguous fields, but rather a relationship of mutual interpenetration and contestation. As they write, the relations between necessity and contingency cannot be conceived as 'relations between two areas that are delimited and external to each other [...] because the contingent only exists within the necessary. This presence of the contingent in the necessary is what we earlier called *subversion*' (114) – and what, in effect, must be called reciprocal subversion. As a result, the centrality of hegemony is predicated on 'the collapse of a clear demarcation line between the internal and the external, between the contingent and the necessary' (142).[13]

What the preceding comments adumbrate is a theoretical relationship which is recalcitrant both to dualism and to monism (in their traditional metaphysical sense). The opposition to dualism is a recurrent theme of the study. Thus, Bernstein's revisionism is chided for embracing a 'Kantian dualism', pitting autonomous ethical subjects against economic determinism. Similarly, Marxist orthodoxy is taken to task for harboring a 'permanent' and 'irreducible' dualism between the logic of necessity and the logic of contingency, with each side being merely the 'negative reverse' of the other. Such dualism, the authors note, establishes merely a 'relation of frontiers', that is, an external limitation of domains devoid of reciprocal effects. Opposition to dualism is also evident in the notion of discursive materiality and the critique of the thought–reality bifurcation. Yet, at the same time, anti-dualism does not vindicate a simple fusionism or a complete elimination of non-identity.

The distinction between 'elements' and 'moments' in articulatory practices is, in fact, predicated on the persistence of a (non-dualistic mode of) non-identity. If articulation is a practice, we read, 'it must imply some form of separate presence of the elements which that practice articulates or recomposes' (93); it must also exclude the complete transformation of elements into integral moments or components. The same kind of non-identical relationship prevails between social formations seen as articulated discursive chains, on the one hand, and 'floating signifiers' constantly exceeding these chains, on the other; and ultimately between discursive practices in general and the '*infinitude of the field of discursivity*' (113). What comes into view here is a term placed midway between identity and total non-identity, a term which some post-structuralist thinkers have thematized under such labels as *intertwining* or *duality*; Heidegger's *Zwiefalt* (two-foldedness) and the Derridean notion of *différance* point in the same direction.[14]

In a prominent manner, the notion of intertwining or duality would seem to be applicable to the relation between positivity and negativity or between the logics of difference and equivalence (as these terms are used in the study). As the authors repeatedly affirm, negativity is not simply a void or a logical negation but a nihilating ferment exerting real effects: 'The presence of the Other is not a logical impossibility: it exists; so it is not a contradiction' (125). The same thought is expressed in the argument that negativity and positivity exist only 'through their reciprocal subversion', and also in the view that antagonism as the negation of a given order operates as the intrinsic limit of that order – and not as an alien force imposing external constraints. Unfortunately, passages of this kind collide with occasional formulations which approximate the interplay to a Sartrean kind of antithesis (of being and nothingness). Small wonder that on such premises antagonism begins to shade over into total conflict – as happens in a passage which finds the 'formula of antagonism' in a 'relation of total equivalence, where the differential positivity of all [...] terms is dissolved' (128).

Flirtation with nothingness is also evident in the statement that experience of negativity is 'not an access to a diverse ontological order, to a something beyond differences, simply because ... there is no beyond' (126). Yet, the fact that negativity is not another objective (or positive) order does not mean that what lies 'beyond differences' is simply nothingness. In fact, if differences were related strictly by nothing, the result would be total segregation or equivalence – and by no means the complex web of relationships thematized under the label of *hegemony*. In Heidegger's vocabulary (which, to be sure, has to be employed cautiously), different elements in order to enjoy a relationship are linked on the level of being – a term denoting a non-objective type of matrix in which positivity and negativity, ground and abyss (*Abgrund*), are peculiarly intertwined.

A similar intertwining affects another oppositional pair closely linked with the nexus of presence and absence: the relation of inside and outside, of interiority and exteriority. On this issue, too, the authors are not always entirely clear and oscillate between divergent conceptions. Thus, in presenting every social formation as a 'delimited positivity', they affirm that 'there is no social identity fully protected from a discursive exterior that deforms it and prevents its becoming fully sutured' (111). The accent on exteriority is further reinforced in a passage dealing with the character of social antagonism. As a witness of the 'impossibility of a final suture', we read, antagonism 'is the experience of the limit of the social. Strictly speaking, antagonisms are not *internal* but *external* to society; or rather, they constitute the limits of society, the latter's impossibility of fully constituting itself' (125).

This formulation, of course, stands in conflict with the notion of limit as a mode of internal subversion or the claim that society is everywhere 'penetrated by its limits' (127). Elsewhere, it is true, the study insists explicitly on the 'irresoluble interiority/exteriority tension' as a 'condition of any social practice,' and on the collapse of a 'clear demarcation line between the internal and the external' (142). This conception, in my view, is more readily congruent with the emphasis on non-essentialist types of antagonism and on the relational quality of hegemony. The discussion of hegemony contains, in fact, a lucid endorsement of this tensional approach. The hegemonic subject, we learn there, 'must be partially exterior to what it articulates – otherwise there would not be any articulation at all'. On the other hand, however, 'such exteriority cannot be conceived as that existing between two different ontological levels'. As a result, to the extent that the term is applicable, exteriority 'cannot correspond to two fully constituted discursive formations' or to 'two systems of fully constituted differences' (135) (that is, to two domains radically exterior to each other).

The external–internal quandary carries over into the conception of democracy – surely a centerpiece of *Hegemony and Socialist Practice*. In this context, the quandary surfaces as the opposition between democracy construed as a system of radical equivalence and democracy as a social formation intrinsically marked by the tension between equivalence and difference. The first alternative is stressed in the historical narrative tracing the emergence and spreading of 'democratic revolution'. Referring to the beginning of this process, the study detects a 'decisive mutation in the political imaginary of Western societies' at the time of the French Revolution, a mutation which is defined in these terms: 'the logic of equivalence was transformed into the fundamental instrument of the production of the social' (155). The same kind of principle is said to govern the subsequent process of democratization:

> The logic of democracy is simply the equivalential displacement of the egalitarian imaginary to ever more extensive social relations, and, as such, it is only a logic of the elimination of relations of subordination and of inequalities' and 'not a logic of the positivity of the social (188).

Not surprisingly, in order to constitute a viable social order, democracy defined in this manner – as a pure 'strategy of opposition' – needs to be supplemented with a 'strategy of construction of a new order' bringing into play the 'element of social positivity' (189). Actually, however, the construal of democracy as radical equivalence or as expression of a purely 'subversive logic' stands in conflict with the conception of 'plural democracy' emphasized in the study – a conception in which equivalence and difference, equality and liberty (or autonomy), are inextricably linked. As Laclau and Mouffe state (in a previously cited passage): 'Between the logic of complete identity and that of pure difference, the experience of democracy should consist of the recognition of the multiplicity of social logics along with the necessity of their articulation' (188). Against this background of tensional experience, the pursuit of pure equivalence emerges in fact as a sign of political deformation – provoking the specter of despotism and totalitarianism.[15]

The latter deformation leads me to a final comment. If democracy involves a complex relationship of forces and groupings (recalcitrant to total opposition or essentialist fixation), then antagonism does not necessarily have to have a hostile and mutually coercive character. If hegemony denotes a non-exclusive articulation – fostering an intertwining of exteriority and interiority – then room seems to be made for a more friendly or sympathetic mode of interaction (which, to be sure, cannot entirely cancel negativity and thus an element of equivalence and power). Against this background it appears possible to reinvigorate the Aristotelian notion of 'friendship' seen as a binding matrix of political life – provided political friendship is carefully differentiated from its more utilitarian and instrumental variants. Extending the study's post-Hegelian leanings, it seems likewise feasible and legitimate to view politics as permeated by ethical concerns or by the Hegelian category of *Sittlichkeit*. Along the same lines, there may be an opportunity today to rethink the Hegelian state – in such a manner that state no longer signifies a positive structure or totality, and certainly not simply an instrument of coercion, but rather the fragile ethical bond implicit in hegemonic political relations. Democracy under these auspices is still an arena of struggle, but a struggle directed not simply toward domination but toward the establishment of a tensional balance between presence and absence, liberty and equality: that is a struggle for mutual recognition (of differences).[16]

Notes

1 It is my assumption that the logical form of the book's argument was contributed mainly by Laclau.

2 In critiquing a class-based essentialism, Laclau and Mouffe locate themselves plainly in 'a post-Marxist terrain' – which does not imply a summary dismissal of Marxism. As they emphasize: 'If our intellectual project in this book is *post*-Marxist, it is evidently also post-*Marxist*' (*HSS* 4). Moreover, the critique of essentialism extends beyond traditional Marxism to other discursive frameworks or 'normative epistemologies':

> Political conclusions similar to those set forth in this book could have been approximated from very different discursive formations – for example, from certain forms of Christianity, or from libertarian discourses alien to the socialist tradition – none of which could aspire to be the truth of society (3).

3 According to the authors, Bernstein's revisionism also supported a gradualist type of reformism – but only for contingent reasons. Basically, the two strategies or approaches do not coincide: 'Thus, in attempting to identify the precise difference between reformism and revisionism, we must stress that *what is essential in a reformist practice is political quietism and the corporatist confinement of the working class*' (*HSS* 30). Compare Bernstein 1961 and Sorel 1950.

4 As the study adds, since …

> all discourse is subverted by a field of discursivity which overflows it, the transition from 'elements' to 'moments' can never be complete. The status of the 'elements' is that of floating signifiers, incapable of being wholly articulated to a discursive chain. […] It is not the poverty of signifieds but, on the contrary, polysemy that disarticulates a discursive structure. That is what establishes the overdetermined, symbolic dimension of every social identity. Society never manages to be identical to itself, as every nodal point is constituted within an intertextuality that overflows it. *The practice of articulation, therefore, consists in the construction of nodal points which partially fix meaning; and the partial character of this fixation proceeds from the openness of the social, a result, in its turn, of the constant overflowing of every discourse by the infinitude of the field of discursity* (*HSS* 113).

5 Compare also their comment:

> The de-centering and autonomy of the different discourses and struggles, the multiplication of antagonisms and the construction of a plurality of spaces within which they can affirm themselves and develop, are the conditions *sine qua non* of the possibility that the different components of the classical ideal of socialism – which should, no doubt, be extended and reformulated – can be achieved (*HSS* 192).

6 The distance from structuralism is expressed in these comments:

> When the linguistic model was introduced into the general field of human sciences, it was this effect of systematicity that predominated, so that structuralism became a new form of essentialism: a search for the underlying structures constituting the inherent law of any possible variation. The critique of structuralism involved a break with this view of a fully constituted structural space. […] The sign is the name of a split, of an impossible suture between signified and signifier (113).

The authors refer in this context explicitly to Derrida 1978.

7 The repercussions of traditional rationalism are found in Hegel's theory of the 'state' and especially in his conception of the bureaucracy as 'universal class' (*HSS* 191). The assessment of Hegel relies strongly on Trendelenburg 1840.

8 Another passage (*HSS* 130) phrases the two logics in the vocabulary of linguistics, associating the logic of difference with the 'syntagmatic pole' of language (the sequence of continuous combinations) and the logic of equivalence with the 'paradigmatic pole' (relations of substitution).

9 Elsewhere the danger of the two social logics is seen in their transformation from a 'horizon' into a 'foundation' (*HSS* 183).

10 Regarding universalism compare these comments:

> The discourse of radical democracy is no longer the discourse of the universal. [...] This point is decisive: there is no radical and plural democracy without renouncing the discourse of the universal and its implicit assumption of a privileged point of access to 'the truth', which can be reached only by a limited number of subjects (*HSS* 191–2).

11 For a critique of the 'foundational' treatment of power or domination in political life see *HSS* 142. As it seems to me, Foucault's later writings point in a similar direction; compare Dallmayr 1984, 1986.

12 For a differentiation of 'praxis' from Weberian categories of action theory compare my 'Praxis and experience', in Dallmayr 1984: 47–76.

13 Another passage presents the external demarcation of the two categories under the image of a 'double void' (*HSS* 131).

14 Compare Heidegger 1967: 36–8, 45–8; 1957; and Derrida 1982. For the notion of 'intertwining' see Merleau-Ponty 1968: 130–55.

15 The tensional view is also endorsed in the assertion that the 'project for a radical democracy' must 'base itself upon the search for a point of equilibrium between a maximum advance for the democratic revolution in a broad range of spheres, and the capacity for the hegemonic direction and positive reconstruction of these spheres on the part of subordinated groups' (*HSS* 189). In part the authors' ambivalence stems from a mingling of two conceptions of politics: namely, politics as 'polity' (or political regime) and politics as 'policy'. For this distinction see Vollrath 1987 and Dallmayr 1987.

16 Compare in this context Dallmayr 1989: 137–57; 1993; 2000: 105–30.

References

Bernstein, E. (1961) *Evolutionary Socialism*, New York: Schocken.

Dallmayr, F. (1984) 'Pluralism old and new: Foucault on power', in *Polis and Praxis: Exercises in Contemporary Political Theory*, Cambridge, MA: MIT Press.

—— (1986) 'Democracy and Postmodernism', *Human Studies*, 10: 143–70.

—— (1987) 'Politics and conceptual analysis: comments on Vollrath', *Philosophy and Social Criticism*, 13: 31–7.

—— (1989) 'Rethinking the Hegelian state', in *Margins of Political Discourse*, Albany, NY: State University of New York Press.

—— (1993) *G. W. F. Hegel: Modernity and Politics*, Newbury Park, CA: Sage.

—— (2000) 'Derrida and friendship', in P. King and H. Devere (eds) *The Challenge to Friendship in Modernity*, London: Frank Cass.

Derrida, J. (1978) 'Structure, sign and play in the discourse of the human sciences', in *Writing and Difference*, tr. Alan Bass, Chicago and London: University of Chicago Press.

—— (1982) *Margins of Philosophy*, trans. Alan Bass, Chicago: University of Chicago Press.

Gramsci, A. (1957) *The Modern Prince, and Other Writings*, New York: International Publishers.

Kautsky, K. (1910) *The Class Struggle (Erfurt Program)*, Chicago: Kerr.

Luxemburg, R. (1906) *Massenstreik*, Hamburg: Dubber.

Heidegger, M. (1957) *Identität und Differenz*, Pfullingen: Neske.

—— (1967) 'Moira', in *Vorträge und Aufsätze*, vol. 3, Pfullingen: Neske,

Merleau-Ponty, M. (1968) *The Visible and the Invisible*, tr. A. Lingis, Evanston, IL: Northwestern University Press.

Sorel, G. (1950) *Reflections on Violence*, Glencoe, IL: Free Press.

Trendelenburg, A. (1840) *Logische Untersuchungen*, Hildesheim: Olms, 3rd edn 1964.

Vollrath, E. (1987) 'The "rational" and the "political": an essay in the semantics of politics', *Philosophy and Social Criticism*, 13: 17–29.

3

POLITICS AND THE ONTOLOGICAL DIFFERENCE

On the 'strictly philosophical' in Laclau's work

Oliver Marchart

The philosophical beyond philosophy

In the proceedings of a conference on deconstruction and pragmatism, Ernesto Laclau once began his contribution by reminding us that he is 'writing here as a political theorist rather than a philosopher in the strict sense of the term' (1996: 47). Laclau does not tell us how we should imagine a philosopher 'in the strict sense of the term'; but we can assume that he seeks to differentiate his own project – which is exclusively concerned with questions of politics and political theory – from the practice of doing 'pure' philosophy, be it in the sense of an academic discipline or a freely floating mode of metaphysical reasoning without any particular realm of application. Laclau's reluctance to present himself as a 'philosopher' might surprise since he regularly locates his theoretical project within the horizon opened up by such arch-philosophers as Heideggger, Husserl, Gadamer, and the later Wittgenstein. While this lineage obviously appears like the genealogical tree of anti-essentialist or post-foundational philosophy – a genealogy which is of definite importance for Laclau – we should not be deceived by it. At least as important as philosophy for the development of Laclau and Chantal Mouffe's discourse theory is, of course, the science of linguistics. Therefore, the most prominent rank in Laclau's referential system is filled with Saussure who, with his differential model of signification, has deconstructed foundational realism, a move later radicalized by Hjelmslev and the Copenhagen school (Laclau 1993), not to mention poststructuralist thought. And finally there is the realm of politics proper – both in terms of political theory and of practical political experience. Here, it is Laclau's experience with Argentinian populism and with the New Social Movements of the 1970s and 1980s that constitutes the background to his theorizing. In an interview, Laclau specifies the role his 'first lesson in "hegemony"' had for the development of his theory:

> That's the reason why I didn't have to wait to read post-structuralist texts to understand what a 'hinge', 'hymen', 'floating signifier' or the 'metaphysics of presence' were: I'd already learnt this through my

> practical experience as a political activist in Buenos Aires. So when today I read *Of Grammatology*, *S/Z*, or the *Écrits* of Lacan, the examples which always spring to mind are not from philosophical or literary texts; they are from a discussion in an Argentinian trade union, a clash of opposing slogans at a demonstration, or a debate during a party congress (*NR* 200).

In his political biography, it may have been the experience of demonstrations and party congresses which taught Laclau his 'first lesson in hegemony', but in his intellectual biography it was of course Gramsci's work that provided him with the means to articulate his practical experience into a coherent framework of political theory and analysis. From the basis of this framework a political project was formulated in turn: the project of radical and plural democracy, by which, again, theory is folded back into practice. Thus, the separation between political theory and political practice, as Laclau holds, 'is largely an artificial operation' since 'theoretico-political categories do not only exist in books but are also part of discourses actually informing institutions and social operations' (1994: 2). Hence, it is important to notice that for Laclau, contrary to what some of his critics claim when they accuse him of formalism or excessive abstraction, the practice of theory, including, I would suggest, the realm of philosophy and science, is far from being disconnected from practical politics. What all these dimensions share, on the most general level, is the very real experience of the slow but steady melting-process of (seemingly) solid foundations. While in the fields of philosophy, science, and political theory all kinds of *foundationalism* came under scrutiny and were deconstructed in what amounts to nothing less than a *post-foundational* horizon shift, the arena of practical politics also witnesses a general weakening of social foundations, a development towards 'disorganized capitalism' (*NR* 58) which goes hand in hand with the emergence of new social actors and a widening of the spaces for strategic forms of acting and thinking. The experience of the absence of 'Ground' (a ground, we must add, which remains present precisely *in its absence*), is the sign of our age, and the 'crisis of essentialist universalism as a self-asserted ground has led our attention to the contingent *grounds* (in the plural) of its emergence and to the complex processes of its construction' (1994: 2). The disintegration of the figure of 'Ground' and the dissolution of all sorts of foundationalism is therefore accompanied by the proliferation of *strategic* forms of construction and negotiation.

This is what characterizes Laclau's work more than anything else. Despite its crystal-clear and 'logical' argumentative procedures, which sometimes give the impression of a deconstructive version of negative dialectics being brought into the argumentative form of scholastic reasoning, the very nature of his thought is decisively *strategic*. What I call strategy emerges from the gaps and fissures that are opened up after the attempt to search for an ultimate foundation has been abandoned. Precisely because there is no such thing as a common ground, divergent elements have to be strategically, that is, *politically*, articulated and new identities forged – which is but another name for *hegemony*. For this reason, Laclau sees 'the development of a theory of hegemony as a precondition for any kind of strategic thinking' (1999: 159). But this *strategic approach* is also what characterizes the specific combination and mutual contamination of the fields of philosophy, science, and political practice/theory as much as Laclau's re-articulation of certain strands within poststructuralism considered incompatible by other theorists:

> In the first place, I see that we need to have some sort of combination of what I would call various branches, various kinds of poststructuralist theory – and not only poststructuralism; for instance, the Wittgensteinian approach is very important to this matter. Deconstruction provides us with a discourse concerning the deepening of the logic of undecidability, which [...] becomes central. Lacanian theory provides us with a logic of the lack, the logic of the signifier, which is also a discourse of enormous importance. I am very much against attempts of simply opposing deconstruction to Lacanian theory. The two can be productively combined in a variety of ways. And I think that the whole conception of a microphysics of power can be complementary to this effort. One should not dismiss the work of Foucault (or, for the matter, of Deleuze and Guattari) too easily, as some people tend to do. So what we have is a very complicated discourse which has to combine traditions of thought that began from very different starting points but that are all converging on a political analysis (1999: 159).

Thus we have seen, in our initial effort to locate 'the philosophical' in his work, that while Laclau is not a 'philosopher in the strict sense', philosophy still remains present in his work, *but only by way of its strategic articulation* with both science (in the form of linguistics and discourse analysis) and a practical as well as theoretico-analytical involvement with politics, for instance with a project of radical and plural democracy.[1] From this perspective, I venture to put forward the main thesis of this chapter. Starting from the observation that philosophy, discourse analysis, and political theory are mutually articulated in Laclau's work, we will be surprised to encounter something which *exceeds* this articulated triad and also exceeds the metaphysical tradition and current philosophizing in the disciplinary sense. While Laclau seems not to be a 'philosopher in the strict sense', there is in fact a moment (an excess) in his work of what I would call the *strictly philosophical* – and what Heidegger would have called 'thinking'. But where exactly to locate the 'strictly philosophical' – that which exceeds philosophy – in Laclau? I would contend that we will find it, amongst other places, in the numerous occasions where Laclau has recourse to the notion of the *ontological difference* – in the radical Heideggerian understanding of *difference-as-difference* (Heidegger 1957), a notion which simultaneously points at *the a-byss of the (non-)ground* (Heidegger 1994) and thus has to be situated within the wider horizon of current post-foundational thinking.[2]

It is here that 'the philosophical' in the strict sense intervenes into the field of 'ordinary' political philosophy.

Before we see how Laclau explicitly theorizes the ontological difference, let us approach the problem by consulting a couple of occasions on which he employs the notion in a seemingly heuristic fashion. In his recent exchange with Judith Butler and Slavoj Žižek, for instance, the 'complex dialectic between particularity and universality, between ontic content and ontological dimension' (Laclau 2000: 58), is said to structure 'social reality itself'. The same distinction is made with respect to *ethical investment* and *normative order*: we can only have hegemony and politics, 'if the distance between the ontic and the ontological, between *investing* (the ethical) and that in which one invests (the normative order) is never filled' (84). Similarly, in a relation of *representation* we have to differentiate between the ontic content to be represented and the ontological function of the principle of representability as such: 'If representation is made possible/impossible by a primordial lack, no ontic content can ultimately monopolize the ontological function of representing representability as such' (71). The very act of *decision*, Laclau holds, must also be understood as being irredeemably split between the ontological and the ontic: 'as required by a dislocated situation, it is *a* decision; but it is also *this* decision, this particular ontic content' (85). *In extenso*, the same must be said about all forms of *identity*, including the identity of social agents and the identity of society (as an impossible totality), as he makes clear in *Emancipation(s)*: Since 'the fullness of society is unreachable, this split in the identity of political agents is an absolutely constitutive "ontological difference" – in a sense not entirely unrelated to Heidegger's use of the expression' (*E* 61). It is because of the primordial 'lack' of all social identity that in a politically dislocated situation (of chaos, civil war, etc.), as Laclau explains with respect to Hobbes, the very principle of ordering will become more important than the content of any proposed concrete order:

> the function of *ordering*, in Hobbes, cannot be the special privilege of any *concrete social order* – it is not an attribute of a *good* society, as in Plato, but an ontological dimension whose connection with particular ontic arrangements is, of its own nature, contingent (2000: 71).

We thus have to take into account 'the distinction between *ordering* and *order*, between *changing* and *change*, between the *ontological* and the *ontic* – oppositions which are only contingently articulated through the investment of the first of the terms into the second' (85). While from one perspective, we can speak about an investment, a necessary intertwining of these terms, from another perspective the gap between them remains unbridgeable. As Laclau explained in an interview:

> If we had a dialogical situation in which we reached, at least as a regulative idea, a point in which between the *ontic* and the ontological dimensions

> there would be no difference, in which there would be a complete overlapping, then in that case there would be nothing to hegemonize because this absent fullness of the community could be given by one and only one political content (1999: 135).

At first sight, Laclau seems to make reference to the ontological difference for heuristic reasons only. It also seems that he comes dangerously close to a metaphysical usage of the ontological difference in terms of a form/content-distinction, thereby remaining within the ambit of metaphysics. But a closer look at his explicit theorization of the notion will reveal that it has nothing to do with the traditional metaphysical version of the ontological difference; rather, it must be located in the Heideggerian trajectory as a dimension of difference *as difference* which, in this more radical or 'strict' sense, plays itself out in the whole of Laclau's body of work, and so lies at the core of his main theoretical categories such as representation, hegemony, order, decision, identity, universalism/particularism, etc. What is more, this 'strictly philosophical' intervention of the insurmountable difference and yet necessary intertwining between ontic and ontological dimension is a specific conceptual way of indicating an absent ground which still remains present in its absence. For this reason, his employment of the Heideggerian notion of the ontological difference *as difference* defines Laclau's work as one of the foremost bodies of post-foundational thought within the field of politics. In the following I will try to substantiate this claim – which may still sound somewhat exuberant and too abstract – in three steps. First, I will show how the 'strictly' philosophical of the intervention of the ontological difference is present in Laclau's frequent usage of the qualifier 'radical'. Second, I will lay out his explicit theorization of the ontological difference; and, third, I will make a case for the expansion of the categorial apparatus of Laclau's theory by indicating where the categories of *the singular* and *the absolute*, so far not present in his work, would have to be located. This will allow us, in a short concluding section, to determine, if only provisionally, the very *status* and place of Laclau's work between and beyond philosophy, science, and political theory.

What's radical in radical contingency?

Let us start with what might seem a detour but will lead us directly into the heart of the problem: the usage of the qualifier 'radical' which regularly appears as Laclau (and, in *HSS*, Laclau and Mouffe) speaks about 'radical freedom', 'radical decision', 'radical contingency', and so on. How are we to make sense of the 'radical way' in which Laclau and Laclau and Mouffe use certain concepts? Is this mere rhetoric? A closer reading will show that the precise role of the notion is to indicate an unbridgeable gap between two levels which cannot be mediated or dialecticized via the logic of either level. In this sense, these levels or dimensions in fact do not simply stand in a relation of exteriority but in a relation of *radical* exteriority. Let's take Laclau and Mouffe's famous example of antagonism. In a situation of antagonism, differential political positions can only relate to others by, in an *equivalential* way, referring to something which they are not. But this 'something' is not a *tertium quid*. It cannot be integrated into the internal chain of differences without affecting the latter's status. Rather, it must be understood as something 'radically' different, incommensurable, threatening, and exclusionary, in so far as it *negates* the positive identity of the internal differences (by turning them into their opposite: equivalence). Under this aspect one can define antagonism – equivalence established by negation – as that which *denies* differentiality as such. The 'radical', hence, indicates exactly this *negatory* dimension of antagonism with respect to the field of differences in the plural.

The argument was extended by Laclau towards a general logic of signification. In this discourse analytic version of the argument, most succinctly presented in his paper 'Why do empty signifiers matter to politics?' (in *E*), Laclau deconstructs Saussure's concept of signification via difference, thereby sharpening the argument as developed in *Hegemony*. He begins with the Saussurian assumption that meaning can only evolve within a system of differences. The possibility of the existence of a system of differences, however, depends on the existence of its boundaries – and these boundaries cannot belong to the system as, in this case, the boundary itself would be just another difference and, consequently, not the very limit of the system of differences and of differentiality as such. Only if we see the outside of the system as a radical outside – and the boundary thus as an exclusionary boundary – can we speak of systematicity or meaning in the first place.

> [I]f the systematicity of the system is a direct result of the exclusionary limit, it is only that exclusion that grounds the system as such. [...] The condition, of course, for this operation to be possible is that what is beyond the frontier of exclusion is reduced to pure negativity – that is to the pure threat that what is beyond poses to the system (constituting it that way) (*E* 38).

As a consequence, the boundary itself cannot be signified, but can only be *manifested* as an interruption or breakdown of the process of signification. The radicality of the radical outside (non-meaning) is not only the condition of possibility for establishing a signifying structure (meaning), it is at the same time the condition of *im*possibility of establishing a structure *as closed totality* (full meaning). In other words, the function of the exclusionary boundary thus consists in introducing an essential ambivalence into the system of differences constituted by the very same boundary. In *New Reflections* this ambivalence (which in *Hegemony* is called 'subversion') is called 'dislocation'. And as such the latter is located *within* the system because what are dislocated are, of course, the internal differences – albeit through a category which comes, as it were, from the outside.[3]

The point not to be missed here is that it is precisely this negative and *radical* dimension of the outside/the antagonism which allows it to fulfil its *constitutive* role vis-à-vis the inside/the system: the outside, in order to be *constitutive*, must be a '*radical* outside'. The same must be said for other important categories within the Laclauian framework such as contingency and undecidability, so that we should not be surprised to find Laclau speaking of '*radical* contingency' and '*radical* undecidability': 'Radical contingency' follows from the revelatory potential of antagonism: 'if antagonism *threatens* my existence, it shows, in the strictest sense of the term, my radical contingency' (*NR* 20). Contingency, therefore, must not be mixed up with pure chance, or accidentality. The status of the conditions of existence of a given significatory system is not merely accidental (a matter of pure chance) but these conditions are contingent to the extent that they cannot be derived from the internal logic or rationality of the system itself – they are *external* in the sense of being *radically* separated from the internal logic.[4] Laclau maintains that 'if negativity is radical and the outcome of the struggle not predetermined, the contingency of the identity of the two antagonistic forces is also radical and the conditions of existence of both must be themselves contingent' (*NR* 20). Contingency, thus, stands to necessity in a relation of subversion: necessity can only partially limit the field of contingency, which in turn subverts necessity from inside. As a result, the demarcation line between the contingent and the necessary is blurred. But the very point of the matter, missed by critiques like Dallmayr as we will see, lies in the fact that – even as the line between the contingent and the necessary is blurred – the existence of this line, that is to say, of the general (i.e. *ontological*) difference between the necessary and the contingent is *not* contingent but necessary: 'as identity depends entirely on conditions of existence which are contingent, its relationship with them is absolute necessary' (*NR* 21). The meaning of the 'radical' in 'radical contingency' lies in the fact that contingency (in its very play with necessity) can never be completely erased by any objectivity or systematicity and, thus, is itself necessary. Or, to put it differently again: while the conditions of existence of any identity/objectivity/system are *contingent* with respect to this system, they are *necessarily* so.

Now, what is introduced into the system by way of radical contingency and radical exteriority (negativity) is *radical* undecidability. The system's constitutive outside – its exclusionary limit – stabilizes the system to some degree, thereby producing the very effect of systematicity (equivalence). Yet, insofar as the outside does this by *negating* the differential character of the system's inside, which is nevertheless necessary for meaning to arise (as meaning arises only through differential relations), the outside injects a necessary ambivalence or dislocation into the system, thus splitting the identity of every element of the system:

> on the one hand, each difference expresses itself *as* difference; on the other hand, each of them *cancels* itself as such by entering into a relation of equivalence with all the other differences of the system. And, given that there is only system as long as there is radical exclusion, this split or ambivalence is constitutive of all systemic identity (*E* 38).

This very split is the locus of undecidability between difference and equivalence. At the same moment in which the identity of the system is affirmed it is also blocked. And it is important to stress once again that the nature of the undecidability of the system's status – caught, as it is, between equivalence and difference – is itself constitutive for the system, i.e. 'radical'.

Fred Dallmayr, in his critique of that alleged internal/external quandary of Laclau and Mouffe's argument tends to overlook this double dimension (the fact that – in order to be constitutive – the mutual subversion of necessity and contingency is itself necessary). He appreciates the undecidable logic, the 'intertwining and mutual subversion of necessity and contingency', difference and equivalence, and he rightly detects the forerunners of this logic between identity and total non-identity in terms 'which some post-structuralist thinkers have thematized under such labels as "intertwining" or "duality"; Heidegger's "Zweifalt" (two-foldedness) and the Derridean notion of "*différance*"' (1988: 44–5). Yet, Dallmayr, while endorsing the 'intertwining' logic of hybridity between inside and outside, remains unhappy with the part of 'radicality', seeing the latter unfortunately colliding 'with occasional formulations which approximate the interplay to a Sartrean kind of antithesis (being and nothingness)' (45). To give an example for such a '[f]lirtation with nothingness', as he puts it, he alludes to Laclau and Mouffe's formula of antagonism as threatening negativity, as symbol of the system's non-being:

> the fact that negativity is not another objective (or positive) order does not mean that what lies 'beyond differences' is simply nothingness. In fact, if differences were related strictly by nothing, the result would be total segregation or equivalence – and by no means the complex web of relationships thematized under the label of 'hegemony'. In Heidegger's vocabulary (which, to be sure, has to be employed cautiously), different elements in order to enjoy a relationship are linked on the level of 'being' – a term denoting a non-objective type of matrix in which positivity and negativity, ground and abyss (*Abgrund*) are peculiarly intertwined (1988: 45).

From a certain perspective, Dallmayr is absolutely correct here. It is true that, for Laclau and Mouffe, inside and outside are completely imbricated, otherwise the system would be either totally open or totally closed. However, exactly *because* the model is the model of 'intertwining', is there not an additional argumentative step required if we want to account for the *tension* between inside and outside? For without this tension one could not reasonably assume any difference between inside and outside at all – they would simply collapse into each other. What is it that allows us to perceive them as *non-identical*, though intertwined? Something of a different nature has to be assumed, something which is *not itself* part of the hybrid play between inside and outside.

So what Dallmayr sees as a deficiency in Laclau and Mouffe's argument (its radical, negatory allusions) is actually an indispensable part of it. It is only with the proviso that the system's outside is a *radical* outside, that we can speak about an outside at all and, hence, about a difference between outside and inside. If we did not make this additional assumption of the radicality/necessity of the limit between outside and inside, where outside would become an internal moment of the inside, and outside and inside would be identical. Only if we assume the radicality of the outside are we in a position to speak about mutual subversion of inside and outside, that is to say, about internal dislocation and retroactive hybridization of the system's limit. In this sense, the 'passage through negativity' (*NR* 213) is required in order to account for relative and always hybridized systematicity. An 'intertwining' without that radical dimension is not an intertwining, but, to put it in a mundane way, a self-identical mess, the night in which all cows are grey. The same must be said about the mutual subversion of contingency and necessity. Yes, 'the contingent subverts the necessary' (*HSS* 128), but this subversion is *itself* necessary. (Which should, of course, remind us of Derrida's claim that deconstruction's 'non-concept' of *différance* – and hence, deconstruction as such (e.g. as justice) – is itself not deconstructible).

Popularized accounts of postmodernism/poststructuralism and versions of pure *anti*-foundationalism that present meaning in terms of an unrestrained pluralism, of a happy play of signification, tend to obfuscate this radical dimension of signification. It is here that the difference lies between Laclau and Mouffe and 'anything goes' approaches or celebrations of hybridity and 'third spaces' *eo ipso*. The Other *as other* is radically inaccessible; the outside is a radical outside – precisely because it is constitutive for the inside – and paradoxically its very radicality is exactly the reason why, eventually, it can never establish itself as pure outside: for it is this radicality which subverts the inside and thus retroactively hybridizes the latter's boundary with the outside. What looks like a paradox can actually be explained in slightly less paradoxical terms by bringing in the ontological difference. At this point, Dallmayr's reference to Heidegger turns out to be crucial. If we decide to differentiate between an ontic and an ontological level, then it is on the ontological level that the categories of 'radicality' (indicating the necessity of the mutual subversion of necessity and contingency, of possibility and impossibility), of constitutive outside, of negativity, etc. are located.[5]

Difference-as-difference

In an article jointly written with Lilian Zac, this seemingly paradoxical relation is explicitly theorized by Laclau in terms of the ontological difference. Referring to Reiner Schürmann's reading of Heidegger's account of *arché*, Laclau and Zac differentiate between, on the one hand, *ontic* nothingness as the source (*Anfang*) of beings which for instance – within a given historic epoch – are absent but could very well be present under different conditions, and on the other, *ontological* nothingness, the 'pull towards absence that permeates presence to its very heart' (Schürmann 1990: 141), as *Ursprung* which has no history. This *Ursprung* – being both 'approaching (*Angang*) and departing (*Abgang*); genesis and *phtora*, rising and declining; being and not being' (ibid.) – is originary *time*. As such it resists reiteration (= spatialization). What is crucial for Laclau and Zac is that if we want to conceptualize the difference between beings and Being as temporal difference – as temporalization – what is required is a 'passage through nothingness' (Laclau and Zac 1994: 29) for nothingness is the 'very condition of access to Being' (30):

> For, if something were mere, unchallenged actuality, no ontological difference would be possible: the ontic and the ontological would exactly overlap and we would simply have pure presence. In that case, Being would only be accessible as that which is the most universal of all predicates, as that which is beyond all *differentia specifica*. And that would mean it would not be accessible at all [. . .]. But if nothingness were there as an actual possibility, any being which presents itself would also be, to its very roots, mere possibility, and would show, beyond its ontic specificity, Being as such. *Possibility*, as opposite to pure *presence*, temporalizes Being and splits, from its very ground, all identity.
>
> (Laclau and Zac 1994: 30)

Here, Laclau and Zac frame the problem in terms of the relation between actuality and potentiality:[6] the actual ontic level of beings can only exist by virtue of relating to something which it is not (yet): potentiality. This potentiality is not to be understood as simply one more possibility on the level of the ontic, but as a possibility which *undermines* actuality – for if actuality reigned completely we would be in a universe where all possibilities are actualized: a desperately overcrowded place. In terms of discourse analysis this universe could be described as a totalized and homogenized system of signification ('society' as closed totality). It is located beyond any *differentia specifica*, which is another way of saying that such system would require a state of pure equivalence – where all differential positivity is cancelled out. If one wants to avoid falling into the trap of assuming total closure, one has to make the 'passage through nothingness'. Yet, nothingness must not be conceptualized in the form of mere indifference, in the sense in which Dallmayr suspects that 'differences are simply related by nothing': the 'nothing' Laclau and Mouffe speak of – a 'nothing' which simultaneously relates *and* subverts differences – has a very real presence. 'Nothing is not merely the absence and lack of beings', as Heidegger puts it, for if the nothing 'were only something indifferently negative, how could we understand, for example, horror and terror before the Nothing and nihilation?' (Heidegger 1998: 45).

In a similar vein, Laclau and Mouffe affirm in *Hegemony* 'that certain discursive forms, through equivalence, annul all positivity of the object and give real existence to negativity as such'. What makes full presence impossible – the 'impossibility of the real – negativity' – 'has attained a form of presence' (*HSS*

129). Thus, negativity or nothingness is very much present in its very absence as it is required for the system of differences if these differences are to achieve some sort of systematicity by entering into a relation of equivalence vis-à-vis 'what they are not'. The outside, 'what they are not', even as it does not *exist* on the level of beings as one more being, very much *insists* in that it subverts that level through the process of *absencing/presencing*. If we managed to completely erase ontological (= radical) nothingness, we would destroy the very effect of (always partial) systematicity and meaning. By reducing ontological nothingness to ontic nothingness, what we achieve is not a more 'realistic' account but a totalized system of pure presence. Here the ontological difference comes into view *as difference*:

> Presencing (*Ursprung*) and what is present, the ontological and the ontic, are irremediably split, but this has a double consequence: the first is that the ontic can never be closed in itself; the second, that the ontological can only show itself through the ontic. The same movement creating the split, condemns its two sides (as in all splits) into mutual dependence. Being cannot inhabit a 'beyond' all actual beings, because in that case, it would only be one more being. Being *shows* itself in the entities as that which they are lacking and as that which derives from their ontological status as mere possibility. Being and nothingness, presence and absence, are the mutually required terms of a ground constitutively split by difference.
>
> (Laclau and Zac 1994: 30)

By now, it should be obvious – as it is once more emphasized in the quote above – that the split between the ontic and the ontological must be conceived to be *radical*, otherwise it would be internal to the ontic, that is to say, it would be part of a system of differences as one more difference. To call the ontic and the ontological 'irremediably split', as Laclau and Zac do, means exactly this: that the difference between the ontic and the ontological is radical, insurmountable and constitutive, i.e. *necessary* with respect to the existence of the differential system of beings. In as much as the system has to refer to something which always escapes its existence, it can never fully constitute itself as totality. This is, as Laclau sees it, the first consequence of the ontological difference. The ontic is rendered impossible by the very instance (the ontological) which makes it possible in the first instance.

Yet, the system's constitutive outside, nothingness, cannot directly be signified from within the signifying system – for in that case it would be already part of it. Because 'nothing' is not mere indifference but insists as an absence which is present, the outside can only *show itself* within the system through the latter's failure to fully constitute itself as totality or pure presence: as 'the system as pure Being' (*E* 39). Hence, the *revelatory* function of dislocation and antagonism is achieved when gaps, breakdowns, interruptions occur on the ontic level of beings. The dislocatory event is accompanied by an effect of unconcealment, and this is the second consequence: the ontological dimension shows itself as lack in the ontic level: 'It is this effect of unconcealment that splits the opposing forces between their "ontic" contents and the character of mere possibility – that is, inception, pure Being – of those contents' (Laclau and Zac 1994: 30).

We are now in a position to evaluate Dallmayr's charge against Laclau and Mouffe of a 'flirtation with nothingness'. In Laclau and Mouffe's approach, being and nothingness do not stand in a relation of antithesis: if we restrict our view to the ontological level, it may even be said that Being (= complete closure of the system) and Nothingness (= complete openness of the system) amount to one and the same thing. The real gap – which some might call the gap of the real – consists in the radical separation between the ontological and the ontic level which does not allow for the level of nothingness – the radical outside – to be reached as such. The latter can only show itself in form of failure or dislocation within the ontic order of beings. For this reason, nothingness is *neither* hypostatized to a black hole *nor* reified or reduced to the inverse category of ontic being. What Dallmayr does not take into account in his reading of Laclau and Mouffe is the *constitutive* nature of the difference between ontic nothingness and ontological nothingness, so he erroneously takes the latter for the former. If, on the other hand, we accept the radicality of that gap, it becomes obvious that Laclau and Mouffe do not adhere to any form of 'negative ontology':

> To assert, as we have, the constitutive nature of antagonism does not therefore mean referring all objectivity back to a negativity that would replace the metaphysics of presence in its role as an absolute ground, since that negativity is only conceivable within such a very framework. What it does mean is asserting that the moment of undecidability between the contingent and the necessary is *constitutive* and thus that antagonism is too (*NR* 27).

If there is a flirtation with nothingness, it will never lead to marriage.

The gap between the particular-universal and the singular-absolute

So how does this somewhat abstract reflection on the ontological difference – which I took as a sign of the intervention of the 'strictly philosophical' in Laclau's work – relate to questions of concrete politics? Is it simply irrelevant for political work – as the charge against Laclau of theoreticism would have it? The answer is, of course, that for a post-foundational political approach it is absolutely imperative to account for the ontological difference, as the latter (in its most radical version) functions as condition of (im)possibility for the play between, for instance, the particular and the universal. This relation has assumed, in Laclau's recent reformulation of his theory of hegemony, the role of a *distinction directrice*. In a nutshell, every particular demand, in order to become politically and, thus, hegemonically effective, has to *universalize* itself: it has to present itself as 'more' universal than its concrete content. And it is only via that excess of universality that something particular can start hegemonizing the social field.

So when Laclau (2000: 58) holds that social reality is structured by 'the complex dialectic between particularity and universality, between ontic content and ontological dimension', our first impression is that he seems to use the ontological difference as a heuristic device in order to explain the relation between form and content of a given hegemonic project. Such a project has to aspire to the *dimension* of universality, and this dimension is logically independent of the project's actual *content* – yet it is related to it since there are *historical* and political reasons for one content, in a given context, to be more successful than another. But again, if we enquire into the *nature* of the relation between ontic content and ontological dimension, we immediately run into the question of *radical contingency* and *necessary (im)possibility*, that is the question of the ontological difference *as difference*. This becomes all the more obvious if we think through the consequences of the argument. If we push the universal to the extreme end of the scale, the particular content will disappear completely: as soon as a project has universalized itself completely, as soon as it has hegemonized the whole field of the social, the latter turns into a closed totality and the project will have assumed not 'hegemony' but absolute power. However, as a side effect exactly of its absolute universality, it will also lose all ontic content, that is, it will be completely emptied of all particular features and objectives since they will already be realized and subsumed under this all-embracing universality. Hence, no need for politics any more. On the other hand, if we push the particular to the extreme end of the scale, we will end up with a situation of pure and total particularism in which no politics is possible either. In this case, every project will be enclosed in its own particular content and will not be able to universalize itself and to articulate that content with other demands.

So where do we encounter the radical line between the ontic and the ontological? Obviously not between more or less universalized particularities. Even a 'relatively' universalized content would still remain at the ontic level. Therefore we have to look for the ontological difference in its radical version elsewhere: It runs, in the 'strict' or 'radical' sense, between those more or less universalized contents on the hand and the *dimension* of universality/particularity *as such* on the other. The latter dimension shows itself in all its radicality at the (unachievable) respective end points of the scale. Being a *dimension*, the ultimate horizon of the universal 'as empty place' functions as both an impossible and a necessary object (and the same must be said about the particular as a *dimension*). In order to distinguish these necessary/impossible limit points of universality and particularity from the 'possible' and always gradual play of universalization/particularization, I propose defining these limit cases as *the absolute* and *the singular*.

Indeed, the singular and the absolute – as impossible limit cases – cannot be easily separated from the aspect of the particular and the universal: this might be the reason why Laclau does not see the need to develop separate concepts –

something I propose to do for reasons of clarification and in order to prepare the terrain for a future comparison of the many other current theorizations of *singularity* (by, for instance, Derrida, Nancy, Negri, Agamben, and others).[7] From the vantage point of hegemony theory, the singular and the absolute are an intrinsic 'aspect' of the play between particular and universal. In some sense, they can even be said to be identical with the latter. And yet they are different in as much as they are *necessarily impossible*: the singular and the absolute are names for that state of particularity/universality which must remain necessarily impossible in order to function as condition for the possibility of the play between the particular and the universal. So it follows that we must assume not only a difference between some particular and some universal, but a more radical difference which acts as the former's (non-)ground: the difference between the two realms of, on the one hand, concrete 'universals' and 'particulars' (which of course are always dialectically linked), and, on the other hand, the singular and the absolute. What we discover at the bottom of the dialectical play between the universal and the particular – with its relative degrees of universalization and particularization of certain demands – is a more radical difference. What we encounter is that very difference *as difference*: the radical gap (which at the same time is a necessary intertwining) between the 'possible' dialectics between universality and particularity on the one hand and the spectre of their impossible limit cases, the absolute and the singular, on the other. This radical difference is named by Laclau in a variety of ways: contingency, freedom, dislocation, radical historicity, etc.

On this basis we have to spell out some important implications for a variety of postmodern or poststructuralist theories which tend to conceive politics under the aspect of ethics. It can easily be perceived that the ontic realization of the ontological limit case of the absolute – which would implicate the complete universalization of a certain demand – would constitute a state of total closure. All poststructuralist thought agitates against this idea. However, while the 'dangerous' consequences of a pretended realization of 'the absolute' are more or less common sense, the obvious consequences regarding the status of *singularity* are regularly ignored. Instead, what one can find is quite often a celebration of singularity *per se*. But if it is impossible to ever reach the limit-case of the absolute then there can be no such thing as pure singularity either. We could even claim that the belief in the possibility to approach something or somebody in its, his, or her 'pure singularity' – *without* recourse to any form of universalization – is *as ideological* as the opposite belief in the possibility of an absolute or closed totality.

To be sure, in a given universal, there will always be a remainder of particularity but this remainder can never constitute a *pure singularity* – for in this case *all* connections to universality would have to be cut off. It follows that the remainder is already part of the dialectics between universality and particularity. For instance, if in a certain situation we identify with the political or social 'underdogs' (the homeless, etc.), we do not identify with a pure singularity. Rather, we identify in as far as we see in them an *exemplary species* of the oppressed and of oppression in general (because of their *inverse* relation towards the hegemonic or ruling class).

Thereby we have always already universalized them and inserted them into the play between particularity and universality. Hence, we have *not* reached the singular or the ontological *dimension* of particularity as such. Of course, there will always be exclusions from the dominant paradigms but as soon as we realize an exclusion *as exclusion*, we establish a connection (if only negatively) to some sort of universality. Does this not also have consequences for Laclau's recent attempt at defining the *subaltern* as those who are excluded from the very dialectics of universality/particularity? To the extent that they are excluded from the dialectics of universality/particularity they are also beyond the realm of politics. Only to the extent that they are perceived as 'subaltern' *with respect* to the 'dominant' classes can they enter the universality/particularity dialectics. The same must be said about Marx's disregard for what he called *Lumpenproletariat* (Laclau 2003). Of course, we can criticize Marx for holding the *Lumpenproletariat* in such contempt, but isn't the term simply an indication of the latter's, in Marx's view, *non-universalizable* and thus *a-political* nature as a (non-)class which is too heterogeneous, impoverished, and 'morally' unprepared to be politicized? Here, a political critique of Marx's stance would significantly differ from an ethical one. The latter would – perhaps in Levinasian or Derridian fashion – call for unrestricted respect towards the singularly heterogeneous, while a political critique would point to the very real possibility of politicizing even a group like the *Lumpenproletariat*. And this is precisely the road Laclau chooses to take (see Laclau 2003; Marchart 2002).

So, Laclau's political realism (founded on his insistence on the insurmountable gap between the realm of the necessarily impossible and the realm of strategic possibilities) refrains from the ethical approach to politics which would respect the other in his/her pure singularity. The ethical injunction to 'accept' the singularity of something or somebody by virtue of that singularity only (to accept the other 'as s/he is'), presents a form of ideological closure which only at first sight seems more sympathetic than its absolutist counterpart. Otherwise, would we not also have to respect the singularly evil or cruel or murderous?[8] Whether somebody who is excluded has been 'victimized' is something which cannot be determined in advance on the basis of the mere fact of exclusion – we just have to think of the perfectly legitimate exclusion of Nazi parties from the sphere of political representation in some countries. Laclau does not give us any indication as to whether he thinks it is possible within the realm of personal ethics to approach the singular, but from the viewpoint of hegemony theory it is evident that such attempts are doomed to failure within the realm of politics. There, even when attention is shifted to the particular remainder, a process of universalization is necessarily enacted. Or rather, the very process of *shifting* the attention to the excluded is already a form of universalization.

Conclusion

I have argued in this chapter that the ontological difference – in the radical Heideggerian sense of difference *as difference* – constitutes the strictly philosophical background of Laclau's categorial framework. I have tried to show how the qualifier 'radical', so prevalent in Laclau's work, is supposed to point at this dimension and to indicate both an unbridgeable gap and a necessary intertwining at the heart of all meaning. It is the resulting *play* of this difference which points at the dimension of a ground which remains present only in its absence. In other words, a theory 'built' on difference-qua-difference does not allow for an ultimate ground to be instituted. Nevertheless, Laclau has provided us with one of the very few post-foundational social theories developed with some internal systematicity. (To combine post-foundationalism with systematicity is not necessarily self-contradictory, if we think of Laclau's notion of the system as an eventually impossible but yet necessary object.) Hegemony can thus be defined as a theory of the strategic moves – and the quasi-transcendental conditions under which those moves can occur – taken on the groundless terrain opened up by precisely the play of difference.

These observations might now put us in a position to better determine, with all necessary caution, the status and place of Laclau's work in relation to philosophy, science, and political theory/practice. Claude Lefort (2000) once described his own ambivalent identity – as somebody to whom the role of a 'philosopher' is attributed – with the medieval formula: *major et minor se ipso*. In a similar sense, Laclau too is *above and beneath himself*, both more and less than a philosopher in the disciplinary meaning of the term. While he is not a 'philosopher in the strict sense' (even as he regularly engages in philosophical arguments and works himself through the philosophical tradition), there is still a moment of the 'strictly philosophical' present in his work, a moment of radicality associated with the thinking of the ontological difference as difference. Why is it important to recognize this? It is important because it affects the very status of the other two dimensions of his work (apart from the philosophical dimension): science and political 'practice', respectively theory. At the beginning of this chapter I said that philosophical motives and arguments in Laclau are always articulated with science (in form of linguistics and discourse analysis) and political theory/practice (in form, for instance, of a project of radical democracy). What is the function of the excess, the intervention of the 'strictly philosophical', into this articulated triad? Far from being a high-brow and redundant *addendum* to his work, I would claim that it does have an important function. The 'strictly philosophical' prevents theory from collapsing into either mere scientism (a positivistic 'counting of words' as in some forms of linguistic discourse analysis) or into some form of journalistic extension of mere activism. In other words, the moment of the 'strictly philosophical' in Laclau functions as a barrier against the closure of his theory into either another version of nominalism/positivism or into a manifesto for blind activism.[9] It should not surprise, then, and this may be taken as a proof *ex negativo*, that nominalistic and adventurist accusations against Laclau of 'theoreticism', 'logicism', or 'formalism' frequently tend to overlook or even denounce the role of the 'strictly' philosophical moment in his theory. Yet without recourse to this moment, it will be impossible to fundamentally rethink and radicalize our notions of contingency, historicity, and freedom.

Notes

1 On one of the rare occasions where Laclau speaks about the status of the object of his thought, he shows a certain scepticism with respect to political 'philosophy': 'If I do not attempt to unify the different approaches [to the problem of politics] under a term like "political philosophy" it is because this would assume the unity of an object of reflection, which is precisely what is in question' (*NR* 69).

2 For an extensive discussion of political post-foundationalism with respect to the difference between 'politics' and 'the political' (or *la politique* and *le politique*) see Marchart 2003c.

3 For a short discussion of the categorial difference between antagonism and dislocation see the Introduction to this volume.

4 If later Laclau refers to the conditions of existence of any contingent identity as 'internal to the latter' (*NR* 24), this could again trigger some confusion. What I said a propos the meaning of interiority/exteriority should be kept in mind however: these conditions are *internal* to the system (say, politics) to the extent that they are not defined by any other system (say, economy). If the political system had its conditions of existence in the economy, it would be determined by the latter and we would find ourselves within the old base/superstructure model. In this sense, the conditions of existence of the system are *internal* to the system. From the viewpoint of the system itself, however, they are external in that they cannot be derived from the internal rationality or logic of the system: if they could, we would find ourselves in a Hegelian universe which unfolds according to the inner logic of the notion.

5 Although, strictly speaking, these categories are already ontic representations of the ontological since the ontological level can never be reached *as such* – that is, without having recourse to its ontic incarnations which, at the same time, corrupt the ontological.

6 See also the work on potentiality by another 'left Heideggerian', Giorgio Agamben (1999).

7 Not all of these current theorizations of singularity are entirely incompatible with the Laclauian framework; as a *radical* event, *the singular* could be theorized as the very moment of the political, even the ethical, as that which comes *from outside* and disturbs (but also partially grounds) the ontic realm of politics or normativity. For an elaboration of this aspect of singularity see Marchart 2003b. It is still important to see, and this will become clear in a moment, that disruption/institution as such does not have a clear political or moral 'content' – it is therefore not possible to tell in advance whether we should or should not 'respect' the event of singularity eo ipso.

8 Similarly, for a debate on terror and terrorism along the lines of a differentiation between the ontological and the ontic see Marchart 2003a.

9 A similar critique of political 'science' or sociology in the empirical sense can be found in Lefort (1988: 11):

> [W]hat is the nature of the difference between forms of society? Interpreting the political means breaking with the viewpoint of political science, because political science emerges from the suppression of this question. It emerges from a desire to objectify, and it forgets that no elements, no elementary structures, no entities (classes or segments of classes), no economic or technical determinations, and no dimensions of social space exist until they have been given a form.

References

Agamben, G. (1999) *Potentialities: Collected Essays in Philosophy*, Stanford: Stanford University Press.

Dallmayr, F. R. (1988) 'Hegemony and democracy: on Laclau and Mouffe', *Strategies*, 30 (Fall): 29–49 (for a modified version of the same article see the previous chapter in this volume).

Heidegger, M. (1957) *Identität und Differenz*, Stuttgart: Neske.

—— (1994) *Beiträge zur Philosophie (Vom Ereignis)*, Collected Works, 65, Frankfurt am Main: Vittorio Klostermann.

—— (1998) *Basic Concepts*, tr. Gary E. Aylesworth, Bloomington and Indianapolis: Indiana University Press.

Laclau, E. (1993) 'Discourse', in R. A. Goodin and P. Pettit (eds) *A Companion to Contemporary Political Philosophy*, Oxford: Basil Blackwell.

—— (1994) 'Introduction', in E. Laclau (ed.) *The Making of Political Identities*, London and New York: Verso.

—— (1996) 'Deconstruction, pragmatism, hegemony', in C. Mouffe (ed.) *Deconstruction and Pragmatism*, London and New York: Routledge.

—— (1999) 'Hegemony and the future of democracy: Ernesto Laclau's political philosophy', interview, in L. Worsham and G. A. Olson (eds) *Race, Rhetoric, and the Postcolonial*, Albany: State University of New York Press.

—— (2000) 'Identity and hegemony: The role of universality in the constitution of political logics', in J. Butler, E. Laclau and S. Žižek, *Contingency, Hegemony, Universality: Contemporary Dialogues on the Left*, London and New York: Verso.

—— (2002) 'Democracy between autonomy and heteronomy', in O. Enwezor, C. Basualdo, Ute Meta Bauer, S. Ghez, Sarat Maharaj, M. Nash, and O. Zaya (eds) *Democracy Unrealized*, Ostfildern: Hatje Cantz.

Laclau, E. and Zac, L. (1994) 'Minding the gap: The subject of politics', in E. Laclau (ed.) *The Making of Political Identities*, London and New York: Verso.

Lefort, C. (1988) *Democracy and Political Theory*, Minneapolis: University of Minnesota Press.

—— (2000) *Writing. The Political Test*, Durham, NC, and London: Duke University Press.

Marchart, O. (1999a) 'Undarstellbarkeit und "ontologische Differenz"', in O. Marchart (ed.) *Das Undarstellbare der Politik. Zur Hegemonietheorie Ernesto Laclaus*, Vienna: Turia + Kant.

—— (1999b) 'Das unbewußte Politische: Zum *psychoanalytic turn* in der politischen Theorie: Jameson, Butler, Laclau, Žižek', in J. Trinks (ed.) *Bewußtsein und Unbewußtes*, Vienna: Turia+Kant.

—— (2002) 'On drawing a line: Politics and the significatory logic of inclusion/exclusion', in U. Stäheli (ed.) *Inclusion/Exclusion and Socio-Cultural Identities*, special issue of *Soziale Systeme*, 8(1): 69–87.

—— (2003a) 'The other side of order: Towards a political theory of terror and dislocation', *Parallax*, 9(1): 97–113.

—— (2003b) 'Umkämpfte Gegenwart: der "Zivilisationsbruch Auschwitz" zwischen Singularität, Universalität und der Globalisierung der Erinnerung', in H. Uhl (ed.) *Zivilisationsbruch und Gedächtniskultur*, Innsbruck: Studienverlag.

—— (2003c) 'Politics and the political: an inquiry into post-foundational political thought', unpublished PhD thesis, University of Essex.

Schürmann, R. (1990) *Heidegger. On Being and Acting: From Principles to Anarchy*, Bloomington: Indiana University Press.

4

POLITICS AS THE REAL OF PHILOSOPHY

Rado Riha

This commentary on Laclau's essay 'Universalism, particularism and the question of Identity' (in *E*) aims to enquire into Laclau's conception of the relationship between the universal and the particular, in connection with the precarious constitution of identity, in order to be able to examine the very specificity of Laclau's intervention which, in my view, consists in the fact that this is an intervention that is at once philosophical and political. My main question will therefore be the following: what consequences can we draw for philosophy from such a duality? Can this duality be justified from the point of view of philosophy itself, in particular as it involves some radical displacements within the field of philosophy? In short, how are we to conceive of philosophy in a way that allows for such a double movement? By engaging in a power struggle to which Laclau himself invites his reader (*E* 22), I will focus primarily on teasing out these questions in order to show the pertinence of my own concern with the specific relation between philosophy and politics which, without being directly addressed in Laclau's essay is, I believe, nevertheless implicitly 'staged' by it.

The main thrust of Laclau's essay as I read it is towards two distinct yet related problems: first, the question of *the subject* insofar as 'the concrete and finite expressions of a multifarious subjectivity' (*E* 20) without a transcendental centre require, according to Laclau, that a new concept of the subject be elaborated that would provide a place for 'concrete finitudes whose limitations are the source of their strength' (*E* 21); second, the question of the *universal* insofar as the relation that the universal holds with the particular is precisely what determines the forming of the identity of both the subject and the community.

Crucial for Laclau is an examination of the extent to which it is possible to play new language games with the universal so as to avoid any entanglement in either an essential objectivism or a relativist particularism (*E* 22). Laclau sets out to show how multifarious subjectivities are incompatible with the perspective of the transcendental subject, as well as with the perspective by which the subject ultimately coincides with the constantly changing subject-positions within a given objective system. In so doing Laclau distances himself from the two perspectives which seem to be inseparable from the modern conception of the universal: he criticizes the universalist perspective for systematically misconceiving the particularist place from which the universal can only be enunciated. At the same time he criticizes the particularist approach for drawing from a perfectly valid premise – the irreducible 'particularist' overdetermination of the universal – an illegitimate conclusion, i.e. the rejection of the very category of the universal, a rejection ultimately sustained in the name of defending the particular.

Based on this sketch it can then be argued that in Laclau's essay, the two issues – the first concerning the subject, the second concerning the universal – are intimately linked, thus signalling that any attempt to recast these two problems requires an elucidation of their conjunction. In what follows I propose to theorize this connection in terms of a triad of the universal, the singular, and the subject. I will argue that the universal can only exist by being supplemented by an irreducible singularity; this supplementation in turn requires, as a condition of its possibility, the advent of the subject, which is but a precarious, finite support for the encounter between radical contingency, or irreducible singularity, and the universal. In saying that the subject is ultimately what makes the universal possible, I wish to indicate that the components of the knot do not pre-exist their knotting; rather, they are only constituted after the fact, i.e. in the process of subjectivation. My central claim at this point is that the knot of the universal, the singular, and the subject sheds light not only on Laclau's conception of the universal but also on the relationship between politics and philosophy, and which can be conceived in terms of the *universalization as subjectivation*.

I

Before I proceed to a more detailed discussion of the construction of the knot of three instances, and consequently of the concept of universalization as subjectivation, I need to first account for the choice of these terms and to justify them within the context of Laclau's theorization of the universal. The construction of the knot is obviously my attempt to make explicit the theoretical consequences ensuing from the *specific form* of Laclau's argument centred around the two main issues of his essay: the subject and the universal. The specificity of this form consists in my view in the fact that two general philosophical issues – the subject and the universal – are theorized as being intrinsically political issues. Yet rather than seeing stylistic idiosyncrasy in Laclau's form of argument, I propose to take it up as an indicator of the solution to the problems at issue.

Laclau argues that his search for a new concept of the subject is motivated by the widespread interest witnessed today in the proliferation of multiple identities: this proliferation manifests itself in the explosion of ethnic and national identities in Eastern Europe and the former Soviet Union; in struggles of various immigrant groups in Western Europe; and in new forms of multicultural protestation in the US (*E* 21). It should be noted, however, that in analyzing the proliferation of particular identities in the present conjecture, Laclau refuses to theorize this phenomenon in terms of mere plurality, arguing that an approach that reduces particularities to the differential dimension they assert paradoxically, yet necessarily, misses the irreducible particularity of the particular (*E* 21–2).

Conversely we can reach the dimension of the *true plurality* of the particular, according to Laclau, only if we think of *plurality as being inherent to the particular itself*. From Laclau's argument it then follows that the plurality is reflected, as it were, in the particular itself, i.e. that the particular must be understood as that which is *in itself* plural. Yet this conception is tenable only to the extent that it is grounded in the idea according to which all identity is *inherently divided*. All differential, particular identity, according to Laclau, is characterized by a constitutive lack. In this sense, for a particular to attain itself, i.e. to assert its 'true' identity, the notion of a 'full', closed identity must precisely be cancelled out.

More important for the purpose of my commentary, however, is Laclau's claim that it is precisely this inherently divided identity that designates the origin, always singular or local, of the universal. If we are to follow Laclau we can then say that, to the extent that the universal is possible at all in the context of the proliferation of identities, it can emerge only as a precarious horizon for the constitution of an always already displaced, transformed, in a word, other identity. In this respect we can say with Laclau that 'the universal is the symbol of a missing fullness' (*E* 28). Universalism can then be considered as a sign of the intrinsic plurality of the particular. What is meant by this plurality is not simply a differential repetition of the One, but rather a form of the appearance of an in-itself impossible One. What Laclau ultimately brings to light is the fact that the universal is in itself inconsistent, not-all, and is, like the particular, without a positive identity.

The second principal issue around which Laclau's theorizing is centred – the possibility of a new kind of universal – cannot be articulated appropriately until the historico-political determination of the universal has been thoroughly assessed. Laclau's inquiry into the universal has to a large extent been incited by contemporary political and social transformations, in particular by a radical problematization, indeed, rejection of Western rationalism as the sole universal paradigm of political and cultural development. Such a critique is obviously not novel. Because of its tendency to systematically limit the domain of the particular, Western universalist rationalism has been denounced as an instrument of domination since the second half of the nineteenth century. If Laclau takes the trouble to cite these well-known facts, however, it is precisely in order to introduce an essential novelty in their interrogation: while fully accepting the classical objection addressed to Western Eurocentrism, according to which the apparent universality of European culture is no more than a particular that at some time has become dominant (*E* 26), Laclau nevertheless insists that the uncovering of the particular overdetermination of the universal only points to the real theoretical and practical problem – that of a 'systematic decentering of the West'. We are confronted here with an operation which, instead of simply rejecting the universal as 'an old-fashioned totalitarian dream' (*E* 26), calls for the *invention of a new kind of universal*. Such invention is only possible once we assume both the topological character of the universal, which refers to the fact that the universal is always linked to the conjecture in which it comes to exist (or to say it with Laclau: the universal cannot exist apart from the particular (*E* 34)), and the fact that this inseparability of the universal from the particular, unavoidable without being necessary, is a result of a historical construction – in short, that it is contingent. We cannot miss the huge political consequences ensuing from the inseparability of the universal and the particular: if the universal is incommensurable with all particular content, as Laclau maintains, this means that political and social struggles can always change the nature of their contingent relationship (*E* 34).

This summary sketch of Laclau's subtle and complex analysis of plurality in terms of a possible decentring of Western universalism should help better to determine my principal task: an examination of the displacements to which the two general philosophical issues are submitted by the very fact of their elaboration within a particular domain – that of politics. To further specify my task, four additional clarifications are needed.

First, Laclau's theorization of the proliferation of plural political and social identities and of the domination of the universalist values of Western civilization must obviously be addressed in its own terms, i.e. as a political intervention. At the same time we should not forget that we are dealing here with a philosophical intervention as well.

While fully admitting that the empirical plurality of particular political and social identities exists independently of all theory, this empirical plurality can nevertheless be asserted as *true plurality* only once the concept of the divided identity has been elaborated. As we have seen, for Laclau to be able to assert the plurality of identities in a given political situation *as a plurality*, it is necessary to conceive it in terms of the expression of an inherently divided identity. This is precisely what I call a philosophical intervention, an intervention aiming, in the final analysis, at determining a political situation with regard to its true being.

By developing the notion of an inherently divided identity, by recasting the relationship between the universal and the particular, Laclau approaches the present socio-political conjecture in a characteristically philosophical manner: he confronts it with a clearly defined conceptual determination or, to venture another formula, with a clearly determined 'norm' of its true being.[1] It is thus this normative 'overdetermination' of a political problematic which justifies my claim that Laclau's is a fully-fledged philosophical intervention.

Second, by stressing Laclau's 'local' (i.e. political) articulation of the general philosophical problem of the subject and the universal, I also wish to stress that the very *form* of the elaboration of the problem must be taken as part of its *material* solution. I will then argue that the new theorization of the subject and the universal that Laclau sets as the aim of his inquiry is already actualized, 'staged' by the very form of his theorization. This is only to indicate that it would be completely erroneous were we to understand Laclau's 'local' elaboration of a general problem either in terms of an application of the universal in a particular field, or in terms of a dialectical mediation between the universal and its particular content.

To designate Laclau's 'local' elaboration of the universal *per negationem* does not, however, help us to fully understand its specificity. To be able to *positively* determine the relationship between the universal and the particular as it is actualized by Laclau's approach, we need to examine Laclau's operation to decentre Western universalism. The 'staging' of the relationship between the universal and the particular through the very form of Laclau's discourse represents, in my view, the practical realization of an implication which is already announced without being fully explored in his deconstructive intervention, an intervention that starts by teasing out the paradoxes of Western universalism.

Laclau's theorization of a new kind of universal – or more precisely, his construction of an asymmetrical relation between the universal and the particular – is rooted in two interrelated propositions. According to the first proposition, the universal is inseparable from the particular, i.e. the universal is always already determined by the particular; according to the second proposition, a particular content remains irreducible to the universal, thus implying that the connection between that content and the universal remains contingent. But the very possibility of putting together these two propositions seems to point to a third one – that which makes this linking possible at all. The inherent 'economy' of Laclau's account of the universal can then be rendered visible in terms of the following syllogism: if we maintain (a) that the universal is necessarily linked to the particular and (b) that their relation is a contingent one, we must draw the conclusion that (c) for the universal to come into existence at all requires contingency, i.e. the irreducibility of the particular. In other words, what remains inseparable from the universal is not simply the particular itself but, rather, the very contingency of its particularity.

I can now try to positively determine the relation between the universal and the particular, as Laclau prompts us to do, by insisting that the particular, while remaining irreducible to the universal and entertaining a radically contingent relation with it, nevertheless operates as an indispensable condition for the emergence of the universal. What is at issue in Laclau's conception of the universal is therefore a universal which can establish itself if and only if it is supplemented by a point of irreducible particularity, i.e. a point of singularity. This paradoxical universal, which because of its vital dependence on the particular presents itself as a horizon in which the particular as particular can only be asserted, calls for an equally enigmatic new name, that of the *singular universal*, which paradoxically joins together two traditionally incompatible dimensions. I will argue that Laclau's elaboration of a general philosophical problem in a particular domain of politics is the perfect example of such an actualization of the singular universal. Laclau's 'practising' of a new kind of universal involves an articulation of three moments: first, in Laclau's perspective, a general philosophical issue (that of the subject and/or of the universal) is inseparable from its 'local', i.e. political actualization; second, from Laclau's elaboration it clearly follows that this general problem cannot be reduced to its local actualization; third, the very co-existence of these two moments then indicates that the irreducible contingency of the particular is precisely what makes it possible for the universal to come into existence.

Third, Laclau's 'local' elaboration of a general philosophical problem involves not only a re-thematization of the subject and the universal but also a re-thematization of the relationship between politics and philosophy. In this sense we could say that Laclau's discourse, by actualizing the concept of the singular universal, practises, at the same time, a *new kind of relationship between philosophy and politics*. Laclau's development of a philosophical, general problem in the field of politics, i.e. a field that remains by definition outside philosophy, can only be properly understood once it is admitted that what is at issue in Laclau's intervention is nothing other than a subversion of philosophy's traditional approach to politics. In theorizing politics, as is well known, philosophy is traditionally confronted with the following dilemma: either to assume the task of examining politics in view of its ultimate truth, or to find itself and its notion of truth determined by politics. Laclau's approach unsettles the very terrain of this dilemma by refusing both the normative perspective which assimilates philosophy to the discourse of the Master, as well as a mere descriptive perspective that reduces philosophy to a sterile academic operation characteristic of what Lacan refers to as university discourse. In this respect Laclau can be said to succeed in avoiding both traps precisely by refusing either to assimilate politics to the application of a philosophical concept, or to consider philosophy as one of the particular fields in which politics exerts its influence.

The following question arises at this point: what is politics for philosophy if it is something other than a domain in which philosophical truths are supposed to be realized, something other than an instance which determines philosophy? Starting with the premise by which the relation between the universal problem and its 'local' (i.e. political) appearance is determined, following Laclau, as an essentially impossible relation,[2] I can characterize the status of politics in Laclau's perspective as follows: for philosophy, politics is that which exists and operates as the point of its *impossible-real*. More precisely, politics is what exists and operates as a site of the real of philosophy; at the same time it is only against the background of this real that philosophy can constitute itself *as* philosophy.[3]

The fact that the philosophical problems of the subject and the universal remain, in Laclau's account, inseparable from the political form in which they appear, while being at the same time incommensurable with it, sheds light on the nature of the relationship between politics and philosophy: for philosophy to be established at all, it must deploy itself in some radical exteriority, this being here the field of politics. Politics as the real of philosophy thus operates as an instance indispensable for philosophy and, at the same time, as an instance in which philosophy as philosophy is already effaced.

It is crucial at this point not to misconceive what is at issue in the new relationship between philosophy and politics that I have tried to reconstruct while staying within the framework of Laclau's account. The realization that philosophy can constitute itself as philosophy only once it articulates politics as the point of its impossibility, in short, as its real, is essential in my view. On the other hand this real can operate as the real only to the extent that it is recognized as such by philosophy – only to the extent that it is the real *for* philosophy. We are clearly confronted here with a paradox because that which constitutes the impossible-real of philosophy is situated nowhere else but in the field of philosophy itself. Yet this is not all. For philosophy to be able to sustain itself, it is forced to articulate, within its own discourse as it were, that which constitutively evades the power of its concept.

This relation between politics and philosophy requires as its precondition that the real of politics is never present in the discourse of philosophy. It can only be evoked through an act by which philosophy is separated from politics as its real. It is this act of separation – through which philosophy establishes itself at a minimal distance from the real, an act by which philosophy is constituted and, at the same time, destituted – that I propose to call the *subjectivation* of philosophy. Yet politics can not operate as the real of philosophy unless philosophy itself is conceived as a discourse for which there is the real as real. From what I have argued so far it should be clear that the subjectivation of philosophy is not to be understood in terms of philosophy's self-presence and/or self-transparence. Rather, we are faced here with an 'empty' gesture of separation through which philosophy articulates politics as its impossible-real. In this sense the subjectivation of philosophy revolves around the question of its capacity to handle the real of politics in such a way as to allow for the real to be affirmed and preserved as such.

I can now return to our second remark concerning a new kind of universal – that of the singular universal – which I presume is already operating within Laclau's discourse. In light of my previous discussion of the relationship between philosophy and politics – this being, in my view, the true stake in Laclau's *mise-en-scène* of the universal – I can now argue that the issue of the singular universal, i.e. the universal constituted through the intervention of a singularity irreducible to the universal, coincides with that of the subject. Laclau is of course not blind to this paradoxical relation of parasitism, insisting that this singularity can be asserted as a concrete finitude only within the incomplete, receding horizon of the universal. If the horizon of the universal remains incomplete (receding, as Laclau maintains), this is precisely because the universal is always already subjectivized; it only exists through a groundless, wholly unjustified yet ceaselessly iterable act of enunciation, thus asserting the irreducible singularity as the site of the universal.[4]

Fourth, Laclau's 'local' elaboration of a general philosophical problem requires that we read Laclau 'with' Kant. To fully understand the implications of Laclau's operation of decentring the universal, I propose to re-examine it within the perspective of reflexive judgement, this being Kant's attempt to re-thematize the relationship between the universal and the particular, a re-thematization developed, as is well known, in Kant's *Third Critique*.[5] But the contrary can also be maintained: the novelty of the universal ensuing from Kant's concept of the reflexive aesthetic judgement can also be better understood in light of Laclau's theorization of the paradoxical relationship between the particular and the universal.

II

My task now is to verify the validity of my interpretation of Laclau's essay and, at the same time, to elaborate in more detail my principal thesis that the link between two of Laclau's issues, the subject and the universal, can be conceived in terms of a conjunction of three instances: the universal, the singular, and the subject. In order to do this I will begin by determining the status of that particular identity to which is attributed the role of the 'exemplary case' in Laclau's construction of differential identity: a subjectivity which asserts its manifold and, for that reason, constantly changing expressions as an actualization of its inherent division, its non-identity.

How, then, are we to understand the 'ontological' status of plural, inherently split identities? Are these identities simply a theoretical construction that must yet realize itself in empirical reality; or, on the contrary, do these identities exist empirically, which means Laclau's theorization would only conceptually unify what is given in its empirical variety? I will argue that the pertinence of my interpretation of Laclau's intervention can only be confirmed if I can show that his construction of plural political identities is neither a philosophical operation prescribing the truth of politics nor an operation that would simply translate the demands of a given political situation into philosophical discourse. It is of course crucial here to show how this construction makes it possible for Laclau to undo the traditional alternative which reduces philosophy either to an instance determining politics or to one determined by politics or, to put it differently, to deconstruct the terrain that makes the alternative between the ontological determining the ontic or the ontic determining the ontological possible.

It is here that a Kantian approach can be of help in our reading of Laclau. The question of the 'ontological' status of plural identities can only be answered by developing the construction of these identities in terms of the Kantian reflexive judgement '*Das ist der Fall* (This is a case of . . .)'.[6] In this respect we could say that plural political identities are precisely what constitutes the case for philosophy, more precisely, a philosophy committed, as in Laclau's case, to both deconstruction and/or Lacanian psychoanalysis. Plural identities in this sense represent for philosophy the impossible-real – in short, a case *of politics as the real*. The construction of plural political identities is therefore never to be taken as a description of a given situation, nor as a normative injunction situating politics in the perspective of the pure 'Ought'. Rather, we are dealing here with an *existential proposition*, i.e. a proposition that postulates the existence of inherently divided identities as a case of what the real of philosophy is. Such an existential proposition allows philosophy to 'register' the effects of its encounter with politics conceived as its real, i.e. to subjectivize itself by handling this real.

That philosophy is capable of handling the real can best be illustrated at the point that I will call the point of the *politicization of philosophy*. I use this term to refer to the situation in which philosophy that thinks politics is subjected, *in an undecidable way*, to the above-mentioned alternative between normativism and descriptivism. That is the situation in which philosophy submits political reality to its command by deciding for politics which possibilities of a given situation are permitted and which must be forbidden; and a situation in which it is political reality itself dictating that philosophy should simply sanction the demands already operating in a given political situation. In the first case the philosophical concept itself 'forces' political reality; in the second case it is political reality which, by means of philosophy, violates philosophy.

The undecidability of this alternative is what constitutes, in my view, the 'normal' condition of philosophy. But it is this inherent undecidability, when assumed, which makes it possible for philosophy to go beyond its 'normal' condition. The constitution of philosophy requires therefore a decision made precisely at the point at which philosophy, in its normal condition, is submitted to its politicization, i.e. to the alternative between philosophy as that instance that determines politics or politics as that instance that determines philosophy. Conversely, by overcoming the state of its politicization, i.e. by deciding the undecidable of the above-mentioned alternative, philosophy at the same time articulates politics as its real while operating *as pure philosophy*.

How can philosophy overcome its politicization? The overcoming of politicization is not to be understood in terms of a defensive, reactive attitude on the part of philosophy. It is not as if philosophy must fence off the temptation to succumb to this or that political interest. A philosophy articulated around politics as its real is not an apolitical, academic philosophy. Rather, it is a philosophy which, while fully aware of the danger of its politicization (this being unavoidable since politicization is a consequence of the undecidability that characterizes philosophy whenever it deals with politics) nevertheless avoids the danger of an illegitimate passage into politics. But we are confronted here with another kind of difficulty. Insofar as philosophy conceives politics as its impossible-real, i.e. as that which constitutively evades the philosophical concept as such, it may appear at first glance that philosophy can avoid its politicization by adopting a stance of modesty and self-restraint. In this sense philosophy could, for instance, maintain that it can never tell the whole truth about politics; that politics to a certain extent represents that which remains unsayable or unrepresentable for philosophy and which, for that very reason, undoes philosophical discourse, renders it not-all. This is not my view, however. Quite the contrary; it is only by asserting itself as a discourse aiming at saying the All that there is a slim chance of philosophy articulating politics as that which is irreducible to philosophical conceptualization.

It is only by going to the limits of sayability that philosophy can, first, recognize that there is nothing in politics itself, no ineffable abyss of unsayability, that can evade or resist philosophical thought. Second, the very fact that philosophy can, in principle at least, say everything about politics, that there is nothing, no irreducible gap, that would separate it from politics, signals that politics, paradoxically, represents for philosophy the instance that evades the grasp of philosophical sayability. Philosophy attains the extreme limits of the power of its sayability by recognizing that it can refer to politics only by making its absence present.

As a consequence, the All that is sayable for philosophy can emerge for philosophy when and only when it declares – after determining in one or another way, explicitly or implicitly, what a true politics is for philosophy – that such a politics also exists. Philosophy thus outlines the extreme limits of its conception of politics as the real through an *existential proposition*, i.e. by declaring that, in a given political situation, *cases of the politics of the real* exist or could exist in the changed circumstances, by postulating – and here Laclau can be quoted as an example – that a politics worthy of the name is a politics that opens up the space for a subjectivity asserting its various expressions as an affirmation of its inherent division, non-identity.

This existential proposition constitutive of philosophy can now be determined in three steps. First, an existential proposition as such is, at one and the same time, a philosophical and political proposition. Such a proposition, that asserts that the affirmation of inherently divided identity is a case of true politics, sets in motion what I have called the politicization of philosophy to the extent that it is undecidable: whether philosophy or politics is speaking. Is philosophy that instance which forces politics to submit itself to what philosophy has determined as a case of a true politics or, on the contrary, is a particular politics that instance which forces philosophy to identify in some particular content that which represents the impossible-real for philosophy itself?

Second, the existential proposition makes it possible for the unlocalizable distance separating philosophy from politics as its real to acquire some precarious localization. We could then say that this gesture of separation creates a void destined to be 'inhabited' by cases testifying to the existence of the politics of the real. And it is only by filling this gap that philosophical discourse can constitute itself as the whole of the saying of the All. What is declared as a case is certainly a point of undecidability between politics and philosophy, a point of politicization of philosophy itself, the point at which philosophy constitutes itself as a coherent and consistent discourse. Yet it is precisely at such a point that philosophy emerges and asserts itself as philosophy.

Third, the declared case is certainly a constitutive moment of the philosophical saying of the All. But that which makes it possible for philosophy to establish itself as the All of sayability – to repeat, the undecidability concerning the instance that postulates the existence of the case of the politics of the real – is at the same time what prevents the closure of the philosophical saying into the whole of saying. The saying of the All which is constituted through the moment of a radical undecidability reveals at the same time the impossibility of the All. In this sense the existential moment is not the moment of the closure of the whole of saying but a sign that the whole of the philosophical saying is in itself impossible, thus signalling a step made by philosophy from saying All to saying not-All.

Philosophy that is grounded in the traversing of its politicization is therefore a philosophy in which the existential proposition is conceived as a constitutive moment of philosophical discourse, indeed, as a place from which philosophy can only speak *as philosophy* and where it can constitute itself as a coherent and consistent discourse.[7] The insertion of such an existential proposition – representing what I have called the undecidable moment of the politicization of philosophy – into philosophical discourse is only possible to the extent that philosophy, by deciding the undecidable, constitutes itself as philosophy separated from politics as its real. This however implies that the existential proposition – by means of which particular moments of a given political situation, say, particular social, political, cultural groups and their demands for particular social and political changes are identified by philosophy as cases of the politics of the real – has the structure of reflexive judgement.

Let me note here that, in a Kantian reflexive judgement deciding that some particular is a case of the rule, of the universal, we are not dealing with an existential statement, nor with a deduction of the particular from the pre-given universal or a deduction of existence from a concept. Rather, with a reflexive judgement we are dealing with a relationship between the particular and the universal, i.e. the rule and the case of this rule, that can only be established by means of the mediation of the judgement. What characterizes the reflexive judgement is the absence of the instance of the universal – a norm or a rule, say – in which such a judgement could ground itself. A reflexive judgement is therefore required whenever we are faced with a situation in which neither the particular nor the universal are given in advance. It is, rather, the act of reflexive judgement which produces, invents as it were, the universal by elevating some particular entity to the dignity of a 'case of the universal'. From the perspective of the reflexive judgement it clearly follows that the universal and the particular are produced simultaneously. The existence of the universal as universal is thus directly dependent upon the capacity of the particular to resist its 'dissolution' into the universal, a particular that insists on its irreducible particularity. A Kantian reflexive judgement is therefore a judgement that provides a solution to the problem of a paradoxical universal that exists only insofar as it is supplemented by an irreducible singularity that subtracts itself from all rules, all norms, all law, a singularity which persists in its pure contingency as something which remains without a reason or cause. In the final analysis the universal that exists only in the form of its proper case is nothing other than a groundless yet unconditional singularity.

The lesson that can be drawn from Laclau's theorization of the problem of the universal indicates that the relationship between the singular and the universal as it is conceptualized in Kant's reflexive judgement always already involves a third instance – that of the subject. One way of developing the subject in the perspective of the reflexive judgement – re-read in light of Laclau's conception of the universal – is to accord it the status of the subject of enunciation such as it has been elaborated by Lacan. The subject of enunciation, within the Lacanian perspective, is nothing other than an empty place that can emerge only once it has been 'cleansed' of all particular incarnations of the subject of enunciation. Insofar as such a subject has no proper place in the Other – because it cannot be designated by any positive predicate or signifier – it is only in the very act of enunciation that the subject of enunciation can find its place.[8] The same holds for the subject of the reflexive judgement; it can only exist in the act of judging that something is a case of the rule or that a particular is a case of the universal. In this sense we cannot say that the act of judgement prescribes a norm of its being to a given reality; nor can a reflexive judgement be considered a result of the decision of the subject pre-existing the act of judgement. On the contrary, the particular (the case) and its universal (the rule) are all the categories supported by the act of judgement: this is a case of the rule.[9]

I can now return to my initial question: how can an intervention such as Laclau's be both philosophical and political? In an attempt to answer this question, I have argued that this 'duplicity' is possible precisely because, first, politics as conceived by Laclau operates as the real of philosophy itself, and second, Laclau's construction of the inherently divided political identity – a construction which makes it possible for Laclau's philosophical discourse to attain politics – is structured as a reflexive judgement. The existential proposition by means of which philosophy constructs a new particularism of our political and social situation in terms of 'the multifarious forms of undomesticated subjectivities' (*E* 20) is an articulation of the universal, the singular, and the subject. Let us see now how these three instances are intertwined in Laclau's account.

The subject, as has already been pointed out, is what takes place in the interval that separates philosophy from politics. Philosophy that thinks politics cannot avoid its subjectivation; where it is inseparably linked to politics, philosophy paradoxically constitutes itself as philosophy separated from politics as the real[10] by the act of decision. Philosophy is thus the empty place of a ceaselessly iterable decision that posits that philosophy can exist only insofar as politics as the real exists. The form of appearance of this, in itself, empty act of decision is an existential proposition, by means of which philosophy identifies as cases of the politics of the real particular moments of a given political situation. The act of decision constitutive of philosophy thus necessarily implies the identification of particular situational elements as those which, for philosophy, represent a case of the politics of the real. It should be noted, however, that it is not the case as it is represented in a given situation which accords to the empty act of decision its particular content, but the case itself.

From the point of view of philosophy, *the singular* articulated with politics is the *instance of the case* of politics as the real. There is a case of the real of politics only insofar as philosophy is capable of *correctly* identifying that which, in a given situation, *represents* the case for it. What I mean by correct identification is not, of course, to be conceived of in terms of its adequacy with political reality. Rather, a philosophy wishing to correctly identify particular moments of a given situation as cases of the politics of the real must, in the very act of identification, preserve the ineliminable incommensurability between the empirical, particular moment of the political situation which represents for philosophy the case, and this case itself. While it is true that there is no such a thing as a case outside the empirical, particular moments that in a given situation represent the case, this case itself is always something more or less than its empirical manifestation. In a sense the case is precisely what can never coincide with what represents it: it is the site of this non-coincidence. It could then be said that the ontological status of the case is an entity which simply cannot be registered under the heading of being, a point of the absolute singularity that operates from within both philosophical discourse and the political situation itself. Yet the case is not the impossible-real of philosophy and of politics in itself. Rather, it operates as such a real on condition that philosophy, as I have pointed out, *correctly* identifies those moments which, in a given situation, represent for philosophy cases of the politics of the real. This brings us now to the third instance involved in the relationship between politics and philosophy at work in Laclau's account – the instance of the universal.

The *universal* at work in the relation of philosophy and the real of politics is an instance established in a procedure through which philosophy identifies what the case is. I can now designate it more adequately as a procedure of *the immediate universalization of the absolute singularity of the case*. We are dealing with a correct identification of the case whenever an existential proposition identifying something as a case of the politics of the real passes the test of the substitution of that moment which, in a given situation, represents the case of the politics of the real. This test consists in the realization that, despite the fact that the empirical representation of the case – the representation of inherently divided identity, say – changes constantly, it always appears to be something other or different, the case is what remains the Same – a case of the inherently divided, impossible identity, for instance. The correct identification of the case must then make it possible for philosophy to engage in an, in principle, endless concrete analysis of concrete circumstances. Such an identification must therefore make it possible for philosophy to constantly slide from that which represents the case of the politics of the real in a given situation, to that which represents the case of the politics of the real in another situation. This sliding from one particular representation to another must however preserve, in all of them, the Sameness of the case. More precisely, it must preserve the case as that which persists in a potentially infinite multiplicity of its essentially incomparable particular representations, i.e. as a point of the Sameness to which no attribute, no predicate applies.

The case is therefore always represented by some particular moment. It is nothing other than the site of the particularity. Something can be established as a case only to the extent that, at this place, any given particularity is equivalent to any other particularity – in short, that it can be considered particularity only insofar as it is immediately universalizable. In this sense the case can be designated as the *Da-Sein*, i.e. the presencing of that kind of universality that Laclau characterizes as 'an always receding horizon resulting from the expansion of an indefinite chain of equivalent demands' (*E* 34). Having said that philosophy, as it emerges from Laclau's account, can only constitute itself by means of an act deciding that philosophy exists if, and only if, there is a case of the politics of the real, I can add now that this act can be realized only as a hazardous wager of philosophy to demonstrate a particular identity which has been identified by philosophy as a case of the politics of the real as an immediately universalizable identity, i.e. substituted by an infinite chain of equivalent particulars.

In conclusion, first, the act of decision constitutive of philosophy is conceivable only in terms of the process of universalization as subjectivation; and second, to the extent that philosophy succeeds in demonstrating the immediate universability of particular identities, the latter exist as a case of the politics of the real, i.e. politics that exists independent of philosophy and outside its domain.

Notes

1 What I mean by such a normative proposition can best be illustrated by the following quotation from Laclau himself: 'a particularism really committed to change can only do so by rejecting both what denies its own identity and that identity itself' (*E* 30).

2 See, for instance: 'The universal is incommensurable with the particular, but cannot, however, exist without the latter. How is this relation possible? My answer is that this paradox cannot be solved, but that its non-solution is the very precondition of democracy' (*E* 35).

3 On account of the fact that philosophy can constitute itself as philosophy on condition that it articulates politics as the real, as that which exists independently or outside philosophy, it is possible to say that insofar as philosophy constitutes itself through an act of separation from the real of politics, its relation to politics is ultimately a relation of non-relation.

4 To maintain that the singular universal is nothing other than a subjectivized universal means that subjectivation, for philosophy, takes the form of universalization, or, what amounts to the same, that the universal can be brought about only insofar as the singularity itself is immediately universalizable.

5 For a more detailed discussion of Laclau's retheorization of the universal within the perspective of reflexive judgement, see Riha 1998.

6 As is well known, it was J.-F. Lyotard (1986) who isolated the judgement 'This is a case of ...' as a central issue of Kant's critical enterprise.

7 In opposition to this procedure, philosophy, in its normal condition, constructs the All of its saying by excluding the point of the enunciation, this being precisely the point of undecidability between politics and philosophy. In other words what evades the philosophical conceptualization of politics in its normal condition is precisely the place from which philosophy speaks as philosophy.

8 I am drawing here on Jacques Alain-Miller's unpublished seminar '1,2,3,4' (1984/5).

9 While it is true that something that has been proclaimed to be the case can only gain reality by 'borrowing' it from the material elements of a given situation, we should nevertheless be careful here and not confuse the reality of the case with a material moment that, in a given situation, represents the case. The gap between the case and that which represents it in a given situation remains irreducible.

10 That is to say, by postulating politics as that which is the real for it, philosophy at one and the same time postulates that another politics, i.e. politics of the real, is possible, thus refusing to assimilate politics with either what can be called the institutionalized politics, i.e. politics of parties and state institutions, or with the 'negative' politics of civil society. It is clear that a

politics of the real represents, for philosophy, that which a given situation, a given set of political possibilities, excludes as inherently impossible and which, for that reason, can assert itself only through the interruption or, to use Laclau's own term, dislocation of the situation. It should be noted, however, that what is involved in the demand for a different, other politics is not an attempt to establish politics either in terms of constituted politics (on the ontic level) or in terms of constituting politics (on the ontological level). On the contrary, such a demand is only conceivable if politics itself is constitutively not-All, thus implying that it cannot constitute itself as Politics, either on the ontic or ontological level.

It clearly follows that a politics of the real cannot be characterized positively. All philosophy can say of it is that it exists (or rather, that it can exist) in one political sequence or another. Politics that is the real for philosophy must not be confused with real politics, politics that pre-exists philosophy, i.e. politics that exists independently of philosophy, outside philosophy. Nevertheless, philosophy can and must make it possible for the politics of the real to emerge as such – not, of course, as the politics of the real but, rather, as politics that is the *real for philosophy*. What is at issue in politics whose emergence philosophy makes possible as the real is not a primordial real of politics but, rather, a real of a different kind, a surpassed real, as it were, as this real can only emerge as a result of philosophical intervention., i.e. of the conceptualization of politics in terms of the real of philosophy. This means that we are dealing on the one hand with the real as a presupposition of the philosophical intervention, and on the other hand with the real which adds itself, as it were, to the preceding real, as the real conceptualized by philosophy as the real for philosophy. The first real, the real of politics, is a presupposition, yet a presupposition which can emerge as such after the fact, once philosophy has added to this presupposition the second real, the real of the philosophical presentation. These two reals are nothing than a logical construction as, in reality, we are only dealing with one real. However, this real in order to allow this redoubling, must be necessarily divided.

References

Lyotard, J.-F. (1986) *L'enthousiasme: La critique kantienne de l'histoire*, Paris: Éditions Galilée.

Riha, R. (1998) 'Plurale Subjekte als konkrete Endlichkeiten oder Wie Laclau mit Kant gelesen werden kann', in O. Marchart (ed.) *Das Undarstellbare der Politik: Zur Hegemonietheorie Ernesto Laclaus*, Vienna: Turia + Kant.

5

THIS UNIVERSALISM WHICH IS NOT ONE

Linda M. G. *Zerilli*

Judging from the recent spate of publications devoted to the question of the universal, it appears that, in the view of some critics, we are witnessing a reevaluation of its dismantling in twentieth-century thought. One of the many oddities about this 'return of the universal'[1] is the idea that contemporary engagements with it are more or less of a piece, and that they reflect a growing consensus that poststructuralist political theories are incapable of generating a viable alternative to the collective fragmentation that characterizes late modernity.[2] The putative return to the universal marks, on this view, both a homecoming to Enlightenment ideals – purified of their more poisonous elements, of course – and a reconciliation of sorts between those who refuted these ideals and those who sought to realize them. Now that 'we' all know and agree that poststructuralism is critically valuable but politically bankrupt; now that we all know and agree that the 'old universal' was indeed a 'pseudo-universal', so the homecoming narrative goes; we can get on with the project of constructing a 'new universal'.[3] This authentic universal would really be inclusive of all people, regardless of race, class, gender, sexuality, ethnicity, nationality, and whatever else attaches to the 'embarrassing etcetera' that, as Judith Butler reminds us, inevitably accompanies such gestures of acknowledging human diversity.

Before signing on to this felicitous agreement about 'the necessity of universalism' we may wish to know whether we have anything like a minimal agreement in language, that is, whether we who speak of this universal are even speaking about the same thing. Apart from the not insignificant problem of translating from a philosophical to a political idiom, the whole question of this agreement is virtually occluded by the rush to rescue politics from the virulent particularisms that admit no common ground or sense of collective belonging. Presented in terms of the familiar binary couple, the choice between universalism and particularism seems settled by merely pointing to global and domestic political realities. Universalism is the only alternative to social fragmentation, wild child of the collapse of communism, the rise of deadly nationalisms, and the multiculturalist romance with particularism. To invoke the name of the universal in any affirmative sense is already to sign on to the political diagnosis and its solution.

One of the many virtues of Ernesto Laclau's *Emancipation(s)* is that it offers both an alternative to the binarisms spawned by the 'return' to the universal (for example, false universalism/true universalism) and a trenchant critique of the original binary couple itself (universalism/particularism). Demonstrating the imbrication of the universal and the particular, Laclau shows why it is a matter not of choosing one over the other but of articulating, in a scrupulously political sense, the relation between the two. He thus explicitly rejects the notion that this relation is one of mutual exclusion, and shows that the tendency to see it as just that has led to the impasse of the contemporary debate, an impasse that is glossed over in some highly visible academic cases by proclaiming the necessary return to the universal. Although the language of universalism as spoken by Laclau searches for some common ground between particularists and universalists, it is more by way of articulating their mutual contamination, that is, how each is rendered impure by the irreducible presence of the other.

The problem of universals

Laclau situates his collection of essays in the context of the increasingly polarized debate over multiculturalism, a debate in which the classical universalism of the philosophical tradition has come under serious question. Reading his essays, one comes to see the deep dependence of the entire contemporary discussion on this tradition, even when its metaphysical assumptions are explicitly rejected (as, say, in the work of Seyla Benhabib) or insufficiently comprehended (as in most of the popularized political discourse). Laclau's book can help us to see that the *political* question of universalism cannot be posed properly as long as it remains tethered to the classical philosophical 'problem of universals'. At stake in sorting out the affinities and the differences between these two idioms of universality, I shall argue, is the question of how we understand intersubjective agreement in a democratic culture. The status of this agreement is, finally, what the debate over multiculturalism and the universal is all about.

I begin with these remarks because Laclau's exercises in rethinking the relation between universal and particular may seem somewhat formalistic to readers who are not accustomed to or even interested in its philosophical dimension. In the context of the national debate over multiculturalism, in which the term universal is a synonym for everything from '*e pluribus unum*' to 'essentialist', it may be difficult to grasp the precise political relevance of a text which is laced with complex philosophical moves. But the political riches of Laclau's text, I submit, arise precisely through its engagement with traditional philosophy and, specifically, its deconstruction of classical universalism. Out of that critique emerges an argument in which the universal looks rather different from the creature one finds in many contemporary returns to it.

Laclau's critique of philosophy interprets the universal and the particular as 'tools in the language games that shape contemporary politics' (*E* 48). He asks, among other things, whether 'the alternative between an essential objectivism and a transcendental subjectivism exhaust the range of language games that it is possible to play with the "universal"' (*E* 22). Although Laclau himself does not elaborate fully on this notion of language games, I want to make use of it as a valuable and appropriate concept for approaching his quarrel with the philosophical tradition.

Derived from Wittgenstein, the concept of 'language game' interrupts the longstanding philosophical debate on the 'problem of universals', exposing it as a pseudo-problem which, as Jamil Nammour puts it, 'trades on the metaphysical assumption that there is language on one side and the "world" on the other' (Nammour 1992: 352). Briefly summarized, this debate concerns primarily the status of the qualities by which we sort and describe particulars. It is governed by the following sorts of questions: How do we justify naming things as we do? Why do we group a collection of particulars under a general term (like chair, house, tree)? For 'realists' the answer is, because those particulars have something in common, some subsistent real entity or *form*, a universal. This something, like the larger objective world in which it exists, is metaphysically distinct from the language we use to describe it, from the standpoint we occupy, and from our interests. For 'nominalists', in contrast, the only thing that the particulars have in common is that they are called the same thing. What they have in common is nothing but a name: two objects *are* chairs because they are both *called* by that name. They share the name, nothing more.[4]

Wittgenstein's intervention unmasks the transcendental terms of this debate. Against realists, he argues that it is impossible to determine the existence of an extralinguistic or nonlinguistic something, a universal form or essence that makes an object what it is and gives sense to our practices of naming. We cannot 'prise words off the world', as J. L. Austin once implored us to do (quoted in Nammour 1992: 348), because even if such a distinction (words/world) did exist, Wittgenstein shows, there is no way to decide whether a Common Property or a Resemblance comes from the side of the world or from the side of language. We simply wouldn't know that we *were* finally outside of language even if we *could* find such a place (which is just another way of saying that we would never know that we had found this place and therefore could not find it). It follows from this critique of realism that, for Wittgenstein, the problem of nominalism is not that it is blind to the extralinguistic quality of the object, its *form* (as the realist contends), but that it is blind to *grammar*, the usage and thus meaning of a word (or 'name') in a language game. As he writes in *Philosophical Investigations*: 'Nominalists make the mistake of interpreting all words as names, and so of not really describing their use, but only, so to speak, giving a paper draft of such a description' (1968: no. 383). Thus to the question, 'How do I know that this color is red?', Wittgenstein gives neither the answer of the realist ('because it *is* red') nor that of the nominalist ('because it is *called* red'). Rather, he responds, 'It would be an answer to say: "I have learnt English"' (1968: no 381).

The notion of language game that Wittgenstein develops in his later works calls into question the transcendental conception of rules and rule-following that underwrites the classical metaphysics of entity and selfsame identity. As Henry Staten observes, what Wittgenstein calls grammar or

> the 'rule for the use of a word' cannot [...] be construed as a form that makes meaning present by predetermining it. And, at the same time, since meaning for Wittgenstein can no longer be simply present, this means that meaning is no longer determined by the 'is,' by the being of the object.
>
> (Staten 1984: 15)

Indeed, for Wittgenstein, writes Staten,

> a rule, where there is a rule, [...] determines but need not itself be determinate. We learn to follow it, obey it, or manipulate it, and yet the rule itself is structurally or essentially indeterminate. A rule is best thought of as an object which happens to be used as a standard of comparison within some practice or other. Because any social practice is carried on by different persons who will vary from each other in their sense of how to apply any given rule, any form of life is always transected by diverging lines of possible practice; a form is a transitive essence always in process of essential variation from itself. On this view a form of life has no self-identical and unitary form, nor does a rule, nor do we.
>
> (Ibid. 134)

Staten's reading is an important corrective to communitarian interpretations of Wittgenstein which both posit 'the agreement of the community as the determinant of correct rule-following' and conceive of a rule as 'having a "*form*" which makes it identical with itself' (ibid. 165 n. 21). These interpretations – which make Wittgenstein complicit with the status quo – merely subsume individual practices of rule-following under an always already existing communal agreement, thereby occluding the heterogeneity of those practices and excluding the possible emergence of new ones. The question of intersubjective agreement is erased *as a question* by being grounded in rules and rule-following practices that are unitary, self-identical, and given in advance. Although not necessarily construed as 'universal' in the strict sense, these forms are cast as universally repeated and repeatable by all members of a given community. They are thus seen as determinate, albeit in a more limited sense.

The notion of language game that Laclau adopts from Wittgenstein is clearly at odds with the latter's communitarian interpreters. In *New Reflections on the Revolution of Our Time*, Laclau (like Staten) emphasizes that 'the rules of [Wittgenstein's language games] only exist in the practical instance of their application – and are consequently modified and deformed by them' (*NR* 22). Indeed, says Laclau,

> if for Wittgenstein every instance of a rule's use *modifies* the rule as such, it cannot be said that a rule is being *applied* [in the sense of communal repetition], but that it is being constantly constructed and reconstructed, between an abstract rule and the instance of its use in a particular context, it is not a relationship of *application* that occurs, but a relationship of *articulation*. And accordingly, if the different instances of an articulated structure have merely differential identities, it can only mean that in the two separate instances the rule is in fact a different one, in spite of its 'family resemblance' (*NR* 208–9).[5]

To think about the universal under the rubric of language game is, for Laclau, to explore the limits and the possibilities of its (re)articulation in various social and political contexts. The universal, as Laclau (*pace* Wittgenstein) says of the rule, is not there to be discovered, followed, or applied; this 'hegemonic act will not be the realization of a rationality preceding it, but an act of radical construction' (*NR* 29). Laclau in no way forecloses the possibility of *articulating* an intersubjective agreement in which the universal has a central place; he simply asks how such an agreement could be possible in the absence of what Staten calls the 'transphenomenal entities' (Staten 1984: 134) that have traditionally been used to ground it. How does one articulate moments of agreement in the absence of a determinate notion of rules and unitary practices of rule-following (to say nothing of God, Reason, or History)? This is the shape of the question of political community after metaphysics. Laclau suggests that we have been looking for answers in all the wrong places because we have not taken seriously enough the meaning of human plurality or, taking it too seriously, namely as an overwhelming problem, the problem of innumerable particulars, we treat plurality as something to be subdued or even overcome by an intersubjective agreement that is grounded in universals.

Hannah Arendt once remarked that Western philosophy would never have a conception of the political because it conceives of Man in the singular, whereas politics concerns men in the plural. Laclau is no Arendtian, but his attempt to shift the discussion of universalism from the terrain of philosophy to that of politics shares this important insight.[6] To rethink the relation between universal and particular in terms of a language game, as Laclau does, must entail a more explicitly political interpretation of that concept than Wittgenstein, the philosopher's anti-philosopher, ever gave it. Although Laclau does not cite Arendt, his critique of the classical universalism of philosophy shares with her rereading of Kant an attempt to develop just this political idiom in which to rearticulate the relation between universality and particularity; an idiom that eschews truth criteria (and rule-following) in favor of opinions formed through contingent practices of publicity. In this idiom the potential moments of intersubjective agreement are anticipated in the context of plurality rather than derived from some notion of an essential commonality or the injunction to reach consensus. For Arendt (following Kant), this idiom is called critical judging: the practice, conducted in the public space of appearances, of assessing particulars without subsuming them under a pregiven universal or rule.[7] For Laclau, as we shall see, this idiom is called hegemony: the reinscription (not the sublation) of particulars into chains of equivalence through reference to the universal as an empty place.

What Laclau and Arendt share, despite their differences, is the view that intersubjective agreement is not there to be discovered in the universality of experience or the sameness of identity. There is nothing that we all share by virtue of being human or of living in a particular community that guarantees a common view of the world; there is nothing extralinguistic in the world that guarantees that we all share a common experience; there is no Archimedean place from which we could accede to a universal standpoint. But if Laclau (like Arendt) refutes the false universality of abstract rationality or common identity, he by no means rejects universalism 'as an old-fashioned totalitarian dream' (*E* 26). Playing a different language game with the universal, however, Laclau does not come home to a universalism which is One. Rather, he reinterprets universality as a site of multiple significations which concern not the singular truths of classical philosophy but the irreducibly plural standpoints of democratic politics. Even those who want nothing to do with this or any other universal, says Laclau, can never quite escape the pull of its orbit.

The limits of particularism

Laclau's critique of the debate over particularism is inflected by the latter's meaning in the heated discussion of multiculturalism. Sympathetic to the insistence on difference that characterizes multicultural projects, but critical of their fence-building tendencies, Laclau wants to reorient these projects in the direction of a concept of the universal that cannot be decided in advance or subsumed under the notion of a dialogical consensus (Habermas) that would transcend all particularisms.

The claim to difference, Laclau argues in chapters 2 and 4 of *Emancipation(s)*, imbricates multicultural groups in the very universalism they refuse. 'The assertion of pure particularism, independently of any content and of the appeal to a universality transcending it, is a self-defeating enterprise' (*E* 26). Laclau gives two reasons for this claim. First, in a complex society (like the United States), no group leads a 'monadic existence' but is situated in a larger context. The identity of the group, as Laclau says of all identity, is differential. It gets articulated in an 'elaborated system of relations with other groups' (*E* 48), not in splendid isolation from them. These relations will be 'regulated by norms and principles which transcend the particularism of *any* group' (*E* 48), such as the language of rights. Moreover, says Laclau, the very assertion of the right of groups to their difference is already an appeal to some universal principle: 'there is no particularism which does not make an appeal to such principles in the construction of its identity' (*E* 26). What this means is that difference, when it is asserted in the political space and discourse of rights, is necessarily entangled in the logic of equivalence: 'If it is asserted that all particular groups have the right to respect of their own particularity, this means that they are equal to each other in some ways' (*E* 49). The only case in which the logic of pure difference would not be contaminated by the logic of equivalence, asserts Laclau, would be in a society in which

> all groups were different from each other, and in which none of them wanted to be anything other than what they are. [...] It is not for nothing that a pure logic of difference – the notion of separate developments – lies at the root of apartheid (*E* 49).

The second reason why pure particularism is self-defeating, says Laclau, is that the assertion of one's differential identity entails 'the sanctioning of the *status quo*'. Inasmuch as the identity of one group is only differential vis-à-vis the identities of other existing groups, it 'has to assert the identity of the other' at the very moment that it asserts its own (*E* 49). Inasmuch as a group 'cannot assert a differential identity without distinguishing it from a context' (that is, a particular set of social relations), it has to reinscribe the very context in which it would inscribe its difference (*E* 27). Multicultural groups which cling too closely to a fantasy of pure difference risk at once ghettoization by, and complicity with, the dominant community. That is why 'a particularism really committed to change', Laclau concludes, 'can only do so [*sic*] by rejecting both what denies its own identity and identity itself' (*E* 30).

The preceding claims are certain to be received as highly controversial. Like his characterization of multiculturalism as a practice governed by an incoherent but dangerous logic of pure difference which, if realized, could only end in 'self-apartheid' (*E* 32), Laclau's apparent reduction of political strategies of separate development to little more than an affirmation of what exists is bound to be criticized as a caricatured and inaccurate portrayal of a complex set of social practices. Some readers may ask: How many existing multicultural groups actually advocate what Laclau calls 'total segregation' and wholly reject, in his words, 'Western cultural values and institutions [as little more than] the preserve of white, male Europeans or Anglo-Americans' (*E* 32)?

Readers looking for a historically and contextually nuanced account of multiculturalism will most likely count themselves among those who find *Emancipation(s)* less than satisfactory. But to accuse Laclau of indulging in the practice of caricature and a highly formalistic mode of argumentation, or of playing into the hands of conservatives and classical universalists, would be to miss the substance of his intervention and to misconstrue the spirit of his critique. Above all, Laclau is concerned to show *both* the limits of particularism for grounding multicultural struggles *and*, as we shall see, the inadequacy of a return to the classical notion of universalism as an alternative to the social fragmentation that is both a cause and an effect of the drive toward particularism. The critique of particularism in *Emancipation(s)* is part of Laclau's broader attempt to situate both it and universality in a language game, and thus to mediate them in ways that are consistent with a political conception of plurality. From Laclau's perspective, the problem of particularism is the problem of identity politics: both assume that members of a specific group ('women', 'blacks', 'gays') are alike in the same way. But what counts as an essential commonality or sameness, as Laclau argued above, is the very identity that condemns the group to marginality and sustains relations of social dominance. The question would be how to articulate political relations of commonality that do not reproduce these other relations of dominance and the terrors of selfsame identity.

Laclau's portrayal of the fantasy of extreme particularism and separate development that governs certain multicultural imaginaries is a sketch of the dark outer limits of the drive for pure difference. Where it has been realized in political reality, this fantasy goes under the name of apartheid. Although he explicitly differentiates the 'new particularisms' (*E* 27) that are collected under the banner of multiculturalism from actual historical instances of apartheid (South Africa), Laclau wishes to call our attention to the possibility that there may be troubling moments of affiliation, unholy places where the aspirations of very different political groups converge in their respective fantasies of absolute difference. Whether Laclau's portrait of multicultural groups is overdrawn is in this sense irrelevant; the importance of the fantasy does not depend on the existence of empirical groups which then enact it in clearly discernible ways. Rather, the fantasy's relevance for the discussion of universalism/particularism as it gets played out in the debate over multiculturalism concerns its position in the production of political identities, namely the filling of lack. That process of filling takes us straight to Laclau's alternative to the self-defeating logic of particularism for building a more viable multiculturalism: his reformulation of the universal as an empty place.

Universal is an empty place

Laclau's critique of particularism is also an argument against Eurocentrism that passes itself off as universalism. He observes how nineteenth-century European culture posed as the 'expression' of 'a universal civilizing function' and how

> the resistances of other cultures were, as a result, presented not as struggles between particular identities and cultures, but as an all embracing and epochal struggle between universality and particularisms – the notion of peoples without history expressing precisely their incapacity to represent the universal (*E* 24).

A question thus arises as to whether the universal, in Laclau's description, is little more than an 'inflated particular', which is precisely how Naomi Schor has recently interpreted his position (Schor 1995: 22). The question is crucial, not least because in the current debate an affirmative answer has become the olive branch with which to negotiate a peaceful settlement of critical differences and to make possible the putative return to the universal. Decrying this inflated particular as a 'false universal', however, implies that there could be such a thing as a 'true universal', which in turn implies that the universal could someday be One.[8]

Although Laclau argues that what comes to signify the universal was once a particular, his position complicates the binary opposition of 'true universal' versus 'false universal' by refusing the notion that there could be an ideal universality which really was fully divested of any trace of particularity. On the contrary, we shall find Laclau maintaining that no universal is without the 'remainder of particularity'. To argue otherwise would be to accept the ideal of a 'pure universality' and its correlate, a 'reconciled society': a totality achieved through the 'realization of the essence of humankind' (*NR* 78), the incorporation or transcendence of all particulars. Laclau shows how this regulative ideal structures the impasse in the polarized debate over universalism versus particularism. Multicultural groups decry universality as 'false' because, in their view, it is not truly inclusive, but also because they see it as an ideal which, if it *were* realized, would obliterate each group's particularity. Universalism is thus rejected not only because, historically speaking, it has been a fraud, an inflated particular, but also because it is no longer desirable even as an ideal. The language of universalism, on this view, cannot provide the terms of intersubjective agreement in a plural democracy.

Laclau's response to these concerns is not to advocate a return to universalism as the only alternative to a war of particularisms; rather, it is to show that the latter, though irreducible, are not incommensurable, and that they can be brought together in the political field, though never made identical with each other, through the articulation of equivalential demands. A conception of the relation between the universal and the particular that would be appropriate to the plurality of a democracy requires a specific kind of political thinking or, in Laclau's terminology, hegemony. To think about this relation in hegemonic terms is to consider it as fundamentally 'unstable and undecidable' (*E* 15) rather than as determined in some way by the (social) structure. Hegemony means that the relation between universal and particular entails not the realization of a shared essence or the final overcoming of all differences but an ongoing and conflict-ridden process of mediation through which antagonistic struggles articulate common social objectives and political strategies. The very fact that commonalities must be *articulated* through the interplay of diverse political struggles – rather than discovered and then merely followed, as one follows a rule – means, first, that no group or social actor can claim to represent the totality and, second, that there can be no fixing of the final meaning of universality (especially not through rationality). The universal cannot be fixed because it 'does not have a concrete content of its own but is an always preceding horizon resulting from an indefinite expansion of equivalential demands'. Put slightly differently, universal is just another word for placeholder of the 'absent fullness of the community'. It can never actually *be* that fullness – not even as a regulative ideal.

To better grasp the distinct political significance of Laclau's reinscription of the universal as an empty place, I want to turn to the third chapter of his text, 'Why do empty signifiers matter to politics?' Starting with a formal question of signification – namely, how can a signifying system signify its own limits? – Laclau rejects the possibility of any 'positive ground' (*E* 38) and argues that 'a radical exclusion is the ground and condition of all differences' (*E* 39). The system, like the subject, is penetrated by a constitutive lack; it can only be the space of differences to the extent that it is bounded by a 'beyond', a limit without which the notion of context, like differential identity itself, would not be possible. What this means, says Laclau, is that the beyond cannot be just another difference but must be something which negates all differential identities, thereby establishing a relation of equivalence among them and establishing the context within which differences can be constituted as such. Just as every identity is constituted differentially – which, for Laclau, means in the first place through relations of antagonism with all other identities – so is the system, in which these differential identities are constituted, itself constituted through antagonistic limits: 'Only if the beyond becomes the signifier of pure threat, of pure negativity, of the simply excluded, can there be limits and system (that is an objective order)' (*E* 38). The empty signifier emerges, then, as that which represents 'the pure being of the system – or, rather, the system as pure Being'; it is 'a signifier of the pure cancellation of all difference' (*E* 38, 37).

This 'act of exclusion of something alien, a radical otherness' (*E* 52) builds on and significantly deepens Laclau's and Chantal Mouffe's earlier notion, in *Hegemony and Socialist Strategy*, of 'social antagonism' as the condition and limit of identity. It is precisely the dimension of antagonism which Slavoj Žižek found so promising in his 1987 reading of *Hegemony*. In Žižek's view, there is a 'homology between the Laclau–Mouffe concept of antagonism and the Lacanian concept of the Real'. Writes Žižek: 'far from reducing all reality to a kind of language-game, the socio-symbolic field is conceived [according to both concepts] as structured around a certain traumatic impossibility, around a certain fissure which *cannot* be symbolized' (Žižek 1990: 249).

Žižek's interpretation invites a reading of Laclau's theory of empty signifiers in which the notion of antagonism as radical exclusion might occasion a rapprochement between 'Lacanians' and 'poststructuralists/postmarxists' – two intellectual camps which are on their way to becoming as opposed as those of universalists and particularists. Although this is not the place to take up the substantive issues of this rather acrimonious debate, I would like to point to one aspect of it which will become relevant to our discussion of the universal as an empty place: namely, the idea – repeated endlessly in Žižek's work – that Lacanians talk about 'the subject', poststructuralists talk about 'subject position', and never the twain shall meet. Why? A primary reason, says Žižek, is that they have two very different understandings of antagonism. As Žižek explains in his commentary on *Hegemony*, the poststructuralist sees antagonism as an external battle between two subject positions or terms (for example, lord/bondsman; man/woman): 'each of them is preventing the other from achieving its identity with itself, to become what it really is'. The Lacanian, in contrast, sees antagonism as internal, the subject's irreducible conflict with itself: 'the negativity of the other which is preventing me from achieving my full identity with myself is just the externalization of my own auto-negativity, of my self-hindering'. The first conception of antagonism, says Žižek, feeds 'the illusion that after the eventual annihilation of the antagonistic enemy, I will finally abolish antagonism and arrive at an identity with myself' (Žižek 1990: 251). The second, 'more radical' notion of antagonism, he adds, exposes the illusion as just that.

> We must then distinguish the experience of antagonism in its radical form, as a limit of the social, as the impossibility around which the social field is structured, from antagonism as the relation between antagonistic subject-positions: in Lacanian terms, we must distinguish antagonism as real from the social reality of the antagonistic fight. And the Lacanian notion of the subject [as 'the empty place of the structure'] aims precisely at the experience of 'pure' antagonism as self-hindering, self-blockage, this internal limit preventing the symbolic field from realizing its full identity: the stake of the entire process of subjectivation, of assuming different subject-positions, is ultimately to enable us to avoid this traumatic experience.
>
> (Žižek 1990: 253)

Disappointed with Laclau and Mouffe's theory of subject positions but enthralled by the possibilities opened up by their notion of antagonism, Žižek seeks, in his own words, 'to supplement the theoretical apparatus of *Hegemony*' with 'two [Lacanian] notions': 'the subject as an empty place correlative to the antagonism; social fantasy as the elementary mode to mask the antagonism' (1990: 259). The Žižekean gesture of supplementation, however, does not merely '*distinguish* antagonism as real from the social reality of the antagonistic fight', it actually folds or collapses the Laclau–Mouffe notion of social antagonism, as the battle between two identities 'presentified' as polar positions in a contingent *social* space, into the Lacanian notion of a constitutive *Spaltung* of the subject. In Žižek's view, the former is merely an illusion produced by the subject's refusal to confront the trauma of the latter, the real. The subject emerges at precisely the limit of the social, its impossibility.

Despite the fact that Laclau himself seems to accept Žižek's appropriation of his (and Mouffe's) work, seeing in it strong theoretical affinities with which to explain 'the dynamic relation between lack and structure' (Laclau and Zac 1994: 33), I want to suggest some reasons why we should at least pause and consider their substantive differences. First, Laclau's reception of Žižek's reading is somewhat puzzling insofar as he repeatedly insists – in the very same book in which Žižek's essay was published – that 'in our conception of antagonism [...] denial [of identity] does not originate from the "inside" of identity itself but, in its most radical sense from outside' (*NR* 17).[9] Although this assertion is aimed at showing 'the limit of objectivity', as we saw above, it is politically significant that Laclau's (and Mouffe's) notion of antagonism precisely does not reduce itself to the original *Spaltung* of the subject but maintains a crucial reference to a remainder which is always historical and contextual, and which gives to antagonism its specifically political dimension. Although Laclau and Mouffe (especially in their recent work on political identities) in no way foreclose a reference to the original division of the subject, their emphasis on the political dimension of antagonism deprives that reference of the all-important status that it has in Žižek's approach.

We can appreciate the stakes for a postfoundational democratic theory in sustaining the difference and the tension between these two notions of antagonism if we turn to a remark that Žižek makes in his commentary on *Hegemony*. Arguing for the more 'radical' (that is, pure) notion of antagonism provided by the Lacanian concept of the real, Žižek writes: 'the Lord is ultimately an invention of the Bondsman, a way for the Bondsman to "give way as to his desire", to evade the blockade of his own desire by projecting its reason into the external repression of the Lord'. To this Žižek adds, 'This is also the real ground for Freud's insistence that the *Verdrängung* cannot be reduced to an internalization of the *Unterdrückung* (the external repression)' (1990: 252). And that is correct – but it is likewise the case that a psychoanalytically informed political analysis (especially a democratic theory concerned with plurality) has also to argue the reverse: the *Unterdrückung* cannot be reduced to the *Verdrängung*. The original division of the subject no more produces the specific form that social antagonisms take than the latter determine the original *Spaltung* through which the unconscious is constituted. The task of a critical analysis which takes account both of the heterogeneity of the subject (psychic division) and the heterogeneity of subjects (social plurality), then, is to relate the complexity of unconscious processes to the repressiveness of cultural norms without reducing one to the other. The same goes for the concept of antagonism.

At stake in maintaining the distinction between the Lacanian and the Laclau–Mouffe notions of antagonism, then, is a democratic theory that does not collapse into sociological or psychological reductionism. I am in no way arguing that the Lacanian real is not relevant to the Laclau–Mouffe concept of social antagonism, only that the issues it raises concerning the status of the subject cannot be substituted for the issues raised by antagonistic social and political relations. These two concepts of antagonism are related, even deeply imbricated, but they are not for all that identical, and the one cannot be accounted for as an 'illusion' which conceals the trauma of the other. What I am arguing is that the field of politics cannot be divorced from the psychoanalytic notion of psychic reality but neither can it be folded into the latter – not for the naive reason that psychic reality is not 'reality', but because the question of intersubjectivity is simply not the same. In politics we have to deal with plurality, with the irreducibility of diverse perspectives implicit in 'the fact that men, not Man, live on earth and inhabit the world', to borrow Arendt's formulation (1958: 7). This plurality, although it cannot exist apart from, is not reducible to, the plurality of (failed) identifications and misrecognitions which make up the subject's psychic reality. The assumption of various subject positions may very well serve to mask the subject's encounter with its own limit, the 'pure antagonism' of which Žižek speaks. But the diversity of subject positions as well as the diverse ways in which they can be occupied or, better, performed (think here of Wittgenstein's notion of the rule), to say nothing of how that performance is indelibly shaped by the space of the public – all this cannot be accounted for by the Lacanian theory of the subject that Žižek proposes in his attempt to redefine the Laclau–Mouffe notion of social antagonism. The political specificity of the particular, the political question of particularisms, and the proliferation of particularistic political identities entail, but are not reducible to, that part of the subject which resists universalization, its Thing. The Real may indeed be the gap that separates the universal from the particular in the register of psychic reality, as Žižek maintains, but in the realm of the political that gap is not reducible to the Real.[10]

We can better understand these distinctions by returning to Laclau's notion of the empty signifier. I said earlier that, according to Laclau, the empty signifier stands for the universal, the *impossible* fullness of the community. In some respects, however, the notion of the *empty* signifier may be misleading. Laclau tells us that it is a particular 'which has divested itself of its particularity' or 'which overflows its particularity' (*E* 22) to stand for the universal. As these two formulations of the process of emptying the signifier of its particularity indicate, it is not always clear what the place of the particular is, finally, in the empty signifier. Is this particular overcome, left behind, transformed? Is the empty signifier, strictly speaking, empty? Actually, none of these formulations captures what Laclau has in mind under the term empty signifier. It is crucial here to recall the distinction he draws between the empty signifier's content and its function. As to the latter, it is 'exhausted in introducing chains of equivalence in an otherwise purely differential world' (*E* 57). As to the former, writes Laclau,

> Precisely because the community as such is not a purely differential space of an objective identity but an absent fullness, it cannot have any form of representation of its own, and has to borrow the latter from some entity constituted within the equivalential space – in the same way as gold is a particular use value which assumes, as well, the function of representing value in general. This emptying of a particular signifier of its particular, differential signified is [...] what makes possible the emergence of 'empty' signifiers as the signifiers of a lack, an absent totality. But this leads straight into the [following] question: If all differential struggles [...] are equally capable of expressing [...] the absent fullness of the community, [...] if none is predetermined per se to fulfil this role; *what does determine that one of them rather than another incarnates, at particular periods of time, this universal function?* (E 42, emphasis added).

This is the crucial political question to ask about empty signifiers. (It is also the question that a strictly Lacanian interpretation of the empty signifier as equivalent to *objet petit a* cannot answer.) We want to know why not all claims to the universal are equally authorized; why the claims of some groups to represent the whole carry more cultural weight than those of other groups. Consistent with his critique of the objectivity of structures, Laclau rejects at once the notion that the particularity of any one group is predestined to be the content of this function (like a universal class) and the notion that the particularity of any other group is constitutively unable to become that content (like women). Does this mean he assumes that each group stands an equal chance of becoming the empty signifier of the community? Naomi Schor appears to think just this when she writes, 'contrary to what Laclau suggests, it is not just any particular that arrogates dominance – women could not just be promoted to the status of the universal subject' (Schor 1995: 22).

Laclau, as it turns out, would quite agree with Schor. He explicitly states that 'not any position in society, not any struggle is equally capable of transforming its own contents in a nodal point that becomes an empty signifier' (*E* 43). The reason is the 'unevenness of structural locations', by which Laclau means not a 'traditional conception of the historical efficacy of social forces' but a radically politicized understanding of the relationship between 'logics of difference and logics of equivalence' (*E* 43). Although Laclau in no way denies that some groups (men, for example) are better positioned socially and politically than other groups (women, for example) to make claims to the universal, he also holds that it is crucially important to foreground the undecidability of (what will come to stand for) the universal, even as one critically examines its historical asymmetry.

> [I]t is impossible to determine at the level of the mere analysis of the form difference/equivalence which particular difference is going to become the locus of equivalential effects – this requires the study of a particular conjuncture, precisely because the presence of equivalential effects is always necessary, but the relation equivalence/difference is not intrinsically linked to any particular differential content. The relation by which a particular content becomes the signifier of the absent communitarian fullness is exactly what we call a hegemonic relationship. The presence of empty signifiers [...] is the very condition of hegemony (*E* 43).

According to Laclau, then, the universal emerges as a 'hegemonic operation [defined as] the presentation of the particularity of the group as the incarnation of that empty signifier which refers to the communitarian order as an absence, an unfulfilled reality' (*E* 44). This competition to fill the lack – which can be defined as any number of things, including the absence of order, the need for unity, liberation, revolution – is structured by relations of power but is by no means determined in advance. 'Politics is possible because the constitutive impossibility of society can only represent itself through the production of empty signifiers', writes Laclau (*E* 44). In other words, if the particularity of any one group *was* in fact predetermined to stand (or could stand indefinitely) for the absent fullness of the community, there would be no such thing as politics.

In Laclau's account, then, the universal is severed from the metaphysics of the subject (which governs the classical understanding of universalism), indeed from the very philosophical category of *the* Subject, and is reinscribed in a political idiom of plurality. This universalism is not One: it is not a preexisting something (essence or form) to which individuals accede but, rather, the fragile, shifting, and always incomplete achievement of political action; it is not the container of a presence but the placeholder of an absence, not a substantive content but an empty place. As Laclau puts it, the

> dimension of universality reached through equivalence is very different from the universality which results from an underlying essence or an unconditioned a priori principle. It is not a regulative ideal either – empirically unreachable but with an unequivocal teleological content – because it cannot exist apart from the system of equivalences from which it proceeds (*E* 55).

Universal can neither precede nor exceed the political, for it is nothing else but a hegemonic relation of *articulated* differences.

Once it is understood that equivalential relations 'do not express any a priori essential unity' (*E* 54) but are themselves politically articulated relations of difference, we can see that 'universal' can never stand for that which persists above and beyond all particularisms. Inasmuch as the universal cannot exist except 'through its parasitic attachment to some particular body' (*E* 72), the particular inhabits the universal as an ineradicable remainder (just as the universal inhabits every claim to the particular). On the one hand, 'the particularity of the particular is subverted by this function of representing the universal'; on the other hand, 'a certain particular, by making its own particularity the signifying body of a universal representation, comes to occupy – within the system of differences as a whole – a hegemonic role' (*E* 53). What this means is that there can be no universal that would be free of all particularity and no particularity without some universal reference – short of a totally reconciled society without politics. But we are back to Schor's objection: the particularity that comes to incarnate the universal may indeed be politically determined and in that sense contingent – but it is not for all that entirely unpredictable, as Laclau well knows. What would it take for 'women' to stand for universal? That is the question feminism poses to Laclau. What would it take to think about women *as* an empty signifier? That is the question Laclau poses to feminism.

Gender-neutral or gender-specific?

Although Laclau's resignification of the universal as an empty place does not address itself directly to the question of sexual difference, his notion of the hegemonic relation between the universal and the particular is of significance for feminism. In some respects, Laclau's argument about the irreducible presence of particularity in universality is precisely the point made by Simone de Beauvoir, who showed that universal is just another word for Man, and that Woman is the remainder of particularity that haunts the masculine subject's claim to transcend all particularisms. Laclau's insistence that this particularity is both contingent and ineradicable can help us to see that the yearning for a gender-neutral universal, which is so often ascribed to Beauvoir, is at once impossible to achieve and necessary to articulate. It is impossible because the universal, inasmuch as it always attaches to some particular body which cannot be fully divested of its particularity, can never be sexually indifferent; it is necessary because even the particularistic claim to sexual difference cannot be made in the absence of a universal reference and the logic of equivalence (which also lends it a more global significance).

Joan Scott has shown that although feminism advocated women's political inclusion by arguing against sexual difference as the condition of their exclusion,

> it had to make claims on behalf of 'women' (who were discursively produced through 'sexual difference'). To the extent that it acted for 'women', feminism produced the 'sexual difference' it sought to eliminate. This paradox – the need both to accept and to refuse 'sexual difference' as a condition of inclusion in the universal – is the constitutive condition of feminism as a political movement throughout its long history.
>
> (Scott 1995: 7)

Every feminist argument for women's inclusion in the universal, then, is also an argument for particularity, sexual difference. Scott's understanding of the paradox which structures feminism articulates in reverse Laclau's claim that every argument for the particular is also an argument for the universal.

Taken together, Laclau and Scott help us to see why the complexity of the current feminist debate over the universal exceeds the opposition 'gender-specific' versus 'gender-neutral' (Schor 1995: 16), which has been mapped out most recently by Naomi Schor in her recent essay on feminism and universalism. However central it has been to the sameness/difference debate in feminism, this opposition is ultimately misleading because, among other things, it cannot account for the ineradicable presence both of the particular in the universal and of the universal in the particular. I have already given some reasons why a gender-neutral universal can never be what it claims (which does not make it any less necessary to articulate), and suggested that the point was not lost on that putatively classical universalist, Simone de Beauvoir. Let me turn briefly to the central problem raised by the idea of a gender-specific universal, as it is elaborated in the work of Luce Irigaray.

'The universal was conceived of as one, on the basis of one. But this one does not exist', writes Irigaray (1992: 65; quoted in Schor 1995: 32). Arguing that the universal effaces sexual difference, Irigaray would counter this universal which is One with a universal which is Two – that is, sexed.[11] Irigaray's project to inscribe sexual difference into the universal is also an attempt to create the possibility for mediation between the sexes (which have heretofore stood in a relation of antagonism). In this respect, her project is not unrelated to what Laclau has in mind when he writes that the universal

> is absolutely essential for any kind of political interaction, for if the latter took place without a universal reference, there would be no political interaction at all: we would only have either a complementarity of differences which would be totally non-antagonistic, or a totally antagonistic one, one where differences entirely lack any commensurability, and whose only possible resolution is the mutual destruction of the adversaries (*E* 61).

From Irigaray's perspective, this is a perfect description of the relation between the sexes: women and men are seen as two halves of a whole and as timeless enemies. The project of a sexed universal, in her view, is precisely an attempt to move beyond 'the old dream of symmetry' and to create an ethical relationship between the genders in which they are no longer 'imagined as being in conflict' (Irigaray 1993: 140). Irigaray's universal differs in significant ways from Laclau's, however, inasmuch as it inscribes not chains of equivalence but, rather (sexual) difference. In the absence of such an inscription, she suggests, the universal subject as well as the collective 'we' that emerge through chains of equivalence will remain androcentric. Thus if the question that Laclau raises for Irigaray is whether we could call universal an inscription in which the logic of difference was not attenuated by that of equivalence, the question that Irigaray puts to Laclau is whether that attenuation does not just reduce to the masculine economy of the same.

Although Laclau is not attentive enough to the concerns raised by Irigaray, his political understanding of the universal as an empty place in which to inscribe chains of equivalence does not foreclose but insists, rather, on the ineradicable place of difference from which every universal claim (including feminist claims) is issued. Shifting the debate over universalism from the philosophical to the political field, moreover, Laclau helps us to see how a particular like 'women' might be articulated as a universal (qua empty signifier) which does not depend on the classical assertion of an essential commonality. If we think about claims to a universal category of women in terms of social practices (like Wittgensteinian language games), we can see them as attempts to generate intersubjective agreement in the absence of pregiven rules or identities. These claims are fully contestable, but not according to the epistemological criteria that has governed the philosophical problem of universals. Likewise, the gendered universal of Irigaray and the gender-neutral universal of Beauvoir are language games which, to the extent that they attain any cultural authority (that is, universality), have to be *articulated*, in Laclau's distinctly political sense of the term. One can well imagine contexts in which 'women' becomes the empty signifier which unites various social struggles in a chain of equivalences; where 'women' – which is a particular not only in relation to 'men' but to all other differential identities – becomes, in Laclau's words, 'the signifying body of a universal representation' (*E* 53).

We can complicate the terms of the feminist debate over universalism (gender-neutral versus gender-specific) by asking this question: under what specific political conditions does a particular mode of difference – including a particular mode of women's difference, since not every notion of women's difference is the same – come to symbolize relations of equivalence? Thinking about women as the empty signifier, we recall that the claim to the universal is not made by a subject that precedes that claim; rather, the claim itself is the articulation of a political identity in a public space. The political identity comes into being through the claim to universality, not the other way around. It is for this reason that feminism has always entailed a dimension of universality.

If Laclau is right when he says that 'all articulation is contingent and [...] the articulating moment as such is always going to be an empty place', the filling of which will be 'transient and submitted to contestation' (*E* 59–60), then any attempt to inscribe the universal will always be confronted and limited by other inscriptions. Politics consists in the mediation of these claims or, as Judith Butler writes, 'how and whether they may be reconciled with one another' (Butler 1994: 18). It is not a matter of weighing each particular claim to the universal against some transcultural or transhistorical universal, or of deciding which claim will be authorized as the 'true universal' according to some preexisting normative, ethical, or cognitive criteria. It is a matter, rather, of mediating the relation between the particular and the universal in a public space, with every mediation remaining open to further mediations. Rather than think the universal as something that is extrapolitical and that can be used to adjudicate political claims, we should think it as the product of political practice. As Laclau puts it:

> The universal is incommensurable with the particular, but cannot, however, exist without the latter. How is this relation possible? My answer is that this paradox cannot be solved, but that its non-solution is the very precondition of democracy. The solution of the paradox would imply that a particular body had been found, which would be the true body of the universal. [...] If democracy is possible, it is because the universal has no necessary body and no necessary content: different groups, instead, compete between themselves to temporarily give to their particularisms a function of universal representation. Society generates a whole vocabulary of empty signifiers whose temporary signified are the result of a political competition (*E* 34).

This universalism which is not One is no ossified rule: a fixed definition which stands outside the public space and serves to order it. This universalism which is not One is no homecoming: a nostalgic return to a lost object which once (supposedly) provided a common origin or ground. When asked, 'what is this new universal?' (Schor 1995: 39), we might say, whatever it 'is' will not be decided in the manner of the epistemologist. And as to the question, 'is there anything in the classic conception of the universal that is worth saving?' (30), we might say that whatever is saved marks the moment of political decision – the judgment that is definite but never final.

Acknowledgement

The author wishes to thank Gregor Gnädig and Alan Keenan for their help with this chapter.

Notes

1 The phrase is Naomi Schor's (1995: 28). Schor 'dates the return of universalism within the precincts of the American academy to November 16, 1991', the day of a conference on 'Identity in Question', which was held at the CUNY Graduate Center in New York (Schor 1995: 28–9).

2 The emphasis here should be on *political* theories. I am not talking about a theory of politics that follows necessarily from something called poststructuralism. As Laclau astutely remarks in his essay, 'Building a new left',

> there is nothing that can be called a 'politics of poststructuralism'. The idea that theoretical approaches constitute philosophical 'systems' with an unbroken continuity that goes from metaphysics to politics is an idea of the past, that corresponds to a rationalistic and ultimately idealistic conception of knowledge. [...] The correct question, therefore, is not so much which is the politics of poststructuralism, but rather what are the possibilities a poststructuralist theoretical perspective opens for the deepening of those political practices that go in the direction of a 'radical democracy (*NR* 191).

3 An example of this homecoming narrative is given in the issue of *differences* on 'Universalism'. In an essay by Naomi Schor, 'the return of universalism' in poststructuralist theory is heralded as a welcome event. Of the penitent anti-universalists, Judith Butler is singled out:

> It is to Butler's great credit that she has continued, in the aftermath of *Gender Trouble* [...], to rethink her positions and has come in a relatively short time to recognize that identity is essential to politics and that the category of the universal cannot be done away with.
>
> (Schor 1995: 27)

In the same issue of *differences*, the title (to say nothing of the substance) of an essay by Neil Lazarus *et al.* (1995), 'The necessity of universalism', leaves little doubt about the consequences of not coming home.

4 My invocation of the opposing camps of 'realists' and 'nominalists' is obviously schematic and contestable; it is meant not to encompass the entirety of Western philosophy but only to highlight certain aspects of Wittgenstein's intervention into the debate over universals and Laclau's appropriation of it. One could equally well construe the debate as being between idealists and realists, or idealists and materialists.

5 The concept of 'articulation' is crucial to Laclau's critique of classical universalism and its attendant notions of essential identity and the objectivity of structures. He argues that all identity is differential and thus contingent: 'Each identity is what it is only through its difference from all the others' (*E* 52); each identity is both affirmed and negated by that which lies outside it and beyond its control. An objective identity is not a self-determining, stable point of reference, then, but 'an articulated set of elements' (*NR* 32). Articulation occurs within discursive totalities which are never self-contained but, like every identity, 'dislocated', that is, 'penetrated by a basic instability and precariousness' (*NR* 109), haunted by an outside which is 'constitutive' in the sense of being both enabling and distorting. The fullness of any identity (and of the social totality) is therefore impossible; it is blocked by what Laclau calls 'the antagonizing force' which is at once the condition of the constitution of identity and its negation. Antagonism is the limit of all objectivity, and thus of the very notion of *form* which governs the problem of universals. Citing Wittgenstein's point that 'the application of a rule always involves a moment of articulation', Laclau asserts,

> while this doesn't mean depriving social practices of *all* their coherence, it nevertheless does mean denying that this coherence can have the rationalistic status of a superhard 'transcendentality'. Thus, it is precisely antagonism which constitutes the 'outside' inherent to every system of rules (NR 214).

6 The difference between Arendt and Laclau is especially stark on the relationship of force to politics. For Arendt, force is by definition apolitical; for Laclau, it is ineradicable and implicit in the very practices of persuasion that Arendt calls political. See Laclau's critique of Richard Rorty in chapter 7 of *Emancipation(s)* for a discussion of the relationship between force, persuasion, and politics.

7 Arendt's account of judging elaborates Kant's notion of 'enlarged thought' (Arendt 1982: 43). In 'Truth and politics', Arendt writes:

> I form an opinion [a judgment] by considering a given issue [or particular] from different viewpoints, by making present to my mind the standpoints of those who are absent; that is, I represent them. This process of representation does not blindly adopt the actual views of those who stand somewhere else, and hence look upon the world from a different perspective; this is a question neither of empathy, as though I tried to be or to feel like somebody else, nor of counting noses and joining a majority but of being and thinking in my own identity where actually I am not. The more people's standpoints I have present in my mind while I am pondering a given issue, and the better I can imagine how I would feel and think if I were in their place, the stronger will be my capacity for representative thinking and the more valid my final conclusions, my opinion (1968: 107; see also 1982: 43).

Laclau does not speak about rearticulating the relationship between the universal and the particular in terms of forming judgments in Arendt's sense. Nevertheless, his notion of the universal as the creation of chains of equivalence whose representative instance is the 'empty signifier' shares Arendt's understanding of representative thinking as the alternative to subsuming particulars under pregiven universals.

8 Naomi Schor raises a similar point when she writes, 'few [feminists] grapple with the fact that to speak of a false universalism logically implies that there is such a thing as a true universalism, unless, that is, one assumes that all universalisms are by definition false' (Schor 1995: 21). But Schor is not quite right: a universalism could be 'false' in the sense of never fully devoid of particularity and yet still stand for that which we call universal. This is how Laclau understands universals in terms of what he calls 'empty signifiers'.

9 In *New Reflections on the Revolution of Our Time*, Laclau gives several examples of antagonism which would fall under the category of subject position for Žižek.

> Insofar as an antagonism exists between a worker and a capitalist, such antagonism is not inherent to the relations of production themselves, but occurs between the latter and the identity of the agent outside. A fall in a worker's wage, for example, denies his identity as a consumer.

This denial, Laclau continues, gives rise to

> two alternatives: either the element of negativity is reabsorbed by a positivity of a higher order which reduces it to mere appearance [as in Hegel], or the negation is irreducible to any objectivity, which means that it becomes constitutive and therefore indicates the impossibility of establishing the social as an objective order (*NR* 16).

Once again, Laclau wants to emphasize the limit of objectivity, but it is significant, I argue, that he does so by way of a notion of antagonism which does not reduce to the original *Spaltung* of the subject.

10 *Hegemony and Socialist Strategy* may be 'the only real answer to Habermas' (Žižek 1990: 259) on these issues, as Žižek claims, but not for the reasons he suggests. The notion of antagonism which Habermas dissolves and Laclau and Mouffe sustain is not so much the basis of a 'political project based on an ethics of the real' (1990: 259), as Žižek would have it – the question of ethics being foreign to their notion of politics. Rather, the Laclau–Mouffe notion of antagonism shows, contra Habermas, that power and conflict cannot be eradicated from politics through the removal of constraints or distortions to intersubjective communication *both* because alterity inhabits every identity *and* because every identity encounters opposition in the form of other identities, other perspectives and opinions which cannot be settled by reference to an extrapolitical ideal of reason or reasonableness or truth.

11 Schor observes that Irigaray's project to inscribe sexual difference in the universal has a 'blindspot': its 'privileging of sexual difference over the racial', which Irigaray herself defines as a 'secondary problem' and difference. Schor notes the blindspot, but she doesn't know what to do about it. Isn't the blindspot itself an example of the ineradicable particular – in this case, racial difference – which inhabits the (gendered) universal? The rhetorical character of the question is not meant to suggest that the articulation of a gendered universal is fundamentally misguided. As I argue, this particular inscription will be mediated by other inscriptions, including those that are so-called gender-neutral or racialized.

References

Arendt, H. (1958) *The Human Condition*, Chicago: University of Chicago Press.

—— (1968) 'Truth and politics', *Between Past and Future: Eight Exercises in Political Thought*, New York: Penguin.

—— (1982) *Lectures on Kant's Political Philosophy*, ed. R. Beiner, Chicago: University of Chicago Press.

Butler, J. (1994) 'Kantians in every culture?', *Boston Review* (October): 18.

Irigaray, L. (1992) *J'aime à toi: Esquisse d'une félicité dans l'histoire*, Paris: Grasset.

—— (1993) 'The universal as mediation', *Sexes and Genealogies*, tr. G. C. Gill, New York: Columbia University Press.

Laclau, E. and Zac, L. (1994) 'Minding the gap: The subject of politics', in E. Laclau (ed.) *The Making of Political Identities*, London: Verso.

Lazarus, N. (1995) 'The necessity of universalism', in N. Lazarus, S. Evans, A. Arnove, and Anne Menke (eds) *differences: A Journal of Feminist Cultural Studies*, 7(1): 15–47.

Nammour, J. (1992) 'Resemblances and universals', in A. B. Schoedinger (ed.) *The Problem of Universals*, Atlantic Heights, NJ: Humanities Press.

Schor, N. (1995) 'French feminism is a universalism', *differences: A Journal of Feminist Cultural Studies*, 7(1): 15–47.

Scott, J. (1995) 'Universalism and the history of feminism', *differences: A Journal of Feminist Cultural Studies*, 7(1): 1–14.

Staten, H. (1984) *Wittgenstein and Derrida*, Lincoln, NE: University of Nebraska Press.

Wittgenstein, L. (1968) *Philosophical Investigations*, tr. G. E. M. Anscombe, New York: Macmillan.

Žižek, S. (1990) 'Beyond discourse-analysis', in E. Laclau (ed.) *New Reflections on the Revolution of our Time*, London: Verso.

Part II

DEMOCRACY

Politics, ethics, normativity

6

IS THERE A NORMATIVE DEFICIT IN THE THEORY OF HEGEMONY?

Simon Critchley

This chapter might be viewed as the history of a disagreement. In May and June 1990, at the end of my first year's teaching at Essex, Ernesto Laclau and I taught a course together on 'Deconstruction and politics'. I was trying to formulate the argument that eventually found expression in the concluding chapter of my first book, *The Ethics of Deconstruction* (1992). My interest in Ernesto's work was less dominated by the way in which the category of hegemony enables a deconstruction of Marxism, of the type executed with such power in *Hegemony and Socialist Strategy*, and much more preoccupied with how hegemony can be deployed in providing both a logic of the political and a theory of political action that could be related to my understanding of deconstruction. Our disagreement turned on the nature of that understanding. My claim was – and still is – that deconstruction has an overriding ethical motivation provided that ethics is understood in the sense given to it in the work of Emmanuel Levinas. At the time, Ernesto was somewhat perplexed by my talk of ethics, arguably with good reason, and he would only talk of ethics in the Gramscian locution of the 'ethico-political'.

That was twelve years ago and since that time I have enjoyed innumerable conversations with Ernesto which have arisen out of a longstanding intellectual collaboration. At the end of this brief history, it might perhaps be concluded that we finally agree, or at least our positions are much closer than they were a decade or so ago. Perhaps, as Wittgenstein speculated, the solution to the problem is the disappearance of the problem. But perhaps not. We shall see.

Politics, hegemony and democracy

What is politics? Politics is the realm of the decision, of action in the social world, of what Laclau, following Gramsci, calls 'hegemonization', understood as actions that attempt to fix the meaning of social relations. If we conceive of politics with the category of hegemony – and, in my view, it is best conceived of with that category – then politics is an act of power, force, and will that is contingent through and through. Hegemony reveals politics to be the realm of contingent decisions by virtue of which subjects (whether persons, parties, or social movements) attempt to articulate and propagate meanings of the social. At its deepest level, the category of hegemony discloses the political logic of the social; that is, civil society is politically constituted through contingent decisions. In my view, the key concept in Laclau's recent work is 'hegemonic universality': political action is action motivated by, or orientated around, a universal term – equality, human rights, justice, individual freedom, or whatever – and yet that universality is always already contaminated by particularity, by the specific social context for which the universal term is destined. I shall come back to this below.

With this definition of politics in mind, the first thing to note is that many political decisions, say decisions at the level of the state administration or those wanting to take over the state, attempt to deny their political character. That is, political decisions attempt to erase their traces of power, force, will and contingency by naturalizing or essentializing their contents; for example, 'Kosovo is, was and always will be Serbian', or 'Macedonia is, was, and always will be Greek', or whatever. Much – perhaps most – politics tries to render itself and its operations of power *invisible* by reference to custom and tradition or, worse, nature and God, or, worse still, custom and tradition grounded in nature and God. Arguably the main strategy of politics is to make itself invisible in order to claim for itself the status of nature or a priori self-evidence. In this way, politics can claim to restore the fullness of society or bring society into harmony with itself – a claim somewhat pathetically exemplified in John Major's wish, after the prolonged torture of the Thatcher years, to govern a country at peace with itself, an England of warm beer, cool drizzle, and cricket.

Now, to understand political action as a hegemonic operation is a priori to understand it as a non-naturalizable, non-essentialistic contingent articulation that just temporarily fixes the meaning of social relations. For Laclau, the fullness of society or the harmonization of society with itself is an impossible object of political desire which successive contingent decisions seek to bring about or, to use Lacan's term that Laclau inherits, to *suture*. So, if a naturalizing or essentializing politics tries to render its contingency invisible by attempting to suture the social into a fantastic wholeness, then hegemony as the disclosure of the political logic of the social reveals the impossibility of any such operation. The moment of final suture never arrives, and the social field is irreducibly open and plural. Society is impossible.

This leads to the significant conclusion that, although the category of hegemony seems at one level to be a simple *description* of social and political life, a sort of value-neutral Foucauldian power-analytics, it is (and in my view has to be) a *normative* critique of much that passes for politics insofar as much politics tries to deny or render invisible its contingency and operations of power and force. To anticipate the topic of this paper, the category of hegemony is both descriptive and normative, a characteristic it shares with much social and political theory. As Laclau would acknowledge, Marx's postulate of a society in which the free development of each is the condition for the free development of all is both a descriptive and a normative claim.

To push this a little further, we might say that only those societies that are self-conscious of their political status – their contingency and power operations – are democratic. What I mean is self-conscious at the level of the citizenry, not at the level of the Platonic Guardians, the Prince, or the latter's philosophical adviser. Machiavelli and Hobbes, it seems to me, were perfectly well aware of the contingency and political constitution of the social, but didn't exactly want this news broadcast to the people. Therefore, if all societies are *tacitly hegemonic*, then the distinguishing feature of democratic society is that it is *explicitly hegemonic*. Democracy is thus the name for that political form of society that makes explicit the contingency of its foundations. In democracy, political power is secured through operations of competition, persuasion, and election based on the hegemonization of the 'empty place' that is the people, to use Claude Lefort's expression. Democracy is distinguished by the self-consciousness of the contingency of its operations of power; in extreme cases, by the self-consciousness of the very *mechanisms* of power. Personally, and parenthetically, I think this is the positive lesson of the US presidential elections in November and December 2000 (this is not to neglect their negative political outcome), where the very meaning of democracy turned on the self-consciousness of the mechanisms of election, from the butterfly ballot in Palm Beach County, to the quasi-theological discussion of the nature of the Floridan 'Chad'. This self-consciousness of the contingent mechanisms of power infected, it seems to me, every layer of the political-legal apparatus, right up to the Supreme Court, and arguably had the beneficial effect of leading voters to raise the Rousseauesque question of the *legitimacy* of their social contract.

Is the theory of hegemony descriptive, normative, or both at once?

In my view, what Laclau's theory of hegemony can teach us is the ineluctably political logic of the social; the fact that politics is constituted by contingent decisions that can never efface their traces of power in the articulation of the meaning of social relations and the attempt to fix that meaning. But the descriptive gain of Laclau's work also has a normative dimension, a dimension which, until very recently, it has done its best to deny. It is this area upon which I would like to focus in the remainder of this chapter, for if I am certainly not writing with the intention of burying Caesar, I do not simply wish to praise him.

Let me go back to the history of our disagreement. In a debate with Rorty, Derrida, and Laclau from 1993 (in Mouffe 1996), I first began to formulate a two-fold critical claim that I sought to sharpen in the following years: on the one hand, in relation to Derrida's introduction of concepts of justice and the messianic a priori, I argued that deconstruction requires the supplement of the theory of hegemony if the ethical moment in Derrida's work is to be more than an empty expression of good conscience. In order for the ethical moment in deconstruction to become *effective* as both political theory and an account of political action, it is necessary to link it to Laclau's thinking, particularly on the question of the decision. However, on the other hand, I advanced the counter-balancing claim that Laclau's theory of hegemony requires an ethical dimension of infinite responsibility to the other if it is not going to risk collapsing into the arbitrariness of a thoroughgoing decisionism. That is, the emphasis upon the irreducibly political constitution of the social could lead to the accusation of voluntarism, where the meanings accorded to social relations depend upon the value-free or value-neutral whims of the subject. Let me now focus on this second claim.

My objection to Laclau can be most succinctly stated in the form of a question: what is the difference between hegemony and *democratic* hegemony? At the level of what we might call a 'genealogical deconstruction', which is how I would describe the analyses of *Hegemony and Socialist Strategy*, the theory of hegemony shows the irreducibly political constitution of the social. In the terminology of the late Husserl, that Laclau adopts in the important opening essay – effectively a manifesto – to *New Reflections on the Revolution of our Time*, social *sedimentation* is simply the masking of the operations of power, contingency, and antagonism. Social and political life, insofar as it overlooks these operations, is a 'forgetfulness of origins' and the category of hegemony permits the *reactivation* of sedimented social strata. What the genealogical deconstruction shows is that the fixing of the meaning of social relations is the consequence of a forgotten decision, and every decision is political.

However, Laclau's work – particularly the parts co-authored with Chantal Mouffe – famously and rightly also invokes notions of 'the democratic revolution' and 'radical democracy' as the positive consequence of the genealogical deconstruction of Marxism. That is, the recognition of contingency, antagonism, and power does not lead to political pessimism *à la* Adorno, or the collapse of the public–private distinction *à la* Rorty, but is rather 'the source for a new militancy and a new optimism' (*NR* 82). As such, we do not stand at the end of history, but rather at its beginning.

Yet, if all decisions are political, then in virtue of what is there a difference between democratizing and non-democratizing decisions? It seems to me that there are two ways of answering this question, one normative and the other factual, but both of which leave Laclau sitting uncomfortably on the horns of a dilemma. On the one hand, one might say that democratic decisions are more inclusive, participatory, egalitarian, pluralistic, or whatever. But if one grants any such version of this thesis, then one has admitted some straightforwardly normative claim into the theory of hegemony. On the other hand, if one simply states in a quasi-functionalistic manner that 'the democratic revolution' and 'radical democracy' are descriptions of a fact, then in my view one risks collapsing any *critical* difference between the theory of hegemony and social reality which this theory purports to describe. I think that Laclau risks coming close to this position when he claims that the democratic revolution is simply taking place, or – more problematically – that *freedom* is the consequence of existing social dislocations. Laclau writes, 'freedom exists because society does not achieve constitution as a structured objective order' (*NR* 44). It is the seemingly causal nature of this 'because' that both interests and worries me. If the theory of hegemony is simply the description of a positively existing state of affairs, then one risks emptying it of any critical function, that is, of leaving open any space between things as they are and things as they might otherwise be. If the theory of hegemony is the description of a factual state of affairs, then it risks identification and complicity with the dislocatory logic of contemporary capitalist societies.

The problem with Laclau's discourse is that he makes noises of both sorts, both descriptive and normative, without sufficiently clarifying what it is that he is doing. This is what I mean by suggesting that there is the risk of a kind of normative deficit in the theory of hegemony. In my view, the deficit can be made good on the basis of another understanding of the logic of deconstruction. Let me return to the two-fold claim outlined above: if what deconstruction lacks in its thinking of the political is a theory of hegemony, which a reading of Laclau provides, then this needs to be balanced by the second claim that what the theory of hegemony lacks, and can indeed learn from deconstruction, is the kind of messianic ethical injunction to infinite responsibility described in Derrida's work from the 1990s.

The ethical and the normative

In a review of Derrida's *Spectres of Marx* from 1995, Laclau seemed unconvinced of the ethical sense that I attached to the notion of the messianic a priori, arguing that no ethical injunction of a Levinasian kind follows from the logic undecidability, and furthermore that democratic politics does not need to be anchored in such an ethical injunction (in *E* 66–83). Needless to say, I do not agree. What is more surprising is that Laclau also does not appear to agree with himself. It would seem to me, on the basis of my reading of Laclau's contributions to a fascinating series of exchanges with Slavoj Žižek and Judith Butler (2000), that his position has changed, and changed significantly.

First, Laclau grants that theory of hegemony cannot be a strictly factual or descriptive affair, both because such a purportedly value-neutral description of the facts is impossible (i.e. all 'facts' are discursive and hence interpretative constructs), and because any apprehension of the facts is governed by normative elements. Strictly factual description – like sense-data empiricism – is an illusion based on some version of Sellars's 'myth of the given'. So, going back to the horns of the dilemma discussed above, the theory of hegemony is not descriptive but normative.

Well, not quite, because Laclau then wants to introduce a distinction that is novel to his work between the normative and the ethical. He writes,

> I would say that 'hegemony' is a theoretical approach which depends on the essentially ethical decision to accept, as the horizon of any possible

> intelligibility, the incommensurability between the ethical and the normative (the latter including the descriptive).
>
> (Laclau 2000: 81)

Let's try and get clear about what is being claimed here. The ethical is the moment of universality or reactivation, when the sedimented and particular normative order of a given society is both invested and placed in question. The emphasis upon both investment and placing in question is important because if the ethical is the moment when the 'the universal speaks by itself', then the specific normative order of a society is always particular. Laclau's claims about the incommensurability of the ethical and the normative entail that there will always be an *écart* between investment and calling into question. Ethical universality has to be incarnated in a normative order, yet that moment of particular incarnation is incommensurable with universality. In language closer to the work of Alain Badiou, we might say that any normative order of 'ethics' is the sedimented form of an initial ethical *event*. Hegemony is the expression of a fidelity to an event, an event moreover that is – and has to be – betrayed in any normative incarnation. We can see that the relation between the ethical and the normative is a – perhaps *the* – privileged expression of the 'hegemonic universality' I spoke of in the introduction to this chapter. Laclau writes, 'Hegemony is, in this sense, the name for this unstable relation between the *ethical* and the *normative*, our way of addressing this infinite process of investments which draws its dignity from its very failure' (ibid.). As Levinas is fond of expressing the difficulty of rendering the Saying in the Said, *traduire c'est trahir*.

A further key aspect of the distinction between the ethical and the normative is that it is echoed in the distinction between *form* and *content*. The ethical is the moment of pure formality that has to be filled, in a particular context, with a normative content. The obvious precursor for such an ethical formalism is Kant, where the categorical imperative can be understood as an entirely formal procedure for testing the validity of specific moral norms by seeing whether they can stand the test of universalization – which raises the question as to how Laclau would respond to the charge of ethical formalism, i.e. Hegel's critique of Kantian ethics in the *Phenomenology of Spirit* and elsewhere. But, I take it, the Lacanian and Heideggerian inflections of this Kantian thought have also been influential on Laclau's understanding of the ethical. In a Lacanian *ethics of the Real*, the latter is the moment of pure formality, a constitutive lack that is filled with normative content when it has become symbolized in relation to a specific content. Finally, the distinction between the ethical and the normative is thought of in terms of the ontological difference in Heidegger, where the ethical would be ontological and the normative would be ontic.

So, it seems that we are obliged to conclude at this stage in our argument that there is, indeed, no normative deficit in the theory of hegemony. More accurately, at the basis of the latter is an irreducible ethical commitment whose scope is universal. In my view, this is good news, and it is the acknowledgement of some such conception of ethics that I have been trying to urge on Laclau since the beginning of our disagreement.

But that does not entail that I fully agree with the position Laclau has reached and, in conclusion, I would like to launch a final series of questions and queries, all of which touch on the attempted distinction of the ethical from the normative.

1 My initial worry with Laclau's new position is that he deconstructs one distinction – the descriptive/normative – only to insist on another distinction – the ethical/normative. Thus, for him, the question becomes that of the relationship between the ethical and 'descriptive/normative complexes' (ibid.). But by virtue of what is this second distinction somehow immune from the kind of deconstruction to which the first distinction was submitted? Logically and methodologically, how can one collapse one distinction only to put in its place another distinction without expecting it also to collapse? I do not see what argument Laclau provides that would protect the second distinction from collapsing like the first one. With this in mind, I would now like to try and deconstruct the ethical/normative distinction a little.

2 Let's look more closely at this distinction between the ethical and the normative and momentarily grant Laclau his premise. Let's imagine that what we have here is an analytic distinction: *de jure*, one can clearly make the distinction that Laclau is after, between ethical form and normative content, universal and particular. But *de facto* it would seem to me that the ethical and the normative always come together; that is, in actual moral life the formal moment of universality is always welded to its concrete particularity. Such, it would seem to me, is the ineluctable logic of the concept of hegemony. Thus, to my mind, it would make more sense to speak of *de facto* moral action in terms of 'ethical/normative complexes', even if one grants *de jure* that an analytic distinction can be made between the ethical and the normative. But if that is granted, then turning around the question, can one still speak of an equally justified *de jure* distinction between the normative and the descriptive even if one grants *de facto* that the two orders are inextricably intertwined? I don't see why not. So in opposition to Laclau's distinction between the ethical and 'descriptive/normative complexes', I think it makes much more sense to speak of a *de facto* 'ethical/normative/descriptive complex', within which one is entitled to make a series of *de jure* distinctions.

3 I think my critical question can be made more concrete by probing the language that Laclau uses to make the ethical/normative distinction and the way in which it runs parallel to the Heidegger's distinction of the ontological from the ontic. Once again, for Heidegger, the distinction between the ontological and the ontic is a *de jure* distinction that isolates distinct strata in phenomenological analysis. For Heidegger, the ontological is the a priori or transcendentally constitutive features – what Heidegger calls 'existentials' – that can be discerned from socially instituted, ontic or a posteriori life. But *de facto*, we have to speak – and Heidegger does speak

– of *Dasein* as a unity of the ontological and the ontic. *Dasein* has precisely an ontico-ontological privilege. I therefore worry about the seeming ease with which Laclau distinguishes the ethico-ontological level from the normative ontic level, as if one could somehow expunge or slough off the ontic from the ontological in ethical. One cannot and, in my view, one should not.

4 There is a separate, but related, problem I have with Laclau's Heideggerian identification of the ethical with the ontological. The assumption behind this identification would seem to be that we can thematize and grasp conceptually the *being* of the ethical, i.e. that the nature of ethics can be ontologically identified and comprehended. It seems to me that Levinas would have one or two important things to say about this identification ethics and ontology, which for him is the defining gesture by virtue of which philosophers from Aristotle to Hegel and Heidegger have understood and – on Levinas's account – misunderstood the ethical. For Levinas, the ethical is precisely not a theme of discourse and therefore cannot be ontologized. It is otherwise than being. But if Levinas seems rather opaque – after all, this is not the place to go into an exegesis of how Levinas, from his pathbreaking 1951 essay 'Is ontology fundamental?' onwards, sought to distinguish ethics from ontology in his attempt to leave the climate of Heidegger's thinking – a similar line of thought can be found in thinkers intellectually closer to Laclau. In Lacan, the ethical is experienced in relation to the order of the Real insofar as a non-symbolizable *Chose* – *das Ding* in Freud – stands in the place of the Real. This *Chose* is precisely something irreducible to ontological categorization, a permanent excess within discursive symbolization. Also, in Wittgenstein, in his 1929 Cambridge lecture on ethics and elsewhere, the ethical is revealed in running up against the limits of language. The ethical is, strictly speaking, something about which nothing can be said. All propositions in the domain of ethics are nonsensical. Ethics is not something ontologically grasped, but rather apprehended in the silence that falls after reading Proposition 7 of the *Tractatus* – and it should be recalled that Wittgenstein acknowledged that the entire effort of the *Tractatus* had an ethical point, a point which could not be expressed in the book itself.

5 Let me stay with the example of Wittgenstein in order to probe further the ethical/normative distinction. In one of his more cryptic remarks on rule-following from the *Philosophical Investigations*, he writes, 'It would almost be more correct to say, not that an intuition was needed at every stage, but that a new decision was needed at every stage *(es sei an jedem Punkt eine neue Entscheidung nötig)*' (Wittgenstein 1958: 75). This quotation would seem to illustrate well the relation between ethics and normativity, namely that there is a rule, which possesses universality, for example the sequence of prime numbers, and yet each expression of the rule demands a decision, an act of continuing the sequence. In this sense, the rule would be 'ethical' and the

particular decision would be normative. But if that is granted, then what is to be gained by attempting to distinguish rigorously between the ethical and the normative? Shouldn't we rather conceive of 'the ethical/normative complex' in similar or analogous ways to the relation between 'a rule' and 'instantiations of following a rule'?

6 Let me come back to a different way of expressing my earlier question as to the difference between hegemony and democratic hegemony. Is the ethical something constitutive of or identifiable within all societies or does it only exist in democratic societies? If it is the former – and I think it is for Laclau – and the ethical exists in all societies, then although this definition would maintain the requirement of strict formality, it might also be accused of banality. If Laclau is making a simple *meta-ethical* point in his talk of the ethical, then one might well ask, 'well, what is the point of making it?'. However, if it is the latter, and the ethical is part and parcel of democratic societies alone, then it seems to me that one has admitted some specific normative content to the ethical. That is, one has consented to describing the ethical in some way or other and recommending a particular description over another. I would be inclined to say that democratic political forms are simply *better* than non-democratic ones: more inclusive, more capacious, more just, or whatever. Now, if there is *some* specific content to the ethical, then the distinction between the ethical and the normative cannot be said to hold; yet, conversely, if there is *no* content to the ethical at all, then one might be entitled to ask: what's the point? Isn't such a meta-ethical analysis rather banal?

7 I imagine that Laclau's critique of my position would be that insofar as it follows Levinas (although, it must be said, an increasingly heterodox Levinas), it admits some specific content to the ethical. This is indeed true. I accept the criticism unreservedly. My position is that on the basis of a certain meta-ethical picture of what I call 'ethical experience', which I trace back to the debates around the notion of the 'fact of reason' in Kant, I recommend a particular normative conception of ethical experience based on a critical reading of a number of thinkers, Derrida and Levinas included.[1] Be that as it may, my question back to Laclau is that, unless one wants to engage in a pure diagnostic meta-ethical inquiry divorced from any substantive normative content, I can't see why one should so insistently want to emphasize the content-free character of the ethical. In my view, formal meta-ethics must be linked to normative ethical claims. One of the great virtues of Laclau's work is that it shows us how to hegemonize a specific normative picture into effective and transformative political action.

Therefore, it would seem that there is still a normative deficit in the theory of hegemony, although it is not at all where I first imagined it to be. So, Ernesto and I still disagree after all, which is perhaps no bad thing as it means that our history can continue.

Note

1 For examples of recent texts where I argue more systematically for this position, see Critchley 2000a, 2000b.

References

Butler, J., Laclau, E. and Žižek, S. (2000) *Contingency, Hegemony, Universality: Contemporary Dialogues on the Left*, London and New York: Verso.

Critchley, S. (1992) *The Ethics of Deconstruction*, Oxford: Blackwell; 2nd expanded edn, Edinburgh: Edinburgh University Press, 1999.

—— (2000a) 'Demanding approval: on the ethics of Alain Badiou', *Radical Philosophy*, 100 (March): 16–24.

—— (2000b) 'Remarks on Derrida and Habermas', *Constellations*, 7(4): 455–65.

Laclau, E. (2000) 'Identity and hegemony: The role of universality in the constitution of political logics', in J. Butler *et al.*, *Contingency, Hegemony, Universality: Contemporary Dialogues on the Left*, London and New York: Verso.

Mouffe, C. (ed.) (1996) *Deconstruction and Pragmatism*, London and New York: Routledge.

Wittgenstein, L. (1958) *Philosophical Investigations*, tr. G. E. M. Anscombe, Oxford: Blackwell.

7

ETHICS AND POLITICS IN DISCOURSE THEORY

Mark Devenney

The Greek word *ethos* and the Latin word *mos* are both commonly translated as 'custom'. They are also the respective etymological roots of the words ethics and morality. Despite their 'customary' meaning, conventional use of these words presupposes the faculty to judge and guide actions with reference to principles which transcend the deliberation of individuals in particular communities. This tacit appeal to a universal law derives from religious and mythical worldviews which subordinate human law to the moral prescriptions of a being(s) or realm whose dictates are only ever approximated. On this account ethics presupposes distinctions between the divine and the human (the ultimate source of the law as opposed to those subjected to the law), the human and the natural, and the human and the animal (those not subject to the law, and therefore never subjects of the law).

It is thus too that ethics is caught up in questions of means–end or instrumental rationality. An ethical act assumes a cut between the human, the divine, and the natural realms, which entails a particular set of (instrumental) relations between them. Adorno and Horkheimer in *Dialectic of Enlightenment* (Adorno and Horkheimer 1985) for example, suggest that early forms of human sacrifice and moral law are ruses of an instrumental rationality: sacrifice to the gods is both an attempt to appease their wrath *and* to establish control over a threatening internal and external nature. The ethical law participates in a process of engendering enlightened humanity, emphasizing the distinction between a civilized/cultured humanity and a natural world which humans use for their own ends. Enlightenment however culminates in the extirpation of any *deus ex machina* and, at least in Adorno's view, the instrumentalizing of not just nature but also of human beings. What's more, enlightenment eventually hollows out all justification of an ethics which relies on some form of metaphysical appeal. On this view a metaphysics bereft of signification appears to provide no guidance for the resolution of ethical dilemmas. Likewise, the confinement of ethics to innerworldly norms seems to render all principles subject to the contingency of choice, and the distinction between strategic and practical reason difficult to draw.

This holds consequences for any discussion of the relation between ethics and politics. Early modern political theory, building on the distinction between the City of God and the City of Man elaborated by Augustine, rests political community on a universal ethics.[1] Likewise, much contemporary political philosophy maintains the distinction between ethics and politics while divesting itself of the religious overtones. Will Kymlicka, writing in *Contemporary Political Philosophy*, for example argues:

> I believe there is a fundamental continuity between moral and political philosophy. First, as Robert Nozick puts it 'moral philosophy sets the background for, and boundaries of, political philosophy. ...' I agree with Nozick that the content of our responsibilities, and the lines between them, must be determined by appeal to deeper moral responsibilities ... Political philosophy is a matter of appeal to our considered convictions.
> (Kymlicka 1990: 6)

This antediluvian strategy situates moral philosophy beyond the fray of political contestation, thus grounding and/or justifying (in no matter how weak a sense) political institutions and actions. Moral philosophy officiates as an ideal 'as if' orienting political and social actions.

Following Adorno's cue this chapter contends that such an ethical reduction of politics is itself politically motivated. In line with a venerable tradition of ideology critique I hold that these arguments veil the political intentions underlying any ethical claim. However, I reject too the political reduction of the ethical, that is, the claim that ethics is simply the strategic exercise of concealed power. Indeed, the key to any political theory worth its salt is an account of justice and its relation to the good life. Political theories which, in refusing all ethics, analyse politics as a strategic game of rational, or irrational, choice hollow out the complexity of tradition and lifeworld. I argue that a contemporary account of ethics has much to learn from absolutist ethics, though the absolutism I defend would be barely recognizable or acceptable to any proponent of absolutism.

This argument is developed through an exploration of the 'join' between politics, ethics, and instrumental rationality in the work of Ernesto Laclau. All ethics, I suggest, entails an instrumental-cum-teleological account of the human and the world – the ethical moment of this entailment concerns the limits of such an instrumental reduction. Or, in other terms, ethics is caught in a double bind. Ethical theory appeals to a moment of non-instrumentalization, a vision of a world in which others are treated as ends in themselves, not as means to an end. Kantian ethics puts this claim at its centre, but it is foreshadowed in Augustine's distinction between the City of God and the City of Man which in turn draws on classical Greek privileging of the Good. For Augustine humans live in time, and are thus subject to change and fickle nature. God however cannot change and is not subject to time. The City of God is a condition in which human identity, subject to the exigencies of space and time, could not be maintained. Indeed we cannot know God. As McLelland writes:

> For Augustine what we call human history is only a moment in the divine scheme of things. God's reason for creating what we call space and time is not all that clear. What is certain is that there was a time, so to speak, when time itself did not exist, and it is equally certain that there will come a time when time itself comes to an end. Time therefore is meaningless to him ... There is properly speaking no 'after' after the last judgement, when the last saved soul enters the city in triumph. There is properly speaking no after the last judgement because nothing ever changes any more. The heavenly city is a city of being not becoming. Eternity is now and forever.
>
> (McLelland 1998: 100)

It is no mistake that this description bears close resemblance to Derrida's (1996) conception of the messianic as a future to come, which is always already here. The logic of the empty signifier in the work of Ernesto Laclau is not dissimilar. If the City of God is a city of pure being, the City of Man is caught between this empty signifier of being which is not subject to contingency and the everyday contingency of a world of becoming. Any human attempt to signify this empty signifier must fail – indeed it is necessary that it should fail both for religious justifications of ethics, and for a post-enlightenment conception of ethics. This suggests that a discussion of ethics should begin with an account of the limits of instrumental rationality and an exploration of the implication of a failure of all signification when confronted by the ethical. I argue that Laclau's analysis of the empty signifier provides both the beginnings of a critique of instrumental rationality, and an account of ethics which addresses the limitations of a metaphysical foreclosure of ethical questions.

Post-Marxism and instrumental rationality

A key tension in Marxist theory during the twentieth century concerned the relation between its ethical and scientific claims. The force of the moral critique of exploitation implicit in Marx's work vies with a deterministic account of capitalist development which is allegedly steered by a fundamental tension between the forces and relations of production. This tension, it is claimed, necessarily ensues in antagonism and revolt against the bourgeois class, and the establishment of a socialist state which unchains the capacity of technological development. An extrapolation of the logic of the capitalist process of production infers that change is inevitable and class identity determined by this structure. From this perspective proletarian struggles are epiphenomenal effects of a more profound tension.

It is thus that the oft unspoken normative anxiety of Marxism is reduced to a strategy: ethical appeals serve to mobilize the masses for their historical task. This strategy neutralizes and naturalizes the force of the performative utterance. Yet the normative or messianic dimension of Marx's analysis acts as a supplement, both giving force to the scientific analysis, and detracting from its systemic purity. The account of exploitation, of alienated labour, the call to arms implicit in the *Manifesto*, derive a performative force from the moral horror implicit in their statement, rather than from a science of history. As Derrida maintains, the messianic solicitation of Marx's work should not be effaced:

> [the] messianic remains an ineffaceable mark – a mark one neither can nor should efface – of Marx's legacy, and doubtless of inheriting, of the experience of inheritance in general. Otherwise, one would reduce the event-ness of the event, the singularity and alterity of the other. Otherwise justice risks being reduced once again to juridical-moral rules, norms or representations, within an inevitable totalizing horizon.
>
> (Derrida 1994: 28)

Laclau and Mouffe's 1985 text *Hegemony and Socialist Strategy* scrupulously deconstructs the deterministic elements of western Marxism, reading the category of hegemony as a supplementary moment which explains why classes have not assumed their historical task and which indicates the limits of Marxism as a privileged science of history. Delineating a logic of hegemony in Marxist theory ensues in the marginalization of determinism, and the privileging of contingency and non-dialectical negativity as *necessary*. However, the deconstruction of the tenuous logic of determinism appears to leave untouched the ethical spectre which haunts Marxism.

Well, this is not quite true: the deconstruction of determinism casts shadow on that spectre but little light. I argue that there is another logic implicit in this text: a 'radical' critique of instrumental rationality. This critique, which disorients any means–end rationality, holds profound implications for any consideration of ethics. At least five arguments concerning instrumental reason are suggested in this and other texts. These suggest a different orientation to the relation between politics and ethics which Laclau has begun to explore in his most recent work.

Instrumentalizing nature

Marx located the source of political transformation and enlightenment in the instrumentalization of nature by human beings. In transforming the external world human beings transform themselves. This relation is both neutralized and naturalized. It is *neutralized* in the unquestioned assumption that the instrumentalization of the inner and outer worlds is the key to the emancipation of human beings from their self-imposed immaturity (to abuse Kant). Discourse theory argues that nature can only ever be considered as articulated within discourse, and that the 'real' of nature resists instrumentalization, that it is always already second nature. There is on this account no nature, 'in itself', but the necessary failure of any discourse to fully instrumentalize a world suggests the threatening potential of a real which cannot be domesticated within any discursive formation. Such a reading provides orientation for an interpretation of environmental politics which avoids the idealization of an original nature, while resisting the assumption common to both Marxist and capitalist modernization that nature is an external object there for instrumental use. Crucially for my argument, 'existence' threatens the security of any discursive organization of the real, pointing to the limits of an instrumental attitude toward an objectified nature.

Instrumentalizing the subject

Discourse theory implies second a critique of the instrumentalization of the 'subject' of politics. Marxists, for the most part, presumed that the working class subject of history would achieve the knowledge necessary to its preordained historical task. This assumption works in at least two related ways: on the one hand a pluralism of subject positions are deemed secondary to class; on the other it is presumed that the subject of knowledge can grasp the concrete through the short circuit of abstraction.

Discourse theory views the subject as both subjected and a source of resistance to subjection. The failure of the subject to fully embody knowledge points to the dislocation of identity, the recognition that the subject is never at home in its own home, and is constitutively impaired in its attempts to instrumentalize both self and other. For Laclau all social structures have a limited ability to predetermine fully constituted subject positions. Likewise subjects do not exist wholly independently of those structures which interpellate them. The condition of possibility of this interpellation is that it can never finally be successful.

Instrumentalized knowledge

If discourse theory implies suspicion about the subject of knowledge, it is also a critique of instrumental or objectivating forms of knowledge. It rejects the assumption that the social is an object which may be simply represented in theoretical discourse. Rather discourse is constitutive of a world for us. The claim to know, in no matter what field, may be read as an attempt to domesticate a constitutive undecidability. Discourse theory is, *in one sense*, a modern version of Kantian transcendental argument, but it side-steps the epistemological question, focusing instead on the conditions of possibility of meaning (or of signification) of any entity – subject or object. For Laclau, the being of any object is contingent upon the forms of discursive signification thereof. Investigating the conditions of possibility of meaning involves also an investigation of the conditions of possibility of the being of objects. The question of objective, or subjective, being only makes sense from within the discursive. Where Kant deduces the transcendental subject of apperception, which both makes human knowledge possible, and limits its reach, discourse theory holds that the being of the object is not stable, but constituted in specific discursive practices.

Instrumentalizing society

Fourth, discourse theory implies a critique of the establishment of purely innerworldly norms, justified solely within the pragmatics of everyday discourse. This follows from the claim that society is an impossible object. It is thus no longer an object which can, at least simply, be objectified for us or which presupposes norms natural to this object. If the representation of society as such is impossible then the various forms of representation of the object society should be viewed as hegemonic attempts to establish political control. In themselves none of these hegemonic projects is possessed of a morality which precedes the political attempt to establish power, what Kymlicka terms our considered convictions which in his view frame political action. Rather, moral discourses are themselves implicated in the struggle for (instrumental) power and control over social and political institutions. As suggested above, such moral discourses are constitutive of certain political claims regarding the status of man, as opposed to nature or animals. This must have ramifications for how we can consider an account of ethics in light of discourse theory.

Instrumentalized language

Discourse theory rejects finally the view that language is merely an instrument with use value, either as a tool of representation or as a tool of communication. Discourse, and by extension language, is not simply a tool for use, but is constitutive of our relation to various worlds, subjective, intersubjective, and instrumental. Laclau writes:

> An empty signifier can only emerge if there is a structural impossibility in signification as such and if this impossibility can only signify itself as an interruption (subversion, distortion, etc.) of the structure of the sign. That is that the limits of signification can only announce themselves as the impossibility of realizing what is in those limits – if the limits could be signified in a direct way, they would be internal to signification, and, ergo, would not be limits at all.
>
> (Laclau 1994: 168)

What is left unsaid in this quote is that the empty signifier points to the impossibility of a purely instrumental relation with the other, and thus of a relation in which language is no longer a means to an end, but an opening toward an other which cannot be reduced to the fixed signification of communication which is semantically guaranteed by some appeal to an ideal of communicative rationality.

These brief suggestions regarding an implicit critique of instrumental rationality in the work of Laclau should indicate that I consider Laclau's work a more fruitful exploration of the limits of discourses of instrumental rationality than that of Habermas, and, as a consequence, of the relation between the ethical and the political. In light of the above let me consider the relation between ethics and politics in Laclau's work, linking this to the question of instrumental rationality.

Discourse theory, ethics, and politics

I have characterized Ernesto Laclau's discourse theory as alluding toward a critique of instrumental rationality in its various guises. I characterized instrumental reason very broadly, as a form of rationality which treats either subjects, objects or language as a means to an end. Laclau's critique of instrumental reason relies ultimately on his account of a structural impossibility in all signification, what he terms the empty signifier, which at the same time makes any signification possible. However, Laclau has also argued that this constitutive undecidability does not entail a particular version of ethics or indeed of politics. Rather this essential contingency is ethically and politically neutral, representing the most general, and for that reason formally empty, conditions of im/possibility of society. This way of presenting the matter is somewhat deceptive and belies a number of important distinctions. While radical democracy may not receive any ethical warranty from such an ontological condition, this does not mean that, to use William Connolly's words, the ontopolitical implications of taking contingency 'seriously' are empty. Two initial points should clarify this.

A consideration of the different positions of the fascist and the radical democrat vis-à-vis undecidability suggests that such an investment not only orients, but also excludes certain forms of institutional, political, and indeed moral articulations. Consider, second, what such an onto-political investment of necessity excludes in terms of possible versions of ethical or moral theory.

The analysis of undecidability is clearly incompatible with one major strand of moral theorization: absolutism. All absolutist versions of the good are incompatible with a theoretical attachment to undecidability. The best known example is Plato's *The Republic*. For Plato moral actions are guaranteed by correct knowledge. In an ideal Republic the knowledge of the guardians of reason approximates knowledge of the absolute good: this knowledge accords to them the right to rule. Plato thus links knowledge, morality, and power. This political argument rests on the claim that there is an ideal form of the good independent of its particular instantiations. True knowledge of morality does not depend on either sensory perception or experience, but is indubitable and absolute regardless of circumstance.

Such a version of moral universalism is incompatible with Laclau's argument on a number of grounds: it privileges a particular version of the good on the basis of a theoretical claim about the nature of all life, that is an ontology of the social; it cannot admit of any other good and ignores its own contingency in linking a theory of knowledge to a theory of morality; perhaps most importantly, the presupposition of an absolute good wholly distinct from its instantiations delinks the good from communal and social life. The bearing of such an account of the good on moral life is impossible to judge, as knowledge of the good is equivalent to experience of an other-worldly realm. This is reminiscent of Augustine's distinction between the Cities of God and Man. In that case the City of God is presented as a realm bereft of time, space, and indeed difference. The bearing of such a realm on human moral laws – which have after all to be articulated in time and space, and with reference to articulated 'proper' bounds (what is proper to the self, what is proper to the state) – is difficult to fathom.

However, we should not too quickly dismiss absolutism. A moral absolutism which makes reference to an-other realm emptied of signification echoes Laclau's analysis of all signification as reliant on what he terms the logic of the empty signifier. Moreover for Laclau this impossible object is the only object of ethical investment. A long and esteemed tradition of ethical enquiry makes a very similar claim – primarily on religious grounds. We will need though to inflect this tradition in a manner which its adherents would reject if its value to a post-Marxist account of ethics is to be determined.

Likewise two other significant versions of ethics/morality are a priori ruled out: subjectivism and objectivism. I generalize for the purpose of argument here. Subjectivist theories hold that morality is a matter of preference, and cannot be objectively determined. However, this subjective relativization of ethics only goes so far, as it cannot acknowledge the relation of subjects exercising ethical preferences to the social and political structures which provide the context of any ethical decision. Moreover subjectivism tends towards a mirror imaging of objectivism in leaving ethics to the arbitrary decision of a fully determinate subjectivity. Such a determinate subject could not take an ethical decision: the decision would be pre-programmed by a subject which pre-exists any decision that may be taken, like a loop in a computer programmed language. Objectivist theories, by contrast, hold that the moral viewpoint admits of universalization and can be known in a similar vein to, for example, the laws of thermodynamics. There are thick and thin versions of such moral objectivism, but all tend to remove the weight of ethical decision, in demarcating appropriate actions and behaviours regardless of context or contingency.

Likewise investment in the onto-political orientation suggested by Laclau's work must reject utilitarianism which assumes the plausibility of determining the greater good, or the maximal pleasure, in a manner which outlaws difference. Consequentialist accounts which presume to determine the moral standing of an action on its outcome cannot admit of the possibility of different forms of outcome, different responses to the same action, and are notoriously slippery in defining precisely how the good is to be both defined and measured. Similar objections might be made against other ethical accounts including deontological and virtue ethics.

Proceeding negatively we may infer that the strict distinction of a theoretical from a normative claim is not plausible. It could though be suggested that my argument presumes too much: an essential contingency does not proscribe any particular ethics but is their neutral condition of possibility. This argument is mistaken. First, it ignores that most moral theories would reject the starting premises of Laclau's analysis. Second, the self-referential nature of Laclau's argument places even the theoretical claims he makes in the realm of contingency. As such they must be subject to argumentative justification and challenge. Third, and perhaps most importantly, Laclau defends an ontology of the social. Any ontology of the social assumes, no matter how deeply they may be hidden, certain normative presuppositions. Laclau's participation in various debates about universality and particularity, radical and liberal democracy, and the limits of tolerance all presume a stronger link than his initial formulation seems to allow. To deny that the account of hegemony and contingency elaborated by Laclau has certain ethical implications would amount to a form of performative self contradiction. However, the acceptance of the argument I have just proposed results in a different version of performative contradiction. It is on the horns of this *aporia*, outlined below, that the ethical weight of discourse theory rests. Let me summarize the view I defend before proceeding to the question of performative contradiction.

First, the discussion of undecidability already contours a debate regarding ethics in certain directions. These contours include *inter alia*: (i) a refusal to endorse the ethical closure of particular communities, as well as the formalism associated with most deontological moral theories; (ii) a recognition that power is a necessary feature of any moral decision; (iii) the conclusion that too rigid a separation of a primitive ontology of the social from morality and sociality repeats Kant's implausible distinction between the epistemological and the moral. Of course Laclau himself would reject such a strict distinction, as his more recent work on ethics makes explicit.

This argument is not wholly incompatible with three key claims Laclau makes regarding ethics in his more recent work. These lend support to my argument but leave unanswered certain questions. Laclau defines the ethical as the moment of the universality of the community. This universality is however both a condition of possibility of any community, as well as its condition of impossibility. For Laclau 'universality' presupposes a logic of the empty signifier which cannot be represented as such. Instead particular discourses struggle to establish their hegemony. He writes:

> The ethical substance of the community – the moment of its totalization or universalization – represents an object which is simultaneously impossible and necessary. As impossible, it is incommensurable with any normative order; as necessary, it has to have access to the field of representation which is possible only if the ethical substance is invested in some form of normative order.
>
> (Laclau 2000: 84)

The ethical is linked then to the presence of empty symbols in the community which make ethical life possible. These empty symbols – for example, equality – are gradually emptied of particular contents as they come to represent a variety of different social struggles. These may well conflict with each other, and compete to give content to the empty symbol. While this 'empty symbol' can never quite become 'empty', it intimates toward a moment of unconditionally empty signification, a signification which (to recall Augustine's characterization of the heavenly realm) would be devoid of any human reference to time, space, or content. This makes clear the grip of metaphysics on Laclau's conception of the ethical as well as the failure of all metaphysics to properly address the ethical. It also indicates that we should not too quickly dismiss absolutist versions of the ethical. Indeed they betray an important element of any post-metaphysical ethical theory.

Laclau argues, second, that particular orders or norms represent an ethical investment through which the universal is incarnated. This follows the logic of his analysis of hegemony in earlier texts. The representation of universality is an ethical moment hegemonically institutionalized. It does not represent the prior existence of an ethical absolute. In this sense it might be said, to refer back to Augustine once more, that the ethical as an impossible reference to a state of being necessarily implies its institutionalization as a state of becoming. There is a necessary, though contingent, relation between the City of Man and the City of God.

Laclau concludes, third, that the object invested in is the *only* object of ethics. This (impossible) ethical object does not dictate the particular forms of ethical investment incarnated in different normative orders. Rather:

> This investment, as it shows no inner connection between what is invested and the social norms which receive the investment, depends on the central category of *decision*, conceived as an act of articulation grounded on no a priori principle external to the decision itself.
>
> (Laclau 2000: 84)

I have indicated that in my view the onto-political orientation implied by Laclau's work does suggest that certain versions of ethics and indeed certain ethical decisions would be precluded if this prior investment in the necessity of contingency has been made. Indeed were Laclau himself not to propose an ethics and a politics broadly compatible with the claims he has made then he would rightly be subject to the charge of performative contradiction, as Habermas would doubtless be quick to note.

This leaves things a little too simple though, for the charge of performative contradiction may be made against this argument, though on different grounds. On my account we presuppose a subject who/that recognizes the contingency of any identification, and takes seriously the impossibility of a finally constituted subjectivity. This entails the exclusion of certain actions, and an argument which justifies this exclusion. But who or what is this subject which makes the investment in such a contingency? Does it/she precede the decision? Well no, for if so there would be no decision proper. Is s/he constituted by the decision? Well not quite, otherwise there would be no subject capable of deciding.

This question of the subject is suggested indirectly in a seemingly innocuous preface to Laclau's discussion of ethics. He writes: '"hegemony" is a theoretical approach which depends on an essentially ethical decision to accept, as the horizon of any possible intelligibility, the incommensurability between the ethical and the normative' (Laclau 2000: 81).

The key issue here is that of decision, more precisely, the *essentially ethical decision* to accept a hegemonic theoretical approach. This ethical decision suggests the type of ontological orientation I suggested above. With such an orientation one could not, at the risk of performative contradiction, engage in certain actions or hold to certain ethical theories. Incommensurability is then the object of ethical investment for the radical democrat. As I indicated, the fascist would not make such an ethical decision, viewing incommensurability as a defect within the body politic. It is overcome through the imposition of an order which seeks to eradicate the distance between the normative order and the impossible object of ethical investment. The decision to adopt a hegemonic approach to politics presupposes a subject that is on the one hand capable of effecting this as a decision, but on the other is not at home in itself. Such a subject is radically disjunctive from the traditional subject of ethics which is either objectively determined in its ethical decision by a prior moral order, or which makes ethical decision as a subject capable of justifying every decision it may make. The ethical subject is instead defined precisely through a failure of justificatory principles, and a responsibility towards this failure.

This characterization of the ethical leaves us on the horns of an *aporia* then. The decision to adopt a hegemonic approach, as ultimately ethical, receives no justification from any prior ethical framework. There is a certain madness in this decision, which is not a decision of the subject, or a decision imposed on the subject. Instead it unhinges the subject. Moreover once this onto-political orientation is invested in it provides no certainty to the subject which has invested precisely in its own uncertainty. The performative contradiction arises because, as Laclau notes time and time again, the logic of the empty signifier does not in itself presuppose an investment in this logic at the level of ethical decisions. In fact, to suggest that contingency is necessary is a proposition of the type 'I am lying'. For if contingency is necessary then this claim must itself be contingent; if necessary then there is no possibility of absolute contingency. The claim that contingency is necessary already presupposes an ethical investment which itself receives no warranty from the mere existence of contingency. So then, two performative contradictions: to make a claim for the necessity of contingency seems, at the risk of contradiction, to refuse the affirmation of certain ethical assumptions; however, to accept this argument is to affirm that contingency is itself not contingent, for it is necessary. This aporetic conclusion is unavoidable, but not disabling. Let me make a few suggestions which lend support to my claim for the exclusion of certain ethical presumptions, and implicit support for others.

The argument for contingency, I suggest, must be defended as *necessary*. If this defence is not made then the relation between the theoretical claims made by Laclau, and particular instantiations of political orders, are impossible to maintain. On these lines we do well to recall that Laclau's original arguments regarding contingency arise from a critique of a very particular tradition, namely Marxism. Indeed the argument itself depends on a particular history and tradition as its condition of possibility. Given this, the dislocation performed by Laclau within and without the Marxist tradition holds implications for the messianic conception of justice briefly alluded to in the comments above. The risk of denying any link between an onto-political orientation and a certain political and ethical orientation is that the account of hegemony becomes simply a theoretical fact – the fact of contingency – which has no bearing on ethico-political debate.

However, the ethical decision to adopt a hegemonic approach (as Laclau expresses it) functions rather differently than for a traditional ethics. For it does not predetermine ethical decisions in advance. It entails serious accounting for every decision, as particular decisions are not prescribed. It entails too that this accounting will only go so far: on the precipice of decision the accounts never quite add up. Nonetheless, while no decision or action is predetermined by this stance, certain ethical decisions *are* excluded if contingency is deemed necessary. This contours the forms of debate appropriate to ethics, without determining what is or is not an ethical decision. Indeed, there is no ethics as such, only an orientation towards the ethical which entails treating contingency seriously, and refusing an absolutism of either the subject or object.

Last, discussion of the ethical implications of contingency is in itself inappropriate if not tied to a politics. For what the radical critique of absolutism demonstrates, irrevocably, is that the ethical does not precede or frame political institutions but is linked to them in an intimate extimacy. Intimate because the only form of realization of 'an ethical life' is through processes of decision and will formation which presuppose this contingency; extimate because no particular order can claim to express or manifest this impossibility. This argument parts with the Marxist assumption that the normative order is the secondary expression of deeper, hidden interests. Rather the ethical radically shortcuts any absolutist or teleological ethics premised on interest.

The defence of radical undecidability then may not issue in a prescriptive definition of the ethical but it does have normative implications. Any claim to represent the ideal should be viewed as an attempt to hegemonize and control an impossibility which resists such final determination. However, we might read this equivocation as suggesting that moral/political theory has to account for this tension, not run from it. Laclau and Mouffe suggest precisely this reading in *Hegemony and Socialist Strategy* when writing:

> This moment of tension, of openness, which gives the social its essentially incomplete and precarious character, is what every project for radical democracy should set out to institutionalize [...] The advancing of a project for radical democracy means, therefore, forcing the myth of a rational and transparent society to recede progressively to the horizon of the social. This becomes a 'non-place', the symbol of its own impossibility (*HSS* 190–1).

This non-place, a symbol of the impossibility of a finally instrumentalized world, is in Laclau and Mouffe's view a precondition of the thinking of radical democracy. It is also, as noted above, a precondition, indeed the very location, of any ethical object and subject. However, the content given to this ethical object depends upon the various forms of normative investment constitutive of particular orders.

Radical democracy proposes then the institutionalization of this uncertainty, the contouring of democratic society in such a way that the place of power is never fully incarnated. This already predetermines certain features of a hegemonic left project. It cannot privilege particular versions of the good, in the way that the Marxian project for example did. Once we begin to consider democratic politics, however, the defence of radical democracy reaches beyond its initial premises to engage in an argument about the efficacy of certain means and ends. It has to make an argument, an argument which in democratic societies will be based on persuasion and agreement between consenting subjects. Moreover the radical democrat precludes the unnecessary exercise of force in the name of truth, as witnessed in various leftist experiments of the twentieth century.

There is a melancholy attached to the realization that democracy is, to abuse Trotsky, the institutionalization of permanent revolution. The melancholic disposition, as Freud argued, laments the lost object while internalizing the pain of that loss against the ego. The danger of this is a narcissistic self-obsession which holds onto the lost object and punishes the ego of the subject. The pained attachment of the revolutionary socialist to the absolutism of a certain spirit of Marxism suggests precisely such narcissistic self-immolation. Melancholy at the social level then points both to the dependence of any political identity on that of the other, and to the dangers induced by a general sense of dislocation for the leftist imaginary. This brings me back to the discussion with which I began this chapter: ethics and instrumental reason. What are the implications of this melancholic attachment to an impossible object for the radical imaginary, and for the relationship between the ethical and the political?

From the City of Man to the City of God: ethics and instrumental rationality

The ethical, as the impossible object of investment is, I have suggested, bereft of any instrumental/means–end rationality. It is also impossible to speak or conceive of. Naming such an impossibility is already to attach a content, no matter how minimal, to the indeterminate. Yet Laclau insists on maintaining the name ethical for this impossible object. Certainly this insistence maintains a relation to absolutist and religious versions of ethical reflection. Indeed Laclau notes as much:

> Naming God is impossible, we said, because, being the absolute *transcendens*, He is beyond all positive determination. If we radicalize the logical implications of this impossibility, we see that even the assumption that God is an entity, even the assumption of Oneness – if Oneness is conceived of as the unicity of an entity – is something which is already an undue interpretation, because it is to attribute a content to that which is beyond any possible content [...] The historical importance of the mystical discourse is that, by radicalizing that 'beyond', it has shown the essential finitude which is constitutive of all experience; its historical limit has been, in most cases, its having surrendered to the temptation of giving a positive content to the 'beyond' – the positive content being dictated not by mystical experience itself but by the religious persuasion of the mystic.
>
> (Laclau 1997: 260–1)

As a consequence, however, any actions, immoral or otherwise, are an expression of God as the absolute, or the ethical as an impossible object. The ethical appears to offer no basis for discrimination between actions, behaviour, or norms. It is wrong to suggest though that this absolute is neutral, or representative of degree zero. Rather it can only 'appear' in forms of signification which seek to represent the universal yet must of necessity fail. It is not, yet it is. This places the ethical in a peculiar position. On the one hand it is an impossible object of normative investment; on the other this impossible object has to rely on constitutively inadequate forms of representation if it is to be made manifest. Moreover, I have argued that investment in the necessity of this impossibility entails the exclusion of certain versions of ethics, and thus the contouring of ethics in particular ways.

Now, all representation relies to some degree on the instrumentalization of language. We cannot then invoke the logic of empty signification as a critique of this instrumental necessity, especially as it is its condition of possibility. What can be done is to argue that once an investment in such an onto-political orientation is made, certain forms of instrumental action can be deemed incapable of accounting for the constitutive impossibility which is their condition of expression. They perform what Derrida once termed a transcendental contraband, veiling their conditions of possibility, in presenting themselves as necessary. Expressed in other terms such discourses either deny the necessity of the transcendental invocation of this ethical moment (and thus deny the constitutive impossibility which infects their performance), or alternatively deny altogether that their forms of expression are particular.

Any process of normative investment in the ethical will have to rely on a means–end rationality. If so, then the ideal of transparency, or the Kantian ethical ideal of the subject as an end in itself, recedes. However it becomes a condition of possibility of conceiving of such a project. In contrast to the Habermasian version of morality which presupposes the possibility of an ideal orienting political practice – symmetrical communication between mature subjects – the ethical is also a condition of impossibility. There is then a secret history to ethical philosophy, a constitutive tension between an impossible reach for transcendence freed of any means–end rationality, and the necessary implication of any moral discourse in instrumental rationality. If so a number of implications for the analysis of instrumental rationality follow.

This argument allows for a determinate analysis of the various modes of instrumentalization in contemporary global conditions. At the start of this chapter I briefly ran through these at the theoretical level, but theory is not isolated from political practice and the forms of instrumentalization noted there find expression in a variety of different contexts and discursive practices. This entails an inflection of the traditional critique of instrumental rationality found in critical theory. Rather than rooting this critique in an ideal of transparent communication we can engage with instrumental forms of reason on their own terms, suggesting that the claim to objective necessity which underlies varies modalities of rationality cannot account for their necessary failure. On this account, then, what critical theorists term instrumental rationality is analysed instead as a particular form of discursive articulation of the social which veils its own conditions of possibility.

I noted earlier that the ethical is caught in a double bind. On the one hand most ethical accounts make reference to an ideal which transcends all particularity. On the other hand ethics has to make reference to particular communities, laws, conceptions of what is proper and what is improper. This tension recalls the classic distinction between the City of Man and the City of God in the work of Augustine. The City of God is a realm devoid of time and space. Properly speaking it cannot be spoken of or conceived. Yet Augustine in the closing books of his *Confessions* constantly runs up against the problem that if God is to have any bearing on the lives of humans then He must be spoken of. This injunction both breaks the prohibition on the representation of God as the ethical Absolute, and keeps the prohibition in place in recognizing that He cannot finally be presented. A contemporary ethics plays a similar game. Caught between determining what is properly ethical and the acknowledgement that the ethical is an impossible object of investment which can never be finally determined, twenty-first-century ethical debates return to questions addressed centuries ago by Augustine. It is this paradox which any defence of radical democracy must take seriously.

This identification with contingency, and thus with an essential value pluralism, distinguishes the radical democrat from the liberal. The liberal endorses value pluralism without acknowledging that this pluralism is constituted by a radical moment of indecision, which undermines the claimed legitimacy of the decision. Thus, the liberal struggles to justify the exercise of force in order to maintain the norms previously endorsed. The radical democrat, in recognizing the contingent foundation of any order and its justification, also recognizes the (illegitimate) violence required for the maintenance of that order. Most accounts of morality and democracy seek principles which either guide the taking of decisions or shift responsibility for decision taking onto the principles. Post-Marxism refuses this necessary link between universal principles of justice and legitimate decision making. The radical absence of such principles does however have implications for political action and choice. An example discussed earlier demonstrates this. Think of the fascist confronted with the spectre of radical contingency. For the fascist, contingency should not be identified with but overcome through the introduction of a principle of order. The fascist identifies with the principle of order as the basis for the organization of political life – the state, the body politic, the fraternity of Aryan man, and the like. By contrast, the radical democrat sanctions contingency as necessary, and, ironically, not contingent. This recognition entails (social) identification with radical contingency and the insistence that all political decisions require justification. A properly ethical decision does *not* rely on any principles or laws which precede it. This has the slightly bizarre consequence that a properly ethical decision would be taken by a wholly indeterminate subject, independent of all social practice. Given that such an ideal of subjectivity is precisely what post-Marxist thought rejects, this ideal of sovereign decision making requires revising. It returns as the condition of possibility for autonomous action *and* the condition of its impossibility. Sovereign decisions cannot be taken, but they must be taken. It is this structure of indeterminacy that opens a realm of freedom in which subjects can begin to question the laws given to them, and recognize that the following of a law presupposes the taking of a decision every time the law is followed. This does not mean that the validity of the legal order is simply suspended. Rather, it is to recognize the violence which goes hand in hand with the forms of legitimation intrinsic to liberal democracies.

Identification with an ultimate contingency implies that the ethical, as an impossible ideal, should be contrasted with any particular normative order which attempts to achieve that ideal. The starting point of a democratic order is the recognition that no principle precedes those principles that we give to ourselves, thus constituting ourselves as a community of selves. This forces the acknowledgement of the contingency of the community of selves thus constituted and the possibility of disruption of the community thus constituted. Connolly terms this a democratic politics of disturbance which requires a constant contestation of all those rules which demarcate the demos, a constant reinvention of the laws which also means their constant amelioration (Connolly 1995). The identification with contingency, and thus with an essential value pluralism, distinguishes the radical democrat from the liberal. The liberal endorses value pluralism without acknowledging that this pluralism is constituted by a radical moment of indecision, which undermines the claimed legitimacy of the decision. Thus, the liberal struggles to justify the exercise of force in order to maintain the norms previously endorsed. The radical democrat, in recognizing the contingent foundation of any order, also recognizes the (illegitimate) violence required for the maintenance of that order. This is why the radical democrat can take responsibility for the decision which underpins the exclusions constitutive of the community and take on the burdensome task of their constant revision.

Note

1 Obviously this is not so for all 'modern' theorists of politics. Machiavelli's *The Prince* for example established the precedence of political rationality over moral qualms. Machiavelli's view, even in *The Prince* though, is ambivalent. The book is written as a handbook advising on how to keep power; nonetheless he does suggest that the maintenance of political order has a moral significance irreducible to the means used to maintain authority.

References

Adorno, T. W. and Horkheimer, M. (1985) *Dialectic of Enlightenment*, London: Verso.

Connolly, W. E. (1995) *The Ethos of Pluralization*, Minneapolis: University of Minnesota Press.

Derrida, J. (1994) *Specters of Marx*, London: Routledge.

—— (1996) 'Remarks on deconstruction and pragmatism', in C. Mouffe (ed.) *Deconstruction, Pragmatism, Hegemony*, London: Routledge.

Kymlicka, W. (1990) *Contemporary Political Philosophy*, Oxford: Oxford University Press.

Laclau, E. (1994) 'Why do empty signifiers matter to politics', in J. Weeks (ed.) *The Lesser Evil and the Greater Good*, London: Rivers Oram Press.

—— (1997) 'On the names of God', in S. Golding (ed.) *The Eight Technologies of Otherness*, London: Routledge.

—— (2000) 'Identity and hegemony', in J. Butler, E. Laclau and S. Žižek (eds) *Contingency, Hegemony, Universality: Contemporary Dialogues on the Left*, London: Verso.

McLelland, S. (1998) *A History of Western Political Thought*, London: Routledge.

8

DEMOCRATIC DECISIONS AND THE QUESTION OF UNIVERSALITY

Rethinking recent approaches

Aletta Norval

> Democratic theorists now take deliberation to be the exemplary practice or activity for democrats, and they gear their arguments toward its realization.
>
> (Sanders 1997: 347)

> A picture held us captive. And we could not get outside of it.
>
> (Wittgenstein 1984: no. 115)

Introduction

The nature and character of democratic decision-making, and the forging of common interests, identities, and wills stand at the center of debates in democratic theory today. Arguments in this respect range from a defense of strategic-instrumentalism in analyses of empirical cases of democratic decision-making, to strongly normative accounts of such processes. This chapter sets out to explore some of the key issues at stake in different approaches to democratic decision-making. It focuses on two approaches that have dominated the debate, namely, the Habermas-inspired model of deliberative democracy and the post-structuralist model of the decision in the theory of radical democracy as articulated in the seminal works of Ernesto Laclau and Chantal Mouffe.[1] It aims to offer a reading of these approaches, while critically examining the central assumptions underpinning them, in order to clear the ground for the articulation of a modified version of deliberative democratic politics, which aims to do justice to the agonistic spirit of democracy.[2] Such a reading clearly cannot proceed from some neutral ground between the two approaches. It is, therefore, important to note that my argument proceeds from a post-structuralist position, and does not assume the existence of a common ground, but seeks to construct it by drawing upon the works of a number of prominent commentators in the field.

At the center of the debate on democratic decision-making are a number of distinct issues, including questions concerning the aims of the decision-making process, the nature of the process itself, the participants in this process, and the conditions under which participation occur. My discussion will concentrate primarily on the nature and aims of the decision-making process, although related issues – such as those mentioned above – cannot and ought not to be excluded from consideration. More specifically, my argument is structured, on the one hand, around the relation between deliberation and the reaching of agreement on the basis of generalizable interests and, on the other, hegemonic argumentation, the decision, and the construction of empty signifiers. I will argue that the former, Habermas-inspired approach fails to offer a workable account of the relation between ideal conditions of deliberation and actual processes of democratic decision-making. As a result, its characterization of the construction of generalizable interests is problematic in that it draws on suppositions excluded from the normative model. The latter approach, exemplified in the works of Laclau and Mouffe, on the other hand, concentrates on the construction of hegemonic outcomes and as a result, does not give sufficient consideration to the extent to which such 'decisions' can in fact be described as democratic. In this case the root of the problem can be located in the overemphasis on the conditions of possibility for decisions specifically, and hegemonic politics more generally. I argue, in conclusion, that a weakened model of deliberation combined with an agonistic view of democratic politics opens the way for a reconsideration of the nature of democratic argumentation and decision-making which makes room for the strongest insights of a post-structuralist inspired politics.

The first two sections of this chapter consist of an overview of issues, organized around the sorts of agreements we may expect to reach in deliberative democracy. They focus, in particular, on the role of generalizable interests and their relation to universality in the reaching of consensual agreements. This is done against the backdrop of recent criticisms of deliberative democracy. Sections III and IV look at efforts to extend this model of democratic decision-making, and explore their implications for the normative assumptions from which deliberative democracy starts. It puts into question the logical status of the conceptual extension of the deliberative model, and reconceptualizes the extension in terms of a Derridean understanding of supplementarity. This opens the discussion out onto the post-structuralist intervention. The next three sections critically discuss post-structuralist accounts of democracy and the role of hegemonization in the construction of generalizable interests and common identities, as well as the manner in which this model seeks to avoid the extreme particularistic implications of some 'post-modernist' approaches. I concentrate here on the writings of Laclau and Mouffe, which have sought systematically to address these issues. I conclude by drawing together the threads of the arguments propounded in each section so as to provide an alternative reading of democratic decision-making, which begins to explore the possibility of combining a weakened model of deliberative democracy with a hegemonic account of democratic politics.

I. Deliberative democracy and its critics

Over the years persistent questions have been raised concerning deliberation, its presuppositions, and its relation to actual democratic practice.[3] Habermas and his defenders have sought to develop responses to these queries and criticisms.[4] Given this it may be appropriate to start with a brief outline of the general parameters of the deliberative model of democracy.[5] To do so, I will briefly survey the uses to which Habermas's writings have been put in contemporary work on democracy. This will be followed by an overview of recent criticisms to which this model has been subjected.

The Habermas-inspired conception of deliberative democracy has been particularly influential in the development of democratic institutions and mechanisms such as deliberative forums, citizens' juries, and deliberative polling.[6] It is not difficult to see why the deliberative conception of democracy offers an attractive model for democratic practice.[7] In contrast to adversarial conceptions of democracy, it places a great deal of emphasis on the joint reaching of consensual agreements. In contrast to aggregative models of democracy, it focuses on the formation of opinions, interests, and democratic wills. Consequently it avoids the pitfalls of assuming that opinions and interests are already in existence, before the making of democratic decisions. Agreements reached under these conditions have the power to legitimate institutions and political principles in a way that the simple aggregation of votes does not, since it places citizens under a publicity requirement: they must offer reasons for their positions and claims, and must defend those reasons publicly. In turn, this emphasis has shifted the focus of theorizing to reflection on the conditions under which processes of decision-making can be deemed democratic. In this respect, the stipulation of discourse rules is taken to provide clear guidance on such conditions. For instance, it allows theorists and practitioners of democracy to argue that a decision will be democratic if and only if no one with the competency to speak and act is excluded from the process; if everyone is allowed to question or introduce any assertion they wish, while also expressing their attitudes, desires, and needs; and if no one is prevented, by internal or external coercion, from exercising these rights (Chambers 1996: 100).

These rules make explicit that under conditions of democratic deliberation we must treat each other as equal partners; that individuals must be given the space to speak; and that we must listen to each other, and justify our positions to one another. Moreover, it seems possible to ascertain in practice whether these guidelines are being followed and, thus, whether any particular process in fact measures up to the standards of democratic practice specified in the model. For instance, in her book *Reasonable Democracy* Chambers fleshes out these conditions in the following fashion. First, approximating[8] the condition of universality means that there should be an absence of barriers excluding people or groups from debate. As many voices as possible should be heard, which means that there is a requirement for a high level of participation (including reading, weighing opinions, having discussions with friends, and so forth).[9] Practically, one has to ask the following questions. Have any groups been excluded? Are there organizations and movements through which the public can voice its opinion? Is there a high level of interest and involvement on the part of all those affected?[10] Second, approximating the conditions of rationality (being persuaded by the force of the better argument) and non-coercion means that agreement must be autonomous.[11] Conditions under which deliberation takes place must exclude both internal and external coercion and should emphasize the need for critical reflection and evaluation.[12] Finally, approximating reciprocity means that we must ask how close we come to maintaining respect and impartiality (Chambers 1996: 208–9). To what extent do participants approach disputes discursively as opposed to strategically? Indicators of sincere acting by participants include consistency in speech, consistency in speech and action, and coherence. Indicators of respect and impartiality include acknowledgement of the moral status of opposing views, a cultivation of openness, and starting from the point of view of reaching possible agreement.

I return to several issues raised by these rules of discourse below. In particular, it is necessary to look more closely at the character of deliberation (*vis-à-vis* strategic bargaining and other modes of communication), and the centrality given to the reaching of consensus or agreement in the process of deliberation. Suffice it to note at this point, that what is at stake in deliberative models of democracy is a very specific conception of practical discourse, which is different from day to day communication. It is a highly specialized, idealized form of discussion aiming to resolve normative disputes to the satisfaction of all. Its motivational premise is to reach agreement (Chambers 1996: 98). It is not agonistic,[13] but dialectical. The assumption is that a clash of opposing forces can move participants forward in a search for a 'common ground' (Chambers 1996: 162).[14] The exact nature of this 'common ground' is precisely what is at stake in the discussion concerning different approaches to universality in the deliberative and post-structuralist conceptions of democracy. I will discuss these differences with regard to democratic decision-making below. However, it should be noted that much of the general criticisms to which the deliberative model has been subjected recently, have tended to focus precisely on a variety of issues related to its account of universality.

Thus, even though deliberative models of democracy are commonly celebrated for their clear practical implications, a spate of critical writings have recently begun to challenge this consensus. David Miller, Lynn M. Sanders, and Iris Marion Young have added their voices to the criticisms made by commentators such as James Tully (Tully 1989; Miller 1999; Sanders 1997; Young 1997). These arguments may be categorized into three broad groups. The first group includes those who begin from within deliberative democratic theory, but who end up rejecting entirely the idea of deliberative democracy. The second group includes those loyal critics who, starting from positions internal to the conception of democracy defended, wish to bolster and strengthen it through their criticism (Chambers 1996; Benhabib 1998). Finally, there are those who criticize deliberative democracy from the 'outside', and aim to develop a conception of democracy starting from very different, if not conflicting, premises. All of these criticisms, in their different ways, can be related to the claims to universality made in the name of deliberative democracy. In concluding this section I concentrate on the first group of theorists, exemplified by the work of Sanders. I deal with Chambers's arguments, representing the second group, in section IV and with those of the third group in the remainder of the sections.

In a recent article, Sanders sets out a series of arguments against deliberative conceptions of democracy. She holds, contrary to received opinion, that where there are tensions between deliberation and democracy they are likely to be resolved in favour of deliberation. If one of the main aims of deliberative theorists is to deepen democracy, it fails since it in fact displays anti-democratic tendencies. These tendencies, Sanders argues, can be ascribed to a variety of factors. To begin with, she draws attention to the fact that the recommendation of deliberation is not, typically, justified by arguments that deliberative democracy is what 'ordinary citizens would themselves recommend' (Sanders 1997: 348). While this may not in itself make deliberation undemocratic, it does open up the possibility of investigating the arguments as to why deliberation may not appeal to ordinary citizens. These may be divided into arguments attaching to the conception of deliberation advanced by theorists of deliberative democracy, and those that relate to issues not addressed or ignored by this conception of democracy, thus seemingly falling outside its scope.

Arguments utilized relating to the conception of deliberation include the connotations of 'rationality, reserve, [...] community, selflessness, and universalism' which, Sanders holds, undermine deliberation's democratic claims. This is so since citizens do not all have the same capacity for articulating their arguments in 'rational' terms. In other words, deliberative democrats, while proclaiming its universality, in fact favour one particular argumentative style over another. This criticism by Sanders is bolstered by arguments relating to issues not receiving sufficient attention by deliberative democratic theorists. The latter pertain to issues of voice, especially where they overlap with an uneven distribution of the material prerequisites for deliberation.[15] Sanders argues in this respect that deliberation requires 'not only equality in resources and the guarantee of equal opportunity to articulate persuasive arguments but also equality in "epistemological authority", in the capacity to evoke acknowledgement of one's arguments' (Sanders 1997: 349). Young raises related problems. She argues that as a consequence of the emphasis deliberative democracy places upon universality and the exclusion of particular perspectives it is, at best, blind to the resource of difference for enriching democratic discussion and, at worst, undemocratic in its overemphasis of apparently universalistic 'public-spiritedness' (Young 1997: 383–406). Rather than seeing a stark opposition between the impartial and unitary on the one hand, and the partial and differentiated on the other,[16] Young argues that democratic dialogue must, of necessity, include critical dialogue among the plurality of socially differentiated perspectives present in the social field (1997: 400–1). Now, if the question of 'universality' is at the root of these problems, it is necessary to look in more detail at some of its dimensions as present in Habermas's theorization of the sort of consensual agreement informing deliberative democracy.

II. Democratic agreement and generalizable interests

The search for agreement is the motivational premise of deliberative democracy.[17] Habermas takes 'the type of action aimed at reaching understanding to be fundamental'; 'other forms of social action – for example, conflict, competition, strategic action in general – are *derivatives* of action oriented to reaching an understanding'.[18] If agreement is the motivational premise of deliberative democracy, the question immediately arises as to what can people agree upon, and how that agreement comes about. If people simply deliberated on the basis of furthering their own interests, then the possibility of agreement would rest on their sharing an interest. However, as pointed out earlier, Habermas refuses to fix interests in advance or to understand them as 'brute facts' (Chambers 1996: 102). Rather, part of what discourse is about is judging what is in one's best interest. As Chambers points out, 'deliberation is really about working out interests we share with each other which can furnish a reason for collectively recognizing [*sic*] a norm. According to Habermas, what we search for in practical discourse are generalizable interests' (1996: 102).

What then are generalizable interests (Chambers 1996: 102–4)? Three characteristics of generalizable interests, of which traffic rules and laws against murder are examples, are of particular importance. First, generalizable interests represent overlapping particular, but not identical interests (i.e. an interest in peace and one in *agape* may lead to agreement on the norm of religious toleration). Second, the conception of interests at work here includes not only material benefits, but also the pursuit of moral ideals. Third, this idea does not presuppose a set of universally true human needs that we attempt to discover through discourse. The idea is that, through criticism, argument, and so on, one can arrive at an interpretation of a collective need. Thus, generalizable interests are open to revision. The central issue with respect to generalizable interests concerns their link to Habermas's 'universalization principle'.[19] For Habermas, justifiable (universalizable) norms are those norms that incorporate generalizable interests (White 1989: 49). The test for such norms is whether the norm is acceptable in actual argumentation to all those who are potentially affected by it.[20]

The nature and character of the process of rational deliberation through which such norms are established, and generalizable interests are reached, is thus of the utmost importance. Habermas provides an account of this process, inter alia, in *Between Facts and Norms*. There he sets out to develop a reconstructive sociology of democracy, which chooses its basic concepts in such a way that it can identify 'particles and fragments of an "existing reason" already incorporated in political practice, however distorted these may be' (Habermas 1996: 287). I will briefly outline his 'process model' of democracy before looking more closely at the manner in which he distinguishes between rational consensus, on the one hand, and bargaining, on the other.

III. A supplementary relation: rational consensus, bargaining and compromise formations

In outlining his process model of democracy, Habermas (1996: 162–5) distinguishes three stages, coinciding with different types of discourse.[21] Stage 1, characterized by *pragmatic* discourse, occurs where experts construct possible programs and their consequences as, for instance, occur in parliament. Expert knowledge is fallible, not neutral and uncontested. Actors make decisions on the basis of hypothetically presupposed interests and value preferences. 'Ought' is relative to given ends and values. Such pragmatic discourses justify rational choices between alternatives, but preferences and interests remain external to these discourses. In Stage 2, characterized by *ethical-political* discourses, value orientations themselves are up for discussion and call for a form of discourse that goes beyond contested interests. At this stage, the hermeneutic self-understanding of participants develops and they become aware of deeper consonances of common forms of life. Thus, there is an overlap between rules of argumentation and membership of a historical community. Examples provided by Habermas include ecological questions, traffic control, and immigration policy. Finally, in Stage 3, characterized by *moral* discourses, contested interests and value orientations are submitted to a universalization test within a constitutional framework of rights. This demands a type of discourse in which there is a stepping back from all contingent existing normative contexts, and a break with everyday taken-for-granted assumptions, so that an 'autonomous will' or rational consensus can be developed.[22]

The nature of generalizable interests, generated in the process of the development of a rational consensus, can be further clarified when contrasted with what is involved in bargaining and compromise formations. Habermas acknowledges that often neither ethico-political nor moral discourses are options. It is here that we move towards bargaining producing compromise formations.[23] Compromise formations arise where it is clear that the sort of agreement required by deliberation cannot be reached since interests continue to conflict. Habermas argues in this respect that the '"basic guidelines for compromise construction must themselves be justified" in discursive terms' (White 1989: 76). This, White argues, makes it possible to distinguish between legitimate or fair and illegitimate compromises, where the latter would be mere disguises for power relations. Whilst in the case of rational consensus, the reasons have to convince participants in the same way, in the case of compromise formations parties may accept a compromise for different reasons. In the latter case, there are no generalizable interests, and power relations cannot be neutralized. As a result, we find bargaining between success-oriented parties willing to co-operate. The discourse principle (D) is still brought to bear, but only indirectly so, since parties use threats and promises (all parties are given the chance to intervene so that (particular) interests have an equal chance of prevailing).[24]

Now, it is important to clarify the implications for democratic will formation implied by the movement from rational consensus to compromise formations and vice versa. Habermas contrasts the democratic process and will formation theorized in his discourse theory with liberal and republican models of democracy (Habermas 1996: 296–302). He argues that the liberal model takes the form of compromises between interests, and the rules of compromise formations are justified in terms of liberal rights with an emphasis on universal and equal suffrage. In the case of republican politics democratic will formation is tied much more closely to the ethico-political self-understanding of the community. Consequently, deliberation draws on the substantive support of a culturally established background consensus shared by citizens. While the discourse model draws on aspects of both the foregoing, it is distinguished from them by the fact that it is not grounded in universal human rights, or in the ethical substance of the community. Rather, as we have seen, it is grounded in rules of discourse oriented to reaching understanding, which arise, in the final instance, from the structure of linguistic communication. The democratic process is thus invested with stronger normative connotations than in the liberal model, but weaker than in the republican case. The emphasis is on the institutionalization or proceduralization of will formation, and the latter is not dependent upon the presence of an active collective citizenry.

The process of democratic deliberation involves all three aspects of practical reason outlined above: its pragmatic, ethical, and moral uses. Democratic deliberation may include and mix together any of these uses of reason. It is thus 'a complex discursive network which includes argumentation of various sorts, bargaining and compromise, and political communication for the purposes of the free expression of opinions' (Bohman 1996: 206). Bohman argues that this conception of democratic deliberation still sets the standard of consensus – that laws must meet the agreement of all citizens, and that the process of law-making be discursive (structured according to mutual recognition of each other as free and equal) – too high. The introduction of compromise as an alternative democratic outcome by Habermas does not, according to Bohman, solve the problem of diverse and potentially conflicting cultural self-understandings entering into the debate on particular issues. I do not wish here to enter into what is already a long-standing debate on the extent to which discourse theoretic principles could be kept pure and free from contamination by any specific cultural content.[25] What is important here is a related question, but one which focuses on the status of the relation between rational consensus and compromise formations: is it logically possible both to introduce modifications and extensions to the conceptualization of consensual will formation, and to retain the absolute primacy of rational consensus over compromise formations? This question can be and has been formulated variously. At its most abstract it concerns the nature of supplementarity,[26] understood here in the Derridean sense, but it also emerges in the attempts to modify discourse theory in the move from ideal to real political discourse.

What is clear in either case is that a discourse of mere 'addition' will not do.[27] A supplement supplements since it fills a lack. It adds something to what was previously considered to be 'full' and complete in itself, otherwise no supplementation would be necessary. Whatever else may be necessary, a relation of supplementarity calls for a reconsideration of the original model. No dualistic ideal/real or theoretical/empirical model would overcome the problem, since such models still depend on a thinking of the original as pure and intact, not recognizing the lack present in it. I will return to these considerations. For the moment it may be more productive to turn to a particularly sophisticated attempt to address some of these problems as they arise in the movement from the ideal presuppositions of communication to the real politics.

IV. From decision rules to ongoing processes

Quite a few commentators on Habermas's discourse theory have recently focused on the question of the movement from the ideal to the real. Indeed, as William Rehg states in his introduction to *Between Facts and Norms*, this book is conceived of as an attempt to bridge normative and empirical approaches to democracy (Rehg 1996: ix–x) and Habermas himself articulates it as a central question, acknowledging that at present 'it is unclear how this procedural concept, so freighted with idealizations, can link up with empirical investigations that conceive politics primarily as an arena of power processes' (1996: 287). Habermas sets about correcting this deficit via a 'reconstructive sociology of democracy' and his process model of democracy referred to above draws on the insights he gains as a result. In this section, however, I will focus on the attempt by Chambers in her *Reasonable Democracy* to work through the problem of the movement from the ideal of undistorted communication to a discussion of 'real' politics. The main question occupying me in respect of her work is whether the modified account of deliberative democracy she outlines can ultimately be reconciled with the idealized presuppositions of Habermas's work, or whether it necessitates a weakening of that model in crucial respects.

Chambers's treatment of the movement from ideal to real is informed by the acknowledgement that real agreements can only ever be an approximation of the ideals set out in the Habermasian model:

> real agreements can never be perfectly universal, they never settle a question once and for all. Through the idea of an ideal communication community we can imagine the conditions of a perfectly rational consensus, but inasmuch as we can never attain the ideal in the real world, the question becomes the degree of *approximation*.
>
> (Chambers 1996: 171, emphasis added)

Everything here depends on how 'approximation' is understood and how precisely it relates to the ideal of a 'perfectly rational consensus'.[28] Before proceeding to investigate this question directly, it is useful to note why Chambers finds it necessary to introduce the idea of an approximation at all. She holds, in common with other commentators on deliberative models of democracy, that the idea of an ideal speech situation is too rigid and narrow 'to capture all that is entailed in a collective evaluation of the appropriateness of a norm'. In particular, she argues, it does not capture the idea that practical discourse is primarily intended 'to be an undertaking in the real (less than ideal) world by real (less than ideal) social actors' (1996: 155). Nevertheless, she regards it as a misunderstanding of discourse ethics to think that we should in all spheres of life strive for the achievement of consensus.[29]

Even though achieving consensus is not the aim of all social interaction there is no disputing the fact that the model of deliberative democracy does indeed privilege consensus over dissensus. I will return to the question of the relation between democracy, agreement, and disagreement below. Here it is necessary simply to say that Chambers gives a negative answer to the question of whether this privileging of consensus (the reaching of full understanding between actors) puts into question the role of pluralism, diversity, and difference within discourse ethics (157). In contrast to liberal pluralists, 'postmodernists', and rational choice theorists, all of whom have objections in this respect, Chambers argues that discourse ethics offers no guarantee that discourse will always be successful. The problem of otherness, disagreement and so on may be permanent features of our collective life, but we cannot draw the conclusion that all problems are of this nature. On Chambers's reading, deliberative democratic theory only argues that deliberation *may* lead to convergence, and this idea is premised on the idea that preferences are shaped by culture and communication. This means that certain types of culture and communication are more likely to promote an interest in co-operative dispute resolution than others.

As noted earlier, this rendering of deliberative democratic theory amounts to a substantially weaker account than Habermas's much stronger claims concerning universalizability. Chambers denies that there is a principled conflict between pluralism and consensual will formation since the search for agreement ignores the fact that 'disagreement, conflict, dispute, argumentation, opposition, in short, naysaying, are *essential aspects* of the discourse process' (158). This claim stands in sharp contrast to Habermas's argument that conflict, competition, and so forth are *derivatives* of action oriented to reaching an understanding, and are thus subordinate, if not supplementary, to it. Thus, even though Chambers concurs with Habermas's view that pluralism,[30] diversity, and difference 'furnish the very conditions that make universalized norms possible' (158–9) in post-conventional societies, she cannot resolve her breach with the basic status accorded to agreement and disagreement respectively in Habermas's work. Chambers's emphasis on the approximation of the real to the ideal also leads her to introduce other modifications to Habermas's model. In particular, she argues that Habermas overemphasizes purely procedural requirements. More attention should be given to citizens' willingness to participate, and to practical discourse understood as a process of interconnected discourses, many of which do not take place in formal settings. These considerations lead Chambers to assert that we need more emphasis on processes of argumentation (196). Nevertheless, this acknowledgement does not lead her to investigate actual processes of political argumentation, or the different kinds of argumentation in which one may engage. Both of these dimensions need to be explored in full if the full consequences of her modifications are to be pursued.

Chambers limits herself to pointing out that people are 'swayed by arguments' (170).[31] This, she points out, happens over time. People often re-evaluate their positions between conversations rather than during them. This gradual, fragmentary process of becoming 'convinced of something' is the product of a web of conversational interaction that includes many exchanges. This emphasis on a 'web of conversations' changes the way in which we think about consensus. Crucially, for Chambers, consensus is no longer conceived of as reached at this or that point, but is a product of many conversations. Thus, practical discourse should be understood as a *long-term consensus-forming process* and not as a *decision procedure*. The latter implies a set of rules that govern closure; as a decision rule, discourse stipulates that full, rational agreement under the ideal conditions of discourse of all affected by a norm constitutes the point of closure. The former is to do with the formation of opinion preceding the making of decisions. This means that 'consensual will formation' should not be understood as the outcome of *one* conversation but must be seen as the cumulative product of many criss-crossing conversations over time. As Chambers's argument shows, the move to actual argumentation entails a considerable weakening of the claims advanced by Habermas (even though Chambers does not focus on these consequences of her argument). In particular, I would claim that the shift from decision-procedures to a long-term consensus-forming process weakens the grip of the emphasis on the 'reaching of rational agreement under ideal conditions of discourse'. It is not only that we need more emphasis on the 'process of argumentation', but this very shift in emphasis also necessitates a re-valuation of the nature of argumentation, its role in democratic politics, and deliberation and its presuppositions.

Several commentators have developed arguments concerning 'political argumentation' and the question of 'deliberation'. Elster (1989) has introduced bargaining as an alternative mode of decision-making to deliberation.[32] Sanders (1997: 369–73) has focused on testimony as an alternative to deliberation in order to overcome the problems associated with 'voice' and epistemic authority she locates in the deliberative model. It is also interesting in this respect to note that she explicitly associates this move with the search for a model of democratic engagement that 'allows for the expression of different perspectives rather than seeking what's common' (371). The pursuit of commonality itself is thus problematized. Others have developed more general positions concerning the role of argumentation in, for instance, policy processes,[33] as well as analysis of styles of argumentation.[34] What these writers have in common is their concern with developing finely grained arguments concerning kinds of argumentation, all of which could be taken to widen the idea of 'deliberation' conceived in the narrow Habermasian sense. As I argued earlier, these conceptual refinements are, more often than not, simply treated as 'additions' to deliberation. Like Elster, Sanders and Chambers fail to explore the consequences of their insights for the very idea of deliberation. They singularly neglect to inquire, for instance, whether any revision in its status as norm is needed, whether a wider conception of argumentation also necessitates re-engagement with the relation between persuasion and deliberation, and between agreement and deliberation. It is to an alternative model of democracy that one needs to turn in order to find a thematization of these and related issues.

V. Post-structuralist conceptions of radical democracy: the place of disagreement

The principal ideas of radical democracy may be related back, on the one hand, to the liberalization of radical tradition (while holding onto the latter's insights into the inequalities of power) and, on the other hand, to the democratization of the liberal tradition.[35] Contemporary radical democrats reject both the instrumental character of liberalism and the anti-political reductionism of much of the Marxist and socialist traditions. They also share three core ideas. They concern, first, the centrality given to the political; second, an emphasis on the construction and articulation, rather than mere aggregation, of interests and identities; and third, the attention given to the process of subject formation in general, and the constitution of democratic identities in particular. However, beyond these broad statements, differences amongst radical democrats inspired by critical theory and post-structuralist thought respectively start to emerge. There are three key areas in which radical democratic theorists differ quite markedly from one another. The first concerns the goal of democratic activity. As argued above, for deliberative theorists the goal of democratic activity is the reaching of a rational consensus. This stands in sharp contrast to radical democrats in the post-structuralist tradition, who are concerned with the disruptive and dislocatory potential of democracy. Secondly, while deliberative conceptions of democracy proceed from a model of unconstrained dialogue, devoid of power and of 'distortions', post-structuralists argue that power relations are intrinsic to their account of democracy. Finally, in contrast to the Habermasian project, post-structuralists make no attempt to specify normative preconditions and foundations for democratic discourse. Whereas deliberative democratic politics, in its strong procedural form as defended by Habermas, immunizes politics against the forces of cultural and ethical life (Benhabib 1996: 9), theorists of agonistic and antagonistic politics view democracy as the incessant contestation over such ethical and cultural questions.

What then, more specifically, do post-structuralist accounts of radical democracy have to offer us? Most centrally, it brings into consideration relations of power, hegemony, argumentation, and an emphasis on disagreement[36] rather than consensus as central to an understanding of democratic processes. Here I will concentrate, first, on the status of disagreement in post-structuralist democratic theory. In the forthcoming sections, I return to how this relates to hegemony and argumentation, as articulated in Laclau's writings, before proceeding to show how this approach may fruitfully be articulated to some of the arguments developed earlier in this article.

The centrality given to disagreement in the post-structuralist theorization of democracy arises directly from one of its basic ontological presuppositions, namely, the 'impossibility of closure' of any identity or structure. This is important, for it affects the status of disagreement in the model, making it not simply an empirical feature of political life, but something arising from a constitutive characteristic of modern society. This *ontological* claim finds different forms of expression in different theorists.[37] For instance, for Lefort the formation of the modern state is marked by a forgetting of the primary division upon which it is instituted. While society can relate to itself only on the condition that it forges a representation of its unity, these representations are secondary accretions, covering over the fundamental breach between 'being' and 'discourse' (Lefort 1986: 196). The moment of the institution of a social order is thus always already that of a particular imaginary regime. Lefort argues that it is here that we find one of Marx's main contributions to our understanding of modern society, for Marx glimpses the illusion which lies at its heart, namely, the idea that the institution of the social can account for itself. But this illusion, Lefort argues, is always subject to failure. Ideology cannot operate 'without disclosing itself, that is, without revealing itself as a discourse, without letting a gap appear between this discourse and that about which it speaks, and hence it entails a development which reflects the impossibility of effacing its traces' (1986: 204). In modern democratic societies, this primary division is not simply effaced, but is marked in a specific manner. Lefort holds that democracy

> is instituted and sustained by the *dissolution of the markers of certainty*. It inaugurates a history in which people experience a fundamental indeterminacy as to the basis of power, law and knowledge, and as to the basis of relations between *self* and *other*, at every level of social life (1988: 19).

Whilst the work of ideology is to cover over this dissolution and to attempt to re-establish certainty, it ultimately is doomed to failure given the constitutive character of social division. Nevertheless, in the case of a democratic regime, the dissolution of the 'markers of certainty' opens a privileged place for the role of dissent, disagreement, antagonism, difference, and all those figures which, in the deliberative model, are indicators of a less than perfect consensus. Other radical democrats of a post-structuralist persuasion share these insights. Jacques Rancière articulates an argument not dissimilar to that of Lefort. For Rancière, anti-democratic politics also entails depoliticization, the demand that 'things should go back to normal' (Žižek 1999: 188).[38] Chantal Mouffe, inspired by Carl Schmitt, similarly argues that the denial of the 'irreducible antagonistic element present in social relations' can have disastrous consequences for the defense of democratic institutions for to negate the political will not make it disappear. It can only lead 'to bewilderment in the face of its manifestations and to impotence in dealing with them' (Mouffe 1993: 140). For all of these thinkers, indeed, disagreement, conflict, and dissensus take their central role from the fact that they arise, and are reflective of, a deeper ontological condition, a condition that is of crucial importance in the formation of democratic regimes.[39]

However, it is of crucial importance to note that, contrary to the manner in which it is often portrayed by deliberative theorists, there is nothing irrational or subjectivist in this emphasis on disagreement. To the contrary, disagreement forms the core of the logic of the political. As with the concept of disagreement itself, 'the political' is characterized variously by different post-structuralist political theorists. As already noted, Mouffe (1993: 2) takes her lead from Schmitt in this respect, arguing that he makes us 'aware of the dimension of the political that is linked to the existence of an element of hostility among human beings'. Politics then becomes an activity aimed at working through the effects of the political in social life, and democratic politics requires an introduction of a distinction between the figure of the enemy and that of the adversary (1993: 4). It is clear that neither in the more general case, nor in the specific case of democratic politics, is disagreement something that escapes a political logic. This is even more clearly articulated in the work of Rancière, for whom politics 'occurs when the egalitarian contingency disrupts to nature pecking order', and when this disruption produces a specific mechanism, namely, 'the dividing of society into parts that are not "true" parts; the setting-up of one part as equal to the whole in the name of a "property" that is not its own, and of a "common" that is the community of a dispute' (Rancière 1999: 18). The disagreement at the heart of the political logic is not one linked to the heterogeneity of language games, as it is for Lyotard. Nor is it a case of participants engaging in an intersubjective relation 'in order to oppose each other's interests and value systems and to put the validity of these to the test' (1999: 44) as for Habermas. Rather, what is at stake is the problem of

> knowing whether the subjects who count in the interlocution 'are' or 'are not', whether they are speaking or just making a noise. It is knowing whether there is a case for seeing the object they designate as the visible object of the conflict. It is knowing whether the common language in which they are exposing the wrong is indeed a common language.
>
> (Rancière 1999: 50)

One cannot therefore, presuppose a mutual understanding as Habermas does. Indeed, *the very possibility of commonality* is what is in dispute in political argumentation and disagreement, and what gets constituted though such argumentation. Rancière argues, for instance, that the utterance 'we proletarians' appeals to a community which is not already realized, and which does not already exist:

> a subject of enunciation creates an apparatus where a subject is named precisely to expose a particular wrong, to create a community around a particular dispute. That is to say, there is politics precisely when one reveals as false the evidence that the community exists already and everyone is already included.
>
> (Rancière 1994: 174)

The disagreement at the heart of the political logic is thus not simply an empirical feature that can be overcome in favour of consensus. It is, indeed, constitutive of that logic, and a marker of its presence in democratic regimes. Drawing on Rancière I would argue that the argument on epistemic authority outlined by Sanders in her critique of the tension between deliberation and democracy cannot be limited to a simple empirical feature of the democratic process. Gaining such authority is not simply a matter of adjusting or rectifying the relation between partners in deliberative discussion, for this model already presumes equality between participants. As Rancière's argument shows, this is precisely what is at stake, what has to be constructed, and what cannot be presupposed. The response by defenders of deliberative democracy, namely, that it simply has to be made 'more inclusive' and that there is no in principle problem with the manner in which it conceives of democracy, is thus decisively problematized.

From this point of view, attempts finally to overcome disagreement are thus based on a misconception of the nature of the political in general, and democratic politics more specifically. This does not, however, mean that disagreement is simply 'given'. As Mouffe has argued, that it is constitutive does not mean that it should not be subject to negotiation. Radical democratic politics precisely aims to encircle and engage with it, without attempting ever completely to supersede it. *How* this is done could be accounted for by means of a hegemonic approach to politics, an approach which precisely aims at (re)creating commonalties and communities of dispute.

VI. A hegemonic account of universalization and the possibility of democracy

A viable account of the construction of generalizable interests must, amongst other things, avoid the extreme particularism and the subjectivism of which so-called 'post-modern' accounts of politics and social life stand accused. One such version can be found in the works of Laclau and Mouffe on radical democracy.[40] Their conceptualization of radical democracy emanates from a post-Gramscian understanding of hegemony. Following Lefort, Laclau and Mouffe argue that a democratic order is one in which the locus of power becomes an empty place, a place that cannot be occupied. No 'individual and no group can be consubstantial with it' (Lefort 1988: 17; see also *HSS* 152–9). The break introduced by the democratic invention is one in which democratic society could be 'determined as a society whose institutional structures includes, as part of its "normal", "regular" reproduction, the moment of dissolution of the socio-symbolic bond'. As Žižek points out, for Lefort, at the moment of elections, 'the whole hierarchical network of social relations is in a way suspended, put in parentheses; "society" as an organic unity ceases to exist' (Žižek 1989: 147–8). It is this suspension that brings to center stage the struggles to occupy the place of power, and so foregrounds a non-foundationalist conception of hegemony.

Their understanding of radical democracy is reached via an elaboration and critique of the concept of hegemony in Marxist theory. Contrary to the dominant understanding in political science of hegemony as domination, Laclau and Mouffe follow Gramsci in his argument that hegemony involves ethical, moral, and political leadership. However, while for Gramsci such leadership ultimately has a class core, Laclau and Mouffe untie the concept of hegemony from its class basis in Marxist theory, and hegemony becomes a form of social relation in which the unity of a political force is constituted through a process of articulation of elements with no necessary class belonging. This unmooring facilitates a two-fold shift in focus. First, it allows the emphasis to shift towards a concern with the construction and deconstruction of political identities and interests in general and, secondly, it opens up a whole realm of theorization of social and political relations based on their contingent articulation. Similar to Rancière's argument outlined above, Laclau and Mouffe thus hold that both interests and identities result from contingent, historical processes of enunciation and articulation.

It is precisely these emphases that have led commentators to argue that an approach that apparently denies the possibility of universalism and necessity cannot but be 'subjectivist' and relativist. However, Laclau and Mouffe have persistently avoided the endorsement of subjectivism, relativism, and particularism. Drawing on deconstructive insights, they argue that, far from such endorsement, making visible the contingency of social relations through a questioning of the logics of necessity dominant in the Marxist tradition leads to a rethinking of both those logics. While their deconstructive account of the Marxist tradition cannot be reconstructed here, it is worthwhile noting that the relation between necessity and contingency is recast as a relation of frontiers. In other words, they are understood as standing in a relation of tension to one another, under conditions in which neither can fully obtain.

This deconstructive logic is also deployed in Laclau's account of the relation between universalism and particularism (*E* 20–35). Instead of viewing universalism and particularism as opposed and mutually exclusive logics, Laclau endeavors to show their imbrication and fundamental interconnectedness.[41] Neither a pure logic of universality nor one of self-enclosed particularity is a possibility here. The latter is ruled out since any appeal to particularity must, of necessity, always already pass through the universal. As Laclau puts it: 'The universal emerges out of the particular not as some principle underlying and explaining the particular, but as an incomplete horizon suturing the dislocated particular identity' (*E* 28). In contrast to conceiving of the relation between the two in terms of incarnation or in terms of a secularized eschatology, an alternative appears, namely, to think of the universal as a symbol of missing fullness, while the particular emerges as the always failed attempt to embody that universal.

This argument provides the link to their non-foundationalist conception of hegemony and democracy. A hegemonic politics is nothing other than a politics of struggle over the occupation of the position of the universal. And, if democracy is possible, Laclau argues, it is because 'the universal has no necessary body and no necessary content; different groups, instead, compete between themselves to temporarily give to their particularisms a function of universal representation' (*E* 35). Moreover, this struggle, as we have seen, is a never-ending one since the place of power cannot be finally occupied. As a consequence, society generates a whole vocabulary of 'empty signifiers' whose function it is to attempt to fill this place temporarily.

To return to our earlier discussion of 'generalizable interests', from the viewpoint of a non-foundationalist hegemonic politics, the very idea of generalizable interests would have to be recast in terms of a hegemonization of particular demands and the construction of empty signifiers. That is to say, particular demands, or identities, may become universalized in and through a process of contingent articulation and political struggle. The universality achieved under these circumstances is not 'merely' that reflecting the status quo or existing power relations. While the dimension of power can never be eliminated, and to seek to do so is to seek to live in a fully transparent society, the universalization of demands arising from a struggle for hegemony must transcend the specific demands and interests of a particular group. This conception of universalization also does not lack a set of standards against which political practices may be evaluated. Whilst these standards are generated by drawing upon and developing the Gramscian conception of hegemony, they must, nevertheless, retain an intra-societal character. In other words, they cannot be specified, as in the case of the conditions of ideal speech, outside any context, even though they are not limited to that context either. To see exactly how this is possible, it is necessary to return to the conceptualization of a Gramscian conception of hegemony.

As noted earlier, hegemony denotes a type of political relation as well as a substantive achievement. In the former case, one is concerned with a type of articulatory relation where persuasion predominates over the use of force. In the latter case, one is concerned with whether or not a particular force has managed to achieve supremacy by imposing its will onto the rest of society through the creation of consent and the incorporation of interests of rival forces.[42] In this respect, it is useful to recall Gramsci's important distinction between economic-corporate struggles, or 'bastard' forms of hegemony, and hegemony proper. In his early works, Gramsci argues that the working class can only become hegemonic if it takes into account the interests of other social classes and finds ways of combining them with its own interests. It therefore has to go beyond economic-corporate struggles in order to become a national force (Mouffe 1979: 180). It is in and through this process of going beyond the specific interests animating a particular group's interventions in the political arena that the universalization of particularistic demands takes place. Without such universalization, we would not have hegemony, but a mere imposition of those demands on subordinate groups. The very process of constructing hegemony thus has a two-fold character. On the one hand, demands are always specific, even particularistic, in that they arise from the experiences and conditions of particular and limited groups. On the other hand, for those demands to become universalized, to function as a horizon in which more generalized demands may become inscribed, they need to be marked by something transcending their particularity.[43] Thus, there is both a contextual and a context-transcending dimension in the process of the hegemonization of a field of demands.

With this we have an account of the construction of interests and identities that fulfil some of the core requirements specified earlier, which are necessary to a theory of generalizable interests. That is, this theorization, with its emphasis on hegemonic universalization, offers an escape from the alleged particularism and subjectivism of post-modern narratives on identities and interests. Moreover, it does not shun the demand for context-transcending criteria of valuation. However, it does avoid positing a model of valuation in such a manner as to construct an unbridgeable gap between the ideal and the real. The theorization of the mutual contamination between universality and particularity, between context-transcending and contextual dimensions of interests and identities undermine the strict separation between these poles without collapsing them into one another.

It is for this reason that, I would argue, a hegemonic account is most suitable to account for the ongoing processes through which Chambers argues convergence and agreement may be achieved, provided that agreement is not here understood as achievable in any final sense. Moreover, there is a clear correspondence between what Habermas characterizes as 'compromise formations' and the sorts of commonalties which may result from hegemonic universalization. However, from the perspective of the latter it has to be emphasized that such commonalties or 'compromise formations' are not second best alternatives and they do not, as for Habermas, leave the identities and interests of participants unchanged. Rather, since they acknowledge and shun the problematic emphasis on rational consensus in a context devoid of political struggle, they also manage to avoid the anti-democratic depoliticizing effects entailed by the deliberative model insofar as it fully accepts the Habermasian strictures.

What is still needed, however, is a more elaborated conceptualization of the relation between hegemonic universalization and democracy. Whereas the Habermas-inspired model ultimately does not succeed in bridging the gap it posits between the ideal and the real, it does provide us with a theorization of generalizable interests which entails democratic agreement as a core feature. From the point of view of a hegemonic account of universalization, democratic agreement can never be entailed by such universalization. There can be no positing of an internal relation between universalization and democratic agreement, however attractive that path may look at the outset. I explore this apparent 'democratic deficit' next.

In his *New Reflections on the Revolution of Our Time* Laclau deepens the discussion of hegemony in a direction that may be useful in addressing the question of the democratic deficit outlined above. This consists of a three-fold radicalization of the model of hegemonic relations discussed above. Each of these levels of radicalization also implies a different articulation of the necessity–contingency relationship (*NR* 27–31). In the first instance, hegemony is understood as the process of fixing the meaning of a floating signifier (such as democracy) around a particular nodal point. Here the field of the social is understood as a war of position in which different political projects strive to 'articulate a greater number of social signifiers around them'. However, contingency only penetrates this conception of hegemony to a limited degree, for while the 'elements' of a discourse may be open to articulation as a result of the empirical inability of one particular force to prevail, the discourse or political project itself is still conceived of as transparent. In the second instance, the political projects themselves are understood as penetrated by contingency. However, as with the former case, contingency is limited since the transparency of the context or structure in which these projects operate is not put into question simultaneously. It is only with the third level of radicalization that the non-closure of the structure is thought, not simply as an empirical result of political struggles, but as 'something which "works" within the structure from the beginning'. In other words, the possibility of final closure obtaining is ruled out in principle, rather than as a result of empirical limitations of actors or projects. In this case both the possibilities for political struggle and hegemonization of demands and the identities of subjects will be penetrated by contingency in the sense that neither would be determined by the structure. The different degrees to which contingency is regarded as penetrating political projects, demands, and identities should now be related to the question of democracy and democratic agreements.

Whilst Habermas's work on the possibility of democratic agreement is informed by the thesis of a movement towards post-conventional morality, there is nothing in Laclau's analysis that allows for what amounts to a teleological logic. For Laclau, the dislocations characteristic of late capitalism are conceived of as resulting in 'an open structure in which the crisis can be resolved in the most varied of directions' (*NR* 50). As a result, any hegemonic rearticulation of the structure will always be eminently political in character. Democracy, whether liberal or radical, cannot be assumed to resolve this crisis in the direction of its own development. This account is thus both more 'pessimistic' than that offered by Habermas, in that it does not presume or entail development occuring in a particular direction, and more 'optimistic' in that it opens up the possibility of a more radical constructionist approach to democracy. Laclau and Mouffe, nevertheless, do not develop their insights into the institution and formation of democratic processes any further. Whilst giving some attention to the specificity of democratic subjectivity, the hegemonic account of politics stands in need of deepening its theorization of the nature of decisions and argumentation in a democratic context. The emphasis on hegemony and contingency, nevertheless, is a crucial starting-point and precondition for the further reflection that is necessary in this respect. It is here that post-structuralist conceptions of democracy may benefit from drawing upon a weakened model of deliberative democracy.

VII. Democratic argumentation rethought

A rethought conception of democracy that will do justice to certain of the central insights of both deliberative and post-structuralist conceptions of democracy will have to give renewed attention to, first, argumentation and persuasion in contradistinction to deliberation; second, the relation between agreement and disagreement in the reaching of democratic decisions; and third, to how both of these are related to underlying conceptions of democratic subjectivity. It is not possible here to flesh out the detailed analyses necessary to develop such a model. This article has had a more limited set of aims, namely to bring two traditions of thought on democratic agreement into critical conversation with one another, so as to open the space for further dialogue. In conclusion, I wish only to sketch out the possible contours of such a dialogue, organized around the themes informing the foregoing discussion, and starting from, as I suggested at the outset, a post-structuralist understanding of politics.

In relation to the issue of the respective emphases on agreement and disagreement in the conceptualization of democracy, I have argued that there is, first, an overemphasis on the reaching of rational consensus in the deliberative model, and second, a conceptual difficulty in reconciling such consensus with the need to introduce other modes of reaching decisions, for instance by means of compromises, into the picture. If the picture of rational consensus holding the deliberative model captive cannot account for a wide variety of features of actual democratic decision-making, as is acknowledged by Habermas, then the introduction of supplementary modes will have the consequence of putting into question that very picture. I have argued that the alternative picture, provided by post-structuralist accounts of democracy, better accounts for the actual processes of decision-making discussed by, for example, Chambers. In addition, it has the advantage of being able to accommodate an enlarged conception of deliberation. That is to say, deliberation, contrary to its strict determination in the Habermasian model, could be understood as a generalized mode of engagement, of which deliberation in the narrow sense, argumentation, bargaining, and so on, are specific embodiments. Such a generalized conception of deliberation would aim to accommodate also the rhetorical features of argumentation, so central to any account of the persuasiveness of the force of argumentation. It is thus not a matter or replacing deliberation understood in the narrow sense, or of merely adding a set of features to it. Rather, an alternative account will have to come to terms with the permeability of the boundaries between such deliberation and the force of rhetoric and persuasion in argumentation. Laclau, in his recent work (2001), has made crucial advances in this direction.

However, the post-structuralist account that I have set out still suffers from two main shortcomings. The first concerns the consequences of its ontological emphasis on disagreement as constitutive of social life in general, and of democracy in particular. The second concerns the lack of attention given to the need to institutionalize democratic arrangements. These two concerns are not unrelated. In fact, it is my contention that the second is a direct, but not necessary consequence of the first. The lack of attention given to the institution of democratic arrangements arises from a carrying over of the emphasis on disagreement from an ontological level to an ontic level. To say this is not to question the ontological status attributed to disagreement. There is today increasingly agreement on the importance of the need to take account of the insights for democracy provided by the post-structuralist emphasis on disagreement. This has taken the form of a far greater centrality given to the need to think the relation between democracy, difference and radical pluralism in deliberative thinking.[44] Having said this, the ontological emphasis has fostered an overemphasis on disagreement also on the ontic level. While post-structuralist theorists have excelled in critical, deconstructive readings aimed at the ontological assumptions of deliberative theory, they have not given enough attention to the need to develop a deconstructive account of the relation between agreement and disagreement at an ontic level. Instead, they have focused exclusively on activities of questioning, disruption and desedimentation in democratic practice. While these are no doubt central, democratic activity cannot be limited to them. As Connolly (1993: 208) has argued, democratic politics is a 'site of a tension or productive ambiguity between governance and disturbance of naturalized identities. It thrives only while this tension is kept alive'. Keeping this tension alive means overcoming the false dichotomy between consensus and contestation at the level of actual democratic practice. Only then will it be possible to construct a democratic theory that combines 'a critique of consent and consensus when they are absent *with a critical engagement of both* when they are present' (213). Since democracy contains the possibility of heightening the experience of contingency, the ethos of democracy is a disruptive and denaturalizing one.

However, and this is what needs to be emphasized and developed in an alternative account of democracy, democracy also acts as the medium in which general purposes become crystallized and enacted. It is only when democracy maintains the tension between these interdependent antinomies that it can function 'as the perfection of politics' (210). Finally, to do so would entail further attention to the actual practices of the institution and maintenance of democratic forms. It is in this respect that post-structuralist accounts of democratic politics can do no better than to turn to the picture of deliberation, and the preconditions for equality in engagement, contained in it. Since both deliberative and post-structuralist conceptions of democracy share the same roots in older models of radical democracy, they also share a concern with equality in all its dimensions that is necessary for effective democratic practice. However, as I have endeavored to show, the model for democratic practice cannot and ought not to be one in which the ideal and the real are divorced from one another. Combining a weakened conception of deliberation with the insights of a post-structuralist conception of democracy which retains an emphasis on universalization can go some way towards meeting these demands.

Acknowledgements

The author is grateful to the Leverhulme Trust for funding the research upon which this chpater is based. She would also like to thank the members of the Essex University Interdisciplinary Political Theory discussion group, as well as of the Ideology and Discourse Analysis Doctoral Programme for their comments on this paper. In particular, she is grateful for the comments by David Howarth, Ernesto Laclau, Sheldon Leader, Yannis Stavrakakis, and Albert Weale, as well as Alejandro Bonvecchi, Alejandro Groppo, Juan-Pablo Lichtmajer, and Lasse Thomassen.

Notes

1 I will not here focus on a third prominent approach, namely, a social choice approach to decision-making. See Miller 1993.
2 Benhabib (1996: 9) has recently noted that this is the theoretical task that is at hand for democratic theorists.
3 See, for instance, Lukes 1982: 134–48; Walzer 1989: 182–96.
4 See Habermas 1982, 1996; Chambers (1996).
5 There is no singular model of deliberative democracy. Recent works have drawn, for instance, both on Habermas and on Rawls. I concentrate on those works taking their inspiration from the former rather than from the latter.
6 See, for instance, the various contributions in Renn *et al.* 1995 as well as Dryzek 1995.
7 It is important to note that commentators differ widely on the role of the ideal speech situation and its relation to democratic practice. Walzer, for instance, points out that while it may be worthwhile to strive for more open debate and a more egalitarian politics, the reasons for doing so *precede* ideal speech rather than emerge from it. Thus, the picture of ideal speech cannot serve as a test of the processes through which these ideas are generated (see Walzer 1989: 194). In contrast to this, Chambers (1996: 9) argues that these idealizations must be presupposed 'in order to criticize the distorting effects of power and domination' .
8 She emphasizes 'approximation', for she holds that the idealizations of the speech situation cannot simply be 'realized' in the real world (Chambers 1996: 9). They need to be translated into practice. This process, I would argue, weaken them considerably.
9 Chambers argues in this respect that Habermas underestimates and downplays the dependence of his conception of discourse on an ethos of citizen participation.
10 This raises the question as to whether this model is simply too demanding. Chambers overcomes this problem by arguing that it is not if it is seen in terms of long-term discussion, rather than as a decision rule. Participation should not be seen as a good in itself (as for republicans) but as having some efficacy and power to shape politics.
11 Who decides whether consent is autonomous? Chambers argues that a theory of deliberative democracy cannot be combined with false consciousness, since it holds that generalizable interests do not exist prior to our entry into discourse. However, deliberative models of democracy assume 'a theory of mistaken consciousness'. That is, people can come to see that they were mistaken to believe such and such to be in their interest (1996: 205). This cannot

be determined from an observer's point of view. Participants themselves must question their motives, look at the genealogy of their beliefs, and ask what interests their arguments serve. Chambers does not address the conditions under which such self-reflexive questioning becomes a possibility. In the final section of this article I will argue that it is only once disagreement, rather than agreement, becomes an essential part of a democratic ethos that such questioning becomes a realistic possibility.

12 External coercion includes threats and bribes, while internal coercion involves psychological pressure, rhetorical manipulation, and deception. Both conceptions of coercion stand in need of further discussion, especially with respect to the conception of subjectivity they presuppose.

13 For a discussion of an agonistic model of politics, see Connolly 1991. For a somewhat broader interpretation of agonistic politics, see Benhabib 1996: 7–9.

14 Such a common ground, Chambers argues, may range from 'agreement on substantive generalizable interests' to an agreement to disagree, or an agreement to settle for a compromise. She holds that 'even in cases where there is no common ground, especially in such cases, we should keep our disputes within the bounds of fair communication. If we do not try to persuade and reason with each other, then we are left with the option of forcing or coercing each other.' (1996: 162–3). This, Wittgenstein would argue, is just playing with words. From the foregoing, it does not seem as if 'common ground' has any limits; thus it has no purchasing power either.

15 Fraser argues that Habermas needs to take account of the economic requirements of deliberative democracy. See Fraser 1992. See also Scheuerman's (1999) discussion of her relation to Habermas.

16 This is a common strategy followed by adherents to Habermas's theory of communicative rationality.

17 Where does an interest in agreement come from? Chambers argues that motivation is here tied to the importance of the norm to the participants and the actions they want to continue. 'If we wish to continue, we must resolve dispute.' (1996: 191) This means that agreement is presupposed by the whole approach. If so, an ambiguity is immediately introduced for agreement becomes both what is presupposed and what is to be sought through the process of deliberation.

18 Habermas, quoted in Chambers 1996: 157. Emphasis added.

19 For a discussion of Habermas' universalization principle, see White 1989: 48–58.

20 This procedure stands in contrast to the Kantian test of the categorical imperative, which can be tested monologically (that is, one can ask oneself if one can will a proposed norm to be a universal law). McCarthy (quoted Outhwaite 1994: 54) argues that the emphasis here shifts from 'what each can will without contradiction to be a universal law to what each can will in agreement to be a universal norm'.

21 It should be noted that Habermas in his 'Postscript' points out that these three aspects should be understood as analytically distinct, but should not be treated as a matter of linear development. See Habermas 1996: 565 n. 3.

22 Ferrara (1996: 127–9) points out that these three types of discourse provide different answers to the question 'What should *I* do?' and 'What should *we* do?'

23 For a discussion by Habermas of Elster on bargaining, see Habermas 1996: 165–7. See also Elster 1998: 5–7.

24 For a critical discussion and contextualization of the U and D principles in Habermas's work, see Ferrara 1996: 131–5.

25 See, for instance, Walzer 1994.

26 Supplementarity here is understood in the Derridean sense. See Derrida 1974, especially part II. For a discussion of supplementarity as infrastructure, see Gasché 1986: 205–12. It is important to note that the deconstruction of a conceptual ordering is thus not simply a matter of inverting the relationship of center and margin. Rather, as Harrison puts it,

> it is a matter of showing, rather, that the distinction between center and margin in question can only be made [...] via a covert dependence on its marginalised component.
>
> (Harrison 1999: 514)

27 Both Habermas and Elster are guilty of this move, and so are countless other commentators. They both assume that the 'original' model of deliberation can be left intact, while 'bargaining', 'argumentation', and so on are 'added' onto the idea of a pure deliberation.

28 It is clear that the ideal speech situation represents only the formal conditions of discourse:

> The philosopher reconstructs the conditions that would have to hold if we wanted to say that an agreement was reasonable and authentic. [...] As a formal representation, the ideal speech situation is drastically limited. It can tell us what would have to be the case for a political norm to be considered collectively binding, but it cannot, by itself, tell us which norms would or would not pass the test. [...] By itself [it] has no content.
> (Chambers 1996: 166)

29 We cannot 'make a living, write a book, teach a class, or run a business discursively'. The ideal speech situation provides guidelines, not for all social interaction, but for the process of deliberation (Chambers 1996: 156).

30 There are numerous issues here in need of further discussion. In particular, we need to look at the concept of pluralism deployed by Chambers and Habermas, both of whom work with a rather weak view of the 'fact of pluralism'. Exactly how weak this is is reflected in what Habermas regards as examples of disagreement, such as traffic rules and basic institutional rules. Habermas holds that there are enough examples to suggest that 'increasing scope for individual options does not decrease the chances for agreement concerning presumptively common interests' (quoted in Chambers 1996: 159). The 'in principle/in practice' dichotomy, the evolutionary view of society underlying the move from 'traditional' to 'post-conventional' societies, and the absence of an account of the subject of 'consensual will formation' all stand in need of further investigation.

31 This is another example of an unexplored possibility. What, precisely, is meant by 'being swayed by arguments'? The same question could be asked of Habermas's failure to engage with the complexities entailed in the idea of being 'persuaded' by the 'force' of the better argument.

32 Several of the contributions to this volume take this further, and develop further conceptual distinction as, for instance, between deliberation and discussion.

33 See, for instance, Majone 1989.

34 See Hacking 1985: Ch. 9.

35 I have discussed this further in Norval 2001.

36 I use the term 'disagreement' here to indicate a plethora of phenomena – including dissensus, conflict, antagonism – conceptualized in very different ways within the post-structuralist tradition.

37 For Laclau (*HSS*) it consists in the thesis of the 'impossibility of society'; for Žižek (1989) in the thesis of the lack in the subject; for Lefort (1986), in the non-closure of the gap between being and discourse, and for Mouffe in the centrality of the political understood in the Schmittian sense.

38 The specific manner in which Rancière accounts for this depoliticization is of special importance, for it directly addresses the question of the speaking subject, and the relation between participants in the process of democratic argumentation.

39 It is important to note that not all radical democrats inspired by post-structuralism conceptualize the relation between this ontological condition and democracy in the same fashion. For Rancière, for instance, there is a direct relation between democracy and the ontological conditions that make disagreement central. For Laclau, on the other hand, dislocation may be one of the conditions making possible the emergence of a democratic regime, but it is not internally related to it.

40 See, for instance, *HSS*, ch. 4; and Mouffe 1992.

41 A similar argument is also present in Balibar's writings on universalism (1995).

42 For an in-depth discussion of the concept of hegemony in Laclau and Mouffe's work, see Howarth 1996.

43 Laclau introduces the terms 'myth' and 'imaginary' to characterize these different processes. For a discussion of the relation between these terms, and a Gramscian conception of hegemony, see Norval 2000.

44 This is reflected in the increasing attention given to questions of radical pluralism and difference within the deliberative tradition. See, in this respect, Benhabib 1996.

References

Balibar, E. (1995) 'Ambiguous universality', *differences: A Journal of Feminist Cultural Studies*, 7(1): 48–74.

Benhabib, S. (1996) 'The democratic moment and the problem of difference', in S. Benhabib (ed.) *Democracy and Difference: Contesting the Boundaries of the Political*, Princeton, NJ: Princeton University Press.

—— (1998) 'Liberal dialogue versus a critical theory of discursive legitimation', in N. L. Rosenblum (ed.) *Liberalism and the Moral Life*, Cambridge, MA: Harvard University Press.

Bohman, J. (1996) 'Critical theory and democracy', in D. M. Rasmussen (ed.) *Handbook of Critical Theory*, Oxford: Blackwell.

Chambers, S. (1996) *Reasonable Democracy: Jürgen Habermas and the Politics of Discourse*, London: Cornell University Press.

Connolly, W. E. (1991) *Identity\Difference: Democratic Negotiations of Political Paradox*, Ithaca, NY: Cornell University Press.

—— (1993) 'Democracy and contingency', in J. H. Carens (ed.) *Democracy and Possessive Individualism: The Intellectual Legacy of C. B. Macpherson*, Albany: State University of New York Press.

Derrida, J. (1974) *Of Grammatology*, Baltimore: Johns Hopkins University Press.

Dryzek, J. S. (1995) 'Political and ecological communication', *Environmental Politics*, 4: 10–30.

Elster, J. (1998) 'Introduction', in J. Elster (ed.) *Deliberative Democracy*, Cambridge: Cambridge University Press.

Ferrara, A. (1996) 'The communicative paradigm in moral theory', in D. M. Rasmussen (ed.) *Handbook of Critical Theory*, Oxford: Blackwell.

Fraser, N. (1992) 'Rethinking the public sphere: A contribution to a critique of actually existing democracy', in C. Calhoun (ed.) *Habermas and the Public Sphere*, Cambridge MA, MIT Press.

Gasché, R. (1986) *The Tain of the Mirror: Derrida and the Philosophy of Reflection*, Cambridge, MA: Harvard University Press.

Habermas, J. (1982) 'A reply to my critics', in J. B. Thompson and D. Held (eds) *Habermas: Critical Debates*, Cambridge, MA: MIT Press.

—— (1996) *Between Facts and Norms: Contributions to a Discourse Theory of Law and Democracy*, Cambridge: Polity Press.

Hacking, I. (1985) 'Styles of scientific reasoning', in J. Rachjman and C. West (eds) *Post-Analytic Philosophy*, New York: Columbia University Press.

Harrison, A. (1999) 'White mythology revisited: Derrida and his critics on reason and rhetoric', *Critical Inquiry*, 25(3): 505–34.

Howarth, D. (1996) 'Ideology, hegemony and political subjectivity', in I. Hampsher-Monk and J. Stanyer (eds) *Contemporary Political Studies*, vol. 2, Glasgow: PSA UK.

Laclau, E. (2001) 'The politics of rhetoric', in T. Cohen, J. H. Miller, A. Warminski and B. Cohen (eds) *Material Events: Paul de Man and the Afterlife of Theory*, Minneapolis: Minnesota University Press.

Lefort, C. (1986) *The Political Forms of Modern Society*, Oxford: Polity Press.

—— (1988) *Democracy and Political Theory*, Minneapolis: University of Minnesota Press.

Lukes, S. (1982) 'Of gods and demons: Habermas and practical reason', in J. B. Thompson and D. Held (eds) *Habermas: Critical Debates*, Cambridge, MA: MIT Press.

Majone, G. (1989) *Evidence, Argument, and Persuasion in the Policy Process*, New Haven: Yale University Press.

Miller, D. (1993) 'Deliberative democracy and social choice', in D. Held (ed.) *Prospects for Democracy. North, South, East, West*, Cambridge: Polity Press.

—— (1999) 'Is deliberative democracy unfair to disadvantaged minorities', paper presented at the Manchester Centre for Political Thought Conference 'New Directions in Democratic Theory', 19 March.

Mouffe, C. (1979) 'Hegemony and ideology in Gramsci', in C. Mouffe (ed.) *Gramsci and Marxist Theory*, London: Routledge & Kegan Paul.

—— (ed.) (1992) *Dimensions of Radical Democracy*, London: Verso.

—— (1993) *The Return of the Political*, London: Verso.

Norval, A. J. (2000) 'Future trajectories of research in discourse theory: Political frontiers, myths and imaginaries, hegemony', in D. Howarth, A. J. Norval and Y. Stavrakakis (eds) *Discourse Theory and Political Analysis*, Manchester: Manchester University Press.

—— (2001) 'Radical democracy', in J. Foweraker and B. Clarke (eds) *Dictionary of Denmocratic Thought*, London: Routledge.

Outhwaite, W. (1994) *Habermas: A Critical Introduction*, Cambridge, Polity Press.

Rancière, J. (1994) 'Post-democracy, politics and philosophy', interview with J. Šumič and R. Riha, *Angelaki*, 1(3): 171–8.

—— (1999) *Disagreement: Politics and Philosophy*, Minneapolis: University of Minnesota Press.

Rehg, W. (1996) 'Translator's introduction', in J. Habermas, *Between Facts and Norms: Contributions to a Discourse Theory of Law and Democracy*, Cambridge: Polity Press.

Renn, O., Webler. T. and Wiedemann, P. (eds) (1995) *Fairness and Competence in Citizen Participation: Evaluating Models for Environmental Discourse*, Dordrecht: Kluwer Academic Publishers.

Sanders, L. M. (1997) 'Against deliberation', *Political Theory*, 25(3): 347–76.

Scheuerman, W. E. (1999) 'Between radicalism and resignation: Democratic theory in Habermas in *Between Facts and Norms*', in P. Dews (ed.) *Habermas. A Critical Reader*, Oxford: Blackwell.

Tully, J. (1989) 'Wittgenstein and political philosophy: Understanding practices of critical reflection', *Political Theory*, 17(2): 172–204.

Walzer, M. (1989) 'A critique of philosophical conversation', *Philosophical Forum*, 21(1–2) (1989–90): 182–96.

—— (1994) *Thick and Thin: Moral Argument at Home and Abroad*, Notre Dame, IN: University of Notre Dame Press.

White, S. K. (1989) *The Recent Work of Jürgen Habermas: Reason, Justice and Modernity*, Cambridge: Cambridge University Press.

Wittgenstein, L. (1984) *Philosophical Investigations*, tr. G. E. M. Anscombe, Oxford: Basil Blackwell.

Young, I. M. (1997) 'Difference as resource for democratic communication', in J. Bohman and W. Rehg (eds) *Deliberative Democracy: Essays on Reason and Politics*, Cambridge, MA: MIT Press.

Žižek, S. (1989) *The Sublime Object of Ideology*, London: Verso.

—— (1999) *The Ticklish Subject*, London: Verso.

9

THE ETHOS OF DEMOCRATIZATION

William E. Connolly

> A different criticism, however, which could be legitimately be directed at my work is that in the passage from classical Marxism to 'hegemony' and from the latter to 'radical democracy', an enlargement of the area of normative argument should have followed – while in my work, this latter enlargement has not sufficiently advanced. [...] I think this is a valid criticism, and I intend to restore the correct balance between the two dimensions in the future.
>
> (Laclau 2000b: 295)

Ethics and democratic politics

I have long been inspired by the work of Ernesto Laclau, even as we express debts to different thinkers and develop our thinking in different vocabularies. Doubtless those latter differences betoken theoretical differences. But that possibility is not my primary concern in this essay. For I agree with Laclau that an important goal of democratic politics is to form 'chains of equivalence', or, as I call them, collective assemblages across differences. I also think that the way democratic intellectuals fashion such connections between themselves can exemplify and inform the more general connections they seek in everyday politics.

My primary concern here is to elaborate a conception of political ethics to see in what ways it makes positive contact with Laclau's thinking. So let me state at the outset some broad similarities in perspective. Both Laclau and I locate ourselves on the democratic left. Each tries to rethink pluralism under new historical conditions of being. Both think that the democratic alliances through which liberals and radicals seek to expand inclusion at any one moment are likely to contain within them unconscious or unarticulated exclusions that may create seeds of future suffering, surprise, conflict, and new calls for significant change. Both think that the 'constitutive outside' of thought and politics carries positive promise for the politics of democratization, as well as setting limits to it at any particular moment. We seek ways to reduce economic inequality by shaking and moving features of a capitalist political economy, thought by many to be immoveable in this respect; neither of us finds socialism as historically defined to provide the best container in which to place that quest. I seek to stretch the horizon of capitalism through a series of changes to make the state supported infrastructure of consumption much more inclusive in health care, education, housing, transportation and retirement, and to improve the conditions of work.[1] Success in these domains requires citizen action across states as well as within them; it could press heretofore existing capitalism to become something other than it has traditionally been. It would doubtless create new troubles too, not easily predictable now.

Finally, neither of us thinks that a ready-made political constituency exists to enact the politics we endorse. The working class does not form a stable unit uniformly predisposed in this direction, partly because of its internal economic stratification, partly because of its pluralization along lines of religion, ethnicity, employment security, age, gender and level of capital investment. The hegemonic assemblage we seek will be drawn from several subject positions in the domains of economic class, religion, age, education level, ethnicity, gender, and sensual affiliation. Whether such an assemblage becomes consolidated has a lot to do with the sensibility and ethos its participants bring to relations between themselves and with others.[2] It also has a lot to do with the extent to which the democratic left participates in a more general ethos of pluralism that includes and exceeds it. If we are not effective in supporting such an ethos the other objectives will suffer immensely.

The political assemblage I pursue, for instance, would incorporate some participants because it speaks to their desperate needs,;others because of more composed economic self-interest; others because of participation in identities supported by the assemblage in religion, ethnicity, sexuality, or gender; others because of religious or nontheistic ethical commitments that inspire them to extend beyond their own constituency needs, interests, and identities; others yet because they fear rises in the rate of crime and urban unrest that would otherwise undermine their quality of life, and most because of some combination of these concerns. The assemblage will be rhizomatic, then, linked through multiple lines of connection, rather than unified by a central political idea or ethical principle which all participants endorse together. Such an assemblage supports the expansion of plurality and the broadening of economic security as two parts of the same agenda.

These, I take it, express some of the lines of connection between Laclau and myself. We are linked through a series of connections across differences that track in microcosm the shape of a larger and more expansive assemblage yet to be consolidated. In this chapter I will explore the ethos of politics most congruent with construction of such an assemblage, leaving a host of other issues to the side. I do not say that the ethos in question guarantees political support for the goals Laclau and I share. Merely that it is worthy of close consideration by a variety of parties who think there is no single ethical source of participation in public life. My thinking, in fact, revolves around a fundamental tension that helps to constitute ethico-political life. Such a tension can be negotiated, but I am doubtful that it can be resolved. The tension is that between the partisan orientation to ethical life an individual or constituency adopts, and the larger ethos of politics they pursue with those embracing alternative sources. The most familiar proposal to contain this tension is, first, to define a general principle, contractual agreement, will of God, or encompassing conception of procedure, discourse, or deliberation that all reasonable people must accept and then to shuffle those aspects of ethical life that exceed that notion into the private sphere. A legion of secular political theorists participates in this project.

My sense, however, is that no single answer to the question of the source and shape of public ethics can be grounded as securely as its most fervent secular and theological defenders contend, partly because *every* particular orientation to ethics contains universal projections in it which infiltrate into the interpretations, inflections, and enactments pursued by its supporters. Neither civic republican nor secular responses to this tension speak adequately to it. So I seek a different way to negotiate the existential tension between a particular ethical orientation and a more general ethos. That involves me in a defense of the credibility of a partisan ethic shuffled to the sidelines today by many partisans of both secularism and civic republicanism. I call it an ethic of cultivation rather than one of command or contract. It touches the civic republican tradition in the way it thematizes the centrality of cultivation. But it is also an ethic that cultivates presumptive appreciation for a protean diversity of being, rather than attunement to an intrinsic purpose already said to be installed in being. In this respect it compromises the republican tradition.

The idea, of course, is not to universalize the ethic of cultivation I endorse, but to propel it onto the public register as one among a series of contestable orientations to public ethics worthy of legitimacy in public life. In the process of defending its legitimacy I also seek to show, through critical work, how the moral sources of public life which others honor are contestable too.[3] Once the contestability of each partisan orientation has been critically supported, the next move is to invite a variety of constituencies to come to terms affirmatively with the persistent element of partisanship in the ethical sources each of us honors. The aim is to fashion an ethos between interdependent constituencies who are unlikely either to leave their partisan faiths in the private realm when they enter politics or to establish it with enough certainty to convince many not already inducted into it. A positive ethos of politics does not grow out of an austere principle of justice or a single logic of deliberation. It grows out of reciprocal appreciation of the element of partisanship in each orientation to public ethics, alongside concerted efforts by numerous parties to overcome existential resentment of this very condition.

I contend, with Laclau perhaps, that this tension between a partisan ethical source and a general ethos has always been with us. Awareness of it becomes sharp during the periods when new drives to unexpected diversity unsettle and disturb the established pattern of diversity. Today is one of those times when that awareness is sharp. It is intensified today in part through the acceleration of the tempo of everyday life: such an acceleration compresses the experience of distance, accentuates interdependencies, and exposes more people on the ground to unfamiliar sources of moral sustenance, exceeding those receiving hegemony during the eras of Christendom, Kantianism, and secularism respectively.[4] The *particular ethical orientation* I embrace makes a strong case both for extending cultural pluralization and reducing economic inequality. The *general ethos* pursued supports a presumptive case for the first objective, but does not go far on its own toward securing the second. That link must be forged through supplemental mixtures of economic argument, political demands, and the cultivation of new sensibilities. The arguments speak to the radical insufficiency of the market to itself, to multiple rationales for a politics of inclusion, to the need for positive state action to protect vulnerable constituencies from the adverse effects of globalization, and so forth. While I have made such arguments elsewhere they will not be reviewed here. The sensibilities to be cultivated will become clear as we proceed.

The basic point to make now is that a general ethos speaking affirmatively to multiple ethical sources does not by itself generate a fixed set of political outcomes. If such connections are drawn too tightly nothing is left to politics itself, and no case could be made as to why losers as well as winners in the political struggle should honor this ethos. If interdependent partisans honoring different moral sources do not negotiate such a general ethos of engagement, however, the possibility of translating social antagonisms into an effective egalitarian democratic assemblage dissolves. This is simply another formulation of the basic tension, the tension between the ineliminability of ethical partisanship in politics and the indispensability of a general ethos of politics to construction of an inclusive democratic politics. The general goal is to support a distinctive ethos of politics, speaking to many people in different subject positions as to needs, interests, and ethical dispositions already touching them. The specific task is to build a broad partisan coalition to support the specific outcomes endorsed, and to do so in a way that expresses and bolsters the larger ethos. For the ethos is important in and of itself to the quality of political life.

The contestability of ethical sources

Let us begin with Kant, for two reasons. First, Kant in the eighteenth century helped to set in motion a series of contemporary, secular orientations to ethics. And, second, his orientation to public morality is openly tied to a specific metaphysical orientation he takes to be undeniable. Today, several advocates of secularism, post-metaphysical politics, non-foundationalism, contractualism, proceduralism and deliberative democracy seek to reoccupy the Kantian position without endorsing the metaphysical perspective in which it was set. I have argued elsewhere, with several others, that none has so far succeeded. Either they pull their position so far away from any particular metaphysical faith that they cannot convince those who do not already concur or they implicitly draw upon a Kantian metaphysic which has become profoundly contestable today. In each of these cases, *the proponents typically give too much primacy to the role of argument or public reason in establishing any ethico-political perspective*. They participate in a mode of intellectualism that underplays the role that affect, embodiment, and sensibility play in inflecting arguments and in the quality of the ethical life itself. Rationalism is only one form such an intellectualism assumes; another is that form of skepticism which presupposes that commitment is impossible unless it can be grounded epistemically.

But Kant himself acknowledged the limits of argument and intellectualism in ethical life. He insisted that argument is insufficient to the grounding of morality and to the quality of ethical life. Listen to Kant speak of practical reason which, unlike empirical understanding and theoretical reason, *is* pure:

> For whatever needs to draw the evidence of its reality from experience must depend for the ground of its possibility on principles of experience; by its very notion, however, *pure practical reason cannot be held to be dependent in this way*. Moreover, the moral law is given, *as an apodictically certain fact, as it were, of pure reason* [. . .] Thus the objective reality of the moral law can be proved through no deduction, through no exertion of the theoretical, speculative, or empirically supported reason; and even if one were willing to renounce its apodictic certainty, it could not be confirmed by any experience and thus proved a posteriori. Nevertheless, *it is firmly established of itself* (1993: 48).[5]

The fundamental character of morality is not established by argument or known by conceptual reasoning: it is recognized apodictically. Pure practical reason, unlike theoretical reason, expresses a dictate flowing from the supersensible realm without being able to theorize it: that morality essentially takes the form of *laws* we are obligated to obey.[6] This logic of recognition is consistent with Kant's thesis that we must project a supersensible realm without being able to know it conceptually. We, rather, *recognize something that flows from it*: again, that morality takes the form of laws we are obligated to obey.

All of Kant's characteristic strictures about the moral necessity to *postulate* a God, the positive political effect of *publicity*, the proper role of *philosophy* in the university, moral *enlightenment*, *universal history*, *perpetual peace*, and *the obligation to pursue cosmopolitanism* reflect the practical implications of this apodictic recognition that precedes, enables, and requires them. Their basis in Kant's work would collapse if the logic of recognition upon which they rest dissolved. For these ideas are not forms of knowledge but (variously) postulates, hopes, and dutiful projections that follow from the undeniable and immediate recognition of the proper form of morality. How strong, then, is the linchpin of Kantian morality? How fragile is apodictic recognition?

I respect Kant for his courage in asserting that no idea of morality cannot be anchored in argument alone. Indeed, I agree with him at this critical juncture, and dissent from his followers who forget the pivotal role of non-argumentative recognition in his very idea of morality. The point of recognition is at once the most crucial and the most vulnerable hinge of his moral philosophy. I join Epicurus, Lucretius, Spinoza, Nietzsche, James, Hampshire, Foucault, and Deleuze, however, in resisting Kant at precisely the point where apodictic recognition anchors the moral arguments he marshals. For, like them, I do not recognize morality to take the form of law in the first instance. And, like them, I deny that I am mad or demented in not doing so. Either something is fundamentally askew with all nine of us, or our dissent, grounded perhaps in a shared resistance to Christian metaphysics, already begins to *disclose* the shakiness of the ultimate, non-argumentative ground of Kantian morality. For if those who do not bestow recognition at this critical juncture are not governed by illusion they pose living counter-evidence to the universality of the recognition Kant projects. Indeed, every time Kant labels a philosopher deluded or worse because he does not respect the Kantian transition from recognition to argument, I treat that same refusal as evidence that Kant himself found it necessary to support the universal recognition he posits by other than apodictic means. Kant is indeed very hard on Epicurus, the gentle soul of pre-Christian Greek life, and Spinoza, the double heretic of early-modern Christendom who grounded ethical generosity and responsibility in *the first instance* in cultivation of joy in life rather than recognition of the lawlike character of morality.

Today many secular philosophers of ethics find themselves in a difficult situation. Either they must surpass Kant in constructing an argument sufficient to ground the public basis of the ethic they endorse or they must devise under unfavorable historical conditions something else to play the role that apodictic recognition plays in the Kantian system. It is not that such proposals have been lacking. The professional journals are littered with them. It is that so far none has commanded the assent of all democrats who otherwise show themselves to be capable of deliberation, argument, reflection, and ethical generosity.

To disclose how this delicate point of transition in Kantian morality is both shaky and contestable is to set in motion the pluralization of legitimate moral sources. It is also to enlarge the role that cultivation of sensibility might play in ethical life. Deconstruction and genealogy help to peel away the appearance of the sufficiency of argument to ethics and the apodicticity of a particular logic of recognition. Their success in these respects helps to explain why so many secular intellectuals seek to marginalize both practices academically and why they are also treated warily by some theologically oriented ethicists. But while these practices are indispensable to formation of a generous ethos of engagement neither is sufficient for the cultivation of the sensibilities needed.

I do not share the view of many secularists that you either can or should leave your fundamental religious, existential, or metaphysical sources of moral inspiration and guidance in the private sphere when you enter public life. I think, in fact, that the secular drive to privatize diverse religious orientations to ethics leads to a depreciation of the dense, layered character of thinking, ethical judgment, and public culture. It fosters a thin intellectualism of public life; an intellectualism that highlights one indispensable element of thinking, identity, and ethical judgment, but casts the others into the shade.

For me the key question of political ethics is not how to get people to be moral if and as they converge on a common moral source. Though that question, of course, is important on occasion. Nor is it how to get people to leave their particular identities and faiths in the private realm when they address public issues. That, too, can sometimes be important to the ethos of public life, as you leave this or that part of your religious or metaphysical baggage in the private realm because it is not relevant to the issue at hand. *But the most compelling ethical issues arise when interdependent partisans honor different sources of ethics and find themselves in situations where the public issues that need to be negotiated implicate those partisan sources*. The question, in such recurrent circumstances, becomes how to craft a generous ethos of engagement between constituencies who honor different sources and inevitably bring chunks of them with them into politics.

The question, as I define it, is difficult to negotiate. But there are important and relevant ways to speak to it. They involve cultural work on the visceral register of intrasubjectivity and intersubjectivity, as well as on the more refined intellectual registers of deliberation, discussion, and debate intimately bound up with the lower registers. One outcome to pursue is the consolidation of more self-modest and generous sensibilities, sensibilities that enable partisans to acknowledge reciprocally and without deep existential resentment the contestability of the faiths that inspire each the most. Such a reciprocal acknowledgment, again when not overwhelmed by resentment against this very condition, softens the edges of antagonisms in the most sensitive domains of faith and identity; it promotes the political possibility of translating them into agonistic differences to be negotiated. The nontheistic, partisan source I embrace is not, certainly, established so confidently that all reasonable people not contaminated by deep prejudice or perversity must recognize, acknowledge, or accept it. Nor is any other confessional, contractual, deliberative, dialogical, or meditative source I have encountered to date.

Here is where political and ethical philosophy becomes very important, but not to consolidate a general ethical scepticism in a world where partisan sources abound and accentuate their mutual contestability. For such a generic scepticism presupposes the primacy of argument to ethics, an issue that needs much further debate. And it carries with it a command to be skeptical about the faith you honor most, making it less likely that you will be able to draw positive energy from that source. To acknowledge the contestability of your faith, however, is to admit that others without your specific fund of experience are unlikely to be instilled with it and to admit that you lack the resources to pull them with assurance into the fold. To acknowledge contestability in this way enables you to build relational modesty into theistic and nontheistic faiths while still drawing nourishment from them: a self-modesty at the level of faith that does not reduce to a generic scepticism impossible to live existentially; an acknowledgment that others too might draw sustenance from putative sources that exceed their epistemological powers to prove or demonstrate.

A partisan ethical source

If one embraces the first two themes, the next thing, perhaps, is to articulate publicly, to the extent possible, the contestable source of ethics you honor most. That is not so easy. It seems doubtful that any individual or a group will succeed in doing so all the way up and down. You might articulate some dimensions. And then a new event could bring out elements that heretofore hovered in the dark, or force a painful modification in the source you acknowledge. And both of these infusions might function as signs that there are still elements in your faith that remain opaque.

The most fundamental source I acknowledge is not apodictic recognition (I resist the dualistic metaphysic in which it is set and the lawlike conception of morality it secretes). Nor is it attunement to a transcendent purpose in being, nor even recognition of the radical alterity of the other. I mention these three because I do bestow agonistic respect upon those who honor them. I admire the integrity that Immanuel Kant, Charles Taylor, and Emmanuel Levinas show in articulating and enacting the sources they embrace. I admire them as prods and interlocutors to the sensibility I pursue.

But I give my heart to a nontheistic metaphysic and a corollary existential faith articulated by Epicurus, Spinoza, Nietzsche, and Deleuze in different ways. The *first* ethical source I acknowledge is neither divine, rational, contractual, dialogical, nor juridical in character. Nor is it entirely reducible to sentiment, emotion, or, worst, 'preference'. It is, rather, a dispositional orientation to being that flows under and through these modalities: existential gratitude for the abundance of being over identity. Each writer listed above reaches this point in his inimical way. Nietzsche, for instance, celebrates the 'religiosity of the ancient Greeks' for the 'lavish abundance of gratitude that radiates from it' (1955: 58). Elsewhere he says that '[s]ome folly keeps persuading me that every human being has this feeling, simply because he is human' (1974: 76–7).[7] Existential gratitude is a source to draw upon and cultivate as you process the sickness, surprises, suffering, and impulse to existential resentment woven into the life of mortals. It is an affective well to mine, say, when you discover a surprising injury your identity, interests, or faith has imposed upon others. Such a fugitive attachment to the abundance of being flows into the identity, interests, principles, codes, and interpretations inhabiting us rather than hovering above them. To cultivate it is to amplify a care for the protean diversity of being already there and to mobilize energies to act upon that care. Such a care infuses decisions with forbearance and generosity rather than providing a set of rules to govern decision. It folds a presumption of receptivity into relations. That presumption in turn is not adjusted through recourse to a juridical moral source above it, but by reference to political interpretations of specific dangers, risks, possibilities posed at the time. Your affirmation of responsibility and obligation, on this view, are not first but second order formations. One way in which this orientation to ethics disappoints systematic philosophers of ethics is that it constructs no architectural system through which to delineate answers to questions settled in advance. It is an ethic-political disposition inserted into shifting contexts of cultural life. Zarathustra and Epicurus express the power of such an immanent source better than others I have read. They underscore a vital source of ethical energy as they point to the constitutive fragility of the ethical life. For the gratitude you or we are able to mobilize at a specific time may not measure up to the level of energy needed. That is the tragic element in the ethical life of embodied mortals.

Such a nontheistic source is layered. It contains, for instance, culturally imbued, affective, proto-thoughts that flow into the higher intellect but are not entirely under its control. It thus bears a family resemblance to the transcendental field in Kant, though it is set on an infrasensible rather than a supersensible register. As such it can be moved and amplified to some degree by tactical means. That's why its proponents and propagandists such as Nietzsche, Foucault, Deleuze, and Stuart Hampshire make so much of self-artistry, tactics of the self, and micropolitics in ethical life. Neo-Kantians, Habermasians, Taylorites, and Lacanians, viewing these arts from the outside, too often misrepresent them as the narcissistic 'aestheticization of politics'. In doing so they recapitulate the reductive reading that Augustine gave of 'pagans' of his day.

It goes almost without saying that my elucidation of this protean, nonjuridical source is both constitutively incomplete and profoundly contestable. Others will articulate the opaque field in question differently, as the oscillating history of the three Euro-Asian religions of the Book discloses. It impresses me, however, that many who find themselves committed either to a religion of the Book or to a nontheistic faith such as Buddhism also point to the importance of the cultivation of generosity. For some, arts of devotion such as prayer and confession form a crucial intermediary between humanity and divinity, while for others going for a long, slow run in the woods or listening to the Talking Heads forges lines of connection between human decisions and somatic energies that infuse and exceed them. You can visit variations on such themes in the work of Charles Taylor, William James, the Dalai Lama, Benedict Spinoza, Jacques Derrida, Hannah Arendt, Henri Bergson, Michel Foucault, and Immanuel Levinas. Such examples encourage me to pursue productive lines of connection across the theistic/nontheistic divide. These oblique connections track at the academic/philosophical level rhizomatic connections across significant difference to be pursued in public life. For, as Epicurus, Buddha, and Zarathustra showed through a diversity of gentle examples, it is possible to cultivate a noble religious sensibility without affirming a God.

Ethos, becoming, and tempo

To be a political theorist drawn to such a perspective is to become more alert to what I call the politics of becoming. Other perspectives as well might encourage you to come to terms with this phenomenon, though you would then inflect it differently. By the politics of becoming I mean that paradoxical politics by which new and unforeseen things surge into being, such as a new and surprising religion, a new source of moral inspiration, a new cultural identity within an existing constellation of established identities such as the introduction of the practice of rights into Christendom, or the placement of a new right on an existing register of recognized rights such as the right to doctor-assisted suicide. The politics of becoming does not always generate positive things. Far from it. But it often emerges out of historically specific suffering, energies, and lines of flight that have been obscure to the dominant or hegemonic formation. In some ethically most important cases the politics of becoming moves from a netherworld below the register of positive recognition, identity, legitimacy, or justice onto one or more of those registers. In doing so it shakes up something in the established social world, moving the hegemonic arguments and identifications through which it had been officially constituted.

In the contemporary world, when the tempo of life has accelerated in several domains, the politics of becoming may be more active, more widespread, and more visible than heretofore. The contemporary era is one in which the most characteristic ethical conflicts of the day arise between the politics of pluralization and the politics of fundamentalization, between two modes of becoming in competition with each other, each spurred on by the acceleration of pace in modern life.

What political virtues are most appropriate to a contemporary world in which the politics of becoming has accelerated, interdependent constituencies honor different moral sources, and partisans are unlikely to have recourse to authoritative arguments sufficient to dissolve these differences? The virtues commended here do not take politics out of ethics, nor do they rise entirely above politics. They, rather, fold an ethical dimension into the experience of identity, the practice of faith, the promotion of self-interest, and the engagements of politics. I note two.

The first is agonistic respect. Agonistic respect is a kissing cousin of liberal tolerance. It is a relation between interdependent partisans who are already on the register of cultural recognition. But liberal tolerance is predicated upon a general public realm where all parties share a general orientation to reasoning, procedure, and deliberation and where they leave their faiths in the private realm. Liberal tolerance is above all tolerance of private diversity; it depends upon more deliberative agreement in the public realm than people can marshal in a late-modern period when Christendom no longer sets the settled, assured background of public life. In a relation of agonistic respect, interdependent partisans do not automatically leave the particular faiths, metaphysics, or fundamental ethical moral sources to which they appeal in the private realm. They might leave pieces and chunks often enough, when a specific issue makes it feasible to do so. That is part of their modesty. But when it is necessary to bring chunks of their fundamental orientations into the public realm, the partisans adopt a certain forbearance and hesitancy with respect to the practical universalizability of those fundaments.

In a fast paced world where multiple faiths intersect, it is important to negotiate oblique connections across multiple lines of difference. But what might a connection look like without devolving either into an individuality without connection or a commonality? Here is one version. Sometimes the diastolic pulse of some corresponds roughly to the systolic beat of others. Here a seed of oblique *connection* is sown between partisans honoring different faiths. Epicurus, a functional nontheist, advised his disciples to subdue worry about what happens *after* death in order to overcome the resentment of human mortality that so often spawns a punitive morality. He thus acknowledged, before the advent of Christianity, a counter-faith inside his faith, one to work on in a way that differs from a Christian quest to salvation but connects to some Christian pursuits of compassion. Several monotheists testify to similar dissonances. What if many can identify a little atheist or theist periodically punctuating a dominant investment of faith? Can such inverted connections occasionally provoke laughter across difference, as each constituency engages an internal *counterpoint* to itself that tempers the *external counterpart* it provides to others? Such laughter may testify to a virtual register challenging every particular confession of it. The structure of such relationships *is* amusing. And the differences across which connections are forged are unlikely to sink into a sea of commonality or to withdraw demurely into the private realm. When the parties mutually acknowledge its complexity without deep resentment, an initial relation of antagonism can devolve into one of agonistic respect. Each knows the source they honor most will be opaque to others. They pursue hard negotiations across difference marked by reciprocal self-modesty and generosity.

The second is critical responsiveness. While agonistic respect is a virtue cultivated between partisans already on the register of public life, critical responsiveness is particularly appropriate to the politics of becoming. It is also most pertinent to a time when the pace of life moves faster than heretofore, the politics of becoming proceeds on more fronts than previously, and citizen action often exceeds state boundaries as well as operating within them. Critical responsiveness is a *presumptive* generosity to new constituencies struggling to move from a place of subsistence below the reach of established recognition, justice, or legitimacy onto one of those registers. It points to the insufficiency of justice to itself in a world where the politics of becoming periodically disturb something in operational understandings of the 'person' and codes of justice.

Both agonistic respect and critical responsiveness are civic virtues that require cultivation and negotiation. They involve tactical work on the lower affective registers of being that filter into the higher intellect but are unsusceptible to its direct regulation. This points to another way in which neither is reducible to liberal virtues, for most liberal virtues are placed on the higher intellectual register rather than also finding expression on the visceral register or sensibility. Critical responsiveness often involves selective work on the visceral register of self-identity. You may modify a gut feeling installed in you, for instance, that your sexuality must monopolize the field of natural or permissible sexualities. Or that your religious faith, so radiant in your experience, expresses the faith others must embrace. Your initial response to a new movement in the domain of religion or sexuality may be to attack it to protect the hegemony of your identity. How could a faith be nontheistic, you might ask, insisting in advance that no space can be created between monotheistic faith and secular orientations that seek to eschew faith. The cultivation of critical responsiveness often involves tactical work on specific elements of our layered identities, then. Such experimental work in turn alters the existential context in which judgments are formed and possibilities of negotiation are considered.

The reciprocal cultivation of such virtues is critical to a generous ethos of politics in another way. By giving something to the visceral registers as already installed in diverse constituencies, the cultivation of these virtues reduces the probability that cultural conflict will become so intense that it cannot be negotiated within a democratic frame. No air-tight protection here is available, however, as Laclau so vividly appreciates. Sometimes a new movement in the politics of becoming aims at confining narrowly the legitimate range of religions, sensualities, ethnicities, etc. Many, for instance, are tempted to respond to the acceleration of pace in late-modern life by trying to slow the world back down. Since they can't slow down the pace of capitalism they pick on more vulnerable constituencies as the source of the problem. In these circumstances it is both important for those who acknowledge the contestability of fundamental sources to come to terms responsively with the conditions that generate such a movement *and* to limit its capacity to de-pluralize the order. Since I cannot now improve upon my response to this issue on a previous occasion, let me quote from a piece that speaks to it:

> 'Doesn't such a vibrant and fluid pluralism generate its own imperatives of delimitation and exclusion?' Yes. Among other things, fundamentalism in the domains of religion, aesthetics, reason, race, sexuality and nationality can be permitted, but none of these movements must be allowed to gain political hegemony. We (Rawlsian, Habermasian, Mouffeian, Foucauldian) pluralists and pluralizers must collaborate to resist the hegemonization of such Schmittian movements. In doing so we can appeal to the contestability of the grounds from which they proceed; we can affirm corollary points of contestability in our own faiths as part of an invitation to forbearance and receptive generosity in political relations; we can appreciate multiple sources from which reflective moral sensibilities might develop; we can show how possibilities for coexistence and selective collaboration among numerous constituencies expand when agonistic appreciation becomes reciprocal across multiple lines of interdependence and difference. But if and when the issue is on the line, we must stand against the violent hegemony of fundamentalism, drawing upon (I now add) the diverse sources of pluralist commitment that inspire us.
>
> (Connolly 1999b: 196)

Thus, despite what you may have heard, I do not now nor have I for decades believed that fundamental antagonism can always be avoided. Or that it is possible to have a political order without limits. It is just that often enough such potential antagonisms can be softened and translated into partial connections across significant difference by ethical means. That is the thing to focus upon first for those who seek to nourish the ongoing politics of democratization. My sense is that the ethos of engagement endorsed here is both worthy of endorsement in itself and most likely to support drives toward a cultural economy of diversity and an economic culture of inclusion.

There are other perspectives from which complementary virtues might be elaborated and cultivated. The idea is to open lines of communication with them, curtailing the tendency of each to see itself as the only source of compassion or generosity or care in public life. The partisan faith embraced here adds another candidate to the list of partisan orientations already in play; and the general ethos pursued signals that it will continue to present itself as a contestable orientation to life.

Such a combination may exert a two-fold appeal to those inspired by Laclau's conception of democratization. Agonistic respect softens the antagonisms he defines as constitutive of democracy; and critical responsiveness opens up productive possibilities in the politics of becoming he and I both find to be vital to the vibrancy of democratic life. Indeed, it is because I listen to Ernesto Laclau when he speaks of 'the distance between the undecidability of structure and the decision' that I offer agonistic respect and critical responsiveness as two virtues to occupy the interval (Laclau 2000a: 79). There are more issues to explore with respect to the particular ethic of cultivation embraced here in relation to the general ethos of pluralism and pluralization proposed. But enough may have been said to launch further conversations with Ernesto Laclau and others inspired by his commendable work on democratic pluralism.

Acknowledgements

Thanks to the Centre for Theoretical Studies at the University of Essex, where the author gave an early version of this chapter in December 1999, and the Centre for Political Philosophy at the University of Sydney where another version was presented. The author has been helped considerably by the discussions at both places. His thinking in this essay is particularly informed by the exchange between Ernesto Laclau, Simon Critchley, Jane Bennett, and himself at the Essex meeting and discussions with Moira Gatens, Paul Patton, and Duncan Ivison in and around the Sydney meeting.

Notes

1 My thinking about how to foster a more inclusive set of consumption practices which allows all members of a political regime to participate in the general cultural and political life it makes available was first developed with Michael Best in our co-authored *The Politicized Economy*

(1976, 1983). Those economic ideas in turn were updated and translated into my current thinking about a democratic culture of pluralism and pluralization in *The Ethos of Pluralization* (1995), particularly chs 3 and 4.

2 Relevant here is the Symposium on Left Conservatism published, in its first draft, in *theory and event* (winter 1998) and its second draft, *as Connolly* 1999c. In the second draft I make a case, against those who give priority to economic redistribution first and foremost, for close interdependence between fostering a more expansive pluralism and developing a more inclusive economic culture. See Connolly 1999c: 47–55, and the pieces by Wendy Brown and Thomas Dumm in that same issue.

3 I will not say much about this part of the project here. But it is pursued with respect to Mill, Tocqueville, Habermas, Benhabib, Walzer, William Bennett, Rawls, and Habermas in Connolly 1995, 1999a.

4 I develop the discussion of the effects on ethico-political life of the acceleration of tempo most in Connolly 2000. There Samuel Huntington and Martha Nussbaum are engaged, the first for the deficiencies which arise when a concentric conception of culture is joined to a stringent territorial model of 'civilization' and the second for arbitrary limits to the politics of becoming posed by the joining of a concentric model of culture to a one-dimensional conception of the universal. My sense is that the double entry orientation to the universal developed there makes positive contact with positions developed by both Ernesto Laclau and Judith Butler in Butler *et al. Contingency, Hegemony, and Universality* (2000).

5 The emphases are added by me.

6 Here is a fascinating way in which Kant's acceptance of Newtonian mechanics affected his conception of morality, not only in elevating the latter above the sensible field but in treating Newtonian laws as analogies to be used in thinking about the moral law. What if, with Nietzsche and Nobel Prize winning chemist Ilya Prigogine, you adopt a philosophy of science that says that nature is not entirely reducible to a fixed set of laws. Now the analogy from nature Kant drew upon to think about morality is compromised. Kant's Newtonianism filters into all aspects of his philosophy, particularly into his flat conception of those parts of human sensibility and inclination that do not reflect the supersensible realm.

7 The second sentence should be read in its larger context:

> But to stand in the midst of this *rerum concordia discors* and of this whole marvelous uncertainty and rich ambiguity of existence without questioning, without *trembling* with the craving and rapture of such questioning ..., that is what I feel to be contemptible, and this is the feeling for which I first look in everybody. Some folly keeps persuading me that every human being has this feeling, simply because he is human. This is my type of injustice.

References

Butler, J., Laclau, E. and Žižek, S. (2000) *Contingency, Hegemony, Universality: Contemporary Dialogues on the Left*, London: Verso.

Connolly, W. (1995) *The Ethos of Pluralization*, Minneapolis: University of Minnesota Press.

—— (1999a) *Why I am Not a Secularist*, Minneapolis: University of Minnesota Press.

—— (1999b) 'Secularism, partisanship and the ambiguity of justice', in E. Portis and A. Gundersen (eds) *Political Theory and Partisan Politics*, Albany: State University of New York.

—— (1999c) 'Assembling the left', *Boundary2*, 26(3): 47–54.

—— (2000) 'Speed, concentric culture and cosmopolitanism', *Political Theory*, 28(5): 596–618.

Connolly, W. and Best, M. (1976, 1983) *The Politicized Economy*, Lexington, KY: D. C. Heath.

Kant, I. (1993) *Critique of Practical Reason*, tr. Lewis Beck, New York: Macmillan Press.

Laclau, E. (2000a) 'Identity and hegemony: The role of universality in the constitution of political logics', in J. Butler, E. Laclau, and S. Žižek (eds) *Contingency, Hegemony, Universality: Contemporary Dialogues on the Left*, London: Verso.

—— (2000b) 'Constructing universality', in J. Butler, E. Laclau, and S. Žižek (eds) *Contingency, Hegemony, Universality: Contemporary Dialogues on the Left*, London: Verso.

Nietzsche, F. (1955) *Beyond Good and Evil*, tr. Marianne Cowan, Chicago: Gateway Editions.

—— (1974) *The Gay Science*, tr. Walter Kaufmann, New York: Vintage Books.

10

ANACHRONISM OF EMANCIPATION OR FIDELITY TO POLITICS

Jelica Šumič

Let me try first to limit the scope of the present essay. It is not my goal to provide in a limited space of a commentary an exhaustive presentation of Ernesto Laclau's work, a complex enterprise in terms of its theoretical stakes, its far-reaching implications for contemporary theorizing of politics, and its unwavering commitment to what Laclau calls 'radical democracy'. An attempt at a comprehensive study of such a remarkable enterprise would require an attentive and detailed reading of his major books, in particular *Hegemony and Socialist Strategy* (written with Chantal Mouffe), *New Reflections on the Revolution of our Time*, and *Emancipation(s)*, as well as a discussion of those theorists whose ideas constitute a source of inspiration for Laclau: Gramsci, Althusser, Lefort, Derrida, and Lacan, to name but the most prominent. In contrast to such a 'totalizing' enterprise, I will consider Laclau's work as a genuine materialist work, comparable in this respect with that of Marx or Lacan – i.e. a work that is by definition 'not-all', unfinishable, and which therefore allows for a partial, fragmentary reading. In what follows I propose to make a number of remarks about Laclau's conception of politics rooted in a fidelity to both deconstruction and emancipation, a 'double fidelity' which Laclau, notwithstanding their many differences, shares with Derrida, that theorist, namely, who virtually equates emancipation with deconstruction.[1]

Fidelity to a signifier

That emancipation is situated at the centre of Laclau's theoretical preoccupations is evidenced, ultimately, by the titles of his two major works, *New Reflections on the Revolution of our Time* and *Emancipation(s)*. But, 'revolution'?, 'emancipation'?, how can one still insist on the performative efficacy of these signifiers in the contemporary socio-political constellation characterized by a more or less pragmatic approach to a political antagonism, an emphasis on the openness to the Other and 'respect' of his/her difference, a dilated conception of 'human rights' as a capital political value, and, consequently, by a broad retreat from the politics of emancipation of the 1960s and 1970s?

It may well be worth asking whether the 'fidelity' to emancipation in an era characterized by its amnesia does not represent a regression in the classical doctrine of emancipation which has collapsed because it has proved to be constitutively unable to develop a relation with specific socio-historical circumstances. And the concomitant question: does not the promotion of emancipation to the centre stage imply that unyielding, dogmatic fidelity as such is subversive, emancipatory? That such a conclusion is inadmissible can best be illustrated with the example of 'revolutionary conservatism'. Clinging to a distressing fidelity to emancipation, such a 'revolutionary conservatism', perseveres in a politics of a complete powerlessness which it tries pathetically to present as a politics of principle.

But secondly and more importantly, the objection of dogmatism fails to address the crucial stake in the fidelity to emancipation, namely an inseparable conjunction of the fidelity to the signifier of emancipation and the contingency of its efficacy. The insistence on the possibility, more, necessity of emancipation in the present situation is not dogmatic, I would argue, to the extent that such a fidelity fully assumes the strictly contingent circumstances in which an emancipatory politics may or may not take place. It is necessary then to ask what can the relationship be between fidelity and contingency. Isn't it rather the case that the (subjective) fidelity cancels out all (objective) contingency? Does not the imperative of fidelity spell out as follows: *Do not give up on your (emancipatory) desire, regardless of all circumstances?*

Alain Badiou provides, in my view, a persuasive answer to this question:

> More than anything else I admire in Pascal his striving to *go against the current* in the difficult circumstances. This should not be understood in a reactionary meaning of the word, but rather as an attempt to invent modern forms for old conviction instead of following the pace of the world and adopting 'portable' scepticism that all eras of transition bring back to life in view of serving the souls too weak to insist on the fact that no historic *speed* is incompatible with the calm will to change the world and to universalize its form.
>
> (Badiou 1988: 245)

Clearly, we are not dealing here with a 'fidelity' for its own sake. On the contrary. The lesson to be drawn from this passage is that such an 'ethics of fidelity', even though a politics of emancipation is far from being obvious in the present constellation, could be far more subversive than all implacable moralist condemnations of politics, more subversive than any seemingly radical proclamation of the 'death' of politics. In a sense, we might say that the reaffirmation of emancipation, insofar as it is rooted in the ethics of fidelity, is subversive simply by being inscribed in the register of rejection.

It is increasingly evident today that any serious attempt at the theorization of contemporary emancipatory politics is faced with the task of demarcating itself from the prevailing trends in contemporary political thought. Laclau's theory of a radical democracy provides one of the most powerful alternatives yet conceived to the various 'postmodern' rejections of all politics and, specifically, that of emancipation, without yielding an inch to the 'realpolitik' prevailing in the last decade of the twentieth century, a politics that advocates the equation of politics and management, ultimately, the global market as our only significant political mechanism.

Laclau's conception of the politics of emancipation begins with a trenchant critique of our current consensus according to which 'the collapse of the communist regimes is supposed to mean humanity's arrival at a final stage where all human needs will be satisfied and where no messianic consummation of time is any longer to be expected' (*E* 76).

On the one hand, Laclau thus claims that the 'age of revolutions' is over, since he fully admits that

> the cycle of events which opened with the Russian Revolution has definitively closed, both as a force of irradiation in the collective imaginary of the international left, and also in terms of its ability to hegemonize the social and political forces of the societies in which Leninism, in any of its forms constituted a state doctrine' (*NR* xi).

On the other hand, however, Laclau's avowed intent, for instance, in *New Reflections on the Revolution of our Time*, is to formulate 'a new politics of the left' in the new historical circumstances. This distinguishes him from a number of other contemporary 'modernist' theorists, who are more concerned to mourn the end of the Enlightenment project than to explore the liberating potential of contemporary 'postmodern' fragmented societies.[2] At the same time, the very gesture of refusing to relinquish emancipation has made him into a rather uncomfortable companion for other postmodernist and/or deconstructivist theorists, who tend to be rather more interested in ominous proclamations of the end of politics.

In this respect, Laclau's theoretical enterprise might be ultimately compared and/or contrasted with several contemporary conceptions of politics recently defined by E. Balibar, J. Rancière, or A. Badiou. For what all these theorists have in common is a refusal of the redemptive conception of emancipation conceived as an endeavour aiming 'at transforming the very "root" of the social' (*NR* 33).[3]

While demonstrating the futility of this now bankrupt concept of emancipation, these theorists remain nevertheless committed to the politics of emancipation and, in so doing, testify to their acute sensitivity to the problem of the reign of liberty and equality in a universe without beyond, that is, in an era in which effective resistance to the global market seems to be finding expression solely in the intolerance of culturally specified identities, from nationalism in Western and Eastern Europe to fundamentalism in countries of the 'Third World'.

The task of the contemporary politics of emancipation, in this view, is to find an alternative to that which presents itself as always already there – but this alternative is no longer a 'once and for all' transformation, a messianic redemption from historical time, so much as a rigorous conception of the possibilities opened up by the very impossibility of what Laclau calls the final closure of the social.

The point I want to stress here is perhaps self-evident, namely that the destiny of politics in a given situation depends on the way in which signifiers such as emancipation, revolution, freedom, equality, etc. are articulated in the field of the big Other. Put differently, to bring into play the signifier of emancipation means simultaneously to bring into play a specific conception of politics.

Thus, for classical political thought, for instance, defined as a theory of different forms of government, as well as for the modern political philosophy which conceives of politics in terms of power and its legitimization, there is no place for emancipation. This notion is considered as a moralist rather than as a political one. And conversely, emancipation is elevated to the dignity of a political concept only for that theorizing which identifies politics with the place of an original dislocation, say, between the institutional and the insurrective moment or, in Laclau's terms, a dialectic of two related, yet contrary, processes: sedimentation and reactivation.

The irreducible gap between the political and the social stems, according to Laclau, from the blind spot of the institution of the social. Every political reactivation at one and the same time detotalizes (de-sediments, he says) the social and installs a new order which it presents as necessary, although it is a consequence of the wholly contingent intervention of politics. This is to distinguish sharply between the inconsistency of the social and the institution of the social. Laclau's 'dislocated configuration' provides an ontological basis for this distinction. Reactivation could then be conceived as a causation that makes specific, but doesn't positively specify its effects. Politics, on this account, always begins in social disruption and disorder. To the extent that reactivation, for Laclau, does not consist in 'returning to the original situation, but merely of rediscovering, through the emergence of new antagonisms, the contingent nature of so-called "objectivity"' (*NR* 35), we might then say, by paraphrasing Badiou, that politics is what happens in society as a subtraction from society. In this sense, politics can be said already to always involve a re-politicization.

Emancipation, to be conceivable at all, requires then as its presupposition an original splitting of the social, a radical antagonism or dislocation which renders the field of the social untotalizable. There are, however, two different ways in which emancipation can be articulated with this division that traverses the social. According to the classical doctrine of emancipation, the chasm de-totalizing the social is present as that outrageous, intolerable situation which 'should not be present at all', which should be eliminated in a wholly 'harmonious society' (*NR* 33).

Any genuine politics of emancipation, by contrast, is only possible by renouncing the temptation to achieve the reconciliation or, which amounts to the same, the closure of the social. It is in fact the very category of 'society' that Laclau finds objectionable to the extent that it implies some sort of totality. For Laclau, on the contrary, such a totality or fullness, to use his own term, remains radically unachievable as there is always at least one moment within the field of the social which evades all attempts at totalization, thus defining what Laclau calls dislocation. Dislocation is a wholly transitory, wholly insubstantial incident that cannot be located in the situation in which it takes place. Part of every situation but belonging to none, the dislocation preserves an ambiguous ontological status. On one account, whenever we conceive of dislocation, it is as specific to a situation. On another account, however, and this is the essential point, it cannot be represented. A situation cannot know of its dislocation. From 'inside' the situation, so to speak, there is nothing to see. The dislocation of a situation will become apparent only retroactively, through what Laclau calls the simultaneous process of desedimentation and reactivation. It is because such dislocation is ineradicable from the social, regardless of the form of its institution, that we can say with Laclau that 'Society does not exist' or, which amounts to the same, that society *in-consists*.

From Laclau's 'ontological' thesis of the inconsistency of the social it necessarily follows that politics is an ever present possibility: this evasive, totally unlocalizable point of dislocation – that is, unlocalizable from the point of view of the established socio-political order – operates as a potential moment of reactivation or re-politicization in any given situation. It remains, however, fully contingent which moment will become the site of reactivation or re-politicization. As such, dislocations have an intrinsically emancipatory potential. It is precisely this conception of dislocation as being, in a situation, the point of impasse, or the point of impossibility, which precisely allows us to reconsider the situation as a whole in light of this dislocation. Dislocation can thus be understood in terms of the real, that elusive instance around which a situation is organized and yet which cannot appear as such, cannot be represented, in that situation. Dislocation is what is insituable for any stable assignation of place; it thereby calls into question the prevailing distributive regime of places and functions as a whole.

In keeping with this conception of dislocation, what I propose to call emancipatory politics always consists in making seem possible precisely that which, from within the situation, is declared to be impossible. The imperative of politics of emancipation is to identify and to isolate the real and to show how the institution of the social is organized around such reality beyond all representation. The very inconsistency of the social thus entails that the politics of emancipation operates in the 'here and now' of any given situation. In a sense, precisely because an emancipatory politics is articulated to the irreducible inconsistency of the social, that is, in the ineliminable dislocation constitutive to politics itself, emancipation can be considered as a permanent, 'eternal' possibility.

From Laclau's theoretical premises it clearly follows that a politics of emancipation is linked to the particularity of the situation in which it takes place. However, the fact that emancipation is situated does not imply that its import is limited by the situation in which it takes place. I will argue that Laclau has not yet sufficiently entertained the idea that, if in its 'being' emancipation is dependent on its situation, in its universalist effects it must be independent of it. This is another way of saying that an emancipatory politics is inherently transcendent: it operates in the situation but it is not of the situation. Insofar as it can only emerge in a given situation as something totally heterogeneous with it, more precisely, as a moment of its extimacy, we might say that the politics of emancipation itself remains entirely incalculable. In this sense we might then say that the demanding task of any politics of emancipation is to be wholly open to chance, to be consistent with the contingency demanding at the same time a specific notion of the subject in consonance with the experience of such a radical contingency.

A number of interesting remarks can be made about Laclau's conception of the subject that suggest other possible interpretations than the one I provide below. Let it be noted that at least one of the things Laclau says about the subject may confirm my interpretation. For instance, Laclau, explicitly states that

> *the location of the subject is that of dislocation*. Thus, far from being a moment of the structure, the subject is the result of the impossibility of constituting the structure as such – that is as a self-sufficient object. Hence also my different conception of the socialist project (*NR* 41, my emphasis).

It is here that I would need to investigate more closely the issue of fidelity as pointing precisely to the convergence of the question of the subject and that of dislocation.

What then are the conditions of a truly contemporary fidelity to emancipation? My sense here is that, as paradoxical as it may at first seem, such an 'ethics of fidelity' is required to keep emancipation viable and effective within the constraints of the existing situation. Without being itself the vehicle of a politics of emancipation, this fidelity provides the space in which politics of emancipation may take place. The fidelity to emancipation may not directly 'install' any particular project of emancipation, as the latter depends both, in view of its content, ideas, and values as well of its emergence, upon the particular circumstances in which it takes place, but it prepares, as it were, the ground for every such establishment. In developing this argument I certainly go further than Laclau in 'complicating' the relation between condition (fidelity to emancipation) and condition (a politics of emancipation in a given situation). In so doing I only wish to stress that the politics of emancipation cannot be conceived in terms of a mere derivation. This does not mean, in my view, that such a politics is entirely autonomous to the extent that the price to be paid for this autonomy is an essential blindness, from the perspective of politics itself, as to its effects in a given situation.

The dislocatory provenance of all politics excludes the possibility of any trans-historical emancipation. Fidelity to emancipation, on this account, is internal to the situation while remaining essentially a-topical. Fidelity to emancipation, however, does not exist prior or above concrete emancipatory projects.

As has been already pointed out, this fidelity can constitute an essential condition for any contemporary politics of emancipation only by renouncing the temptation to turn emancipation into an agalma and, as its corollary, to adopt the pathos of the 'guardian' of an emancipatory ideal. Second, inasmuch as the fidelity to emancipation insists on the possibility of emancipation anytime and anywhere, regardless of all circumstances, irrespective of all demands of the reality, it is obvious that such a subjective maxim is tenable only at the cost of its blindness. This blindness is precisely its anachronism.

Anachronism as a constituent of the fidelity to emancipation, however, by no means involves a dogmatic, i.e. inflexible, stand with respect to a particular situation. Anachronism does not involve rebellion at any cost. Rather, what I am dealing with here is a stand which, through its dislocation with respect to the demands imposed by the 'laws' of the situation, testifies – at the level of the subject – to the radical contingency of the given socio-politico-ideological order, in other words, to the dislocation constitutive to the situation itself in which the emancipatory project has to come into existence.

Anachronism of emancipation

It is no doubt one of the great merits of deconstruction to emphasize precisely this 'ontological' aspect in anachronism. As a mode of appearance of the structural dislocation, of the irreducible division that traverses the social, anachronism is an exemplary case for the efficacy of deconstruction itself. Anachronism, in this sense, figures as a constitutive component of deconstruction, since, as Laclau points out, 'the existence of this chasm is what makes deconstruction possible' (*E* 74). At the same time, Laclau convincingly argues that anachronism is also a constituent of politics itself. He pursues this important point with the following words: 'Time being "out of joint", dislocation corrupting the identity with itself of any present, we have a constitutive anachronism that is at the root of any identity [...] at the very heart of the constitution of the social link' (*E* 74). Anachronism, we could say, represents in Laclau's view the 'quilting point' of deconstruction and the political, i.e. of the logic of the irreducible redoubling, that Derrida calls the logic of spectrality, and the hegemonic logic, this being, according to Laclau, the logic of politics proper.

I cannot but agree with Laclau when he maintains, in keeping with Derrida, that deconstruction is that operation destined to uncover the constitutive dislocation that inhabits all politico-social configuration and which the established order strives to conceal, that dislocation namely without which 'there would not be politics but just a programmed, predetermined reduction of the other to the same' (*E* 67).

On one account, anachronism is not emancipatory in itself, rather, it only points to the structural inconsistency of the social, indicating in this way that any socio-political arrangement that emerges within this undecidable terrain remains irreducibly contingent, non-groundable. On another account, however, the liberating effects of anachronism cannot be denied either. Contemporary politics of emancipation is therefore confronted with the task of recognizing the irreducible undecidability of any institution of the social 'and tak[ing] full advantage of the political possibilities that this undecidability opens' (*E* 65).

The question which arises at this point is the following. Does it mean that we are dealing here with a contingent convergence of the logic of deconstruction and the logic of the political or, rather, with their mutual implication? This is the key question, whose answer is the precondition for solving the problem of the possible relationship between deconstruction and emancipation.

In opposition to the prevailing idea of the mutual belonging together of emancipation and deconstruction, which can be found in both Derrida's and Laclau's recent texts, I will argue that the articulation between deconstruction and emancipation implies a contingent rather than a necessary relation. Moreover, I will try to show how the assumption according to which deconstruction itself is considered a possible condition for emancipation represents an obstacle for drawing the most radical implications from Laclau's theorizing of politics and, more specifically, politics of emancipation.

While it is true that Laclau repeatedly argues in favour of such a compatibility of the logic of spectrality and the logic of hegemony, nevertheless he hesitates to entirely endorse their assimilation. On the one hand, the relationship between deconstruction and hegemony can be conceived in terms of a mutual 'parasitism':

> Deconstruction and hegemony are the two essential dimensions of a single theoretico-practical operation. Hegemony requires deconstruction: without the radical structural undecidability that the deconstructive intervention brings about, many strata of social relations would appear as essentially linked by necessary logics and there would be nothing to hegemonize. But deconstruction also requires hegemony, that is, a theory of the decision taken in an undecidable terrain: without a theory of the decision, that distance between structural undecidability and actuality would remain untheorized.
>
> (Laclau 1996: 59–69)

Hence, the most important lesson that deconstruction may teach a theory of politics is that it shows the necessity of a hegemonic operation defined as 'a contingent intervention taking place in an undecidable terrain' (*E* 89), and, at the same time, constitutes the conditions of visibility of such an operation.

If deconstruction provides an answer to the question how it is possible that any situation is both inconsistent, not-all, and a solid relation of its representation, hegemony provides tools to describe choices made by various politics. What any such hegemonic intervention chooses is a certain way of 'fixing' the inconsistency of the social, where the very possibility of such an intervention implies that there is no way to calculate the 'correct' choice. Simply put, deconstruction produces the social as the still untotalizable horizon of any totalization established through the hegemonic intervention.

Hegemony, on this account, presupposes the contingency of the structure, more precisely, 'the inherent distance of the structure from itself' (*E* 92). However, the fact that the social is inhabited by an original lack, its undecidability, is not visible as such. It can only be made visible after the fact, retroactively, precisely through the hegemonic intervention involving a conflict between various contents in their attempt to fill the structural gap. The very possibility of a hegemonic intervention thus signals that there is no specific content predetermined to play this filling role, which means that the 'chosen' particular content can be seen as equivalent to other possible contents (*E* 92). A hegemonic operation, to take effect at all, thus demands a certain degree of *de-particularization*. This making indifferent of differences between particular contents, however, can only be achieved through the primacy of what Laclau calls the 'logic of equivalence' over the 'logic of difference'.

It is at this point precisely that the crucial distinction between the logic of hegemony and spectral logic can be pointed out. Given the importance of Derrida's contribution to Laclau's political philosophy, it is worth paying this distinction the attention it deserves. A hegemonic relation is spectral and, at the same time, irreducible to the logic of spectrality. It is spectral insofar as, by choosing a particular content to signify the universal, it causes the splitting of the former between its own particularity and 'a general function of filling that is independent of any particular content' (*E* 93). On the other hand, what eludes the logic of spectrality, what deconstruction fails to recognize, is precisely 'the very fact that other bodies compete to the incarnating ones, that they are alternative forms of materialization of the same "spirit"' – in short, it cannot recognize the 'autonomization of the latter which cannot be explained solely by the pure logic of spectrality' (*E* 71). This rehabilitation of the universal sets Laclau's approach apart from the prevailing deconstructivist rejection of this category.

Through his emphasis on the autonomization of the universal, Laclau opened up a new field of inquiry into contemporary theorizing of politics and emancipation. The importance of this point will only fully be understood once we have considered Laclau's conception of the relationship between the universal and the particular. It may be worth developing this particular dimension of the more general relation of hegemony and deconstruction in a little more detail, given its strategic prominence in so much of Laclau's recent work.

According to Laclau, the domain in which the universal is most obviously and compellingly at stake is politics. This fact alone corroborates, in a sense, the profound insight of Laclau's account. Laclau convincingly argues how autonomy of the universal principle can emerge out of its constitutive impossibility. The fact that fullness is constitutively unachievable signals that it is absent yet needed, as a consequence, as it cannot have any content of its own, any form of self-representation – it can only be represented inadequately, through a series of particular contents that 'assume, in certain circumstances, a function of representation of the impossible universality of the community' (*E* 71).

The question, then, is how and when can a particular body 'carry' the universal as we never know in advance what quality, what particularity, which signifier, is capable of becoming the support of the universal. If the universal at stake in politics is always the result of a hegemonic struggle, this means that there can be no intrinsic relation between the universal and the particular qualities of the instance in which it is embodied. Laclau thus preserves without the slightest reconciliation the gap between the universal and the particular. The universal, in Laclau's view, 'can exist only through its parasitic attachment to some particular body; but that body is subverted and deformed in its own particularity as it becomes the embodiment of fullness' (*E* 71). This connection of parasitism and subversion has far-reaching consequences for Laclau's conception of emancipation.

Nevertheless, Laclau's position is equivocal on this point: on the one hand, a hegemonic relation is a relation of support, that is, the relation between the universal to be represented and the particular that fulfils the function of representing is wholly external. In this sense, we cannot go from the particular to the universal, even if the latter seems to be 'supported' by the former. On the other hand, however, it is – at least to a certain degree – also a relation of transitivity.

To illustrate this somewhat abstract arrangement, Laclau cites as example (used by Derrida himself), the irreducible gap between the 'anachronistic' language of revolution and the revolutionary content. In opposition to Marx, who postulated the necessity of the transcendence of their chasm, Laclau and Derrida firmly stress that the inadequacy or, rather, the anachronism of language with respect to the content of revolutions remains inevitable. But for that very reason, the anachronistic emancipatory language which appears to Marx inappropriate for expressing demands of the present situation is precisely in its inappropriateness appropriate. On this account, then, every revolution is necessarily forced to express itself in an 'anachronistic language', more, the split between 'phraseology' and 'content', instead of being an obstacle to the politics of emancipation, constitutes a permanent condition for emancipation. Conversely, the realization of Marx's requirement for the coincidence of the 'content' and 'phraseology' would only lead to the death of emancipation.

In a sense, we might say that the 'phraseology' in its very inadequacy, in its very anachronism, is a stand-in for the Revolution as such. Or, to say it with Laclau: 'The old revolution is present in the new one, not in its particularity but in its universal function of being *a* revolution, as the incarnation of the revolutionary principle as such' (E 72). To put it another way: what the new revolution includes is simply the void of the universal Function in the previous revolution.

Once admitted that the universal has no content of its own, the only option left to the universal principle, if it is to come to exist, is to fully assume the impossibility of ever achieving its coincidence with 'language'. It is precisely because of its failure to adequately 'express' it that anachronistic language, according to Laclau, is capable of representing, more, incarnating, the universal principle. The universal of emancipation is thus embodied not through the transparency of language, but rather through its opacity, through what I propose to call *the materiality of the signifier*. In this sense, we might say that every language, in its relation to the content to be 'expressed' through it, is 'anachronistic'.

The constitutive role of 'anachronistic' language can thus be explained with the help of Laclau's concept of the 'empty signifier'. The function of the empty signifier is usually explained as follows: it is a signifier capable of representing, not, of course, the totality, the Whole, but, rather, its impossibility, precisely to the extent that we are dealing here with a signifier without a signified, devoid of all meaning, of all content of any kind (*E* 36). It should be noted that it is not its 'emptiness' which qualifies a given signifier for the function of the 'empty signifier', that is, of the placeholder of the impossible totality, as it is not difficult to show that no signifier, the empty signifier notwithstanding, is ever fully empty.

Laclau certainly makes a valid point by arguing that no operation of emptying can do away with what he calls 'the remainders of signifieds', that zone of opacity that links an empty signifier to a particular situation in which such a signifier is to take effect. The remainder of signifieds as that which, in Laclau's view, remains as a residue of the operation of emptying, as such points to the empty signifier's contamination with the existing signifieds, making it in this way intrinsically problematic.

Where my conception of the empty signifier differs from Laclau's concerns the ways in which we both conceive of what I propose to call the materiality of the signifier. It is here that we would need to investigate more closely Laclau's conception of the universal.

What a signifier cannot by definition be stripped of, in my view, is not the remainder of signifieds, rather, it is the very materiality of the signifier which, however, only emerges as the ineradicable residue of the operation of emptying. Yet, this 'pathological' dimension of the signifier, to use a Kantian term, this 'flesh', of the signifier, this 'ineradicability' of the particular, is not something that 'corrupts' the signifier and, ultimately, prevents it from legitimately assuming its symbolic mandate – that is, to operating as representative of the representation, a *Vorstellungsrepräsentanz*, of the absent fullness, of the impossible totality, as deconstructivists would have it. Rather, it is that which makes it possible to perform this function.

The paradox of the 'empty signifier' then consists in that the function of representing is performed thanks to that which makes the representation impossible, that is to say, through a paradoxical, one is tempted to say 'immaterial materiality', of the signifier, a materiality that is by definition undeconstructible. This means that if the empty signifier remains undeconstructible, if it does not abide by the 'rules of the game' established by deconstruction, this is precisely because, at this point, it operates no longer as a signifier. The empty signifier, inasmuch as it coincides with the name, transgresses the register that is proper to it to 'fall' so to speak in the register of the real.

The empty signifier thus points to an excess or surplus in the autonomous working of the signifier. This surplus, however, is not related to the remainder of signifieds, as Laclau suggests, but rather to something inherent in the signifier, something 'within' the signifier itself (whether sound or letter). And it is precisely this 'materiality' which leads to its going beyond, exceeding, or surpassing itself. Thus, if I use this term (the materiality of the signifier), it is simply to emphasize the nonsensical nature of the signifier, the very existence of signifiers apart from and separated from any possible meaning or signification they might have; it is to emphasize the fact that the signifier's very existence exceeds its significatory role, that its substance exceeds its symbolic function. And only by being reduced to its mere being, 'its being there', its mere presence, can the empty signifier operate as representative of the representation of the impossible universality.

The signifier's being goes beyond its 'designated role' which is to signify. It is in this sense that we might then say, by paraphrasing Lacan, that rather than referring to 'the fact of having meaning' the empty signifier should be used to refer to 'the fact of having effects Other than meaning effects', namely that of naming and thus creating a new referent. The empty signifier defies the role allotted to it, refusing to be altogether relegated to the task of signification. In a certain sense, the empty signifier is associated with the name – the name, in Lacan's terminology refers to the material, nonsignifying face of the signifier, the part that has effects without signifying.

Empty signifier is the name that has no referent in the situation. Such names are terms which 'will have been presented' in a new situation, in the situation considered, hypothetically, as transformed by the hegemonic intervention. The empty signifier is a term which creates its referent. Empty signifiers upset established significations, so as to leave the referent empty, in a place that will have been filled in a new situation. The production of an empty signifier is an absolutely creative moment, a moment with no links to what is already established: the transformation of an anonymous, perfectly insignificant proper name (say, Peron, to use Laclau's example) into a representative of the Whole.

The essential point is that, without any direct relation to an already existing object or situation, the empty signifier intervenes or interrupts but does not 'represent', or 'interpret'. The creation of the empty signifier is an active intervention rather than reactive. It is the moment of 'forcing' or positing the conditions of the very intervention. In this sense it could be said that the empty signifier by deciding the undecidable creates a new situation.

Laclau is certainly right in claiming that what is named, the content of the empty signifier, is immanent to the situation, what Laclau refers to as the remainders of signifieds, but the naming itself, as act, changes the situation as a whole. By insisting on this 'umbilical cord' linking the empty signifier to a given situation, Laclau seems to neglect this other, creative, aspect of the empty signifier.

The issue of the materiality of the signifier thus 'condenses' in a sense two aspects of emancipation: anachronism – this being but another name for a more general Laclauian term, that of the structural dislocation – and the universal.

How then are we to articulate this mutual belonging of the universal and dislocation? This question is all the more complicated in that the issue of the universal has as its horizon the destiny of emancipation (*E* 13).

The first conclusion that can be drawn from this mutual implication of the universal and dislocation can thus be formulated as follows. If there is no universal outside its 'embodiment', this means that there is an irreducible dislocation between the universal and the 'body' chosen to hold its place. Here, I propose to take another step in this direction. It is not enough to affirm the dislocation of the universal and the particular. My own view is that this dislocation is indeed grounded in a 'more original' dislocation of the universal itself, that is to say, in the dislocation between the impossible, yet always already anticipated universal, the universal represented, according to Laclau, by the empty signifier, and an incorporated, yet by this very fact always already subverted, universal.

This is also evident from the specific temporality of the universal. Generally speaking, the time of the universal is always 'out of joint', 'derailed', because the universal, in this sense, is either an anticipation of itself or is delayed with respect to itself in that it is always inadequately represented or subverted by each of its concrete 'incarnations'. As a consequence, the universal is therefore necessarily situated in the interval between these two temporal modes. In this sense of the universal it can only be said that 'it will have been'. The point that I am trying to make here is that the hegemonic relation – which according to Laclau is the only conceivable modus of the presentation and the representation of the universal – is secondary to, or parasitic on, the inherent dislocation of the universal. That said, it is only possible to insist with Laclau on the fact that there is no universal outside its concrete 'incarnations', if we recognize that the hegemonic relation is secondary to, or, in Laclau's words, parasitic on, the inherent dislocation of the universal. To put it in yet another way, the hegemonic relation as such is already an attempt to solve the inherent deadlock of the universal itself.

This allows us to postulate two different levels of the universal: the universal as the point of impossibility within the constitutively inconsistent social and that particular instance which, because of its 'out-of-jointness' with respect to the established order, fills the void of the absent universal. This particular thus transformed represents that dimension which de-particularizes all particularities, transcends the horizon of the particularities by making their differences indifferent. The empty signifier as the result of a hegemonic relation can be said to reveal and, at the same time, conceal the split inherent to the universal. On this account, such a signifier signals that the universal comes to exist as a 'universal singular', peculiar to but unlimited by the contents of the situation in which it takes effect, thus allowing the singular universal to escape its specification exclusively in terms of a given situation through a kind of subtraction from the particularities of that situation. Only as such, i.e. deprived of an established place, can the singular universal then be open, non-exclusionary, i.e. 'offered to all'.

The empty signifier thus fulfils a two-fold function: the first being the traditional role of the master signifier whose principal role is to totalize an inconsistent, incomplete multiple into a consistent structure. In the field of politics this means that the empty signifier, by introducing a new distributive regime in the social, 'stabilizes' the floating of the existing signifiers by 'fixing' the relations between them and, as a consequence, determines the affinity between given signifiers and their signifieds. But there is also what I propose to call the function of the de-totalizer. This function is of capital importance for any contemporary politics of emancipation inasmuch as it is precisely this signifier which makes it possible for a community 'for all' to come into being.

This distinction between the two functions of the empty signifier, however, seems to be neglected to a certain degree by Laclau. Nowhere is the 'mutual parasitism' of hegemony and deconstruction more obvious than in the ambiguous status of the empty signifier. Insisting as he does on the conjunction of deconstruction and hegemony as the sole model for theorizing politics, Laclau refuses to recognize that he is making use, under one and same name, of two quite different sorts of the universal. As part of his emphasis on the open-ended, untotalizable character of the social, he tacitly adopts precisely a deconstructivist notion of universality as a forever incomplete, potential, or ongoing process. The perspective of hegemony, on the other hand, seems to privilege the role of the 'totalizer' as the principal role of the universal.

I want here to address some of the questions arising from Laclau's conception of politics in terms of the convergence of hegemony and deconstruction. I propose to look at the conjuncture of hegemony and deconstruction, and suggest that this conjunction can be discerned further in order to locate its emancipatory potential. I believe that Laclau has not yet sufficiently entertained the idea that, in order to contribute to a contemporary theory of emancipation, it may well be necessary to pass beyond the very terms of the universality debate as posed in the perspective of the conjunction of deconstruction and hegemony. It might be useful to address this problem from another angle, or indeed from the perspective of an altogether different approach than a deconstructivist.

According to Laclau, the universal at stake in politics is always a particular universal, always the result of a pure hegemonic intervention. That is, there can be no intrinsic relations between the universal as the empty form of totalizing and the particular qualities of the instance 'chosen' to fulfil the task of representing the absent universal. His theory of hegemony provides the opportunity for the distinction between the two aspects of the universal, the form and the content, but does not itself explain the precise relation between the two. Laclau's position on this point begs many questions. What kind of relationship is there, for example, between the remainders of signifieds and the capacity of the particular elevated to the dignity of the universal to renounce its difference? What is neglected in Laclau's account of the universal, I would argue, is precisely the way in which the universal *transcends* these differences, makes them indifferent.

In light of the danger of conflation of different conceptions of the universal implicit in the deconstructivist approach, I would want to add a different kind of emphasis in my attempt to sketch out the problems that concern Laclau's theorization of a politics of emancipation at the level of its intersection with the universal.

Clearly, Laclau's theory appears to be a radical departure for any serious work on the politics of emancipation, in particular as, departing from the constitutive inconsistency of the social, it inscribes politics in the register of the 'not all', a horizon without 'beyond', thus providing necessary theoretical tools for addressing the issue of politics in the present situation of globalization. The question is then: is there adequate space for a concept of the universal ('for all') within an ontology founded on the undecidability of the structure. More precisely, taking Laclau's conception of politics, what sort of status, in short, are we to accord to what I refer to as the politics of emancipation? Such questions point directly to perhaps the most unsettling one of all, the status of hegemony as the sole model of politics.

Needless to say, any political situation, left to itself, presents several orientations, several ways of resolving differences. This multiplicity, as such, remains a matter of the relation of forces, of alliances, of conjunctures, and never a matter of 'fidelity'. A political movement, resistance, or mobilized outrage, presents politics conceived as a bundle of more or less antagonistic positions competing for dominance. In this sense, politics in terms of hegemony thus represents so many efforts to do what can be done in the situation of the de-sedimentation of the socio-politico-ideological order as we know it. What are the criteria for distinguishing different politics, all rooted in the logic of hegemony, in particular if we acknowledge, as we must, that these criteria remain immanent to their situation?

The problem is that the logic of hegemony is consistent with both the politics of emancipation and its negation. Laclau's conception of hegemony provides little space, say, for distinguishing between the communitarian promotion of a particular identity and a reactionary protection of the same identity. How can the hegemonic logic be consistent with a radically egalitarian definition of a politics of emancipation? Clearly, a politics of emancipation recognizes that, in order to be effective, it must respect what is possible within the objectivity of the situation. It is a matter of dealing with the situation at hand. In this sense, an emancipatory politics, to be efficacious at all, cannot escape the constraints imposed by hegemonic logic. Nevertheless, the obvious problem with any theory of emancipation, including a theory of radical democracy, I would insist, is that it sits uncomfortably with the whole logic of hegemony. Laclau's theory of radical democracy, in the final analysis, his fidelity to emancipation, cannot be derived solely from the assertion that nothing is allowed into existence that does not undergo the test of undecidability.

If every form of politics is conditioned by a process that, by de-sedimenting the social, re-activates what Laclau calls 'the political moment of its originary institution' (Laclau 1996: 47), what then is the status of a politics of radical democracy which seems to turn politics toward emancipation as its 'atemporal destiny'? In anticipation of the more systematic discussion to come, I would argue that, to some degree, Laclau avoids addressing the question of his own fidelity to the politics of emancipation testified to by his ambition to formulate a theory of radical democracy. This question, however, is of capital importance in my view as it is precisely this fidelity to emancipation which seems to be pointing towards what, in particular political projects, transcends time and situation, and saves politics from the trap of 'historicism'; the trap of a deconstructivist as well as pragmatist conception of politics that seeks to reduce politics to the historical determination of socio-political arrangements.

Laclau would no doubt argue that his concept of the political in terms of the dialectic of sedimentation and reactivation is sufficiently broad to account for all the sorts of politics at issue. The problem is precisely how to account, on his definition of politics, for the particularity of politics of emancipation as politics among others. This point in the argument must not be pressed too far. If Laclau is indeed able to sustain that making visible of the 'dialectic' of the sedimentation of the social and the reactivation of the political is crucial for our understanding of the working of the politics of emancipation (*NR*: 34–5), then it seems that he has a way of linking the specificity of emancipation with the fact that the formulation of any politics, emancipatory included, is historically contingent. In this sense, I would argue that there is today no question more compelling in theorizing about politics than the question of the articulation between emancipation and the de-totalization of the social.

The fidelity to emancipation, which operates here as an axiom rather than a programme to be realized, is then, in more strictly Laclauian terms, nothing other than the fidelity to reactivation. Laclau thus seems to be suggesting that all true politics of emancipation acts as 'guardian' of this dislocation, and, as a consequence, of what is not counted by the established order. Politics of emancipation designates here nothing other than a continuous reactivation of this dislocation, a reactivation aiming, ultimately, at the detotalization of the social. This, of course, is not to be understood in the sense of a total destruction of the social fabric but rather in the sense of the institution of a community 'for all', a community in which what is at stake is precisely the predicate determining the belonging to the community, the demarcating line between inside/outside, Us/Them.

So the real question comes down to this: how are we to conceive a contemporary politics of emancipation once it is admitted that all politics is rooted in the incompleteness of the social and, as a consequence, that all political order established in such an untotalizable society remains constitutively contingent, a sedimented result of a series of contingent articulations, as Laclau puts it? Is fidelity to emancipation simply a matter of choice, ultimately, due to one's personal preference or must it rather come from some further, undefined injunction?

In response to this question I would argue that to be faithful to emancipation is not a matter of choice between various political regimes, because it is choice itself that constitutes the framework for the distinction of these regimes. At the same time it is a blind spot that constitutes a theory, yet a spot that can be theorized only at the cost of its inconsistency. On this account, fidelity to emancipation is that 'surplus' which distinguishes a politics of emancipation from any other 'hegemonic' politics. Certainly, politics of emancipation is only possible if, refuting the appearance of necessity, we recognize that there is a field of possibilities. But, to paraphrase Badiou, a choice to break with what is the case must begin with a break with oneself.

Notes

1 Laclau, on the other hand, while fully acknowledging that deconstruction may be of help to a theory of radical democracy by radicalizing its trends and arguments, refuses categorically to join Derrida in his attempt to recognize in emancipation the manifest destiny of deconstruction (*E* 59).

2 It is precisely for that reason that Laclau criticizes Habermas who, in the name of a final rational reconciliation, such as has been outlined by the Enlightenment project of modernity, rejects a 'nihilistic' postmodernity, neglecting in this way an important emancipatory potential of both, the postmodern society as well as of its postmodern theorizing. Against Habermas Laclau thus states:

> Our position, however, is exactly the opposite: far from perceiving in the 'crisis of reason' a nihilism which leads to the abandonment of any emancipatory project, we see the former as opening unprecedented opportunities for a radical critique of all forms of domination, as well as for the formulation of liberation projects hitherto restrained by the rationalist 'dictatorship' of the Enlightenment (*NR* 3–4).

3 Rather than simply dismiss the concept that has become embarrassing, as witnessed by today's prevailing approach to the problem, we should, as Laclau reminds us very pertinently, preserve the concept on the condition, however, that the formulation of a new politics of emancipation takes as its point of departure the deconstruction of what Laclau refers to as the classical notion of emancipation. While showing that this concept involves a series of logically incompatible claims, Laclau maintains that:

> this should not lead us [...] to the simple abandonment of the logic of emancipation. It is, on the contrary, by playing within the system of logical incompatibilities of the latter that we can open the way to new liberating discourses which are no longer hindered by the antinomies and blind alleys to which the classical notion of emancipation has led (E 2).

References

Badiou, A. (1988) *L'être et l'événement*, Paris: Seuil.

Critchley, S. (1998) 'The hypothesis, the context, the messianic, the political, the economic, the technological: on Derrida's specters of Marx', *Acta Philosophica*, 2: 81–108.

Laclau, E. (1996) 'Deconstruction, pragmatism, hegemony', in C. Mouffe (ed.) *Deconstruction and Pragmatism*, London and New York: Routledge.

Derrida, J. (1994) *Specters of Marx: The State of the Debt, the Work of Mourning, and the New International*, tr. P. Kamuf, New York: Routledge.

Part III

HEGEMONY

Discourse, rhetorics, antagonism

11

ENCOUNTERS OF THE REAL KIND

Sussing out the limits of Laclau's embrace of Lacan

Jason Glynos and Yannis Stavrakakis

We've plugged our 'lacanometer' into Ernesto Laclau's theoretical corpus. Eyes raised in expectation, we wait to see where on its scale the pointer will come to rest. Just how far is Laclau willing to go in appropriating Lacanian categories in the service of his hegemonic approach to discourse analysis? Or, to put it in Freudian terms, what measure of truth shall we attribute to the lapsus haunting a recent publication: a textual condensation of the two authors' names ('Laclan')?[1]

Framing our essay in this way, the question clearly takes for granted a certain reading of Laclau's theoretical trajectory, namely, his increasing readiness to take on board many crucial Lacanian insights. Theoretical affinities with Lacanian thought are evident from at least the time of *Hegemony and Socialist Strategy*, if not earlier. Since then, such affinities have been subject to further exploitation (mainly in *NR* and *E*). There is often a straightforward terminological cross-over. Think, for example, of terms like suture, identity, identification, and the subject-as-lack. But there is also an apparently close conceptual affinity, even when the names of terms are not shared. Think, for example, of the nodal point, the empty signifier, the radically excluded, the impossibility of society, or the notion of an outside that is constitutive of the inside (roughly corresponding to the Lacanian concepts of the *point-de-capiton*, the master signifier, the *objet petit a*, the impossibility of the sexual relation, and extimacy). Indeed, conceptual affinities such as these make up a fairly extensive reservoir, from which Laclau does not hesitate to draw in elaborating further his discourse theoretic approach to political analysis.

An early example of such conceptual cross-fertilization concerns the already-mentioned nodal point, as developed in *Hegemony and Socialist Strategy*. The nodal point functions as a central category in discourse theory, a category developed at the intersection of Lacanian theory and political analysis:

> Any discourse is constituted as an attempt to dominate the field of discursivity, to arrest the flow of differences, to construct a centre. We will call the privileged discursive points of this partial fixation, *nodal points*. (Lacan has insisted on these partial fixations through his concept of *points de capiton*, that is, of privileged signifiers that fix the meaning of a signifying chain. This limitation of the productivity of the signifying chain establishes the positions that make predication possible – a discourse incapable of generating any fixity of meaning is the discourse of the psychotic.) (*HSS* 112).

This is not to argue, of course, that during the mid-1980s Lacanian theory is already the main theoretical reference in Laclau's or Laclau and Mouffe's work. The relative importance of Lacanian argumentation was to increase in Laclau's subsequent work partly due to the whole dialogue that took place after 1985 – between Laclau and Žižek for instance – and which left its distinctive mark in Laclau's work – most notably in *New Reflections on the Revolution of our Time* and in *Emancipation(s)*.[2]

This account suggests a fairly high reading on our 'lacanometer', a hypothesis further confirmed by the fact that Laclau has explicitly acknowledged a strong Lacanian influence upon his work. As he clearly points out in a 1993 interview, although 'Lacanian theory played an important role in my theoretical trajectory at least from the beginning of the eighties [...] this influence has increased during these last years' (Laclau 1993: 58). This has led him to a very important redefinition of some of the categories of his theory of hegemony (one can think of the shift from a conception of subjectivity in terms of 'subjects positions' to acknowledging the importance of an understanding of subjectivity in terms of the subject-as-lack), a redefinition put forward in *New Reflections*. Moreover, he has also actively defended his Lacanian 'turn' in the most uncompromising terms. In a recent exchange with Judith Butler and Slavoj Žižek, he finds himself 'allied with Žižek against Butler in the defence of Lacanian theory' (Laclau in Butler *et al.* 2000: 281), concluding that Butler's 'objections to incorporating the Lacanian Real into the explanation of hegemonic logics are not valid' (Laclau in Butler *et al.* 2000: 182).

Nevertheless, such an account of the relation between Laclau and Lacan should also raise suspicions. Our worry is that it suggests too much convergence, almost to the point of obscuring potential – and potentially fruitful – divergences. It is precisely these potential disjunctions we wish to start exploring in this essay. Why, for example, the almost complete and conspicuous absence in Laclau's work of Lacanian categories such as fantasy, and, perhaps more importantly, *jouissance*? Are their absence the effect of a conscious eclecticism that judges them appropriate only to the clinic? Can they be safely ignored without violating even a minimal fidelity to Lacan's thought? In view of their central importance to many Lacanian scholars it would seem reasonable to expect some sort of response. All the more so since these categories and theoretical logics constitute the kernel of Lacan's understanding of the real, that is to say, of a central Lacanian category that we have just seen Laclau defending against Butler's objections. After all, these categories are also central to other theorists who otherwise share many common theoretical assumptions and aims with Laclau in the fields of social and political theory.

It is clear, to refer to just one example, that Slavoj Žižek and Ernesto Laclau's exchanges over the last decade or so have provoked each other to their own mutual annoyance and benefit, thereby also making possible some of the most exciting new developments in social and political theory. Nevertheless, despite some common aims and assumptions, and even despite some fairly caustic exchanges mostly related to their respective political standpoints,[3] it remains unclear precisely where the differences between Laclau and Žižek should properly be located, at least in relation to Laclau's use (or non-use) of Lacanian categories. We feel that there are several issues that need to be made explicit and which may force Laclau to better refine his position on this matter. This is not to suggest, of course, that Lacanian social theorists themselves are capable of resolving these questions in any definitive way. The more direct purpose of this paper is to force such issues onto the agenda in a way that may prompt Laclau to develop further his own position, and even advance (or destabilize) frontiers drawn by Lacanian social theorists like Žižek.[4]

It will come as no surprise after these introductory paragraphs that, though any number of categories could have been chosen for our purposes, we have chosen to explore a subset of issues as they relate to the category of the *real*. Not only is this category central to Lacan's thought and to self-confessedly Lacanian social theorists, it is one to which Laclau himself attaches special import, as his aforementioned response to Butler demonstrates. The real will function as the conceptual axis along which our 'lacanometer' will be aligned. It thus becomes crucial to specify more precisely the way this real in Lacan's work is understood both by Laclau and by other (Lacanian) scholars.

There are a lot of points in Laclau's work where one can find direct references to, or analogies drawn with, the category of the real in Lacanian theory. A good starting point in probing the relation between Laclau and Lacan is the category of the real conceived negatively as the limits of signification. This is because we believe that their theoretical affinities are strongest here, sharing as they do a kind of negative ontology. We then move on to examine a couple of further points where their affinities become progressively less clear and potentially divergent. These will be considered first, in terms of the means by which the real is positivized for the social subject; and second, in terms of the means by which the real provides a kind of 'positive' satisfaction or enjoyment for the social subject.

Negative dimensions of the real: the limits of discourse

Clearly, Laclau's work aims at showing the discursive nature of social objectivity: it understands human reality as socially constructed and articulated in discourse.

This is a constant theme which runs through most of his work. In *Hegemony*, for example, it is argued that 'every object is constituted as an object of discourse' (*HSS* 108) while ten years later Laclau will introduce his edited volume on *The Making of Political Identities* by acknowledging that 'a dimension of construction and creation is inherent in all social practice' (Laclau 1994: 3). Here Laclau is in complete agreement with Lacan who also argues that 'every reality is founded and defined by a discourse' (Lacan 1998: 32).

Neither Laclau nor Lacan, however, are content with this banal constructionism. Such a position can only be the starting point for a complex understanding of human experience. Indeed, they are both interested in showing that human construction is never able to institute itself as a closed and self-contained order. There is always something which frustrates all efforts to reach an exhaustive representation of the world – whether natural or social. One can approach this constitutive frustration by speaking of the *limits of discourse*, often associated with notions like 'incompleteness of identity' (poststructuralism), 'impossibility of society' (Laclau), or 'the lack in the Other' (Lacan).

Registering this constitutive limit is exactly what prevents the assimilation of Laclau and Mouffe's discourse theory into an idealism wherein human experience is reduced to social construction. Indeed, according to Laclau and Mouffe, to argue that all objects are constituted as objects of discourse has *nothing to do* with the question of whether there is a world external to thought or whether we can come to know this external world. Events like earthquakes or the falling of a brick certainly exist independently of our will. However, whether their specificity as meaningful objects will be constructed *as* an earthquake or a falling brick, or understood in terms of 'natural phenomena' or 'expressions of the wrath of God', depends upon the discursive articulation interpellating the social subject. What is denied here 'is not that such objects exist externally to thought, but the rather different assertion that they could constitute themselves as objects outside any discursive conditions of emergence' (*HSS* 108). In other words, we are dealing with two distinct orders: discursive being and extra-discursive existence. Stressing the importance of the first for human societies does not put into question the irreducibility of the second. It is simply to say that the latter assertion adds little to our understanding of the logics and mechanics of discourse.

Thus, the limits of discourse are *internal* to discourse itself, even if these end up being inextricably intertwined with notions of extra-discursive existence/reality. If it is never possible to fully grasp what escapes discourse, this is not because of some epistemological barrier that can be progressively overcome in an asymptotic fashion. Rather, it is because this barrier is ontologically *constitutive*. In this view, discourse is in a constant state of *tension* – a tension which is *internal* to discourse.

The aforementioned distinction between discursive being and its internal limits, therefore, seems to be analogous to the Lacanian distinction between 'reality' and the 'real'. In a very Lacanian way reality corresponds to the discursively constructed identity of objects whereas the real names what is *impossible* to articulate in discourse. Reality is what a social subject constructs utilizing its symbolic and imaginary resources.

> Canceling out the real, the symbolic creates 'reality', reality as that which is named by language and can thus be thought and talked about. The 'social construction of reality' implies a world that can be designated and discussed with the words provided by a social group's (or subgroup's) language.
>
> (Fink 1995: 25)

The real is what remains outside this field of representation, what remains impossible to symbolize. In fact, the gap between the real and reality is treated as *axiomatically* unbridgeable. Why? Because it serves to account for human *desire*, our unending (ultimately failed) attempts to colonize and domesticate the real with reality, to represent the real in discourse.

Negative indices of the real: dislocations

In Lacanian theory, although this real is *ex definitione* irreducible to the field of construction and representation, it nevertheless shows itself indirectly through the kinks and inconsistencies of the latter's functioning. From a psychoanalytic point of view, then, the limits of every discursive structure (of the conscious articulation of meaning, for example) can only be shown in relation to this discursive structure itself (through the subversion of meaning). Using Thomas Kuhn's vocabulary, we could say that a discursive 'anomaly appears only against the background provided by the paradigm' (Kuhn 1962: 65). Hence Freud's focus on the formations of the unconscious – dreams, slips of the tongue, symptoms, etc. – the places where ordinary conscious meaning is distorted or disrupted and where another dimension – the unconscious – makes its presence felt.

The psychoanalytic idea of distortion or disruption as a negative index of the real is fully endorsed by Laclau's discourse theory. Although in *Hegemony* Laclau and Mouffe explicitly reject 'the distinction between discursive and non-discursive practices' (*HSS* 107), they do not focus on the dialectic between the field of discursivity and its extimate real *per se*. In *Emancipation(s)*, however, Laclau could be said to be doing precisely this. His article on empty signifiers, for example, makes crystal clear a shift of emphasis which began with his 1990 *New Reflections on the Revolution of our Time*. The emphasis shifts from signification and discursive articulation to the *limits* of signification. Although the category of *antagonism* was conceived as a limit to objectivity in *Hegemony*, *New Reflections* conceives antagonism as already a discursive articulation. *New Reflections* introduced the category of *dislocation* as a remedy, and his article on empty signifiers could be said to be a kind of formalization of this move.

According to Laclau's account in this latter article, if what are at stake here are

> the limits of a *signifying system*, it is clear that those limits cannot be themselves signified, but have to show themselves as the *interruption* or *breakdown* of the process of signification. Thus, we are left with the paradoxical situation that what constitutes the condition of possibility of a signifying system – its limits – is also what constitutes its condition of impossibility – a blockage of the continuous expansion of the process of signification (*E* 37).

Laclau even goes on to explicitly link his treatment of the issue with the Lacanian problematic of the real:

> we are trying to signify the limits of signification – the real, if you want, in the Lacanian sense – and there is no direct way of doing so except through the subversion of the process of signification itself. We know, through psychoanalysis, how what is not directly representable – the unconscious – can only find as a means of representation the subversion of the signifying process (*E* 39).

In Lacanian terms, then, it is the real which can never be adequately represented, which can only show itself through the disruption of any attempt (symbolic or imaginary) to represent it. And Laclau seems be in full agreement with this part of the argument. In fact, it can be argued that his concept of dislocation, first developed in *New Reflections* following Žižek's critique of the concept of antagonism, seems to be designed to account for what in Lacanian terms we could describe as 'encounters with the real' (Stavrakakis 2000a): while antagonism falls on the side of the imaginary-symbolic order of reality, dislocation falls on the side of the real order. In this view, dislocation becomes the index of the negative dimension of the real as limit of discourse.

Positive dimensions of the real

One must not forget, however, that in Lacanian theory the real is not only associated with moments of disruption, with traumatic or dislocatory experiences. First of all, the real in-itself is not disruption or lack. Disruption is certainly one way of *showing* the constitutive inability of the symbolic to represent the real, of demonstrating the symbolic order's lack of resources. But this lack is not simply a lack of symbolic resources; rather, it is a lack of the *real*, in particular, a lack of real *jouissance*: 'the lack inscribed in the signifying chain through which the Other, as the only possible site of truth, reveals that it holds no guarantee, is in terms of the dialectic of desire a lacking in *jouissance* of the Other' (Lacan and the École Freudienne 1982: 117). In this sense the lack in the Other is a lack of *jouissance*, of a pre-symbolic real enjoyment or satisfaction which is always posited as lost. What is lost is the part of ourselves that is sacrificed when we enter the socio-symbolic system – a system that regulates the discursive articulation of need in demand (thus introducing the crucial dimension of desire).[5]

Second, real disruption, the lack of the real is usually positivized (imaginarized) and presented in fantasy as an object of desire – what Lacan calls the *objet petit a*, the object-cause of desire.[6] Fantasy promises to cover over the lack in the Other, it promises an encounter with our lost/impossible *jouissance*. Fantasy offers us the object-cause of desire as the metonymy of our (lacking) fullness. The paradox of this *objet petit a* is that it embodies, in a double movement, the lack in the Other together with the promise of its filling.

Positive indices of the real I: empty signifiers, master signifiers, **objets petit a**

What is Laclau's position *vis-à-vis* these two important aspects of Lacan's conceptualization of the real? Let us start with the second point. As we will see, it is possible to argue here that Laclau's work takes a direction which brings him very close to the Lacanian approach. In Laclau, dislocation, any encounter with the real which disrupts the discursive field, is not only something traumatic – an experience of negativity – but also the condition of possibility for social and political creation and re-articulation. In other words, dislocation also has a productive dimension.[7] As far as the nature of dislocations is concerned, therefore, it is clear in *New Reflections* that dislocations are, at the same time, traumatic/ disruptive and productive. They are traumatic in the sense that 'they threaten identities' but they are productive in the sense that they serve as 'the foundation on which new identities are constituted' (*NR* 39). Dislocation qua encounter with the impossible real functions as both the limit and condition of identity formation. This dislocation, for Laclau, is *positivized* in what he calls an 'empty signifier'.

If our continuous experiences of dislocation reveal that the full closure of the Other is impossible, that the real is ultimately unrepresentable, that lack is an irreducible characteristic of socio-political reality, this does not mean that closure, fullness, or full representation disappear from political discourse. Politics comprise all our attempts to fill in this lack in the Other: 'although the fullness and universality of society is unachievable, its need does not disappear: it will always show itself through the presence of its absence' (*E* 53). And this is precisely where Laclau's category of the empty signifier becomes relevant:

> In a situation of radical disorder 'order' is present as that which is absent; it becomes an empty signifier, as the signifier of this absence. In this sense, various political forces can compete in their efforts to present their particular objectives as those which carry out the filling of that lack. To hegemonize something is exactly to carry out this filling function (*E* 44).

Laclau suggests, moreover, that signifiers other than 'order' can function in a similar way, signifiers like 'unity', 'revolution', etc. 'Any term which, in a certain political context becomes the signifier of the lack, plays the same role. Politics is possible because the constitutive impossibility of society can only represent itself through the production of empty signifiers' (*E* 44).

The important thing to note here is that these internal – though productive – real limits of signification are positivized from a Lacanian perspective too. At the symbolic level, these are positivized in the form of structurally significant signifiers called master signifiers; while at the imaginary level, these are positivized in the form of the *objets petit a*. Clearly, therefore, there is an immediate theoretical affinity holding between Lacan's positivizations of the real and Laclau's positivization of the limits of signification in terms of 'empty signifiers'. What both gestures have in common is the acknowledgement of the need to positively index these limits in the psychic economy and the discursive identity of the social subject.

From a Lacanian perspective, then, consider this formulation by Žižek:

> Out of the free-floating dispersion of signifiers, a consistent field of meaning emerges through the intervention of a Master Signifier [...] [E]very language contains a paradoxical element which, within its field, stands in for what eludes it – in Lacanese, in every set of signifiers, there is always 'at least one' which functions as the signifier of the very lack of the signifier. This signifier is the Master Signifier: the 'empty' signifier which totalizes ('quilts') the dispersed field ...
>
> (Žižek 1992: 102–3)

But from a Lacanian perspective not only is there a symbolic positivization of lack, there is also an imaginary positivization: '*Objet [petit] a* is a kind of "positivization", filling out, of the void' (Žižek 1993: 122). Thus, this *objet petit a* 'is simultaneously the pure lack, the void around which the desire turns and which, as such, causes the desire, *and* the imaginary element which conceals this void, renders it invisible by filling it out' (Žižek 1994: 178–9).

What is clear, therefore, is that both a Laclauian and a Lacanian approach attach great importance to the need to positively index the real in the subject's psychic economy. What is less clear, however, is what precise relation Laclau's empty signifier has to the Lacanian categories of master signifier and *objet petit a*.[8] This acquires special, and potentially fruitful, significance, given the Lacanian claim that 'the subject ($) is constitutively split between S1 [the master signifier] and a [*objet petit a*]; it can represent itself in S1, in a signifier, only in so far as the phantasmatic consistency of the signifying network is guaranteed by a reference to *objet petit a*' (Žižek 1996: 79).

Positive indices of the real II: jouissance *structured in fantasy*

We would like to suggest that one reason for this unclarity comes from the 'non-encounter' between Laclau and Lacanian theorists at the level of *jouissance*.[9] To our knowledge there is no reference in Laclau's work to the concept of *jouissance*. Perhaps, however, this is due to the overall mode of Laclau's embrace of the Lacanian real – an embrace framed in formal, structural terms rather than substantive terms. For as Jacques-Alain Miller has recently put it, '*jouissance* presumes the body; *jouissance* needs the body as its support, thus Lacan called it a substance. In Aristotle's tongue it's *ousia*; 'where *ousia* is, so is substance' (Miller 2000a: 13). So if the decision to forego any discussion of *jouissance* is a conscious decision on Laclau's part – and it would be very interesting to know whether it is – there is no doubt that prima facie objections could be summoned to support this decision. For in talking about *jouissance* one is always walking on the threshold of essentialism. Indeed, 'there is no exaggeration in positing Lacan's teaching as being animated by the difficulty of thinking about the subject as lack-in-being, that is, as a certain kind of non-being, together with *jouissance* as substance' (Miller 2000a: 13) – an especially poignant and potentially productive difficulty for anyone working within the broad field of anti-essentialist political theory. However, one should not forget that, even if thinking about the real qua *jouissance* seems to flirt with a certain essentialism, it nevertheless remains 'essentially' unrepresentable and always in a state of irresolvable tension with the socio-discursive field. Hence the whole issue seems to hinge on the particular advantages, insights, or problematizations the category of *jouissance* can offer to a discursive approach to politics such as the one advanced by Ernesto Laclau.

First of all it is necessary to point out that the category of *jouissance* and Lacan's continuous engagement with the field of enjoyment in both clinical and theoretical work should not be treated as a mere *supplement*, some kind of optional conceptual extra that can easily be bracketed, leaving intact and ready for appropriation the rest of Lacan's theoretical edifice (mainly his theorization of signification and symbolic articulation and their limits). This is not because of any kind of old-style essentialism. The problem is that, without taking into account enjoyment, the whole Lacanian framework loses most of its explanatory force. For example, what can possibly account for the constitutivity of desire (both in personal life and in the variety of political identifications) if *jouissance* is not accepted as the absent cause of human desire? Furthermore such enjoyment helps us answer in a more concrete way what is at stake in socio-political identification and identity formation, suggesting that support of social fantasies is partially rooted in the *jouissance* of the body.[10] What is at stake in these fields, according to Lacanian theory, is not only symbolic coherence (and/or dislocation) and discursive closure (and/or impossibility) but also *enjoyment*, the *jouissance* (a lost/impossible *jouissance* no doubt) animating human desire. Indeed, from a psychoanalytic point of view, socio-political symptoms persist exactly because they provide the social subject with a form of enjoyment. This explains why it is so hard to dis-articulate or displace such symptoms.

A couple of examples will reveal how *jouissance* can serve as an important explanatory ingredient in various socio-political phenomena, starting with advertising discourse. If advertising attempts to stimulate, to cause, our desire, this can only mean that the whole mythological construction that it articulates around the product is a *fantasy* and, furthermore, that this product serves or functions as an object that can satisfy our desire. Such a fantasmatic scenario must provide the coordinates within which our object-cause of desire appears, our *objet petit a*.[11] The condition of possibility for this complex play is, of course, the loss, the prohibition, of a mythical pre-symbolic *jouissance*. Such a (castrating) event posits *jouissance* as lost, thereby permitting the emergence of desire; a desire that is structured around the unending quest for the lost/impossible *jouissance*. Fantasy is a construction that stimulates, causes desire, because it promises to extinguish the lack created by the loss of *jouissance*.

It is a piece of this enjoyment that is promised in slogans like 'Enjoy Coca-Cola' – a slogan that Lacan himself had associated with what he called *le sujet de la jouissance*. In other words, within the advertising universe, every experience of lack is projected to the lack of the product that is being advertised; that is to say, to a lack that one simple move promises to eliminate: the purchase of the product. Advertising fantasies reduce the constitutive lack in the subject to the lack of the product that it simultaneously offers as an *objet petit a*, as a promise for the final elimination of this lack. Thus, advertising fantasy attempts to exorcise the *malaise* of everyday life by reproducing the system within which this *malaise* is constitutive.

The harmony, however, promised by fantasy cannot be realized; the *objet petit a* can function as the object-cause of desire only insofar as it is lacking. As soon as we buy the product we find out that the enjoyment that we get is partial, that it has nothing to do with what we have been promised: '"That's not it!" is the very cry by which the *jouissance* obtained is distinguished from the *jouissance* expected' (Lacan 1998: 111). And with every such experience a lack is re-inscribed in the subject. But this resurfacing of the inability of fantasy to lead us to a full satisfaction of our desire does not put in danger the cultural hegemony of advertising in late capitalist societies. As Slavoj Žižek often reminds us, the aim of fantasy is not to satisfy our desire, something that is ultimately impossible. It is enough to construct it and support it as such: through fantasy we 'learn' how to desire. As far as the final satisfaction of our desire is concerned this is postponed from discourse to discourse, from fantasy to fantasy, from product to product. It is this continuous displacement that constitutes the essence of consumer culture. The important 'by-product' of this process is, of course, a specific structuration of our desire. It is this particular *economy of desire* articulated around the advertised product qua *objet petit a* that guarantees, through its cumulative metonymic effect, the reproduction of late capitalism within a distinct 'promotional culture'. In other words, the hegemony of the market depends, to a large extent, on the hegemony of this particular economy of desire, on the hegemony of this particular *administration of enjoyment*.[12]

But advertising discourse is just one, and perhaps not the most important or revealing example. Another crucial example concerns the phenomenon of racism. In *Television* Lacan replies to the following question posed by Miller:

> – [W]hat gives you the confidence to prophesy the rise of racism? And why the devil do you have to speak of it?
> – Because it doesn't strike me as funny and yet, it's true. With our *jouissance* going off track, only the Other is able to mark its position, but only insofar as we are separated from this Other. Whence certain fantasies – unheard of before the melting pot.
>
> Leaving this Other to his own mode of *jouissance*, that would only be possible by not imposing our own on him, by not thinking of him as underdeveloped.
>
> Given, too, the precariousness of our own mode, which from now on takes its bearings from the ideal of an over-coming (*plus-de-jouir*), which is, in fact, no longer expressed in any other way how can one hope that the empty forms of humanhysterianism (*humanitairerie*) disguising our extortions can continue to last?
>
> Even if God, thus newly strengthened, should end up existing, this bodes nothing better than a return of his baneful past.
>
> (Lacan 1990: 32–3)

Miller takes up these comments in his seminar *Extimité*, which leads him to argue that racism, as a hatred of difference, is founded on 'the fact that the Other takes his *jouissance* in a way different from ours' – something reflected in racist discourse.

> All the arguments employed by racists to justify their hatred ultimately focus on the way in which the Other obtains some *plus-de-jouir* that he does not deserve; either he does not work, or he works too hard, or he eats smelly food or he has too much sex, etc.[13]

It follows from this line of argumentation that intolerance and racism are directly associated with the intolerance towards the *jouissance* of the Other (Evans 1998: 21).

Clearly all these insights are crucial not only for the analysis of racism but also for the analyses of all sorts of discourses of hatred. In *Tarrying with the Negative*, Slavoj Žižek conducts a masterful analysis of nationalism around this same Lacanian insight, building on Miller's idea of what he calls 'the theft of enjoyment': 'The question of tolerance or intolerance [. . .] is located on the level of tolerance or intolerance toward the enjoyment of the Other, the Other as he who essentially *steals* my own enjoyment' (Miller in Žižek 1993: 203, our emphasis). Nationalist hatred is explained then as a way societies or social groups attempt to deal with their lack of enjoyment, attributing this lack, this structural impossibility, to the action of an external force, the national enemy or the general Other who is fantasized as enjoying more (having already stolen what is thought of as 'essentially ours'). It follows therefore that 'the hatred of the Other is the hatred of our own excess of enjoyment' (Žižek 1993: 206).

Given this background, it should come as no surprise to find *jouissance* acquiring special importance for those contemplating seriously theories of ideology and, especially, critiques of ideological discourse. For in this view, 'the element which holds together a given community cannot be reduced to the point of symbolic identification: the bond linking together its members always implies a shared relationship toward a Thing, toward Enjoyment incarnated', an enjoyment structured in fantasies and directly linked to the hatred of Others (Žižek 1993: 201). In *The Sublime Object of Ideology*, Žižek's first book, which also includes a foreword by Laclau, the analytical extraction of enjoyment in social fantasies is described as the second step in a two-pronged approach to the analysis of ideological discourse. It constitutes a crucial step in that it situates discourse analysis (the first step) in relation to the problematic of enjoyment. For in Žižek's view, fantasmatically-structured *jouissance* functions as the support for our discursive articulations and symbolic identifications (Žižek 1989: 125). This is increasingly being acknowledged by researchers working within the broad field of discourse analysis, including the research programme in *Ideology and Discourse Analysis* initiated by Laclau.

A recent example of such work is David Lewis's PhD project on the discursive construction of 'New Age Travellers' within the New Right imaginary in Britain. Lewis's analysis of New Right discourse (both of primary material and the secondary bibliography on the issue) and the way New Age Travellers (NATs) are demonized within this political imaginary reveals that what sustains this whole public/official discursive edifice is an 'exposition' of their mode of enjoyment, a mode of *jouissance* which is presented as excessive and thus threatening for the social order. Moreover, as Lewis argues,

> in the construction of NATs the perception that they are the possessors of a surplus of *jouissance* becomes linked with the perception that they are the thieves who have stolen the *nation Thing* which constitutes a full British identity [...] NATs are thus presented as being guilty of a whole plethora of thefts.

from shoplifting to 'stealing' the aesthetic *jouissance* of a beautiful rural idyll (Lewis 2000: 10–11).

Given that our own *jouissance* is structured around how we think the Other takes its *jouissance* (Žižek 1993: 206), and given that *jouissance* sustains our public/official discourse (Glynos 2001a), we immediately see the significance of categories like *jouissance* and fantasy for the critique of ideology. From this perspective, it is possible to articulate political theory with praxis by linking the critique of ideological discourse with an ethico-political shift that parallels the Lacanian 'crossing of the social fantasy'. The potential (and still speculative) benefit of this psychoanalytically-inspired intervention is that Lacanian theory also offers us a typology of enjoyment modes, i.e. the different ways a subject relates to *jouissance* through fantasy.[14]

> What psychoanalysis can do to help the critique of ideology is precisely to clarify the status of this paradoxical *jouissance* as the *payment* that the exploited, the servant, receives for serving the Master.[15] This *jouissance*, of course, always emerges within a certain phantasmic field; the crucial precondition for breaking the chains of servitude is thus to 'traverse the fantasy' which structures our *jouissance* in a way which keeps us attached to the Master – makes us accept the framework of the social relationship of domination.
>
> (Žižek 1997: 48)[16]

In that sense, the importance psychoanalysis attaches to the notion of the real qua fantasmatically-structured *jouissance* suggests that symptomal analyses of the discursive or interpretative kind, though perhaps a necessary prerequisite, are often not sufficient to effect a displacement in the social subject's psychic economy. We often encounter cases in which a subject fully acknowledges the contingency of his/her situation, a subject who accepts how things could be otherwise and how an even minor change (in behaviour, attitude, etc.) would lead to a different life visited less by suffering. Yet the subject can't help him/herself; she cannot stop repeating. Why? Lacan's answer is, as should be clear by now, *jouissance*, the same *jouissance* that animates the consumerist desire that sustains late capitalism, the same *jouissance* that supports racist, nationalist, and New Right discourses – in fact discursive structures in general.

The structure of fantasy defines a mode of *jouissance* that often resists all interpretive/deconstructive strategies. Thus if psychoanalytic intervention (and, by extension, political intervention) is to have any effect in these cases, it must aim between the lines, so to speak, at the ineffable *objet petit a*, at the whole field of *jouissance*. This is ultimately what is at stake in working with a concept such as that of the Lacanian real. An articulation of this problematic of the real qua *jouissance* with Ernesto Laclau's discourse theory would, in our view, enhance our understanding not only of ideological processes, but also of the conditions of ethically relevant and politically effective ideological critiques.[17]

Notes

1 The lapsus is made by Glyn Daly or by the copy-editor of the *Journal of Political Ideologies*. See Daly 1999: 236 n. 15.

2 For a detailed examination of the evolving relation between Laclau's theoretical and conceptual apparatus and Lacanian theory along these lines see Stavrakakis 2000b.

3 See, in this respect, the exchanges between Laclau and Žižek in Butler *et al.* 2000.

4 Although, of course, Žižek's continuously shifting positions and his insatiable drive to apparently transgress himself, make any such project extremely difficult.

5 For a detailed presentation of the various definitions and nuances of *jouissance* in Lacanian theory see Evans 1998 and Miller 2000b.

6 The object-cause of desire is, of course, a bit more complex than we make it out to be in this paper. For, as Žižek points out,

> [t]he *object petit a* is not what we desire, what we are after, but, rather, that which sets our desire in motion, in the sense of the formal frame which confers consistency on our desire: desire is, of course, metonymical; it shifts from one object to another; through all these displacements, however, desire none the less retains a minimum of formal consistency, a set of phantasmic features which, when they are encountered in a positive object, make us desire this object – *objet petit a* as the cause of desire is nothing other than this formal frame of consistency.
>
> (Žižek 1997: 39)

On this point see also Žižek 2000: 20–1.

7 One should not fail to notice here the analogies with the conception of power Foucault advances in his later work, especially in the first volume of *The History of Sexuality*.

8 For an exploration of possible links between discourse theory and psychoanalytic theory see Glynos 1999, 2000a, 2000b, 2001a; Stavrakakis 1999, 2000b.

9 Indeed what is also curious is the fact that Laclau has never referred to the Lacanian category of master signifier (despite the terminological and theoretical affinities it shares with Laclau's empty signifier and nodal point); while he has mentioned the *objet petit a* (despite the latter's inherent link to *jouissance*). Can one not sense here a certain reluctance of Laclau to follow a Lacanian direction?

10 More specifically, perhaps, this *jouissance* of the body can be seen as rooted in the circulation of drive around bodily orifices:

> The very delimitation of the 'erogenous zone' that the drive isolates from the metabolism of the function (the act of devouring concerns other organs than the mouth – ask one of Pavlov's dogs) is the result of a cut (*coupure*) expressed in the anatomical mark (*trait*) of a margin or border – lips, 'the enclosure of the teeth', the rim of the anus, the tip of the penis, the vagina, the slit formed by the eyelids, even the horn-shaped aperture of the ear ...
>
> (Lacan 1977: 314–15).

11 On the relation between the subject's lack, the extimate *objet petit a*, and the lack in the Other, see Žižek 1992: 162; 1993: 48; 1994: 178.

12 This account of the function of advertising discourse is based on the more detailed argument presented in Stavrakakis 1999 and 2000a. For a related discussion of the relation between capitalism and desire in Žižek's work, see Glynos 2001b.

13 On this point see Žižek 1994: 70–4, where he relates hatred at the level of the id-*jouissance* to hatred (or evil) at the levels of the superego and ego.

14 It is impossible within the context of this short paper to develop a sophisticated account of the different modes of *jouissance* discussed by Lacan in his long theoretical trajectory. For a first approach to this complex issue see Miller 2000b. In fact, some of Miller's categorizations of *jouissance*, what he calls for example 'discursive *jouissance*', would be crucial in further exploring the links between *jouissance* and discourse. The same applies to the whole Lacanian problemetic of *lalangue*, of a field in which language and enjoyment are coupled together forming the phonematic *jouissance* from which discourse is eventually 'extracted'.

15 On this point, see Žižek's discussion of the opposition Fool/Knave (Žižek 1997: 46–8).

16 This, therefore, throws open a whole new way of conceiving the notion of phenomenology, at least as it relates to the analysis of fantasies, an analysis of forms of socio-symbolic transgression-enjoyment. Žižek explores the status of such a phenomenology in the following way:

> Phenomenology is now reasserted as the description of the ways in which the Real shows itself in phantasmic formations, without being signified in them: *it is the description, not interpretation*, of the spectral domain of mirages, of 'negative magnitudes' which positivize the lack in the symbolic order. We are thus dealing here with the paradoxical disjunction between phenomenology and hermeneutics: Lacan opens up the possibility of a radically non-hermeneutical phenomenology – of a phenomenological description of spectral apparitions which stand in for constitutive non-sense. In so far as the respective domains of *meaning* (accessible to hermeneutics) and symbolic *structure* (accessible through structural analysis) form two circles, the phenomenological description of fantasy is thus to be located at the *intersection* of these two circles.
>
> (Žižek, 1997: 217–18)

17 For a discussion of the relation between politics and ethics from a deconstructive and psychoanalytic perspective, see Glynos 2000c.

References

Butler, J., Laclau, E. and Žižek, S. (2000) *Contingency, Hegemony, Universality: Contemporary Dialogues on the Left*, London: Verso.

Daly, G. (1999) 'Ideology and its paradoxes: dimensions of fantasy and enjoyment', *Journal of Political Ideologies*, 4(2): 219–38.

Evans, D. (1998) 'From Kantian ethics to mystical experience: an exploration of jouissance', in D. Nobus (ed.) *Key Concepts of Lacanian Psychoanalysis*, London: Rebus.

Fink, B. (1995) *The Lacanian Subject: Between Language and Jouissance*, Princeton: Princeton University Press.

Glynos, J. (1999) 'From identity to identification: discourse theory and psychoanalysis in context', *Essex Papers in Politics and Government: Sub-series in Ideology and Discourse Analysis*, 11: 1–16.

—— (2000a) 'Sex and the limits of discourse' in D. Howarth, A. Norval and Y. Stavrakakis (eds) *Discourse Theory and Political Analysis*, Manchester: Manchester University Press.

—— (2000b) 'Sexual identity, identification and difference', *Philosophy and Social Criticism*, 26(6): 85–108.

—— (2000c) 'Thinking the ethics of the political in the context of a postfoundational world: From an ethics of desire to an ethics of the drive', *Theory and Event*, 4(4) http://muse.jhu.edu/journals/theory_and_event/v004/4.4glynos.html.

—— (2001a) 'The grip of ideology: a Lacanian approach to the theory of ideology', *Journal of Political Ideologies*, 6(2): 191–214.

—— (2001b) '"There is no Other of the Other": symptoms of a decline in symbolic faith', *Paragraph*, 24(2): 78–110.

Kuhn, T. (1962) *The Structure of Scientific Revolutions*, Chicago: Chicago University Press.

Lacan, J. (1977) *Écrits: A Selection*, London: Routledge/Tavistock.

—— (1990) *Television*, New York: Norton.

—— (1998) *The Seminar. Book XX. Encore, On Feminine Sexuality, The Limits of Love and Knowledge, 1972–3*, New York: Norton.

Lacan, J. and the École Freudienne (1982) *Feminine Sexuality*, London: Macmillan.

Laclau, E. (1993) 'Ernesto Laclau: a theoretical trajectory', an interview with Y. Stavrakakis and D. Zeginis, *Diavazo*, 324: 56–62.

—— (1994) 'Introduction', in E. Laclau (ed.) *The Making of Political Identities*, London: Verso.

Lewis, D. (2000) 'The construction of "New Age Travellers" in official and popular discourse' (PhD Colloquium, Department of Government, University of Essex).

Miller, J.-A. (2000a) 'The experience of the real in psychoanalysis', *Lacanian Ink*, 16: 7–27.

—— (2000b) 'Paradigms of *Jouissance*', *Lacanian Ink*, 17: 10–47.

Stavrakakis, Y. (1997) 'Field note on advertising', *Journal for the Psychoanalysis of Culture and Society*, 2(1): 139–41.

—— (1999) *Lacan and the Political*, London: Routledge.

—— (2000a) 'On the critique of advertising discourse: a Lacanian view', *Third Text*, 51: 85–91.

—— (2000b) 'Laclau with Lacan: comments on the relation between discourse theory and Lacanian psychoanalysis', *(a) the journal of culture and the unconscious*, 1(1): 134–53.

Žižek, S. (1989) *The Sublime Object of Ideology*, London: Verso.

—— (1992) *Enjoy your Symptom!* New York: Routledge.

—— (1993) *Tarrying with the Negative*, Durham, NC: Duke University Press.

—— (1994) *Metastases of Enjoyment*, London: Verso.

—— (1996) *The Indivisible Remainder*, London: Verso.

—— (1997) *The Plague of Fantasies*, London: Verso.

—— (2000) *The Fragile Absolute*, London: Verso.

12

'TAKING UP A TASK'

Moments of decision in Ernesto Laclau's thought

J. Hillis Miller

In the political thought of Ernesto Laclau, as in that of Walter Benjamin, Paul de Man, or Jacques Derrida, with whom Laclau may be instructively compared, a central question is how a movement from a less just to a more just society may be imagined to occur or does occur. How does political change, change that is not just a rearrangement of old forces and ideological commitments, happen? This is a major problem, perhaps *the* major problem, for any political theory. How do we get to something different as opposed to just more of the same old injustice and inequitable distribution of goods, powers, and privileges, slightly reorganized? Laclau's names for the kind of change he hopes for are 'hegemony' (borrowed from Gramsci) and 'emancipation(s)', the latter the name of one of Laclau's books. Revolutions and successful 'declarations of independence' are one form of such change, but small-scale events of this kind may happen whenever effective (political) decision is taken by an individual. For Laclau, it almost seems to be the case that all decision is political or has an essential political dimension. How do such events, political change for the better, happen to happen?

Before sketching and offering a critique of Laclau's answers to these questions, let me characterize three features of Laclau's thinking (and his stance as a person) that I find particularly attractive. One is a remarkable generosity of spirit, an openness to other ways of thinking that is accompanied by a rigor in sticking to his own commitments. Laclau thrives on discussion and even on controversy. He sees it as a way to make his own thinking more rigorous and less open to objection, but he also has a genuine curiosity about other ways of thinking that is unusual in its breadth. An example is his invitation to me to contribute to this book. This invitation was initiated by discussions we had at the University of California at Irvine in the fall of 1999 about his essay for the book on Paul de Man's materialism, *Material Events*, published by Minnesota late in 2000. I had taken issue with some aspects of Laclau's use of rhetoric, in particular his notions of catachresis. His response was both to change his essay somewhat and to ask me to extend what I had to say by writing this present essay.

A second salient feature of Ernesto Laclau's thinking about politics is his quite remarkable project of appropriating rhetorical theory, especially so-called deconstruction (as a particularly exigent rhetorical theory), to think about how political change for the better might occur. Laclau's hypothesis is that the play of forces within a given political situation takes place – materially, concretely, in actuality – according to displacements, substitutions, equivalences, differentiations, and condensations that may be accurately described in terms drawn from the most sophisticated rhetorical theories of our time, those, for example, of Gérard Genette, Paul de Man, or Jacques Derrida. If Jacques Lacan's originality, following Freud, was to see that the unconscious is structured like a language, a language, moreover, in which tropological displacements are essential, Ernesto Laclau's originality, no less bold and challenging, has been to hypothesize, and then to argue persuasively and patiently, that the political field too is structured like a language, or to be more precise, like a tropological system.

The third attractive feature of Laclau as a person and as a writer is his cheerful confidence that political change for the better is possible. He remains optimistically certain that this can happen. His work is devoted to thinking out how and why this may be. But Laclau's work is not just neutrally descriptive, a mere 'political science'. He wants his teaching, writing, lecturing, and conversing to be politically effective, to work to bring about change, to have what speech act theorists would call a performative as well as a constative dimension.

The way Laclau answers the question of how political change for the better may occur is complex and rigorous, expressed somewhat differently in different essays, and consequently not all that easy to express fairly and accurately in a few paragraphs. I shall base my brief account primarily on three characteristic essays, 'The politics of rhetoric' (2000). 'Deconstruction, pragmatism, hegemony' (1996), and 'Why do empty signifiers matter to politics?' (*E* 36–46). Central to Laclau's thought is a concept of 'hegemony', appropriated from Gramsci and from the Russian social democrats, then refashioned, defined anew, and redefined by Laclau in many books and essays. The word is used in a way that seems odd to someone unfamiliar with its Gramscian or Laclauian use. Normally we think (or *I* think) of hegemony as the name for the (often unjust) domination of an already existing ruling power, whether within a given nation state or as exercised outside the state, for example in imperialism or colonialism. 'Hegemony' is another name for sovereignty. Laclau uses the term quite differently, to name the way a contingent group within a given society (the working class, say, or certain individuals within it in the case of the Russian revolution or a certain group within the Communist Party in Italy after World War II) 'takes upon itself the task' of political emancipation from unjust ruling powers. Here is one example: 'The relationship by which a sector takes up tasks that are not its own is what the Russian social democrats called *hegemony*' (2000: 245). Later in the same essay Laclau quotes Togliatti, leader of the Italian Communist Party, in an essay of 1957:

> The proletariat becomes a national class insofar as it takes on these problems [the problems of the entire society] as its own and thence comes

> to know, by the process of changing it, the whole reality of national life. In this way it produces the conditions of its own political rule, and the road to becoming an effective ruling class is opened (248).

How is this 'taking up a task' not one's own possible? How does it happen? It is here that Laclau makes brilliant use of 'deconstruction' to define a given society or social situation, say that within a given nation state at a particular time, as an incomplete or undecidable structure, something not fashioned, as language is for de Saussure, as a complete and self-contained system of similarities and differentiations, but something structurally incomplete, heterogeneous, and open-ended, something non-totalizable, without clearly defined or definable limits. It always 'contains' (or excludes) at least one element which is necessary to the prospective totality of the system but which both belongs to the system and is outside it. This one (at least) additional element is what Laclau calls the 'hegemonic suture'. Laclau often uses the couplet 'impossible/possible', or the deconstructive term 'undecidability' to characterize this situation. In the essay on de Man ('The politics of rhetoric') he appropriates de Manian and Genettean insights into the undecidable 'logic' (his word) of the relations among metaphor, metonymy, synecdoche, and catachresis to define this impossible/possible political system. After commenting in some detail on one of de Man's most important and challenging late essays, 'Pascal's allegory of persuasian', Laclau observes:

> Now, this succession of structural moments coincides, almost step by step, with the logic [!] of hegemony that I have tried to describe in my work and which I see operating in the texts of Gramsci [...] To start with, the condition of any hegemonic suture is the constitutive non-closure of a system of political signification [...] vis-à-vis the excluded element (2000: 234).

The excluded element is the 'hegemonic suture', equated here with the Pascalian zero as defined by de Man, or with what Laclau elsewhere calls an 'empty signifier' (*E*, passim) because it refers to something outside the system and something, moreover, that is proleptic, anticipatory, evermore about to be, like that 'democracy to come (à venir)' of which Jacques Derrida often speaks. Laclau continues:

> [A]ll differences within the system establish relations of equivalence between themselves. And equivalence is precisely that which subverts difference. So the 'beyond' which is the condition of possibility of the system is also its condition of impossibility. All identity is constituted within the unsolvable tension between equivalence and difference (2000: 234).

Equivalence and difference, as Laclau knows and shows, are logical transpositions of the tropological terms 'metaphor' and 'metonymy'.

Laclau makes strategic use of the traditional recognition within rhetorical theory that the borders among the various master tropes tend to blur, so that a synecdoche is a little bit metaphorical, as well as a little bit metonymical, and so for the other tropes. This slippage in a given social system gives Laclau the 'play' that he needs to find in it to make possible new acts of hegemony. An act of hegemony is a moment when a contingent or metonymical segment within the non-totalized, heterogeneous whole takes upon itself the task of representing the whole, in a movement which might be defined tropologically as a step by which a contingent metonymy becomes a synecdochic metaphor, part standing for whole and acting politically in the name of the whole toward a better future, like the Italian Communist Party in Togliatti's description of its task.

One big question, perhaps, for Laclau's political theory the biggest, remains. How does this 'taking up of a task' occur, actually, historically, materially? It occurs by what Laclau, following Derrida, following Kierkegaard, calls 'the madness of decision'. As Laclau explicitly recognizes in one place, 'The madness of the decision is this blind spot in the structure, in which something totally heterogeneous with it – and, as a result, totally inadequate – has, however, to supplement it' (1996: 55). As I have already hinted, the one of the three branches of the trivium (grammar, rhetoric, and logic) that dominates in Laclau's work is logic. The opacities or irrationalities of tropes, however subtly and flexibly Laclau treats them, tend to get reassimilated by him to logic, assimilated to what he calls, more than once, the 'logic of hegemony'. Of course it is an 'impossible/possible' logic, and therein lies its strength. Nevertheless, the co-presence of possibility and impossibility is defined by Laclau from the perspective of more or less traditional logical assumptions. Tropes in general combine possibility and impossibility, as in the false equivalences of metaphor. They are irreducibly 'illogical' or 'alogical'.

The madness of decision is accurately to be described as a 'blind spot' because the predominantly logical thinking of Laclau's argumentation cannot command those moments of decision, rationalize them, or illuminate them with the light of reason. Often Laclau more or less takes for granted the way a given social group at particular moments in history and in a particular nation state has taken up tasks that make it an adequate/inadequate representative of the whole and so has performed acts of emancipation. The bourgeoisie in Czarist Russia was weak and, moreover, fearful above all of the proletariat. What in Western European countries was a stage in which the bourgeoisie defeated and replaced the aristocracy and its feudal structures, was in Russia, as in a somewhat different way in China, bypassed directly to a working class revolution. The job was there to do and they did it, in a way that was fundamentally to be defined by the manifold contingencies of the situation. It just happened that way, in an immensely complex and overdetermined way.

More, however, can be said than this about Laclau's theory of how emancipatory political change occurs. Laclau wants to avoid, in one direction, any remnant of what he sees as the now outmoded Marxist materialist determinism that believes all historical change is predetermined by inviolable materialist laws necessitating the ultimate withering away of the state and the dictatorship of the proletariat, in short, the Marxist millennium. In the other direction Laclau wants to avoid any return to a pre-existing transcendent source, any universal principle justifying the power and authenticity of those irruptive events that more or less abruptly change the course of history. That is one reason why he is hostile to any ethical justification for political change, such as, for example, that Levinasian theory, endorsed, Laclau observes, by Simon Critchley. The latter holds political engagement to be a response made by a demand of the other. '[...] I do not see,' says Laclau, 'in what sense an ethical injunction, even if it only consists of opening oneself to the otherness of the other, can be anything else than a universal principle that precedes and governs any decision' (1996: 53). Laclau, on the contrary, wants political decision to be singular, particular, contingent, not justified by any universal principle, therefore a 'madness'. Laclau espouses what he calls 'deconstruction' not because deconstruction is an ethics, but because it is in his view fundamentally a politics:

> Deconstruction is a primarily *political* logic [!] in the sense that, by showing the structural undecidability of increasingly large areas of the social, it also expands the area of operation of the various moments of political institution. [...] The central theme of deconstruction is the politico-discursive production of society (1996: 58–9).

This is a powerful appropriation of deconstruction, but I should call it as much a performative positing as a constative description. 'I declare', says Laclau in effect, 'that the central theme of deconstruction is the politico-discursive production of society.'

Just as Laclau opposes Levinas and the notion of an ethical exigency behind politics, so he must oppose the notions of violence as they are expressed in Georges Sorel or, in a different way, in Walter Benjamin. 'The politics of rhetoric' contains a forceful and exigent rejection of Sorel's idea, in *Reflexions sur la violence*, that the revolutionary general strike alone can function as a metaphorical totalization bringing about the 'grandeur' of the proletariat and the formation of a dominating proletarian revolutionary will. Walter Benjamin, in 'Zur Kritik der Gewalt', though in other ways critical of Sorel, appropriates for his own Marxist-messianic thinking Sorel's notion of the general strike as an example of divine lawbreaking and law-instituting violence. That violence, for Benjamin, is based on what Derrida in *Force de loi*, borrowing the phrase from Montaigne, calls 'the mystical foundation of authority'. Such violence ruptures social continuity and makes way for a radically new social order: 'Violence, violence crowned by fate,' says Benjamin, 'is the origin of law (Ist nämlich Gewalt, schicksalhaft gekrönte Gewalt, dessen Ursprung)' (Benjamin 1978: 286; 1977: 188). Benjamin's term 'fate' (*Schicksal*) is a catachresis for the manifestations of the nameless power that, for him, lies behind all identifiable acts of violence, whether they are mythical violence or divine violence, lawmaking, law-preserving, or law-destroying in the name of justice.

Laclau, on the contrary, sees Sorel's concept of the revolutionary general strike as a false and dangerous metaphoric totalization:

> The attempt to ground the revolutionary will in a metaphoric totalization that would avoid the particularization of hegemonic variations ends in failure. [. . .] [I]t is only through the pure, irreducible event that consists in a contingent displacement not retrievable by any metaphoric reaggregation that we can have a history, in the sense of both *Geschichte* and *Historie* (2000: 243).

Laclau's thinking is radically secular and this-worldly, immersed in the contingency of social and historical things as they are. He will have nothing to do with any spooky ideas of a law-destroying, law-installing divine violence, nor with the notion of a call from the other, from my neighbor, for ethico-political action.

How, then, for Laclau, does the 'madness of decision' occur. A full discussion of this is presented in 'Deconstruction, pragmatism, hegemony'. Laclau follows more or less closely (and explicitly cites) Derrida's theory of decision in *Force de loi*. As for Derrida, so for Laclau, a decision made rationally, on the basis of already existing principles, laws, or rules is no true decision at all, but a preprogrammed commitment – in no way an exercise of freedom. '[T]he decision,' says Laclau, 'cannot be *ultimately* grounded in anything external to itself. [. . .] [T]he decision has to be grounded in itself, in its own singularity' (1996: 52–3).

A salient difference from Derrida must be noted at just this point, however. The madness of decision, for Derrida, as for example instanced in Abraham's decision to obey God's injunction and sacrifice his beloved son Isaac, discussed by Derrida in *Donner la mort*, is a response to a call from 'le tout autre', the wholly other. Laclau, as I have shown, will have nothing to do with such spectral notions. They constitute, for him, a recourse to pre-existing religious or ethical principles.

Nor does Laclau accept or even make any reference, in his essay on de Man, to de Man's explicit claim, for example at the end of his discussion of Rousseau's *Social Contract* in 'Promises (*Social Contract*)' (a political essay if there ever was one), that it is not men or women as self-conscious, thinking, and choosing subjects that promise, instigate, or initiate political change, but rather language itself, operating on its own, independent of man's or woman's conscious will:

> The redoubtable efficacy of the text [Rousseau's *Social Contract*] is due to the rhetorical model of which it is a version. This model is a fact of language over which Rousseau himself has no control. Just as any other reader, he is bound to misread his text as a promise of political change. The error is not within the reader; language itself dissociates the cognition from the act.
>
> (de Man 1979: 277)

It is not quite true to say, as Laclau does in his characteristically generous essay on de Man, that de Man's 'untimely death' prevented him from contributing to political theory by 'anything that he had to say about politics' (2000: 251). De Man had a quite specific and rigorous political theory, but it is one quite different from Laclau's, which is probably why Laclau does not have anything to say about it. His goal in 'The politics of rhetoric' is to stress the positive contribution de Man's rhetorical theory can make to Laclau's own theory of hegemony.

That leaves my question still unanswered. How, for Laclau, does a decision that initiates political change, when a person or group hegemonically takes upon itself a task that exceeds its contingent situation, come about? If it happens neither by a Benjaminian act of divine revolutionary violence nor by a de Manian performative enacted by language itself, how then, for Laclau, does it happen? The answer is given by Laclau's theory of the subject, as worked out in *New Reflections on the Revolution of our Time* and in 'Deconstruction, pragmatism, hegemony'. Laclau recuperates, however carefully and prudently, a notion of the deciding and acting autonomous subject. For Laclau politically effective decision is made by a subject. Laclau's deciding subject, however, is defined subtly and circumspectly, also with considerable originality, in spite of the acknowledged indebtedness to the Lacanian theory of the self as lack and to a transformed mode of the psychoanalytical notion of identification. For Laclau, as for Derrida in a somewhat different way, the subject does not precede the decision, but is brought into existence by the decision itself in an act of self-grounding or auto-generation. The subject, says Laclau, 'is the distance between the undecidability of the structure and the decision' (1996: 54). What that undecidability is, we already know. It is the impossibility for any social structure to close itself off as a complete and self-contained system. This means that a given social structure has freeplay for many possible next stages. 'Undecidability [is] the distance between the plurality of arrangements that are possible out of [a given structural moment] and the actual arrangement that has finally prevailed' (ibid.). Another way to put this is to say that a fundamental contingency characterizes a given social structure. What Laclau calls 'dislocation' is 'the trace of contingency within the structure' (ibid.). The actual arrangement that has finally prevailed has done so because of a decision by a self-grounding and self-constituting subject that quite arbitrarily and freely has chosen one possibility out of the many that exist. This choice is what Laclau calls a contingent intervention that works according to a 'logic (!) of supplementarity' (ibid. 55). The self and the decision are identical, or the subject comes into existence in the madness of decision: 'This moment of decision [...] is the moment of the subject' (ibid. 54–5). The subject is what it decides to do, when it takes up a given political task that is in no way imposed on it but is, freely and without justification, chosen: 'The moment of the decision, the moment of madness, is this jump from the experience of undecidability to a creative act, a fiat which requires its passage through that experience' (ibid. 54). In a significant figure, a figure that has a Sartrean ring to it, to my ear at least, Laclau compares the subject that decides to God: 'To take a decision is like impersonating God. It is like asserting that one does not have the means of being God, and one has, however, to proceed as if one were Him' (ibid. 55).

It is just here that Laclau's appropriation of the term 'identification' is crucial. The deciding subject is fundamentally characterized as lack. It gives itself content by identifying itself, madly, without justification or reason, with the futurity of some social group, political party, or with some specific historical task. The subject, in the act of decision that constitutes it, identifies itself with its absent or proleptic fullness. This identification is not entirely free. It is determined by the contigent possibilities available in a given historical situation. 'We have seen,' says Laclau,

> that the absent fullness of the structure (of the community in this case) has to be represented/misrepresented by one of its particular contents (a political force, a class, a group). This relation by which a particular element assumes the impossible task of a universal representation, is what I call a *hegemonic* relation (ibid. 59).

I have cited so many of Laclau's own words in discussing his theory of the deciding subject in order to do at least partial justice to the complexity and rigor of his thinking. My citations nevertheless indicate that behind that complexity remains the powerful spectral presence of the good old-fashioned subjectivity, self, or ego that freely decides in a given historical situation to take upon itself a task. In a somewhat similar way, J. L. Austin's theory of the performative speech act depends on the notion of the self-conscious ego or 'I' in full possession of its faculties that in a given situation says 'I promise' or 'I bet' or 'I do' or 'I choose'. In the end Laclau's theory of political change for the better cannot do without the recuperation of the subject or 'I' that decides, arbitrarily and without justification, but nevertheless rationally and logically in the midst of what Laclau calls 'regulated' madness, to undertake some specific historical task: 'The madness of the decision is, if you want, as all madness, a regulated one' (ibid. 57).

As opposed to the divine violence that initiates the revolution for Benjamin, or the decisive 'saying yes' in Derrida's thought that is a response to a demand from the 'wholly other', or the power language has to act performatively, on its own, even against the subject's wishes and intent, in de Man's political thought, political decision for Laclau is made by a somewhat coolly calculating or rationally logical 'I' that sees its chance to intervene in the historical process and takes it. Confidence that this is possible may be what gives Laclau's political thought its attractively optimistic side.

Though Laclau mentions at the beginning of 'The politics of rhetoric' 'the performative dimension' of the 'generalized rhetoric' he admires in Paul de Man's work and is appropriating for his own political theory, he does not follow this up in the course of his essay on de Man. Confronting de Man's radical theory of performatives, a crucial feature of his later work, or Derrida's similarly radical speech act theory, so essential to his theory of the 'event', would allow a further measure of the distance between Laclau and Derrida or de Man, in spite of his generosity toward them and willingness to appropriate features of their work. For Derrida or de Man, a decision is always in one way or another a performative speech act, and speech acts are not amenable to the logic of constative statements or to any other logic. For Derrida or de Man, and for me too, a speech act, for example a decision, is 'mad' not because it is arbitrary and unjustifiable, but because it does not belong to the order of cognition. You can never know what a speech act is going to bring about. It is in this region of thought that Laclau's use of the term 'catachresis', in spite of his modifications of his essay's original draft, would still differ from mine. A catachresis is an irrational positing, as when, for example, Laclau says 'I call this *hegemony*'. It is irrational not because it is an act of madness to decide to call this hegemony and not because, as Laclau says, a catachresis names a proleptic nothingness, but because you cannot know whether or not it refers to something. A catachresis, like a political decision, is a leap in the dark that may or may not name something really there, just as political decision may or may not make things better.

I imagine Ernesto Laclau might well agree with the last clause of that sentence, but he still seems to believe that one can logically distinguish good political decisions from bad ones and that one can work consciously to make good ones, taking up the tasks that are at hand and thereby performing acts of hegemony that are possible/impossible. These acts have, after all, for Laclau, a sort of contingent sovereignty.

References

Benjamin, W. (1977) 'Kritik der Gewalt', in *Gesammelte Schriften*, vol. 2, 1, ed. R. Tiedemann and H. Schweppenhäuser, Frankfurt am Main: Suhrkamp.

—— (1978) 'Critique of violence', in P. Demetz (ed.) *Reflections*, New York and London: Harcourt Brace Jovanovich.

de Man, P. (1979) 'Promises (*Social Contract*)', in *Allegories of Reading*, New Haven: Yale University Press.

Laclau, E. (1996) 'Deconstruction, pragmatism, hegemony', in Chantal Mouffe (ed.) *Deconstruction and Pragmatism*, London: Routledge.

—— (2000) 'The politics of rhetoric', in B. Cohen, C. Cohen, J. H. Miller and A. Warminski (eds) *Material Events*, Minneapolis: University of Minnesota Press.

13

COMPETING FIGURES OF THE LIMIT

Dispersion, transgression, antagonism, and indifference

Urs Stäheli

Ernesto Laclau and Chantal Mouffe have successfully re-introduced the notion of discursive limits as one of the key concepts of poststructuralist political theory. For Laclau and Mouffe, the figure of antagonism underlies such diverse forms of discursive limits as Peronism in Argentina, the apartheid system in South Africa or Thatcherism. The antagonistic constitution of these political discourses has been shown very clearly in discourse theory and also in empirical studies (e.g. Norval 1996); however, what has been neglected is the question of discursive limits, which do not – at least not openly – share the antagonistic design of the examples mentioned. Think for example of the welfare state: on the one hand, there is a clear boundary separating those who are entitled to the benefits of the welfare state and those who are excluded from it. In this case, the limit separating those 'inside' and those 'outside' the welfare state is more than visible, but it seems that this limit is not necessarily antagonistically constituted. In a similar sense, discourses such as legal discourses are based upon drawing limits between the law and that which is external to the law, but what these limits exclude is not necessarily seen in terms of antagonism: that which is beyond the horizon of the law may simply be a piece of art which is not in any antagonistic relation at all to the logic of the legal discourse.

These empirical examples point to the central question whether antagonism is a general structure of all limits or whether only particular types of limits are antagonistic. In order to tackle this problem, I want to explore postfoundationalist theories, which try to work without the idea of necessary antagonistic limits. In principle, there are two logical possibilities which lend themselves to the idea of non-antagonistic limits: on the one hand, one might try to conceptualize discourses as regularities without clear limits; on the other hand, one might conceive of discourses with clear limits which are, however, non-antagonistic. It is with the first option that my exploration of limits starts. Michel Foucault's concept of *dispersion*, best represented in archaeological discourse analysis (Foucault 1972), does indeed try to speak of discourses without clear limits. However, it is the 'early', 'pre-archaeological' Foucault who introduces the concept of *transgression*, which provides one of the best criticisms of archaeology. This reading of Foucault with and against Foucault prepares the ground for re-examining Laclau and Mouffe's concept of antagonism. If we accept the difficulties of a concept of discourse with no clear limits, we have to discuss the second alternative: are there discourses based upon a constitutive difference that is not antagonistically coded? Drawing from Niklas Luhmann's systems theory, it is argued that, on the one hand, one has to introduce 'indifferent' differences in order to avoid an over-politicization of social and political theory. On the other hand, however, the assumption of necessarily antagonistic discursive limits tends to de-politicize the discursive construction of antagonisms.

I. Dispersion of discursive statements

My discussion of Foucault – which does not, incidentally, follow a chronologically linear path – starts with Foucault's *Archaeology of Knowledge*. The reason for this is that archaeology challenges the very assumption that discourses must have limits. Often it is used in order to criticize the question of discursive limits as such, i.e. the assumption that discourses are based upon a constitutive distinction.[1] What I would like to explore is whether Foucault does indeed introduce such a concept of discourse and whether this attempt is successful.

The *Archaeology of Knowledge* starts with a powerful and devastating critique of traditional modes of thinking which allow us to establish discursive boundaries. What is left after this critique is neither a founding subject, nor a theme or an object guaranteeing the unity of the discourse. Still, Foucault speaks about discursive formations. How does he grasp the unity of a discursive formation? A discourse is a multitude of statements, which belong to the same system of formation. Foucault is strongly opposed to approaches which presuppose an essence or an abstract rule that guarantees the unity of a discursive formation. Rather, what he is interested in is the 'system of dispersion' (Foucault 1972: 38), i.e. certain regularities of statements. Yet the term 'system of dispersion' is a paradoxical one, since it links the idea of a *system* with the idea of mere *regularity*. What kind of system does Foucault presuppose in order to avoid the idea of systemic limits? Let me dwell on two dimensions of the paradoxical notion of a 'system of dispersion'.

First, Foucault uses the weak notion of dispersion in order not to end up with the concept of totality. Discourses, it seems, are like landscapes, consisting of different materialities (e.g. wood, stone, human bodies) that are structured by the frequency of their occurrence. A landscape changes without clear lines of demarcation. There might for example be a large number of houses in a narrow space, surrounded by some solitary buildings; in this case, we wouldn't know how to draw a distinction between the village and its surroundings. What density of development is sufficient for us to speak of a village? Speaking about the 'happy positivism' of discourse analysis, Foucault refers to a form of analysis, which does not ask for a unifying principle. We will never know where the village ends and that is why we have to be content with a mere description of discursive events.

Still, the question remains of how to delimit those fields of regularities that constitute discursive formations. This leads me to the second dimension of the paradoxical notion of 'systems of dispersion'. Discourses are not just accidental groupings of statements, but they are systems governed by 'rules of formation' (Foucault 1972: 38). Yet how is it possible to determine the limits of a discursive formation if it is merely defined by the dispersion of statements (*HSS* 276)? To put it differently: how does Foucault grasp the systematicity of a discursive formation, which would only allow him to assume that there are discursive formations?

A possible Foucauldian answer might emphasize that a discourse is also based on the principle that not everything has been said: there are constraints delimiting the range of possible statements. Foucault mentions the example of the grammar and vocabulary of a language, which contain many combinations that have not been realized: 'One has to look for the principle of non-filling of the field of possible formulations' (Foucault 1972: 173). The discourse presupposes a horizon of that which is in principle sayable. At the same time, Foucault is very eager to stress that the unsaid is not a repressed and subversive level. There is no text below the discourse, since this would leave the level of positivity. Instead discourse analysis describes successfully realized discursive structures. Still, there is something which haunts the discourse; something which one might call, from a systems theoretical point of view, the medium of discourse: that which circumscribes the horizon of possible statements without becoming actualized. The horizon of the discourse is 'made up of all the formulations to which the statement refers (implicitly or not); [...] there can be no statement that in one way or another does not reactualize others' (ibid. 98). Thus, Foucault has to presuppose a field of reference, which he defines in a relational manner.

What remains unclear in Foucault's notion of discourse is precisely the field of the unsaid, which functions as a horizon, as a space of the possible. Concepts such as the unsaid occupy a crucial theoretical position in Foucault's work, since they allow him to define discursive 'elements' (i.e. of statements) in a non-atomistic and anti-essentialist way. Foucault takes great pains to grasp the concept of statements in a relational way. However, what becomes clear, first and foremost, is what the concept negates. A statement is neither a proposition, nor a sentence, nor a combination of signs, nor a speech act (ibid. 115 passim). Foucault suggests a non-substantialist definition. In so doing, he reverts oddly enough to a *functional* explanation: a statement is not a unit, but a 'function which crosses a field of structures and possible units' (ibid. 126–7). In a structuralist vein, he suggests that one proceeds from the differential *value* of statements. The value is defined in terms of a particular position within processes of exchange and circulation. Thus, Foucault has to presuppose a circular network of exchange relations in order to define statements as basic units of a discourse. However, we do not learn much about the general structure of this network, although the functional definition of statements depends on such a concept. Foucault leaves the presupposed 'system', 'field', 'medium', or 'horizon' un(der)theorized – which is also responsible for his sometimes rather static conception of discourse.

Foucault's attempt to define an open model of discourse that is able to account for heterogeneity is caught up in a difficult theoretical problem. On the one hand, he wants to establish a pure and positive archaeological discourse analysis which simply describes the dispersion of statements. From this point of view, a discourse has no clear limits; there are only local limits, but not a limit which is constitutive for the discourse as such. Rather than developing a general discourse theory, Foucault suggests an archaeological discourse *analysis*, which works without a proper *theory* of discourse. Foucault's solution is a pragmatic one: instead of exploring the theoretical problem of discursive limits, he analyses discourses. Yet Foucault's discourse analysis has to imply quite important concepts that are not in line with the methodological ideal of a pure description of discursive events. It is from this point of view that one may become uneasy with a definition of discourse, which comes quite close to a functionalist model. Foucault implicitly introduces a notion of totality, which he wants to avoid; yet it seems that the system's side of the 'systems of dispersion' is the secret winner of the battle. Of course, this hidden idea of a system produces theoretical effects, not least since it somehow has to guarantee the identity of a discourse without being able to account for its exterior as a constitutive feature.

II. Discursive transgression

In contrast to the standard reading of Foucault, I want to suggest that Foucault's early work on literature provides a concept of discursive limits, which can also be used for discourse analysis – moreover, a concept of the limit that is necessary for discourse theory if it wants to grasp discourse in a difference theoretical manner. In Foucault's writings on Bataille and Blanchot, transgression plays a crucial role.[2] It is here that boundaries are problematized and that they become the central focus of Foucault's work. Very often Foucault's early work is criticized for developing a naïve perspective on an excluded, which is identified with phenomena such as madness or avant-garde literary practices. The early Foucault is often attacked for a longing for otherness. Although one might agree with some of these criticisms, it is important not to overlook the important contribution he makes in thinking the limits of discourse, which is most clearly elaborated in his work on literature.

The question which Foucault explicitly raises – and which haunted even his *Archaeology of Knowledge* – is how to conceive of the limit of a discourse. Here, Foucault comes much closer to Laclau's question of how to conceptualize the systematicity of the system. In order to represent the totality of the system within the system, a self-referential operation is required: the system has to refer to itself in order to account for its own systematicity. Thus, Foucault is confronted with the difficult problem of conceptualizing the self-reference of the system as well as something which escapes the self-referential circle. To put it differently: is it possible to escape the self-referentiality of a closed system if one introduces a necessary self-reference? If self-reference becomes a self-sufficient theoretical figure, then every possible thinking of the outside is always already 'internalized'. Thus Foucault attacks the Cartesian reflexive discourse for re-integrating the dimension of exteriority into the discursive framework. Foucault struggles with a notion of discourse which would allow him to think an outside of the discourse that is not just an internal construction or the negation of the discourse. In a way not dissimilar to Derrida's early writings on the excess of meaning, Foucault draws upon Bataille to think the transgression of discourses in a non-dialectical manner. Transgression challenges and problematizes boundaries. Transgression introduces an empty space within the discourse, which shows itself in many different theoretical figures such as the ecstatic eye, the will to power and the self-reference of language.

Foucault explains these figures in his work on language where he tries to locate the being of language in the 'centre' of the discourse. The being of language corresponds to the unsayable, a void within the discourse, a disruptive silence. For this reason, Foucault sometimes speaks about an 'archaeology of silence', i.e. an archaeology of that which is not sayable within a discourse, but still necessary for the constitution of the discourse. This 'archaeology of silence' is also an 'archaeology of the invisible'. But it is neither the invisibility of the blind spot (as we know it from Luhmannian systems theory), nor the silence of the repressed (as we know it from Foucault's work on madness), which concerns the early Foucault. Rather, he shows how this invisibility leaves and dislocates the order of the visible. Foucault distinguishes between two different relations towards exteriority: on the one hand, the commentary, which tries to repeat the murmuring that is external to the discourse; on the other, a language which always remains exterior to itself. The invisibility of the invisible is exemplified by the latter dimension: the emptiness, the gap, and the fissures within the visible.

It is important to note that Foucault refers to an invisibility which radically leaves the realm of the visible. He illustrates this invisibility when discussing two concepts of the eye, drawing from Bataille's famous novel of the eye. First he explains the Cartesian model of the eye:

> Lying behind each eye that sees, there exists a more tenuous one, an eye so discreet and yet so agile that its all-powerful glance can be said to eat away at the flesh of its white globe; behind this particular eye, there exists another and, then, still others, each progressively more subtle until we arrive at an eye whose entire substance is nothing but the transparency of its vision.
>
> (Foucault 1977: 45)

The Cartesian observation of observation escapes any constitutive intransparency, eventually leading to the pure self-reference of total vision whose only substance is transparence. Thus, there is nothing that remains constitutively invisible, nothing which could not be seen by another eye, and no mediality which would interrupt this transparency. 'Cartesian invisibility' is only the empirical fact that something is not observed, but not the actual structure of unobservability. All observations are based upon the idea of a last eye; an eye without substance guaranteeing that there cannot be anything constitutively intransparent. The second approach – and this is the approach Foucault subscribes to – is the Bataillean. Now the eye has lost its privileged place of observation. What is left is 'only a small white ball, veined with blood ... only an exorbitated eye to which all sight is now denied'. Instead of the observing eye 'only a cranial cavity remains, only this black globe which the uprooted eye has made to close upon its sphere, depriving it of vision' (ibid.). The eye has lost its proper place through violence. The uprooted and ecstatic eye symbolizes the invisible invisibility which Foucault's interrogation of boundaries wants to grasp by pushing language and the visible at their limits.

The problem of the limit arises in these early works as the question of a *pure self-reference*. One of the reasons why Foucault's work on literature in particular focuses on this self-reference is undoubtedly that the early Foucault is not speaking about a particular discourse (e.g. medical discourse), but generally about language or the visible and the stain therein. That is why it becomes possible to speak about the being of language as the limit of the discourse (this is a theoretical figure which Foucault resumes in other works; e.g. when referring to the experience of pure order). Foucault abandons these figures of pure self-reference in archaeological discourse analysis, since he restricts his analysis to particular fields of power/knowledge. By focusing on the working of a particular discursive formation, he analyses discursive constraints such as subject positions or strategies of object formation without accounting for the limits of the discourse (and not just limits within discourse). For archaeological discourse analyses, there are basically two possible ways of dealing with this problem: either one adapts the general model of exteriority to historically concrete discourses and fills the role of exteriority with excluded minorities; or one abandons the 'metaphysical' thinking about outsides and exteriority. Foucault has pursued both strategies. The first strategy is most clearly elaborated in *Madness and Civilization*, where the exterior is essentialized. The second strategy is established in the *Archaeology of Knowledge*, emphasizing the dispersion of discursive events.

Yet this celebration of positive dispersion presupposes that it has been possible to identify the dispersed statements. And it is here that the functional definition of discursive units presupposes what Foucault wants to avoid on the historical level: a closed totality which enables the discourse theorist to identify statements.[3] It seems to me that Foucault's earlier work on literature could be helpful in tackling this question. Thus, I have suggested, instead of reading Foucault in terms of a linear history of theoretical progress (from transgression, archaeology, genealogy to the theory of the subject and governmentality in his late writings), it is Foucault's early work on language and transgression which may help us to tackle the problem of discursive boundaries. What becomes clear is that there are at least two general models of the limit in Foucault's work. First, Foucault criticizes the Cartesian model of the *cogito* in thinking of the closure of discourses. Instead, the model of the 'I speak' is more useful, since it points to the being of language, to a space within the discourse that transgresses it. Foucault's 'archaeology of silence', then, tackles the problem of how to think the closure of discourses without the Cartesian model of self-reflection. Instead, a *self-reference* is introduced which threatens the very closure it produces. The speaking of the speaking points at an exteriority which cannot be reduced to an internal commentary and which is always based upon a primary violence disrupting the self-referential closure (Foucault 1977: 48).

In juxtaposing the archaeological and the transgressive, Foucault confronts us with the question of how to link these two aspects. This is not due to the need to soften ruptures in Foucault's work. Rather it has been raised by the implicit functionalism of archaeological discourse theory. If we do not want to introduce a model of totality through the back door, then a theoretical strategy is required which loosens the potentially functionalist grip of archaeology. Thus, the question I would like to discuss is: how can we integrate the figure of a pure and transgressive self-reference into a general model of discourse? In what follows I want to read Laclau's notion of discourse and Luhmann's notion of system as two answers to the problems raised by Foucault's discourse theory.

III. Antagonistic limits

Laclau and Mouffe (*HSS*) have criticized Foucault's discourse theory heavily. Their main point is that Foucault is unable to think discursive limits and that this is why his use for political and social theory is seriously restricted. Moreover, Foucault still assumes the existence of a 'non-discursive' realm, which contradicts the de/constructivist stance of Laclau and Mouffe. It seems that Laclau has become even more sceptical about Foucault in his more recent work. Whereas *Hegemony and Socialist Strategy* still tried to establish its concept of discourse by working through Foucault, now Laclau has become a very distant 'neighbour' of Foucault's: 'Moreover, the work of Foucault has had only a very limited influence on my own approach, and I feel towards it only a very qualified sympathy' (Laclau 2000: 285). While I agree with Laclau and Mouffe's emphasis on discursive boundaries, I have tried to show that even the *Archaeology of Knowledge* has to presuppose discursive limits without properly theorizing them. This may result in a fatal import of non-theorized limits in order to grasp the identity of discursive formations. Against this background, Foucault's work on literature becomes more attractive, since it develops a concept of the limit as self-referential figure. Foucault's distinction between the commentary on the exterior of a discourse and the self-referential interrogation of boundaries is much closer to Laclau and Mouffe's work than the *Archaeology of Knowledge*.

Laclau's argumentative context is not a Foucauldian one, but rather the attempt to propose a discourse theory which tries to overcome the tension between deconstruction and Lacanian psychoanalysis. Although these theoretical resources are very heterogeneous, they share one common feature: both establish their theoretical position through a thorough discussion of the question of limits and boundaries, linking the problem of the limit to that of self-reference. Thus Derrida's notion of 'constitutive outside' of any distinction has become as crucial as Žižek's Lacanian notion of the Real.[4]

The different emphasis of Laclau and Mouffe is due to their interest in the working of discursive boundaries.[5] A discourse is an attempt to deal with unarticulated discursivity by providing partial fixations of meaning. It is the construction of discursive limits which becomes constitutive to every discourse: 'The very possibility of signification is the system, and the very possibility of the system is the possibility of its limits' (*E* 37). Every discourse is therefore based on a constitutive exclusion which enables a vast chain of equivalences: 'All these differences are equivalent to each other, as far as all of them belong to this side of the frontier of exclusion' (*E* 38). The equivalential elements share the same beyond of the system which is *per definitionem* that which transgresses the meaning horizon of a system: '[L]imits only exist insofar as a systematic ensemble of differences can be cut out as *totality* with regard to something beyond them' (*HSS* 144). Laclau explains the condition of possibility and impossibility of this totality by means of the concept of the empty signifier. The empty signifier symbolizes the systematicity (e.g. pure order) of the system, since it represents that which links all elements of a system: a chain of equivalences constitutes itself by referring to the same empty signifier. Since the empty signifier tends to cancel the differences between the differential elements of a discourse, it introduces a negativity into the system which points at its exteriority. The empty signifier itself points at the pure being of the system: its emptiness stands for the impossible totality of the system (i.e. for the often totalitarian dream of a system with no outside).

Thus, in discourse theory there can be no discursive system without an empty signifier pointing at a pure self-reference which reinforces and questions the limits of the system at the same time. The self-reference is always also a disruptive self-reference. Precisely by introducing a moment of meaninglessness into the system, the self-referential closure produces dislocations and cracks within the discursive system. This concept of systemic closure is very close to Foucault's attempt to think the exteriority of language or the visible. Think for example of the 'speaking of speaking' and the empty cranial place of the eye which has lost its ability to see – instead it has become pure matter; or a wobbling white mass. However, in contrast to Foucault, these concepts are no longer restricted to extraordinary experiences such as erotic excess or elite artistic practices. Rather, Laclau and Mouffe's discourse theory takes this as a general problem of every social and political discourse – and it is a matter of political articulation whether ecstasy comes about or not.

Still, there are also problems with Laclau and Mouffe's discourse theoretical suggestion of thinking discursive limits. Laclau qualifies the relation to the exterior as necessarily antagonistic. The constitutive outside of a discourse always indicates an antagonism:

> [A]ntagonism and exclusion are constitutive of all identity. Without limits through which a (non-dialectical) negativity is constructed we would have an indefinite dispersion of differences whose absence of systematic limits would make any differential identity impossible. But this very function of constituting differential identities through antagonistic limits is what, at the same time, destabilizes and subverts those differences (*E* 52–3).

Every identity needs a frontier and that which is beyond this frontier threatens the identity within the frontier. In an antagonistic relationship the exterior is represented in the system as that which *threatens* the full constitution of the system. Laclau refers here to the well-known deconstructive argument that the condition of possibility is at the same time the condition of impossibility. However, he characterizes this impossibility as an *antagonistic threat* – and I think it is here that the discourse theoretical argument becomes problematic.

If Laclau's introduction of a constitutive threat is taken seriously, it implies that any system has to be antagonistically constituted since it is only an antagonism which provides a totalizing effect. However, in his work after *Hegemony and Socialist Strategy*, Laclau has introduced the important distinction between dislocation and antagonism. Dislocation means that 'every identity is dislocated insofar as it depends on an outside which both *denies* that identity and provides its condition of possibility at the same time' (*NR* 39, my emphasis). Yet it seems that Laclau cannot escape from a circular construction of the relation between antagonism and dislocation. Even in the aforementioned definition of dislocation he refers to an outside which *denies* the identity. Thus, what is crucial is to think the impossibility of a system in terms *prior* to an antagonistic denial.

Put differently, the problem is whether the difference between the interiority and exteriority of a discursive system is already an antagonistic relation, or whether antagonism is a specific historical configuration of a dislocated system. In the latter case, one may well assume that every system is potentially dislocated, while the dislocation is not necessarily antagonistic. Decoupling antagonism and dislocation, then, may help us to think the antagonistic articulation as a contingent historical result which is not pre-given with the differential and paradoxical foundation of a system. Only dislocations are an effect of the differential constitution of the system, whereas antagonisms are a particular articulation of a dislocation.[6]

IV. Non-antagonistic limits in systems theory

If we take seriously such an attempt of strictly separating dislocation and antagonism, we have to be very careful not to think of dislocation as an inherently threatening force. It is here that discourse theory might learn from Niklas Luhmann's systems theory; and for this reason I would like to introduce the systems theoretical conception of systemic limits before I proceed with the discussion of the distinction between dislocation and antagonism.

Luhmann (1996) tackles the problem by introducing the system/environment distinction on several levels of his theory. One may distinguish the two most important ones by referring to their operative or observational dimension. First of all, a system creates a distinction between the system and its environment by blindly connecting certain events. The connections of operations produces the system's boundary. The relation to the environment on the operative level, then, is remarkably non-antagonistic: there is no threat which is created by the environment – it is just ignored. The 'unmarkedness' of the exterior – this might be an ugly, but appropriate term – characterizes the relation to the environment on the operative level of the system. One of the advantages of distinguishing between the marked and the unmarked side of a distinction is precisely that one does not have to qualify the unmarked side. To put it differently, the unmarked side is not threatening *per se*. And it also escapes a dialectical conception which would think the other side of a distinction as a negation of the positive side. However, this stream of operations only constitutes itself as a system by being observed by itself. It is here where the self-reference of the system becomes important. Luhmann tries to grasp this self-reference with the figure of the re-entry, i.e. the distinction between the marked (the stream of events) and the unmarked (everything which does not link up to this stream of events) is 'represented' on the marked side. It is only the re-entry of the distinction within itself which allows an observation of that which is simply ignored on the operative level. Luhmann puts this very clearly in *Die Gesellschaft der Gesellschaft*: 'The system/environment distinction occurs twice: as distinction *produced* by the system and as distinction *observed within* the system' (1997: 45).

Only the second usage of the distinction (the 'copied' distinction) allows the construction of a particular environment. Now the unmarked becomes a non-antagonistic negation of the system – Luhmann calls this the *Negativkorrelat* (negative correlate). Thus, on the observational level, the environment is constructed with reference to the system. This distinction also helps us to distinguish between two different relations to the environment. The environment of operations is a pure exclusion of the unmarked which is not reflected upon and which is on a level prior to the observation of the environment as negative correlate. In contrast to Laclau's notion of discursive systems this negation is not necessarily a threat. The *Negativkorrelat* does not imply an antagonistic relation; and it depends on the particular system whether it constructs its relation to the environment not only in negative, but also in antagonistic terms. The latter, then, is not ontologically given, but the effect of a particular observation. Only now may the environment be constructed as a threat to the system. The construction of the threat, then, is an observational operation of the system itself. It is not a force which exists outside the system, but rather a result of the system's management of its own precarious foundation on a difference. This threefold distinction between blindness (unmarkedness), negative correlate, and antagonistic observation of the environment may help us to tackle the problem of the circular relation between dislocation and antagonism in discourse theory.

V. Interrupting the circular structure of dislocation and antagonism

We have seen that there is an urgent need in discourse theory to account for discourses which are not antagonistically constituted. Discourse theory was too quick to generalize its political notion of discourse. But – as I have tried to show – Laclau's attempt to find a solution to the problem results in a vicious circle. Recalling our discussion of the re-entry of the system/environment distinction into itself, it becomes apparent that Laclau is tackling a similar problem to the one Luhmann does.

> This implies that a formation manages to *signify itself* (that is, to constitute itself as such) only by transforming the limits into frontiers, by constituting a chain of equivalencies which constructs that which is beyond the limits as that which it is *not*. It is only through negativity, division and antagonism that a formation constitutes itself as a totalizing horizon (*HSS* 143–4).

Laclau/Mouffe describe the re-entry of the system/environment distinction in terms of a transformation of *limits* into *frontiers* (cf. Norval 1997). The last sentence of the quote also hints at three important steps of such a process – although in a somewhat unordered way. One can distinguish between division, negativity, and antagonism in order to explain the antagonization of a discursive system. First, there have to be discursive moments which are interlinked: discursive events (i.e. just by operating) produce a *division* and the linkages become possible since they refer to themselves. They constitute an equivalential chain which now draws a limit to the *negativity* of the exterior. What is important is that this construction of what is beyond the limits should not be confused with an antagonism. Thus we have to account for a discursive limit; otherwise we would end up in a pure dispersion of events as in Foucault's archaeology. Instead, the pure exclusion allows us to draw a boundary. It is at this level that the problem of dislocation arises, which systems theory, in turn, cannot really grasp (Stäheli 2000). One of the very advantages of the concept of dislocation is precisely that it has neither to rely on Foucault's sometimes rather essentialist vocabulary of transgression, nor to presuppose that there are always already 'happy' articulations of discursive events, as in Luhmann's systems theory.

By introducing the possibility of a non-antagonistic boundary, it becomes possible, as Norval (1997: 12) has postulated, to separate the *differentiation* of a discourse from the political logic of *antagonism*. The differentiation produces a field of indeterminacy: '[T]he side of identity formation can be regarded as one of *indeterminacy*' (Norval 2000: 223). Yet I think Norval throws the baby out with the bathwater when she concludes that for this reason discourses are no longer based upon a constitutive exclusion. Her attempt to relativize the logic of antagonism weakens the idea of a constitutive outside and replaces this concept with the vague idea of indeterminacy. However, Norval rightly emphasizes the need to separate conceptually the idea of discursive differentiation from antagonism. Thus what I want to suggest is that the idea of exclusion and of chains of equivalencies constituting the limits of systems be retained, since one tends otherwise to give up some of the most valuable assumptions of Laclau and Mouffe's discourse theory – possibly ending up with a hidden notion of totality such as in Foucault's archaeology of knowledge. What is needed instead is therefore not to weaken the conception of discourses which is based upon the equivalence of discursive moments, but rather to arrive at a deeper understanding of different layers of discourses. This requires us to disarticulate two arguments. The exclusionary nature of any discourse is not automatically antagonistic, yet the constitutive exclusion creates dislocations of the discourse in question. In a certain way, discourses close themselves by connective operations – as is suggested by systems theory – which leave the exterior unmarked. A discourse only becomes antagonistic if the dislocations are articulated in an antagonistic way. To put it in systems theoretical terms: the discourse has to observe and describe itself as antagonistically constituted in order to become an antagonistic discourse. This argument allows us to historicize antagonisms and to maintain, at the same time, the general assumption of the constitutive outside.

It is only if a discursive system constructs that which it excludes as a threat to itself, that the system becomes antagonistic. The construction of the exteriority of the system then transforms that which is seen as the ungraspable outside to a concrete threat to the system. Now it has to attribute the internal inconsistencies and undecidabilities to an instance external to the system. Alternatively the system may either ignore these inconsistencies or attribute these to itself, creating a fully internalized antagonistic structure. In this respect, Slavoj Žižek has emphasized very clearly two different sorts of antagonism: on the one hand, the antagonism which blocks any identity, and on the other hand, the *externalization* of the 'intrinsic, immanent impossibility' (Žižek 1990: 252). It is precisely this impossibility of identity which I suggest terming dislocation in order to prevent conceptual confusions. Dislocations do not require an antagonistic force in order to occur, but they are also based upon the constitutive exclusion of any system. It is this exclusion which Luhmann explains as the blind operation of the system which always leaves an unmarked side. However, in contrast to Luhmann, this necessity of unmarking always already implies the impossibility of a proper marking. The mark is always already dislocated – not least because it has to be iterated and articulated. Thus, in contrast to Norval, the separation of dislocation from the political logic of antagonism does not force us to abandon the differential constitution of discourses and to introduce a field of indeterminacy. Rather, it leads us to think of dislocations as effects of an impossible pure self-reference, of the blockage of discursive self-reference and of pure operativity.

Laclau has put this relationship very clearly in an interview where he stresses that the category of dislocation is logically prior to that of antagonism. In order to perceive an enemy there has to be a primary symbolic identification. It is only this position which allows one to construct an enemy (Laclau in Stavrakakis 1998: 184). To put it in systems theoretical terms: the construction of an enemy presupposes the self-referential operating of the system.[7] Thus we have to distinguish between two different versions of the outside of a discursive system. On the one hand, there is the outside which shows itself in dislocations. This radical outside 'does not share a common measure or foundation with the inside of the structure' (*NR* 44). Put differently, dislocations are the failure of any structure to fully close upon itself. Thus, dislocation is not just an empirical imperfection, but designates the impossibility of closure.[8] Second, we have to be careful not to confuse dislocation with 'the presence of antagonistic forces' (*NR*: 40).

Let me summarize my argument on discourse theory. Laclau and Mouffe emphasize that discourses are constituted by a primary exclusion. This exclusion distinguishes between the equivalential moments of a discourse and that which cannot be put in a relation of equivalence. The closure of the discourse is generated by an empty signifier, signifying the impossible totality of the discourse. Instead of presupposing an unexplained discursive field or system, as Foucault does in his *Archaeology of Knowledge*, Laclau tries to account for this problem from the very beginning. This prevents discourse theory from implicitly essentializing the totality of a discourse. Instead, it becomes possible to think the 'being' of a discourse in terms of a chain of equivalence of discursive differences. Thus, the problem of the discursive limit is a problem within the discourse – best exemplified with the notion of the empty signifier – which concerns each discursive difference. The limit of the discourses is reproduced by each discursive moment since it has to be equivalent, and to exclude the non-equivalent. Whereas Foucault's writings on literature prepared a similar argument, in discourse theory the problem of exteriority is successfully moved away from the exclusive sphere of avant-garde literature.

At the same time, a problem arises which has been identified by many students of discourse theory. Does the primary exclusion, which is constitutive for the discourse, necessarily imply an antagonistic relationship? Drawing upon systems theory, I have tried to show that the basic self-reference of a discourse is characterized by an indifference towards the unmarked, non-equivalential moments. If we take this argument seriously, then we have to relativize the status of antagonism. Antagonism is now a particular articulation of that which a discourse has to exclude. In this respect, Laclau's overpoliticized concept of antagonistic discourses has to be limited; at least, that is, if we are interested in developing a social theory based on the concept of discourse. This theoretical decision has to be taken, if discourse theory wants to widen its theoretical and empirical focus and if discourse theory is no longer content with analysing political discourses in a narrow sense.

In contrast to Žižek who argues for the separation of a general concept of Antagonism (with a capital A) from historical antagonisms, it is not necessary to presuppose an ahistorical kernel of the Real which dislocates a discourse. Rather, the dislocation which is given with the primary exclusion of any discourse is a product of the closure of a discourse. In this respect, it is probably more useful to revert to deconstructive arguments which emphasize the immanent aporetic structure of discursive systems which are based upon the 'logic' of iterability. And we can learn from systems theory that the possibility of being perturbated also depends on the complexity of a system.

Thus, what any discourse analysis of political antagonisms has to clarify are the historical conditions of possibility for an antagonistic articulation. Antagonism itself, then, becomes a discursive event, which has to be explained and which we cannot presuppose. Such a discourse analysis has to account for the discursive strategies which are employed for *constructing* an antagonistic articulation of a discourse. It is in this sense that the political finds itself placed prior to and after antagonism at one and the same time. Since there are no natural antagonisms, it is the very construction of antagonism which becomes the potential site of the Political. Instead of presupposing that there is a pre-'existing' antagonism, which has to be analyzed, it becomes necessary to show the discursive strategies constructing a particular antagonism. The analysis of antagonisms, then, becomes a 'conjectural science', which is interested in the manifold attempts at antagonistically coding discourses.

Notes

1 This is why Lawrence Grossberg (1996: 95) seems to be rather unhappy with Laclau and Mouffe's reading of Foucault: 'Laclau and Mouffe have reread Foucault as if he were Derrida. Foucault's notion of the regularity of dispersion becomes an ensemble of differential positions; the rarity of discourse becomes exteriority as an excess found in the surplus of meaning.'

2 Cf. Saghafi (1996) for a reading of the early Foucault very close to the one suggested here.

3 The functional definition of the statement implies the existence of a discursive field or horizon. The notion of a field has a necessary function in Foucault's discourse analysis since otherwise it would be meaningless to talk about a function: there must be a totality within which an statement is functional. That is why Foucault resorts to the paradoxical term 'systems of dispersion'. But how is it possible to maintain a moment of heterogeneity if one resorts – implicitly – to a functional definition of statements? Now, one might argue that the *Archaeology of Knowledge* relativizes its functionalism in its last sections. It is here that Foucault starts an ironical game with the position of the author by interviewing himself. However, this carnivalesque masking of the author does not help much if we are interested in obtaining a concept of discourse useful for social theory.

4 It is only if we read Foucault's work as a New Functionalism, as has been suggested by Neil Brenner, that Laclau and Foucault become compatible once again. Discourses and Dispositifs integrate different functions with a common target, whereas Laclau's discursive systems are unified by a common boundary which demarcates their horizon. Still, important differences remain: 'Foucault differs from Laclau and Mouffe, of course, in his complete rejection of their interpretive focus in favor of the analysis of anonymous flows of functions between tactics and targets' (Brenner 1994: 706).

5 Such a re-figuring of discourses creates theoretical costs of its own. One might call this the semiotic bias of Laclau's discourse theory. Whereas Foucault is able – at least with the concept of dispositif – to integrate practices of very different nature, Laclau and Mouffe use the deconstructed model of the sign as their point of departure.

6 Further elaboration on the relation between dislocation and antagonism is discussed in Norval (1997, 2000) and Dyrberg (1995: 24), who suggests that antagonisms exist '*vis-à-vis* systems'.

7 Discourse theory also assumes that 'Closure is the condition of meaning as far as, all identities being purely differential, they need the system in order to constitute themselves as identities' (Laclau 1996a: 220). At the same time, this closure is impossible, since no systemic element can ever become meaning-*full* due to its 'ultimate dislocation' (ibid. 205).

8 '[N]o system can be fully protected given the undecidability of its frontiers [...]; but this is tantamount to saying that identities within that system will be constitutively dislocated and that this dislocation will show their radical contingency' (Laclau 1996b: 54).

References

Brenner, N. (1994) 'Foucault's New Functionalism', *Theory and Society*, 23: 679–709.

Dyrberg, T. (1995) 'Discourse analysis as systems theory' (unpublished paper) Roskilde.

Foucault, M. (1972) *Archaeology of Knowledge*, London: Tavistock.

—— (1977) *Language, Counter-Memory, Practice: Selected Essays and Interview*, Ithaca: Cornell University Press.

Grossberg, L. (1996) 'Identity and cultural studies: Is that all there is?', in S. Hall and P. du Gay (eds) *Questions of Cultural Identity*, London: Sage.

Laclau, E. (1996a) 'The death and resurrection of the theory of ideology', *Journal of Political Ideologies*, 1(3): 201–29.

—— (1996b) 'Deconstruction, pragmatism, hegemony', in C. Mouffe (ed.) *Deconstruction and Pragmatism*, London: Routledge.

—— (2000) 'Constructing universality', in J. Butler, E. Laclau and S. Žižek (eds) *Contingency, Hegemony, Universality*, London: Verso.

Luhmann, N. (1996) *Social Systems*, Stanford, CA: Stanford University Press.

—— (1997) *Die Gesellschaft der Gesellschaft*, Frankfurt am Main: Suhrkamp.

Norval, A. (1996) *Deconstructing Apartheid Discourse*, London: Verso.

—— (1997) 'Frontiers in question', *Acta Philosophica*, 2: 51–67.

—— (2000) 'Trajectories of future research in discourse theory', in D. Howarth, A. J. Norval and Y. Stavrakakis (eds) *Discourse Theory and Political Analysis. Identities, Hegemonies and Social Change*, Manchester: Manchester University Press.

Saghafi, K. (1996) 'The "passion for the outside". Foucault, Blanchot and exteriority', *International Studies in Philosophy*, 28 (4): 79–92.

Stäheli, U. (2000) *Sinnzusammenbrüche: Eine dekonstruktive Lektüre von Niklas Luhmanns Systemtheorie*, Weilerswist: Verlbrück Wissenschaft.

Stavrakakis, Y. (1998) 'Laclau mit Lacan', in O. Marchart (ed.) *Das Undarstellbare der Politik*, Vienna: Turia + Kant.

Žižek, S. (1990) 'Beyond Discourse Analysis', in E. Laclau, *New Reflections on the Revolution of our Time*, London: Verso.

14

THE POLITICAL AND POLITICS IN DISCOURSE ANALYSIS

Torben Bech Dyrberg

Conceptualizing the political

One of the major themes running through the works of Ernesto Laclau and Chantal Mouffe has been to grasp the significance and specificity of the political. The attempt has been to conceive the political as constitutive as opposed to being subsumed under or derived from other, say economic or cultural, 'logics'. It is in this context that the concept of hegemony plays a key role in the unravelling of ground, order, and meaning (*HSS* 193).

The leitmotif has been that it is crucial for emancipatory politics to be founded on democratic values, which again have to be rooted in an understanding of the specificity and autonomy of the political. The reason why this is important is that the political makes a difference – it is a form of power which cannot be reduced to procedural rules, and which cannot be superimposed upon by social logics. Nor is it a self-annihilating vision of its elimination as in the case of certain strands of liberal, communitarian and emancipatory discourses. The concept of hegemony has played a central role in advancing a non-reductionist and hence non-essentialist conception of the political, which revolves around the political mechanisms at work in the ordering of social relations. Especially in Laclau's later writings, emphasis has been given to what I will refer to as two analytical levels claimed to be operative in the logic of hegemony: the political refers to the terrain in which articulations take place, and politics refers to the structuring of articulations.

To conceptualize the political requires a transcendental move, which holds, on the one hand, that the two levels mutually condition each other and, on the other, that the political can be conceived apart from its contingent manifestations in the political regime and political community. This is discussed as the articulation between particular and universal, where the point is that, although present in each other, they are also distinct. The concept of the political is thus analytical. To argue on those lines signals the importance of breaking 'with the false alternative "ahistorical transcendentalism/radical historicism"' (Laclau 2000b: 201), alias objectivism and relativism. The argument concerning the contingency of social constructs can only be sustained by accepting the 'dialectic between necessity and contingency: as identity depends entirely on conditions of existence which are contingent, its relationship with them is absolutely necessary' (1990a: 21; see also Laclau 1993a: 284; *HSS* 114). The transcendental move and the contingency argument are thus correlative. It is because they mutually condition each other that objectivism and relativism are no longer a relevant alternative for the analytical conception of the political

'Our whole analysis', says Laclau (1990c: 212–3), 'goes against an objectivist conception and presupposes the reduction of "fact" to "sense", and of "the given" to its conditions of possibility. This "sense" is not a fixed transcendental horizon, but appears as essentially historic and contingent.' The reduction mentioned here implies inserting particulars in more encompassing wholes to get at the structuring of political identity. This further implies making sense of the political as dealing with context from the viewpoint of common concerns and governmentality. Reduction is not then opposed to diversity. On the contrary, to get at the political aspect of the discursive field of co-existing differences is an attempt to grasp the hegemonic structuring of particulars, and not to derive or deduce the latter from the former.

The deconstruction of the objectivity of the social runs parallel to seeing the political as constitutive as opposed to being epiphenomenal to the logics of, say, market and culture. This implies taking issue with, for example, liberal and functionalist conceptions according to which the political is defined as a necessary evil whose role is to supplement non-political logics insofar as they become dysfunctional for society. Politics is thus assigned the task of 'damage control' (*ex post* as well as *ex ante*), as when economic, political, and social destabilization associated with market failure, class struggle, and normative disintegration (anomie) is in 'need' of regulation.

Seen against this background it is important for Laclau and Mouffe to argue that the political has a specificity and an autonomy of its own – and that it is 'freestanding' as Rawls would say. The idea is to grasp the political as a practical dimension of the ordering of the co-existence of contexts, and that this ordering of differences is an act of creation. The social qua social – social whole or totality – entails a recoiling or self-referential movement, which *is* the political. There are two steps in Laclau and Mouffe's argument. The first concerns what it means to talk about the discursive structuring of social relations, the second what makes this structuring political.

As social order cannot be provided with a pre- or extra-discursive ground, it has to be created politically. This calls for the recognition that 'the impossibility of a universal ground does not eliminate its need: it just transforms the ground into an empty place which can be partially filled in a variety of ways (the strategies of this filling is what politics is about)' (Laclau 1995b: 158). The need is not, obviously, for a universal ground, but for conceptualizing the political function of this need – how the political is assigned a universal function *vis-à-vis* order. It is in this light that the substitution of ground with horizon should be seen, where the latter serves as the matrix for discussing the logic of hegemony (Laclau 1993a: 295). The idea is to outline a viewpoint or an analytical concept that is able to capture the political function as overarching compared to political structure, and at the same time as being an integral part of the plurality of contexts.

The concept of the political revolves around how discourses take form, partly, in relation to each other, their frontiers (Laclau 1990b: 160), and partly, internally, that is, in relation to the elements constituting them. The aim is to outline a concept of political ontology that sees politics as an actualization of potentials, which at the same time structures them. The potential cannot then pre-exist its actualization, but is produced retroactively, which is similar to, for instance, a Foucauldian take on power as the ability to make a difference, where ability is not a given potential, but is construed retroactively in the making of difference, that is, in practice. Here it is important to grasp, first, how limits constitute identity, which is where the concept of antagonism plays a central role; and second, how context is delimited, which evokes reference to totality, and hence to self-reference and autonomy.

Hegemonic logic and the two levels

There is a higher-order level of the political – its function of articulating particular and universal – and a lower-order level concerned with politics – the political structuring of hegemonic relationships. To grasp the political and politics along these lines implies, first, that the political has to be disentangled from its spatial and temporal binding to regime forms and hegemonic relationships in general. In other words, to avoid essentialism, the *function* of the political must not be reduced to its historically contingent *structuring*. Second, the political is the practice of articulating particular and universal, which, as a matrix for politics, has a spatial and a temporal dimension, neither of which has form or content a priori. Third, the attempt to fill the gap between universal and particular is a political act that depends on the articulation of hegemonic forces, which means that decisions exceed the structure that conditions them. '[T]he positive content of the empty universal is', says Žižek (1997: 240n.), 'provided by the subject who, by an act of abyssal decision, *identifies* the (empty) Universal with some particular content which hegemonizes it'.

There are two reasons for conceiving politics in terms of hegemony. First, politics deals with the co-existence of incommensurable and hence irreducible differences, which cannot be ordered automatically, or founded on an Archimedean point. Second, in politics there can be no truth claims to be settled as there can be no recourse to extra-political moral or epistemological foundations such as the free and rational individual, the common good or 'philosophical experts' (*HSS* 183; see also Rawls 1995: 174). In politics, references to the rational and the normative are put between brackets. Instead, there is a principle to be complied with, namely the irreducible and in this sense 'factual' nature of pluralism that conditions politics, which for that reason has to be coped with, instead of being a problem that has to be solved or done away with. It is in this respect that contingency and facticity make up the bottom line of the transcendental move.

The anti-objectivist thrust of the logic of hegemony concerns the political creation of order out of disorder. The hegemonic relation – defined vis-à-vis the political function – is marked by 'a reciprocal contamination between the universal and the singular or, rather, the never ending and never totally convincing impersonation of the former by the latter' (Laclau 1996a: 59; see also Laclau 1992b: 89; Mouffe 1993: 13). It is the political function of universalizing particularity and particularizing universality that forms the hegemonic logic (Laclau 2000b: 188–9, 208).

The political is a historical a priori that pertains to every society, which means that the modern structuring of the political is a particular embodiment of the political function. Mouffe (1993: 3) states this succinctly when saying that

> the political cannot be restricted to a certain type of institution, or envisaged as constituting a specific sphere or level of society. It must be conceived as a dimension that is inherent to every human society and that determines our very ontological condition.

This insight can only be sustained by distinguishing the political as a higher-order function from the lower-order structuring of this function.

At this juncture, it is important to distinguish between the conditions of hegemonic relationships and actual hegemonic relationships (Laclau 1993a: 283–8; 1993c: 227; 1994: 175; 1995a: 89–90; 1996a: 59; *HSS* 104, 153):

1 *The condition of a hegemonic relationship*: the constitutive split and the reciprocal contamination between particular and universal.
2 *The actual hegemonic relationship*: the particular becomes the signifier of the absent (communitarian) fullness of society.

The question is wherein the specificity of the political consists, given the argument that hegemony 'defines the very terrain in which a political relation is actually constituted' (Laclau 2000a: 44; see also 2000d: 3). (1) conditions but is unable to determine (2), which is a contingent structuring of (1), that is, of the political terrain in which politics is 'a practice of creation, reproduction and transformation of social relations' (*HSS* 153). Articulation is a broader category than antagonism that cannot define the political structuring of hegemonic relationships in an undecidable structure, which involves decisions that articulate the actual and the potential. Decisions play an important role in the relation between the political and politics. They link (1) and (2), that is to say, what conditions the actual and the actual itself. The latter actualizes the former, which means that it actualizes a function that has neither content nor goal.

The actualization of the potential, which at the same time forms it, is the strategical moment of politics *par excellence*, which emphasizes that decisions are made in what Foucault calls 'a complex strategical situation' (Foucault 1981: 93; see also 1979: 215). Laclau similarly refers to decisions as systematizing the possibilities of actualization thus shaping the political terrain (Laclau 1995a: 92–4; 1996a: 52–3). The politics of frontiers, or the politics of becoming, is a play within bounded varieties, and the possibility of binding what is not yet bounded. The actual draws upon its potentials, meaning that it is contingent upon its becoming, that is freedom.

The political cannot be conceptualized at the level of the structuring of hegemonic relationships, because that would imply conceptualizing it at the ontic level, which would block understanding the political as an ontological category. Otherwise put, the political overflows the structuring of hegemonic relationships, thus showing that they were brought about in a political act, which in turn is an argument for both contingency and freedom. The actual realizes *and* blocks the potential because actualization, as the becoming of the potential through decisions, is an actualization of specific possibilities, and hence an elimination of others. Realization and blockage are two sides of the same coin in that the former, by attaining a determinate form, entails blocking others. As the link between actual and potential, politics revolves around limits and hence mechanisms of inclusion/exclusion. Three points should be mentioned here.

First, the political is an ordering principle of the hegemonic structuring of contexts and social orders, which does not have any content, goal, or need built into it, just as it does not have the capacity to cause or determine anything. This is the political stripped of its embeddedness in contingent articulations. Second, the political is immanent in the doubling of the social – meaning that it is both within and above it – by being the constitutive principle of co-existence, which refers to empty universality. This is 'essential for any kind of *political* interaction, for if the latter took place without universal reference, there would be no political interaction at all' (Laclau 1995b: 160; see also 2000d: 6–7; 2000b: 208). Third, hegemonic relationships shape identity, forms of life, rules, and so on, *vis-à-vis* limits that realize and block identity. The political function is defined independently of the structuring of hegemonic relationships in which politics is, for instance, seen as located in the state, the public sphere, or in conflicts.

Dislocation, antagonism, and identity

Antagonism is a type of relation where 'the presence of the "Other" prevents me from being totally myself. The relation arises not from full totalities, but from the impossibility of their constitution' (*HSS* 125, see also 122–7; Laclau 1990a: 17–8, 27). This impossibility means that 'the negativity of the other which is preventing me from achieving my full identity with myself is just an externalization of my own auto-negativity' (Žižek 1990: 252–3), which has an affinity to dislocation in Laclau and event/rupture/pure distance in Foucault. Antagonism indicates 'that certain discursive forms, through equivalence, annul all positivity of the object and give a real existence to negativity as such' (*HSS* 128–9) which is what Žižek refers to as 'the positive embodiment of our own self-blockage' (1990: 253).

It is necessary to distinguish between antagonism and negativity, which is analogous to the distinction between structure and function: the latter is presupposed by the former, but it is also shaped by it. In antagonism – 'a relation wherein the limits of every objectivity is *shown*' (*HSS* 125; see also Žižek 1997: 217) – *what* is shown, and *how* it is shown are intimately connected. What is shown is conditioned by how the political terrain is structured, that is, how 'certain discursive forms' are contingently ordered around fundamental deadlocks of co-existence. This ordering comes about everywhere in all sorts of ways, which require engagement in complex strategic situations.

The spread of nationalist, racist, and populist sentiments and strategies in European politics illustrates how a political terrain is taking form by antagonizing otherness, and hence contouring a full identity that is taking shape in relation to this triad. The nationalist dimension focuses on the European Union, globalization, international elites, and so on, as those forces destroying the unity of the cultural and the political nation. The racist dimension focuses on strangers, primarily Muslims, which make up a subversive force endangering the cultural nation and the unity and will of the people. Finally, the populist dimension construes enmity in terms of the Establishment's alliance with internal and external enemies that antagonize nation, culture, and people (Dyrberg 1999, 2000).

Antagonism plays a constitutive role in structuring and representing deadlocks by simultaneously stigmatizing enemies and eulogizing a national, cultural, and popular identity allegedly given beforehand, which is, however, taking shape retroactively in this encounter. In looking at the far right, one is typically confronted with strong resentment and hatred against the threats to 'our' identity. The externalization of auto-negativity and its 'embodiment' in the other is an exclusionary limit structuring the political terrain and the articulations within it, thus fixing the identity of both self and other. Having said this, however, it does not follow that antagonism defines the political, as the latter is prior to form/content, which in turn means that antagonism cannot be *the* structuring principle of identification.

Antagonism is a discursive structuring of the hegemonic terrain, which simultaneously constitutes and blocks identity. The other is itself a limit experience, as it were, which is constructed as the stumbling block for 'being what one is'. However, this blockage of the possibility of somehow fulfilling one's identity also triggers this imaginary identity in the first place. The reason is that this blockage is embodied in the imaginary figure of an 'authentic' identity, which cannot but remain elusive (e.g. national or cultural identity). The representation of the other in antagonism is a positivation of negativity that is prior to any representation (Laclau 1996b: 35n). This shows the deadlocks of co-existing differences which signify 'the obstacle preventing a society from reconciling with itself' (Laclau 2000d: 6).

Antagonism shows the split between the actual and the potential in which the latter is sought hegemonized by the former as an actuality that is prevented from being what it is. The self-referential or recoiling nature of negativity, triggered by the blockage of identity, is shown in what Foucault (1981: 155) calls the 'fundamental reversal' of power/knowledge where 'to be what one is' is a retroactive imposition of an imaginary fullness. Fullness is a metaphorical effect of the potential yet-to-be-realized that is prompted by the blockage of this potential (Žižek 1985: 16; 1989: 158, 175; 1990: 251–4; Dyrberg 1997: 145–55). Actualizing the potential is an act in the sense that it cannot be read off from structure, which is why the decision is an irreducible moment in the process of rendering the potential actual.

Antagonism is the negation of identity and the attempt to cope with it by binding and thus making sense of potentials yet-to-be-realized whose actualization is blocked. The other as the name of what blocks identity can find an outlet in all sorts of practices and be expressed in all sorts of ways. Since the articulation between the actual and the potential is prior to what is articulated, the actual qua actual has to pose the potential in a circular fashion by imposing it as that which it itself presupposes. This is a hegemonic act, which is similar to the relation between the social and the political, where the latter, as mentioned, resides in the doubling of the former.

It follows not only that there is a gap between the actual and the potential, which can only be bridged in the fundamental reversal of positing one's presuppositions, but also that actualization is always-already blocked. It is on this background that notions such as limit, blockage, contingency, and the other should be seen, all of which revolve around antagonism. The circular structuring of identity cannot ever fully encircle itself, because it is sparked off by its impossibility of completion (Foucault 1981: 152–6; Žižek 1989: 160, 161–78, 183, 224–31; 1992: 170–2, 179–86). This is the reason why dislocation, analytically speaking, is prior to antagonism. When dislocation is seen in terms of temporality, possibility, and freedom (Laclau 1990a: 39–45), it is a disclosure of unbounded varieties or the potential, and hence the contingency of decisions taken in an undecidable terrain. The three aspects of dislocation are vital for the political function of articulating particular and universal in which political reason as opposed to axiomatic rationality plays a key role.

The political importance of the concept of dislocation for antagonism lies in the latter being a vehicle in hegemonic attempts to deal with the self-blockage of the subject by internalizing the potential as a blocked actuality still-to-be. Put differently, dislocation is the condition of possibility for antagonism and for politics in general. Politics does not only deal with conflicts of interests, but is basically concerned with dislocations between the potential and the actual, and the structuring of the potential as an actuality to come in relation to deciding authoritatively in matters of common concerns. In actualizing the potential the subject is engaged in a strategic maneuver to bind time and space, which positions it. To structure the potential, and hence to systematize actualization vis-à-vis decision-making, is the main feature of the politics of hegemonic systematization of differences.

Antagonism and the politics of systematizing differences

To speak of discourse as a system of differences means that various differences have been constructed as being part of a system. This implies three things.

First, the system cannot be a common denomination of an extra-discursive unity of its elements, but is instead a reduction of reality. To render reality intelligible implies blocking signification, and this means that reality overflows every attempt of systematization. The system is thus contingent on what conditions the systematization of differences in the first place, namely the reduction of reality, and the surplus of meaning and the struggles between these that are likely to accompany this reduction (*HSS* 111). By systematizing the actualization process the system binds, spatially as well as temporally, the potential, but it is not able to bind what conditions it in the first place.

Second, the nature of a system cannot be read off from the structure of reality because the being of the latter is discursive and because identity is always embedded in various discourses, which prevents it from being sutured. Identity as well as the construction and destruction of systems are governed by another logic, namely that of difference and equivalence. In the construction of a system, differences are construed as equivalent vis-à-vis the system, whereby the system performs a double task: it organizes them as elements, or rather moments, which are different, but it also binds them together in a way that subverts their differences. Signification and hence order can only arise by binding the free variation of differences.

Third, the constructed nature of system means that it is hegemonic in two senses. It is a systematization of differences imbued with calculations, which are conditioned by the politics of universalizing the particular and particularizing the universal. The system is moreover hegemonic by aiming to systematize actualization processes, which implies a retroactive binding of time that is inseparable from a specific structuring of space. Since identity can only exist in processes of identification, the identity of the system requires an ongoing temporal and spatial structuring.

These three aspects of system indicate that it is an impossible object in the same way as society is (*HSS* 95–6, 98–9). It is a metaphor of an absent totality or the reference point of an impossible tantalization process.[1] System is an overdetermined effect of the articulation between its elements. To say that political strategies are concerned with systematizing differences conveys that what makes a strategy political is its attempt to articulate part/whole and past/future. The question is how this is done, and how totalizing effects are structured.

The political dimension of a strategy concerns how systems position themselves in relation to one another and to their parts. Systematizing differences is an ongoing political process, which is the context and vehicle of antagonism. It is presupposed by antagonistic parties when they use the strategic metaphors of a system in political struggles, or when they address the authorities of a system. The political process can take several forms: it can be fast or slow, turbulent or steady, fragile or stable, rapidly changing or highly sedimented. It can also be conflictual or consensual, hierarchical or egalitarian, dominating or liberating. What matters here is that the political aspect of these processes cannot be linked to one side of the distinctions, for instance, that it is turbulent, conflictual, hierarchical, and dominating as opposed to steady, consensual, egalitarian, and liberating. The distinction between the political and the social does not run along these lines, which belongs to the lower-order structuring of social relations (Bang and Dyrberg 1993a: 13).

System, hegemony and antagonism

> Without limits through which a (non-dialectical) negativity is constructed we would have an indefinite dispersion of differences whose absence of systematic limits would make any differential identity impossible. But this very function of constituting differential identities through antagonistic limits is what, at the same time, destabilizes and subverts those differences.
>
> (Laclau 1995b: 151–2)

Laclau's argument is important for two reasons: by distinguishing between difference and differential, and by approaching negativity in terms of systematic limits, which it describes as a function. Antagonism cannot be opposed to difference, since the former is a particular structuring of the latter; otherwise it would be a contradiction of terms to speak of 'antagonistic differences' (Laclau 1981: 177). Difference is an overarching category that refers to the relational construction of identity. What are opposed then are antagonistic and differential identities.

Here, at the lower-order level of structuration, we find the two poles of antagonistically and differentially constructed identities, where the former shapes the latter by playing a central role in effectuating systematic limits. These are described as a function, but it is not, needless to say, a functionalist type of function, because it does not operate with a telos defined in relation to a societal whole. Instead, it is a political function that revolves around the systematization of differences (Bang 1998: 285), which has both an ontological and an ethical dimension.

In talking about limits as constitutive for identity, Laclau is referring to the political function of the hegemonic systematization of limits. The political concern with order focuses on the articulation between identity and context: how are differences to be articulated to make context possible, and which differences are, and which are not, politically acceptable? Politics revolves around the articulation of limits, which deals with governing co-existing differences. A system could not exist if it was not concerned with and did not govern the limits defining it. This in turn indicates the importance of political authority. Thus the political is a function of the articulation between identity and context, which effectuates limits: $P = f\{a(I + C) \rightarrow L\}$.

The system conditions and situates antagonism as the terrain in which it occurs, but antagonism is also constitutive of system in the sense that it shapes, changes, and undermines it. If the relation between two agents (*A* and *B*) develops into an antagonism, the former differential relation between them is replaced by one in which A constructs various elements as moments in a chain of equivalence that represents the negation of A, its impossibility of being what it is. Insofar as *B* occupies this place of the negation of A, it has come to symbolize the presence of the other that prevents A from fulfilling its identity. The situation is this: $B \equiv \sum(b_1, b_2, \ldots, b_n) \equiv$ non-A. *B*'s identity takes form in the negation of A, which is construed in a chain of equivalence among various elements: $\sum(b_1, b_2, \ldots, b_n)$ symbolizing the negation of A: non-A. Antagonism plays a constitutive role for identity by structuring limits, some of which consist in naming a political enemy, but a limit could also be a rupture or the bottom line of acceptability.

Identity takes form in these processes because the systematization of differences partially subverts them due to the equivalential logic. As a metonymic chaining of elements, the logic of equivalence cannot account for antagonism, meaning that it cannot account for the constitution of a system. The system effect – the political institution of the system – consists in delineating the limits of the system, which cannot themselves be signified by the system, for in that case they would have to be internal to its identity. That is, they would be differential moments *in* the system, whereby they could not be the limits *of* the system. But neither can these limits simply remain external, for in that case they could not make an impact on the system. It is the systematicity of differences that accounts for these differences as differences, and hence their partial subversion in chains of equivalence (Laclau 1994: 168–71).

The only way in which a system can signify itself, and thus achieve identity and autonomy, is by blocking the signification of the system. The blockage that sparks off self-reference Laclau calls exclusionary limits, which are antagonistic as opposed to differential. '[W]hat constitutes the condition of possibility of a signifying system – its limits – is also what constitutes its condition of impossibility – a blockage of the continuous expansion of the process of signification'. It follows that 'if the systematicity of the system is a direct result of the exclusionary limit, it is only that exclusion that grounds the system as such' (Laclau 1994: 168–9; see also 1992a: 133; 1992b: 89; 1995b: 151–2).

The two types of limits are relative to wider contexts into which systems are inserted, and it is this relativizing of exclusionary limits that accounts for the forging and displacing of antagonism. Politics as the systematization of differences is an ongoing practice, which requires that the equivalential logic creates a spatio-temporal enclosure that is able to frame signification and identification, which in turn is what underpins the persistence of systems or discourses. This makes it possible to systematize the actualization of potentials, which triggers a circular process in which the system recognizes itself 'as it is'. It is only by positing its own presuppositions in this way that self-reference can get off the ground. This is the reason why identity takes shape in a recoiling movement, and systems or discourses are autonomous in relation to each other.

Equivalence mutates particulars by way of systematizing them, meaning that they can only be identified in relation to a system, which at the same time subverts their differences. Systems of differences are both medium and outcome of the constructions of chains of equivalences. They are medium because these constructions do not take place in a vacuum, but are articulated with conventions, traditions, values, rules, commitments, social positions, and so on. They are also outcome because they take form, undergo changes, and are subverted in these processes. When *A* and *B* are symbols of each other's impossibility of being what they are, both a temporal and a spatial dimension are evoked. This is due to the hegemonic attempt to bind the potential as an actuality still-to-come, and as an actuality latently present.

A hegemonic systematization of actualization depends, as mentioned, on its ability to articulate spatial and temporal metaphors. Space is a binding of time, and opposite, time can only exist if it is ordered spatially. If time was not discursively ordered, it would appear as a dislocation of space.[2] Dislocation is a rupture in the political systematization of differences, that is, structures of signification and identification relating to the co-existence of differences. The articulation between time and space necessitates reconsidering the question of order. Whereas liberals and Marxists typically hold that politics plays a supplementary role vis-à-vis social order, Laclau and Mouffe argue that politics creates temporary order in a general disorder – that order 'exists only as a partial limiting of disorder' (*HSS* 193; see also March and Olsen 1989: 16, 159, 162; Bang 1998: 283–4, 286). In the words of Laclau (1993a: 291), 'the need to "fill in the gaps" [in politics] is no longer a "supplement" to be added to a basic area of constitution of the identity of the agent but, instead, becomes a *primary* terrain'. This is the reason why politics cannot simply be a response to societal dysfunctions, or a neutral frame for regulating conflict. Politics as a primary terrain revolves around the act of systematizing differences, which means that the political is ingrained in the structuring of the social, or it is a dimension of social relations.

Antagonism poses and presupposes the system vis-à-vis limits, which constitutes the system as medium and outcome of hegemonic articulations. The system that conditions and situates antagonism also points towards the possibility of dissolving it, because the structuring of the system through limits to other systems is an ongoing articulation that might displace it. The contingency of the politics of systems calls for terms such as strategy, reason, and decision to deal with forging and displacing antagonism. What conditions hegemonic power struggles – the widening of the horizons for political strategies – also signals their contestability. When an antagonism is articulated with other systems it is articulated with other systematizations of time and space. This triggers dislocations between incommensurable differences, which 'free' temporality, possibility, and freedom from their particular structuring in systems. These ruptures can be the result of antagonistic power struggles, but the opposite is also possible when dislocations render new articulations possible and hence new ways of forging hegemonic blocs (Laclau 1990a: 39–44, 46, 60).

Dislocatory effects are built into hegemonic relations where the widening of equivalential chains is required for the success of hegemonic strategies. However, the more they aspire to speak in the name of wider contexts or society, the more their identity will tend to get blurred because it gets increasingly difficult for these parts to identify themselves as belonging to the same system. This allows the possibility of re-articulating these elements in points of resistance to how they are formed in the hegemonic blocs (Laclau 1990a: 76–7, 80–1; 1992a: 132–5; 1992b: 90; 1993a: 287; 1993b: 435; 1994: 175; 1995b: 153–5; Foucault 1981: 99–102). The ability of a hegemonic bloc to forge exclusionary limits and hence to sustain its identity will thus weaken as these limits tend to become indistinct and contoured as a horizon of values, forms of life, and ways of doing things ingrained in practical day-to-day rule-following.

Final remarks on the political and politics

The political is a hegemonic terrain, which is an empty place of inscription in the sense that it has neither form nor content, just as it is not equipped with goals or needs. This is the reason why the political cannot determine the structuring of discursive forms, that is, politics. Moreover, the political cannot have a specific location in society, just as it cannot be the prerogative of certain agents, notably elites. It is rather an ontology of potentials geared toward the articulation of identity and context, which revolves around governing limits. The political can be seen as potentials of actualizations vis-à-vis systems of differences, which insert politics in a temporal and spatial matrix.

Politics is the practice of structuring the political function, which consists in instigating directions in the hegemonic terrain, and to actualizing the potential through articulations where systematic limits are delineated. It is in these processes that the identity of the subject is given in relation to its spatial and temporal insertion into systems of differences. These processes are open in the sense that they cannot be determined a priori as, for instance, discourses of order or of progress, which are reading principles that operate as an organizing nexus for grand narratives (Laclau 1995b: 159–60). Politics as the filling of the empty place of identity has to be seen in relation to the blockages inherent in the actualization of the potential. This so because actualization revolves around negativity that sparks off self-referential processes, thus providing systems with identity and autonomy. Politics in general and political authority in particular are concerned with speaking on behalf of the system thus delineated (Easton 1965: 54).

To talk about the primacy of the political means that systems are political constructs. The impossibility of the social regulating itself in the absence of political ordering shatters emancipatory visions of the end of politics regardless of whether they are coined in liberal, Marxist, or communitarian terms. Anti-political conceptions of emancipation typically assume that the political supplements social logics, such as market and culture, when they fail. This is, for instance, envisioned in a self-regulating market coupled with procedural rules or in a normatively integrated community. Visions of the end of politics – and hence the inability to grasp the political as an ontological condition – are inscribed in the structures of political modernity, which attempt to bind the political to a procedural set-up, normative order, rights, truth, and so on, by equipping it with origin and telos as well as form and content (Bang 1998: 289). This goes hand in hand with confining the political to particular locations where attempts can be made to render it law-like and by the same token controlled by political elites.

It is this neglect of 'the political [...] as a dimension that is inherent to every human society and that determines our very ontological condition' (Mouffe 1993: 3) that shapes elitist views of politics as the never-ending struggle for domination, as well as emancipatory views for which the elimination of domination is unthinkable without the withering away of politics. The concept of the political in Laclau and Mouffe's work does not succumb to either elitism or an emancipation coined in terms of 'freedom from' political power, and the protective views of democracy that go with it. They take up the political problem and democratic challenge to give way for a more wide-ranging view of politics as types of practices that can take place everywhere, and which do not have to be caught up in strategies of control, domination, hierarchy, and the like.

Democratic theory has to be based on political ontology: the political is a spatial and temporal function of articulating part/whole and future/past; and politics is a structuring of this function, which remains incomplete because hegemonic forces cannot fill the gap between particular and universal because they are conditioned by it. Dislocation – temporality, possibility, and freedom – is another name for this impossibility of suture, which as a condition of possibility of form cannot itself have form. It has to be presupposed though to underpin the contingency argument, and hence a *political* concept of freedom. This is what defines the political nature and value of democracy, which is decisive not only for democracy but also for a political take on emancipation: that things could be different *and* better. It is in this sense that Laclau and Mouffe's contribution to political theory presents a democratic challenge related to the co-existence of differences whether in the political regime or in the political culture.

Notes

1 'The category of "social totality" certainly cannot be abandoned because, so far as all social action takes place in an overdetermined terrain, it "totalises" social relations to some extent; but totality becomes now the name of a horizon and no longer of a ground' (Laclau 1993a: 295). See also Laclau 1990c: 213; 1992b: 89–90; 1993c: 231–2; 1994: 168–71; 1995a: 94; 1995b: 152–3; 2000c: 291–2; *HSS* 1985: 103–5, 186–8, 191; Lefort 1986: 220, 303–5; Žižek 1991: 81–3, 99–100).

2 In Gasché's discussion of the relation between time and spacing 'differance as temporalizing is inseparable from, though not identical to, differance as spacing, since the becoming-time of space is the condition proper of spacing' (1986: 198). For a critique of the time/space dualism in relation to the concept of political authority, see Bang and Dyrberg 1993b: 17.

References

Bang, H. P. (1998) 'David Easton's postmodern images', *Political Theory*, 26(3): 281–317.

Bang, H. P. and Dyrberg, T. B. (1993a) 'The political in the social: an ontological turn of political and democratic theory', *Working Paper*, Department of Social Sciences, Roskilde University.

—— (1993b) 'Hegemony and democracy', *Working Paper*, Department of Economics, Politics and Public Administration, Aalborg University.

Dyrberg, T. B. (1997) *The Circular Structure of Power: Power, Politics, Identity*, London: Verso.

—— (1999) 'Racisme som en nationalistisk og populistisk reaktion på elitedemokrati', in T. B. Dyrberg, A. Dreyer Hansen and J. Torfing (eds) *Diskursteorien på arbejde*, Copenhagen: Roskilde Universitetsforlag.

—— (2000) 'The politics of racism, nationalism and populism – the Danish case', paper presented at the ECPR Conference.

Easton, D. (1965) *A Framework for Political Analysis*, Englewood Cliffs, NJ: Prentice-Hall.

Foucault, M. (1979) *Discipline and Punish: The Birth of the Prison*, New York: Vintage Books.

—— (1981) *The History of Sexuality*, volume 1, *An Introduction*, Harmondsworth: Pelican Books.

Gasché, R. (1986) *The Tain of the Mirror*, Cambridge, MA: Harvard University Press.

Laclau, E. (1981) 'Populistischer Bruch und Diskurs', 'Anhang' in E. Laclau, *Politik und Ideologie im Marxismus: Kapitalismus – Faschismus – Populismus*, Berlin: Argument-Verlag.

—— (1990a) 'New reflections on the revolution of our time', in E. Laclau, *New Reflections on the Revolution of our Time*, London: Verso.

—— (1990b) 'Letter to Aletta', in E. Laclau, *New Reflections on the Revolution of our Time*, London: Verso.

—— (1990c) 'Theory, democracy and socialism', in E. Laclau, *New Reflections on the Revolution of our Time*, London: Verso.

—— (1992a) 'Beyond emancipation', in Jan Nederveen Pieterse (ed.) *Emancipations, Modern and Postmodern*, London: Sage.

—— (1992b) 'Universalism, particularism and the question of identity', *October*, 62: 83–91.

—— (1993a) 'Power and representation', in M. Poster (ed.) *Politics, Theory, and Contemporary Culture*, New York: Columbia University Press.

—— (1993b) 'Discourse', in R. Goodin and P. Pettit (eds) *The Blackwell Companion to Contemporary Political Philosophy*, Oxford: Blackwell.

—— (1993c) 'The signifiers of democracy', in J. H. Carens (ed.) *Democracy and Possessive Individualism*, New York: State University of New York Press.

—— (1994) 'Why do empty signifiers matter to politics?', in J. Weeks (ed.) *The Lesser Evil and the Greater Good*, London: Rivers Oram Press.

—— (1995a) 'The time is out of joint', *CONTENTS* (Summer) this article first appeared in *Working Papers 2*, Centre for Theoretical Studies, University of Essex, 1995.

—— (1995b) 'Subject of politics, politics of the subject', *differences: A Journal of Feminist Cultural Studies*, 7(1): 146–65.

—— (1996a) 'Deconstruction, pragmatism, hegemony', in Chantal Mouffe (ed.) *Deconstruction and Pragmatism*, London: Routledge.

—— (1996b) 'Universalism, particularism and the question of identity', in E. Laclau, *Emancipation(s)*, London: Verso.

—— (2000a) 'Identity and hegemony: the role of universality in the constitution of political logics', in J. Butler, E. Laclau and S. Žižek (eds) *Contingency, Hegemony, Universality: Contemporary Dialogue on the Left*, London: Verso.

—— (2000b) 'Structure, history and the political', in J. Butler, E. Laclau and S. Žižek (eds) *Contingency, Hegemony, Universality: Contemporary Dialogue on the Left*, London: Verso.

—— (2000c) 'Constructing universality', in J. Butler, E. Laclau and S. Žižek (eds) *Contingency, Hegemony, Universality: Contemporary Dialogue on the Left*, London: Verso.

—— (2000d) 'Power and social communication', unpublished paper, University of Essex.

Lefort, C. (1986) *The Political Forms of Modern Society*, Cambridge: Polity Press.

March, J. G. and Olsen, J. P. (1989) *Rediscovering Institutions: The Organizational Basis of Politics*, New York: Free Press.

Mouffe, C. (1993) *The Return of the Political*, London: Verso.

Rawls, J. (1995) 'Reply to Habermas', *Journal of Philosophy*, 42(3), 132–81.

Žižek, S. (1985) 'La société n'existe pas', *L'Ane*, (Oct–Dec).

—— (1989) *The Sublime Object of Ideology*, London: Verso.

—— (1990) 'Beyond discourse analysis', in E. Laclau, *New Reflections on the Revolution of our Time*, London: Verso.

—— (1991) *For they Know Not What they Do*, London: Verso.

—— (1992) *Enjoy your Symptom! Jacques Lacan in Hollywood and Out*, New York and London: Routledge.

—— (1997) *The Plague of Fantasies*, London: Verso.

15

HEGEMONY, POLITICAL SUBJECTIVITY, AND RADICAL DEMOCRACY*

David Howarth

While the concept of hegemony has been employed with good effect to account for a wide range of social phenomena at the descriptive and explanatory levels, it remains under-theorized in mainstream political science and political theory.[1] Compared with a range of cognate concepts such as power, domination, leadership, and force, not to mention democracy, freedom, or the state, rigorous conceptual clarification has not been undertaken. This means that its different usages have not been fully explored, and there has been little effort to relate the concept to the different theoretical fields and traditions in which it functions. One consequence of this neglect is that hegemony has usually been equated with states of domination and political supremacy, in which case other dimensions of the concept – questions pertaining to political strategy or normative concerns about different forms of political rule – have largely been occluded. Whether in ordinary language usage, in descriptions of party politics or changing state forms, or whether employed as the obverse of radical and plural democracy, the concept is usually made synonymous with sedimented forms of political order, the stifling of difference, and the durability of established political power.[2]

One exception to this rule is the work of Ernesto Laclau, who has developed a sophisticated and compelling concept of hegemony by articulating structuralist, post-structuralist, and psychoanalytic thought with the Marxist tradition of political theory.[3] Although Laclau's work has provoked considerable debate, it has often tended to be of a typically 'either/or' variety: either his work has resolved all the problems associated with the concept and its application, and thus requires very little further investigation, or it has no relevance at all, and should be immediately rejected. In the too rapid desire to praise or condemn, much of the richness of Laclau's problematic has been lost, with careful analysis of its sources and the unanswered questions it raises foreclosed.

Against this background, this chapter examines Laclau's account and its implications for the analysis of politics, subjectivity, and democracy. I begin by relating Laclau's concept of hegemony to the Marxist theoretical tradition, showing how it offsets a number of problems in this body of discourse, after which I reconstruct three models of hegemony evident in his writings, raising questions in need of further elucidation. I then evaluate key aspects of Laclau's resultant social ontology, arguing that his concept of subjectivity and political agency needs further specification; that his conception of society remains too focused on what I call the ontological, rather than ontical, level of analysis; and finally that the relationship between the normative and explanatory dimensions of his project is largely implicit and in need of greater clarity.

Deconstructing Marxism

A full study of the concept of hegemony would begin by constructing a grammar of its employment in various fields of thinking – American political science, international relations theory, and in ordinary language. I want, however, to confine myself to its emergence in the Marxist tradition, as it is this system of thought that forms the backdrop for Laclau's writings, and it is here that most work has been done to develop a coherent conception. As to its 'origins' in this field of thinking, Perry Anderson (1976) has carefully examined the emergence of the concept in debates in Russian social democracy, and it is not necessary to rehearse his story here. Suffice it to say that the concept of hegemony came to fill a hiatus in the classical Marxist account of historical development. The need for the Russian working classes to hegemonize other social classes, by taking on tasks such as the struggle for liberal democracy which were not essential to it, arose because of the under-development and structural weakness of the national bourgeoisie, itself a product of the 'combined and uneven development' of international capitalist social relations. Its quintessential expression was the Leninist conception of hegemony in which the vanguard party was to establish political leadership amongst an alliance of social classes in order to bring about a series of short-term and essentially instrumental gains (cf. Lenin 1968: 117, 279). In these accounts, however, the hegemonic relation remained primarily a contingent and externally conceived connection between political forces, and there was no ultimate weakening of the foundational meta-narrative of the Marxist tradition.

It was left to Antonio Gramsci to develop a more positive conception of hegemony. In brief, he provides a novel account of class rule in capitalist society by insisting that ruling groups need to win the consent of the governed by establishing authority and legitimacy in 'civil society', and not just by virtue of their economic position or control over the government and state. In Gramsci's terms, therefore, a ruling class must achieve 'intellectual and moral leadership', and not just 'political supremacy', if it is to govern effectively and efficiently. This re-conceptualization of the nature and dynamics of class rule leads Gramsci to develop a new political strategy. As against Lenin's object of constructing temporary alliances between distinct classes in a bid to overthrow class rule, he argues that particular social classes must transcend their narrow economic interests by elaborating a new ideology or 'common sense' (Gramsci 1971: 134, 161, 180–

5). This means that different classes and social groups must come to share a common set of political objectives based on a new sets of beliefs and practices by forging a 'collective will'. For Gramsci, then, politics ceases to be a zero-sum game conducted by classes with fixed identities and interests, and becomes more a process of constructing relationships and agreements – 'equilibria' as he calls them – between divergent groups and strata. It occurs, moreover, largely on the terrain of civil society, and consists of 'winning over' agents and groups to certain ideological and political positions – Gramsci's famous 'war of position' (Gramsci 1971: 238–9).

Laclau's concept of hegemony arises out of a deconstructive reading of the Marxist tradition, especially a critique of Gramsci's texts. He discerns a crucial ambiguity in Marxism between, on the one hand, a necessary logic of historical development and, on the other, a supplementary set of concepts and initiatives designed to open a space for contingent political intervention, which disrupts the dominant essentialist conception. This ineliminable tension is manifest in three fundamental aspects of Gramsci's approach: his commitment to a fundamental social class bringing about significant social change; the centrality of a 'decisive economic nucleus' as both the object of political struggle and determinant of the ideological and political superstructures; and his strong separation of the roles of coercion and consent in accounting for the capitalist state and class hegemony (see Howarth 2000a: 99–100). While the first two aspects require the Marxist notions of a unified social totality with predetermined laws of motion and development, the latter is a product of Gramsci's tendency to posit binary oppositions – traditional versus organic intellectuals; domination versus hegemony; state versus civil society; East versus West – while privileging one term over the other. Thus, even though Gramsci strives to reconcile the state and civil society by introducing the concept of the 'integral state', he nevertheless tends to identify the state with coercion and repression, and civil society with the manufacture of consent and the practice of hegemony.

Three models of hegemony

Arising from his deconstructive reading of Gramsci and the Marxist tradition more generally, Laclau has developed three models of hegemony.[4] In his earliest writings, drawing on Louis Althusser's structuralist rethinking of historical materialism, he argues that hegemonic practices are conducted by 'fundamental social classes', which aim to transform society in line with their interests and values (*PIM* 109 n. 37, 141 n. 56). In developing this model, he challenges the orthodox Marxist view that all ideological interpellations, especially appeals to 'the people' or 'the nation', have a 'necessary class belonging', arguing that they are contingent elements, which can be articulated by competing hegemonic projects endeavouring to endow them with a particular class inflection (*PIM* 100–11). More particularly, he stresses the strategic importance of articulating popular-democratic and populist discourses, which are organized around the contradiction between 'the people' and 'the state/power bloc', with traditional socialist demands, though he does not challenge the overriding importance of class forces in ultimately fixing the meaning of popular struggles.

In *Hegemony and Socialist Strategy*, Laclau and Mouffe present us with a second model. Drawing principally on post-structuralist conceptions of language and society, as developed by theorists such as Derrida, Foucault, and Lacan, they argue that the identities of *all* 'ideological' elements, and the social subjects they interpellate, are contingent and negotiable (*HSS* 105–14). Indeed, the open-texturedness of social relations is a central condition of possibility for articulatory practices and political subjectivity occurring at all. These assumptions are predicated on an ontological distinction between, on the one hand, a discursive field of overdetermined identities and, on the other hand, endeavours by different political projects to construct finite and limited discourses. Two further conditions of possibility are necessary for hegemonic practices to occur: the existence of antagonistic political forces and the instability of the political frontiers that divide them (*HSS* 136). Hegemonic practices thus presuppose a social field riven by antagonistic relations, and the presence of contingent elements – or 'floating signifiers' as Laclau and Mouffe call them, borrowing from Levi-Strauss – that can be articulated by opposed political projects (Howarth 2000a: 110).

The practice of hegemony is conceived as a metonymical operation involving the displacement of one set of demands from one social site to another, or from one group to another. For instance, a student organization or movement that begins to take up and articulate the demands of workers or peasants, which stand in a contiguous or neighbourhood relation to them, can be seen to be endeavouring to establish a hegemonic relationship between the two constituencies (see Howarth 1995a: 195–201). The major aim of hegemonic projects is to construct and stabilize systems of meaning or 'hegemonic formations' which, on a societal level, are organized around the articulation of *nodal points*. The latter are defined as privileged condensations of meaning that partially fix the identities of a particular set of signifiers. To use a somewhat stylized example, it might be argued, following the work of Andrew Gamble (1990) and Stuart Hall (1983, 1988), that Thatcherite hegemony in the 1980s was organized around the nodal points of a 'free economy' and 'strong state'.[5]

Laclau develops a third model of hegemony in his more recent writings. This development is partly a response to Slavoj Žižek's important critique of *Hegemony and Socialist Strategy*, which centres on perceived failings in Laclau and Mouffe's theory of subjectivity (Žižek 1989, 1990). Žižek argues that their post-structuralist theory of discourse dissolves the concept of subjectivity into mere subject positions within a discursive structure, in which case their radical concept of antagonism is blunted. In order to explicate and assess this criticism, it is necessary to say a little more about Laclau and Mouffe's theory of antagonism. In brief, this conception is directed against objectivist accounts of social conflict that conceive antagonisms as the clash between social agents with fully constituted identities and interests, where the task of the political analyst is to describe the causes, conditions, and resolution of conflict. For instance, Eric Wolf's (1971) classic study of peasant rebellion suggests that the penetration of capitalist relations into 'traditional' peasant communities provided the necessary dislocatory conditions for such events, and that it was the alliances between two groups of social actors – alienated '"rootless" intellectuals', on the one hand, and 'middle peasants and poor but "free" peasants' on the other – which generated the peasant uprisings themselves (Wolf 1971: 282–302; see also Duverger 1972; Gurr 1970; Marx 1977).

As against this view, Laclau and Mouffe argue that social antagonisms occur because social agents are *prevented* from attaining their identities (and attendant interests) by an 'enemy' who is deemed responsible for this 'failure'. Their recasting of Wolf's arguments results in the view that peasants expelled from their land by capitalist farmers and forced to become workers are literally prevented from 'being peasants', thus experiencing a blockage of identity. This 'failure' of identity is a mutual experience for both the antagonizing force and the force that is being antagonized, and the task of the discourse analyst is to describe the ways in which the identities of agents are blocked, and to chart the different means by which these obstacles are constructed in antagonistic terms. In the case of peasants expelled from their land, such an investigation would examine the different ways peasants constructed the landlords or the state as the 'enemy', as well as the different symbolic resources they deployed to oppose such enemies (see Howarth 2000a: 105).[6]

Žižek's critique of this conception stresses that social subjects are not antagonized by external 'others' who threaten their identity. Instead, the subject is inherently and ontologically divided, such that antagonisms are a projection of this inner division (*Spaltung*) onto an external other. Drawing explicitly on Lacan's theory of subjectivity, he argues that the subject's various identifications with external objects are predicated upon, and occlude, an originary lack or void at the heart of subjectivity: 'the subject is precisely correlative to its own limit, to the element which cannot be subjectified, it is the name of the void which cannot be filled out with subjectification: the subject is the point of failure of subjectivation' (Žižek 1990: 254). This lack is ontological, first, because we can only become subjects by identifying with an external and essentially alien system of signifiers which can never represent us adequately and, secondly, because the signifiers with which we identify in the symbolic order are always incomplete, marked as they are by an outside or 'real' that always escapes them (Lacan 1977: 155–6; Žižek 1989: 174–5). Žižek claims that this division produces a radical and ineliminable antagonism at the heart of subjectivity, and he criticizes Laclau and Mouffe's conception of antagonism between opposed subject positions on the grounds that it implies that antagonistic relations could ultimately be transcended in the name of a final emancipation – the workers, for instance, might succeed in overthrowing the owners of capital and bring about a socialist utopia.

In what he calls a threefold radicalization of the concept of hegemony, Laclau responds to this criticism in *New Reflections on the Revolution of our Time* by extending the contingency of discursive elements to both the subjects of hegemonic projects *and* to social structures. Leaning more heavily on Derrida's deconstructive readings of metaphysical texts, and Lacan's conception of a symbolic order haunted by a 'real' that always escapes it, structures are now conceptualized as 'undecidable' entities, which are both constituted and threatened by a discursive exterior, and the problem of subjectivity is addressed by introducing a split between subject positions *within* a discursive structure, and political subjects that actively *constitute* structures. This requires, in turn, the introduction of the concept of dislocation to account both for the disruption of symbolic orders and their concomitant identities, and the opening up of spaces within which creative political subjects emerge to identify with new discourses. Dislocations are thus defined as those 'events' or 'crises' that cannot be represented within an existing discursive order, as they function to disrupt and destabilize symbolic orders (*NR* 72–8). This enables Laclau to inject an 'extra-discursive' dynamism into his conception of society, and his later writings suggest that late- or post-modern societies are undergoing an 'accelerated tempo' of dislocatory experiences (Howarth 2000a: 111). This 'accelerated tempo' is caused by processes such as commodification, bureaucratization, and globalization, all of which can be seen as the contemporary manifestations of what Marxists such as Trotsky called 'combined and uneven development' (see Löwy 1981).

An important corollary to the accelerating rhythm of dislocations is a greater role for political subjectivities, which emerge in the spaces of fractured structures, and whose decisions reconstitute dislocated orders. In order to capture these new forms of identification, Laclau introduces the concepts of myth and social imaginary. Myths are new 'spaces of representation', which are designed to make sense of and suture dislocations; if they successfully conceal social dislocations by inscribing a wider range of social demands, they are transformed into imaginaries. A collective social imaginary is thus defined by Laclau as 'a horizon' or 'absolute limit which structures a field of intelligibility', and he gives examples such as the Christian Millennium, the Enlightenment, Marxism, and positivism's conception of progress as examples (Howarth 2000a: 111).

Finally, in his most recent writings, most notably the collection of essays entitled *Emancipation(s)*, Laclau's third model of hegemony is further refined by the introduction of the concept of *empty signifiers*. Contrasting floating and empty signifiers, in which the former are seen as ambiguous elements always 'overdetermined' by a plurality of meanings in a discursive field, an empty signifier is 'a signifier without a signified', and developing the concept of nodal points, empty signifiers are possible not because of a surplus of meaning, but because of the structural impossibility of signification as such. In Lacanian terminology, they exist because of the 'lack of being' in any symbolic order. This impossibility arises out of the inability of any internal linguistic difference to represent the systematicity of the system as a whole. Paradoxically, therefore, it is only a signifier that negates a system of differences which enables the system to represent itself. It is this signifier – the empty signifier – that constitutes both the possibility and the impossibility of any signifying chain.[7]

With respect to the conceptualization of hegemony, Laclau argues that '[t]he presence of empty signifiers [...] is the very condition of hegemony' (*E* 43). This is because 'the hegemonic relationship' refers to the way in which a particular signifier ('people', 'nation', 'revolution') is emptied of its particular meaning and comes to represent the 'absent fullness' of a symbolic order. Thus, in social terms, the empty signifier comes to play the universal function of representing an entire community or social order. For instance, Laclau argues that the idea of 'order' in Hobbes's philosophy functions as an empty signifier because Hobbes is not interested in proposing a particular sort of order to overcome the insecurities of the state of nature, but the need for order as such. In this sense, the signifier 'order' acquires a universal function, and various political projects attempt to incarnate or embody this idea in their endeavours to become hegemonic (*E* 45–6).

One crucial question concerns *which* particular signifier comes to play the role of an empty signifier. Rejecting deterministic solutions in which economic logics are seen to play this role, Laclau argues that no signifier is predetermined to incarnate the (impossible) symbolic unity of a community or society. Instead, he proposes that it is the 'unequal distributions of power' that partly determines which signifier in any particular society will play the role of the empty signifier. In this regard, Laclau specifies three theoretical conditions that have to be satisfied for their emergence and functioning. These are the *availability* of potential signifiers and their *credibility* as means of signification and interpellation. A third condition, not mentioned by Laclau, would be the presence of *strategically placed agents* who can construct and deploy empty signifiers to advance their projects (see Griggs and Howarth 2000). Moreover, he stresses that the idea of 'unequal distributions of power' does not reintroduce a form of economic or structural determinism through the back door, as these inequalities of power are themselves the product of previous hegemonic struggles and operations. Finally, as against the charge that this theorization is the result of a priori reasoning, he argues that only careful empirical investigation of particular historical conjunctures can determine *how* and *why* any particular difference can and does perform this role (Griggs and Howarth 2002: 47).

Evaluation and critique

My genealogy of Laclau's concept of hegemony has charted a threefold movement. The initial Gramscian/Althusserian model put forward in his early writings gives way to the essentially post-structuralist conception in *Hegemony and Socialist Strategy*, whereas in Laclau's most recent writings we see the emergence of a more Lacanian slant with the introduction of a radicalized political subjectivity and the addition of 'empty signifiers' as the condition of existence for the establishment of hegemonic orders. In evaluating these models, I want to focus on two central questions. First, what are we to make of the internal development of his ideas on hegemony? Second, how plausible and coherent is his overall conception of hegemony?

With respect to the first question, it is evident that the shift from the first to the second models has evinced most debate amongst critics and commentators.[8] However, it is not my intention to revisit these (sometimes hostile and bitter) encounters. As I shall argue below, much of the critique has either operated at the inappropriate level of abstraction, missing the fact that Laclau's political theory functions in large part on the ontological, rather than ontical plane, or it has remained stuck on the futile query as to whether Laclau's theory of discourse is materialist or not. Again, I believe that this concern is largely a red herring although, as I shall endeavour to show below, when discussed at the appropriate level of abstraction – this time the ontical level – it does raise questions that need further elaboration.

Instead, I want to focus on the shift from the second to the third model of hegemony. In this regard, as against Anne Marie Smith's recent suggestion that there is an essential discontinuity between the second and third models (Smith 1998: 74–83), I think there are important continuities between the two models, in which model three is best seen as a further refinement and extension of ideas presaged in model two. Hence the introduction of concepts such as myth and social imaginary are best understood as endeavours to account for different modalities of hegemony construction, and are best placed alongside Laclau's usage of Husserl's concepts of sedimentation and reactivation to distinguish between politics and society (*NR* 33–6). The areas where there is a significant change of emphasis concern Laclau's theory of political subjectivity, as well as the addition of the concept of an empty signifier at the expense of nodal points; both aspects will be carefully scrutinized in my assessment of Laclau's social ontology and his account of political agency. In short, for purposes of evaluation, I will take the third model as a final statement of Laclau's theory, viewing models two and three as complementary moments in the development of a theoretical whole, and I shall note any discrepancies as I evaluate different aspects of the synthesis.

Turning to the second question, I think any satisfactory conception of hegemony ought to address three main aspects of politics. It must address the political activity of constructing hegemony; the character of the resultant social formations; and it should furnish us with the normative criteria for distinguishing between hegemonic and non-hegemonic practices and formations. In order to evaluate Laclau's account of hegemony, it is possible to translate my three criteria into three questions. How convincing is his account of hegemonic practices? What is his underlying conception of society? To what extent does he provide the normative means to distinguish between hegemonic and non-hegemonic formations, and to advance a viable political project compatible with the underlying contours of their theory? I shall assess each of his answers to these questions in turn.

Hegemonic practices and political subjectivity

With respect to hegemony as a form of political practice, Laclau's second model presents the logic of hegemony as a social practice involving the disarticulation and rearticulation of 'floating signifiers' in a social field criss-crossed by social antagonisms. In the third model, by contrast, hegemonic operations involve 'acts of radical construction' by political subjects which actualize latent possibilities inherent in undecidable social structures. In the latter case, hegemonic practices always involve the emergence of political subjects whose task is to reconstitute structures in new forms.

This is undoubtedly the strongest and most convincing aspect of Laclau's theorization, and it opens up a number of important lines of theoretical and empirical inquiry into the construction of political alliances, coalitions, and forms. One query, however, centres on Laclau's conception of subjectivity, and there are two opposite lines of criticism worth considering. On the one hand, some critics argue that his approach amounts to nothing more than 'an absolute voluntarism' or 'subjectivism', which privileges the role of the human subject above structural constraints. This line of attack focuses on the way Laclau and Mouffe supposedly give priority to the 'logic of contingency', such that 'almost anything is possible' (Osborne 1991: 210). From a diametrically opposite point of view, Žižek (1990: 250–1) and Močnik (1993: 155) argue that Laclau *reduces* questions of human subjectivity and political agency to mere Foucauldian 'subject positions' within discursive structures, in which case the subject is just 'spoken for' by pre-existing discursive structures.

Ironically, with respect to the question of structure and agency, Laclau has striven to find a middle path between these two critical positions. He rejects essentialist approaches to subjectivity, in which individuals are deemed simply to maximize their interests, or in which agents are reduced to the role of reproducing pre-constituted structures.[9] Instead, he argues that while human beings are constituted as subjects within discursive structures, these structures are inherently contingent and malleable. Once their 'undecidability' becomes visible in dislocatory situations when structures no longer function to confer identity, subjects become political agents in the stronger sense of the term, as they identify with new discursive objects and act to re-constitute structures.

This reasoning makes a powerful contribution to the so-called structure/agency debate (cf. Giddens 1984; Hay 1995). However, one remaining difficulty concerns the positing of an unconditional subjectivity that is literally able to 'create' meaningful structures (see *NR* 29). While this conception accounts for extreme or 'limit' situations such as revolutions when a thorough restructuring of social relations may occur, even here Laclau's thesis ought to be qualified by the fact that most revolutionary movements and agents are conditioned by existing ideological traditions and organizational infrastructures, a qualification that is half-acknowledged in Laclau's later writings when he argues that certain discourses need to be 'available' and 'credible' if movements and political agents are to emerge and construct new social orders (*E* 43).

A second difficulty concerns the question of taking a decision itself. In this regard, Laclau tends to regard decision-making, the emergence of political agents, and the creation of new social orders as equivalent. However, this collapses the distinction between different kinds of decision-making, such that a distinction needs to be made between decisions taken *within* a structure and decisions taken *about* a structure. These two modalities of decision-making are best viewed as two ideal-typical forms of subjectivity that bound a spectrum of possible forms of decision-making, in which concrete acts can be located according to the degrees to which they produce structural effects. For example, it is evident that consumers in free markets or politicians in parliaments are continuously taking decisions without necessarily questioning or creating new structural contexts in which these choices are made. However, in revolutionary situations collective political subjects may clearly 'take decisions' about the creation and formation of new social structures. With the kind of qualifications noted above, these are the situations in which Laclau's novel theorization of structure and agency becomes applicable. What this means is that, rather than a general theory of a radical political agency, we need to remain sensitive to the specific historical contexts in which different kinds of subjectivity come into play. The criterion for this analysis depends on the kinds of decision that get taken, and the circumstances in which they are taken (Howarth 2000a: 121–2).

Laclau's conception of society

A related difficulty concerns Laclau's account of social structures, and this brings us to his underlying conception of society. There has been a plethora of criticisms directed at Laclau's claim that social structures can be made equivalent to discursive structures, and that social relations are analogous to texts or linguistic systems.[10] More concretely, it has been asserted that social structures are purely contingent and dispersed entities; that structures are reduced to language; and that the analysis of social and political institutions is not possible within his approach. Indeed, I have also added a dissenting voice about the over-hasty equation of social structures with undecidable philosophical texts (Howarth 1996). However, it is important to separate out as judiciously as possible the real from the bogus attacks.

At the outset, it is important to stress that Laclau's category of discourse does not involve a distinction between 'linguistic' and 'non-linguistic' elements of social life, nor does it entail a distinction between 'ideas' and their 'material' conditions. In this regard, it is worthwhile noting that their approach depends on the trope of catachresis. That is to say, he 'creatively misapplies' the concept of discourse to encompass all dimensions of social reality and not just the usual practices of speaking, writing, and communicating. This displacement is, of course, characteristic of a number of different approaches to social and political analysis. One has only to think of the way in which rational choice theorists model social and political behaviour on the behaviour of firms and private markets, or the way in which models of communication have been used to develop systems approaches to society and politics (see Deutsch 1963; Friedman 1953; Olson 1965).

Nevertheless, the key issue we have to discuss is *how far* we can extend Laclau's resultant analogy between language and society (cf. Wittgenstein 1969: 23–9). In this respect, it is important to begin by distinguishing between what I shall call the ontological and ontical dimensions of their analysis. Following Heidegger (1962: 31–5), I use the ontological dimension to refer to the implicit assumptions presupposed by *any* inquiry into specific sorts of phenomena, whereas the ontical level designates research into specific sorts of phenomena themselves. For instance, one might as a political theorist be interested in describing, classifying, and comparing different types of political institution, whether it be the effects of electoral systems on party systems, or the relative democratic performance of parliamentary and presidential regimes. Instead, by contrast, one might be interested in putting into question the very concept of a political institution, or trying to set out criteria as to what *counts* as a political practice or activity. Whereas, in Heideggerian terms, the former type of inquiry conforms to the ontical level, and accepts the agreed standards of political theory and political science, the latter can be seen to be conducted at the ontological level and explores the conditions which make possible political analysis itself.

Using this distinction, it is clear that much of Laclau's conception of society is not concerned with the nature of specific *types* of object, practice, institutions, or even concrete discourses, that is, the conduct of *ontical* analysis about particular sorts of entities. Rather, it is concerned with the necessary presuppositions of *any* inquiry into the nature of objects and social relations (Mulhall 1996: 4). In short, he is concerned with *ontological* questions, and seeks at this level of inquiry to criticize other ontologies, while developing an alternative conception. His aim is thus to affirm the meaningfulness of all objects and practices; to show that all social meaning is contingent, contextual, and relational; and to argue that any system of meaning relies upon a discursive exterior that partially constitutes it. As Laclau (*NR* 185) puts it, '[t]he primary and constitutive character of the discursive is [...] the condition of any practice'. Thus his central claim that 'society is an impossible object of analysis' seeks to exclude essentialist, objectivist and topographical conceptions of social relations (whether put forward by positivists, materialists, or realists), while developing a relational conception of society in which concepts such as antagonism and dislocation are constitutive (see Howarth 2000a: 112–13).

At this level of analysis, the analogy between social relations and language yields a number of distinct advantages. The structuralist model of language enables him to develop a relational conception of society, which avoids the determinism and reductionism of Marxism and positivism, while Derrida's and Lacan's critique of the structuralism model enables him to show how the 'complex dialectic' between the logics of contingency and necessity can account for the structuring of social relations by hegemonic practices. Finally, the equivalence he establishes between society and language enables him to draw upon the full range of literary tropes and figures to explain a range of social phenomena and events (Howarth 2000a: 116–17). Thus, for instance, he is able to rethink the concepts of social antagonism and 'the structuring of social spaces' by making use of the logics of equivalence and difference, which are drawn in turn from the difference between paradigmatic and syntagmatic relations in linguistic theory (*HSS* 127–34).

On the ontical level, by contrast, his investigation ought to focus on the characterization of different forms of discourse or kinds of social formation, as well as an explanation of their emergence, functioning, and change. In this regard, however, there are four areas of Laclau's conception that need further attention. First, he tends to over-emphasize the ontological dimension at the expense of the ontical. This means that the concepts and logics run the danger of appearing too thin and formalistic, and are in need of being articulated with a range of thicker concepts and logics. Consider for instance Laclau's concept of practice, which is central to his social ontology. While at an abstract level, he is surely correct to stress the articulatory and discursive character of all social practices – if only as a minimal condition of their intelligibility – it does not follow that these two conditions exhaust their character.[11] To take what might appear as a trivial example: buying a 'Free Nelson Mandela' T-shirt at a rock concert in South Africa during the 1980s is a concrete social practice that presupposes a historically specific set of economic and legal relations (a market economy, money as a means of exchange, property law, etc.), and articulates together economic, political, and cultural aspects of a social practice in a mutual interweaving, that is, it represents an economic transaction, an act of political defiance, signifies a particular cultural identity, and so on. The point, in short, is that while the discursivity or meaningfulness of the practice is a necessary condition of its intelligibility both to practitioners and observers, it is not sufficient to characterize the practice as such.[12]

If this is the case, then Laclau's concept of articulation can be expanded not only to define a kind of social practice that establishes 'a relation among elements such that their identity is modified as a result' (*HSS* 105), but also at a descriptive and explanatory level to include the way in which the political analyst is able to grasp the concrete ontical level as 'a rich totality of many determinations and relations' (Marx 1973: 100). The concept of articulation at the levels of both social ontology and theoretical explanation thus provides the essential starting point for connecting the ontological and the ontical levels without subsuming the concrete under the abstract, or falling back into an atheoretical empiricism when analysing concrete conjunctures (see Poulantzas 1973: 13). However, this requires the elaboration of a series of 'middle ranging' concepts and theories about political institutions and economic organizations in specific historical contexts (see for example Held 1995), and the specification of strategies and practices to govern this articulation. With respect to the former, some work has been undertaken from a discourse theory point of view (see Torfing 1998), while the latter task has benefited from the later Wittgenstein's thoughts about applying a rule and the Aristotelian notion of phronesis (see *NR* 208–9).

In a related vein, a second difficulty is that the basic constituents of Laclau's social ontology at the ontical level remain too indeterminate. Although he distinguishes between 'moments' and 'elements' of a discourse at the ontological level, he does not specify or give examples of these categories. In Laclau's earlier work (*PIM* 92–100), 'elements' are explicitly understood as ideological components such as 'militarism', 'statolatry, 'anti-clericalism', 'nationalism', 'anti-semitic racism', 'elitism', and so forth, which make up ideological discourses such as Italian fascism or Peronism. However, in his later writings elements are sometimes used in a narrow sense to refer to signifiers such as 'justice', 'order', 'democracy', or 'the free world' (*E* 36–46, 56–65), while at other times they refer to the central components of any social formation, such as the 'economic', 'political', and 'ideological' dimensions of society (*NR* 21–6). Laclau owes us some clarity with regard to this aspect of his social ontology.

A third query pertains to the ambiguity surrounding the category of dislocation. While it is clear that this category goes a long way in addressing Žižek's important critique of the third model of hegemony, it remains suspended between at least two possible meanings and functions. On the one hand, Laclau uses the category to draw attention to the 'always already' dislocated character of all social identities, that is, because all identity is marked by a constitutive outside that both makes possible that identity and prevents it from achieving closure it is by definition dislocated (*NR* 39). On the other hand, the category is akin to events or experiences that make visible the contingency of social identities – caused for instance by processes of commodification, bureaucratization, and so on – and thus functions as 'the very form' of temporality, possibility, and freedom (*NR* 41–3). In short, Laclau has to disambiguate and clarify what might be called the ontological (Dislocation 1) and historicist (Dislocation 2) dimensions of the category. To use Heideggerian terminology, Dislocation 1 captures something of our 'being-thrown' (*Geworfenheit*) into a world of signification (or discourse) over which we have little or no choosing, whereas Dislocation 2 is more like an 'event of Being' in which the contingency of this world is disclosed, and other options and choices become possible.

Finally, there is a certain degree of conceptual imprecision regarding the relationships between certain categories of Laclau's social ontology. One possible source of confusion concerns the relationship between nodal points and empty signifiers in the transition from the second to the third model of hegemony. In Laclau's political theory, as with Lacanian theory, the conceptual relationship between these basic ontological categories raises a number of queries. To begin with, it is not clear whether the empty signifier is simply synonymous with the nodal point, a refinement of the original concept, or picks out and captures different aspects of social reality. Moreover, even though the character of the displacement in Laclau's texts might not be altogether clear, the distinction does bring important implications for his overall social ontology: while the second model seems to imply a plurality of nodal points linked together in a discursive formation or historical bloc by hegemonic practices,[13] the third model suggests that the unity of a social formation is constituted by an empty signifier that establishes the meaning of the other signifiers, that is to say, it performs the totalizing function of linking together the elements of the system.[14] If this is so, then a question is raised as to *how* the empty signifier can perform this function.

That is to say, how do signifiers such as 'justice', 'order', or 'the free world' function to unify and sediment a wide range of practices and discourses? Are they symbolic condensations or representations of unity, equivalent to the role that the monarchy or the constitution performs in the United Kingdom and United States respectively, or do they actively produce 'society effects' by constituting the ensemble of social relations making up concrete social orders?

The sum total of these aporias at the ontical level, and in the relationship between the ontical and the ontological, results in a significant under-theorization of 'hegemony as form' – the sense in which we might say that a particular political project has become hegemonic or to use Gramsci's terms 'become state' (Gramsci 1971: 268), that is, the extent to which a political project has been partially successful in universalizing its particular set of political demands and values, thus naturalizing its vision of social order and rendering invisible the tensions and contradictions it contains.[15] It is here that a whole range of issues and questions need to be posed and explored. They include, *inter alia*, the need to construct a *typology* of different kinds of historical bloc at varying levels of abstraction (e.g. liberal democratic, authoritarian, authoritarian populist, totalitarian, etc.);[16] the importance of examining the *conceptual* connections between hegemony, power, and domination; and lastly the task of explaining the logics and processes by which hegemonic projects endeavour to *institutionalize* themselves. With respect to the latter task, Laclau has already introduced the concept of sedimentation to account for the 'forgetting of political origins' and the stabilization of social relations, but this concept needs to be supplemented with what Derrida calls the 'logic of iterability' so as to account for the active production of social orders through the interweaving of continuous and discontinuous elements (see Howarth 1995a: 195–8, ch. 6; 1995b).

Normativity, radical democracy, and the question of critique

I want, finally, to turn to some of the normative and critical questions surrounding Laclau's conception of hegemony. A number of related issues are raised in this regard, which I can only touch upon in these concluding remarks. One such issue concerns the alleged 'normative deficit' in Laclau's theory of hegemony. For instance, Simon Critchley (1998: 809) holds that if Laclau and Mouffe's theory of hegemony 'is simply the description of a positively existing state of affairs, then it risks identification and complicity with the logic of contemporary capitalist societies'. He goes on to argue that Laclau and Mouffe's theory runs the risk of 'collapsing into a voluntaristic Schmittian decisionism' and thus needs to be supplemented by an explicitly formulated ethical framework. He draws on the writings of Emmanuel Levinas and Jacques Derrida to develop an ethics of 'infinite responsibility' to the face of the Other (Critchley 1992; see Howarth 2000a: 123).

Critchley is correct to raise doubts about the division between describing, evaluating, and justifying in Laclau's writings, as at times it appears that the various logics in his texts are simply analytical tools with little or no normative content, which can be applied to all cases without exception. Careful inspection of his arguments show, however, that the genesis of his conception of hegemony *does* presuppose a certain normative orientation, especially as it emerges out of his deconstructive reading of the Marxist tradition. Take for example his critique of Leninism. Whereas Lenin's conception of hegemony is little more than a temporary tactical alliance between classes and groups pursuing a limited end – the overthrow of the Tsarist regime for example – Laclau invokes the idea of democratic (rather than authoritarian) practice and the work of Gramsci to develop a quite distinct political theory. For him, hegemonic practices presuppose a degree of autonomy and difference amongst the different components of an 'alliance', such that the identities of different groups have to be retained. Hegemony thus requires the modification of identities and interests as a new set of relationships are constructed, as well as the institutionalization of a more universal democratic and pluralist ethic amongst the social actors themselves (Howarth 2000a: 123–4).[17]

Furthermore, practitioners of discourse theory do not claim to be conducting 'value free' or 'objective' investigations. It is a basic assumption of the perspective that the discourse theorist is constituted as a subject (just like any other subject) within a particular discursive formation and within a specific tradition (Laclau 2000: 293–5). Moreover, the values of the discourse theorist are revisable in the light of political argument and ethical reasoning. What is challenged, however, is the claim that values can be *derived* or *deduced* from the philosophical assumptions and social ontology of discourse theory (Laclau 1988: 23). In this sense, an anti-foundational perspective does not determine a certain set of political and ethical positions, though it does rule some positions out – those based on essentialist presuppositions for example. The assertion and justification of values is thus the result of an articulatory practice, rather than a necessary entailment (Howarth 2000a: 124). Thus Laclau and Mouffe's (*HSS* 192) own proposal for a plural and radical democracy, built as it is around the extension of demands for liberty and equality into greater and greater areas of social life, seeks to recognize and incorporate a sense of its own contingency and precariousness: 'This moment of tension, or openness which gives the social its essentially incomplete and precarious nature, is what every project for radical democracy should set out to institutionalize' (see also Mouffe 1989, 1992, 1993, 2000). Lastly, in certain passages Laclau and Mouffe also restrict the scope of the application of hegemony to those 'modern' forms of social formation, as he puts it, 'when the reproduction of the different social areas takes place in permanently changing conditions which constantly require the construction of new systems of difference' (*HSS* 138).

In all these respects, then, the clear line between description and explanation, on the one hand, and normative evaluation, critique, and justification, on the other hand, is blurred in Laclau (and Mouffe's) writings. However, it is equally true that the logic of hegemony has been generalized into a more universal tool of analysis – functioning at the ontological level – and can thus be applied to the construction of all forms of social order. In other words, although their concept of hegemony emerges as a strategic concept designed to advance a particular project for radical democracy, it has been extended into a general theory of politics.

How is it possible to tackle and resolve this evident tension? Here I think one has to introduce a distinction between, on the one hand, a logic of hegemonic practice that is not restricted to modern democratic societies, and on the other those hegemonic practices which are attendant upon the articulation and defence of the project of radical democracy. With respect to the latter, the affirmation of radical democracy requires that democratic practices are built into the very project itself; without this immanent relation, the project runs the risk of internal incoherence. This distinction is not without consequence for Laclau's conception of hegemony. In the first place, some of the conditions for hegemonic practices have to be relaxed. In particular, the division between authoritarian and democratic practices introduced to criticize a Leninist conception of hegemony ought *not* to apply to the general logic of hegemonic practices, as they constitute general logics of political activity. Secondly, the case for radical democracy has to restrict and limit the general operation of hegemonic practice to only those practices that are commensurate with the fostering of autonomy and difference within alliances and coalitions. It goes without saying that further elaboration of this particular project for radical democracy, in conjunction with its justification vis-à-vis other radical critiques of radical democracy, such as the deliberative models of democracy articulated by Jürgen Habermas and his school, or William Connolly's project of 'agonistic democracy', which draws upon Nietzsche and Foucault, is still required.[18]

Conclusion

This chapter has analysed the development of Laclau's theory of hegemony by charting the emergence of three models of hegemony, all of which correspond to particular theoretical problematics and address concrete political issues. In so doing, I have subjected the third and most advanced model to what might be called an immanent or deconstructive critique that seeks to supplement aspects of the original conception and explore latent possibilities therein. At an explanatory level, I employed Heidegger's distinction between the ontological and ontical dimensions of inquiry to raise questions about Laclau's overall social ontology. More particularly, I offered thoughts about reconfiguring the structure/agency dialectic so as not to fall into a decisionistic conception of the subject, raised questions about the conceptual relationship between empty signifiers and nodal points, as well as the role of the empty signifier in producing society effects, and stressed the need to disambiguate and refine the category of dislocation. I also suggested a set of research tasks, which this ongoing research programme might examine in the future. Finally, on a normative level, I considered the so-called normative deficit in Laclau's writings, arguing that there is an implicit normativity in their various conceptions of hegemony which render some political articulations of his work incommensurable, and I offered some thoughts in defence of his project for radical democracy.

Notes

* Parts of this chapter build upon and rework arguments presented in Howarth 2000a.

1 For studies in politics and international relations that deploy the concept of hegemony to analyze their empirical objects of investigation, see Cox 1987; Gamble 1990; Hall 1988; Hay 1996; Howarth 1997, 2000b; Howarth *et al.* 2000; Knutsen 1999: 59–72; Norval 1996; Smith 1994.

2 This is true in mainstream political science (see Dahl 1971: 7–13; Rothchild 1986; Sisk 1995: 52–4) and international relations (see Keohane 1984), and even for those radical theorists who generally support the elaboration of a more nuanced conception of hegemony (cf. Connolly 1995: p. xxi).

3 This chapter focuses primarily on Laclau's writings, though many of his ideas were developed jointly with Chantal Mouffe. I have thus chosen for the most part to use Laclau as the proper name for this body of work, and use the term 'Laclau and Mouffe' only where their work is published jointly.

4 These three models correspond to three different theoretical problematics and their concomitant political orientations. In the 1970s, Laclau (*PIM*) mainly used the writings of Gramsci and Althusser to criticize and rework Marxist theories of politics and ideology, and his work was directed at advancing what might be called the traditional socialist demands of the working classes. In the 1980s, the theoretical nodal point around which his work revolved was post-structuralism, especially the writings of Derrida and Foucault, and he recast his political standpoint around a project for radical democracy (*HSS*). In the 1990s, Laclau's work was more strongly structured around psychoanalytic theory, particularly the work of Lacan and Žižek, and his (and Chantal Mouffe's) politics were oriented around constructing 'contingent universals' and an 'agonistic pluralism' in the face of a perceived fragmentation of Leftist politics caused by the rise of new forms of particularism (*NR*; *E*; Butler *et al.* 2000; Mouffe 1992, 1993, 2000). This schematic periodization of Laclau's work and its concerns should not of course be hypostatized; it merely presents in ideal-typical form the changing emphases of his work over the last three decades.

5 In a similar vein, Fredrik Sunnemark has shown how the signifiers 'God' and 'Jesus' function as nodal points in Martin Luther King's civil rights discourse in the United States during the 1960s. See Sunnemark 2001: 123–6.

6 In this regard, Laclau and Mouffe introduce the logics of equivalence and difference to account for the production of political frontiers and the structuring of social spaces. See Howarth 2000a: 106–7.

7 I have used this concept to examine the emergence and logic of the black consciousness movement in South Africa, showing how the category of blackness functioned as an empty signifier in its discourse (see Howarth 1997, 2000b).

8 See Aronowitz 1992; Dallmayr 1989; Geras 1987, 1988, 1990; Osborne 1991; Sim 1998; Wood 1986.

9 The former perspective is characteristic of rational choice and 'game theoretical' models of politics (see Olson 1965), while the latter of structuralist and structural functionalist conceptions (see Althusser 1971).

10 Cf. Aronowitz 1992: 175–92; Best and Kellner 1991: 200–4; Clegg 1989: 178–86; Howard 1987.

11 It should be noted that Laclau does mention other types of social practice – political, social, hegemonic, and so on – in elaborating his theory. In theoretical terms, they are characterized principally as articulatory and discursive.

12 This tension between the ontological and the ontical is also evident in Laclau's distinction between the 'field of discursivity' and 'concrete discourses', in which the former is understood to 'indicate the form of its relation with every concrete discourse', that is, 'it determines at the same time the necessarily discursive character of any object, and the impossibility of any given discourse to implement a final suture' (*HSS* 111).

13 Laclau and Mouffe (*HSS* 136) put it in the following terms:

> A social and political space relatively unified through the instituting of nodal points and the constitution of *tendentially* relational identities, is what Gramsci called a *historical bloc*. The type of linking joining the different elements of the historical bloc – not unity in any form of historical a priori, but regularity in dispersion – coincides with our concept of discursive formation.

14 As Laclau (*E* 40) puts it, 'there can be empty signifiers within the field of signification because any system of signification is structured around an empty place resulting from the impossibility of producing an object which, none the less, is required by the systematicity of the system'.

15 In Stuart Hall's terms, the degree to which a project has made possible 'the taking of [a] "leading position" [...] over a number of different spheres of society at once – economy, civil society, intellectual and moral life, culture', when it has succeeded in 'winning [...] a strategic measure of popular consent', and the extent to which it has established the 'security of a social authority sufficiently deep to conform society into a new historic project' (Hall 1988: 7).

16 Cf. Held 1995; Lefort 1986; Poulantzas 1973, 1978.

17 These arguments are elaborated in more detail in Laclau 1992; Smith 1998: 177–202; Zerilli 1998.

18 See Connolly 1995; Habermas 1996; Howarth 2001a, 2001b; Norval 2001; Thomassen 2001.

References

Althusser, L. (1971) *Lenin and Philosophy and Other Essays*, London: New Left Books.

Anderson, P. (1976) 'The antinomies of Antonio Gramsci', *New Left Review*, 100: 5–81.

Aronowitz, S. (1992) *The Politics of Identity: Class, Culture and Social Movements*, London: Routledge.

Best, S. and Kellner, D. (1991) *Postmodern Theory: Critical Interrogations*, London: Macmillan.

Butler, J., Laclau, E. and Žižek, S. (2000) *Contingency, Hegemony, Universality: Contemporary Dialogues on the Left*, London: Verso.

Clegg, S. R. (1989) *Frameworks of Power*, London: Sage.

Connolly, W. E. (1995) *The Ethos of Pluralization*, Minneapolis: University of Minnesota Press.

Cox, R. W. (1987) *Production, Power, and World Order: Social Forces in the Making of History*, New York: Columbia University Press.

Critchley, S. (1992) *The Ethics of Deconstruction: Derrida and Levinas*, Oxford: Blackwell.

—— (1998) 'Metaphysics in the dark: A response to Richard Rorty and Ernesto Laclau', *Political Theory*, 26(6): 803–17.

Dahl, R. A. (1971) *Polyarchy: Participation and Opposition*, New Haven: Yale University Press.

Dallmayr, F. (1989) *Margins of Political Discourse*, Albany: State University of New York Press.

Deutsch, K. W. (1963) *The Nerves of Government: Models of Political Communication and Control*, New York: Free Press.

Duverger, M. (1972) *The Study of Politics*, London: Nelson.

Friedman, M. (1953) *Essays in Positive Economics*, Chicago: University of Chicago Press.

Gamble, A. (1990) *The Free Economy and the Strong State*, London: Macmillan.

Geras, N. (1987) 'Post-Marxism?', *New Left Review*, 163: 40–82.

—— (1988) 'Ex-Marxism without substance: A rejoinder', *New Left Review*, 169: 34–61.

—— (1990) *Discourses of Extremity: Radical Ethics and Post-Marxist Extravagances*, London: Verso.

Giddens, A. (1984) *The Constitution of Society: Outline of a Theory of Structuration*, Cambridge: Polity Press.

Gramsci, A. (1971) *Selections from the Prison Notebooks*, London: Lawrence & Wishart.

Griggs, S. and Howarth, D. (2000) 'New environmental movements and direct action protest: the campaign against Manchester Airport's second runway', in D. Howarth, A. J. Norval and Y. Stavrakakis (eds) *Discourse Theory and Political Analysis: Identities, Hegemonies and Social Change*, Manchester: Manchester University Press.

—— (2002) 'An alliance of interest and identity: explaining the campaign against Manchester Airport's second runway', *Mobilization*, 7(1): 43–58.

Gurr, T. R. (1970) *Why Men Rebel*, Princeton: Princeton University Press.

Habermas, J. (1996) *Between Facts and Norms: Contributions to a Discourse Theory of Law and Democracy*, Cambrige: Polity Press (tr. William Rehg).

Hall, S. (1983) 'The great moving right show', in S. Hall and M. Jacques (eds) *The Politics of Thatcherism*, London: Lawrence & Wishart.

—— (1988) *The Hard Road to Renewal*, London: Verso.

Hay, C. (1995) 'Structure and agency', in D. Marsh and G. Stoker (eds) *Theory and Methods in Political Science*, London: Macmillan.

—— (1996) *Re-Stating Social and Political Change*, Buckingham: Open University Press.

Heideggar, M. (1962) *Being and Time*, Oxford, Basil Blackwell (tr. J. Macquarrie and E. Robinson).

Held, D. (1995) *Democracy and the Global Order: From the Modern State to Cosmopolitan Governance*, Cambridge: Polity Press.

Howard, D. (1987) 'The possibilities of a post-Marxist radicalism', *Thesis Eleven*, 16: 69–84.

Howarth, D. (1995a) 'Black consciousness in South Africa: resistance and identity formation under apartheid domination', unpublished PhD thesis, University of Essex.

—— (1995b) 'The discursive construction and character of black consciousness ideology in apartheid South Africa', *Essex Papers in Government and Politics* (Sub-Series in Ideology and Discourse Analysis), 8.

—— (1996) 'Theorising hegemony', in Ian Hampsher-Monk and Jeff Stanyer (eds) *Contemporary Political Studies 1996*, Glasgow: PSA UK.

—— (1997) 'Complexities of identity/difference: The ideology of black consciousness in South Africa', *Journal of Political Ideologies*, 2(1): 51–78.

—— (1998) 'Discourse theory and political analysis', in E. Scarborough and E. Tanenbaum (eds) *Research Strategies in the Social Sciences: A Guide to New Approaches*, Oxford: Oxford University Press.

—— (2000a) *Discourse*, Buckingham: Open University Press.

—— (2000b) 'The difficult emergence of a democratic imaginary: black consciousness and non-racial democracy in South Africa', in D. Howarth, A. J. Norval and Y. Stavrakakis (eds) *Discourse Theory and Political Analysis: Identities, Hegemonies and Social Change*, Manchester: Manchester University Press.

—— (2001a) 'Democratic Ideology', in B. Clarke and J. Foweraker (eds) *Encyclopaedia of Democratic Thought*, London: Routledge.

—— (2001b) 'Inclusion/exclusion', in B. Clarke and J. Foweraker (eds) *Encyclopaedia of Democratic Thought*, London: Routledge.

Howarth, D., Norval, A. J. and Stavrakakis, Y. (eds) (2000) *Discourse Theory and Political Analysis: Identities, Hegemonies and Social Change*, Manchester: Manchester University Press.
Keohane, R. O. (1984) *After Hegemony: Cooperation and Discord in the World Political Economy*, Princeton: Princeton University Press.
Knutsen, T. L. (1999) *The Rise and Fall of World Orders*, Manchester: Manchester University Press.
Lacan, J. (1977) *Écrits: A Selection*, London: Tavistock.
Laclau, E. (1988) 'Building a new left', *Strategies*, 1: 3–21.
—— (1992) 'Universalism, particularism, and the question of identity', *October*, 61: 83–90.
—— (1996) 'The death and resurrection of the theory of ideology', *Journal of Political Ideologies*, 1(3): 201–20.
—— (2000) 'Constructing universality', in J. Butler, E. Laclau and S. Žižek, *Contingency, Hegemony, Universality: Contemporary Dialogues on the Left*, London: Verso.
Lefort, C. (1986) *The Political Forms of Modern Society: Bureaucracy, Democracy, Totalitarianism*, Cambridge: MIT Press.
Lenin, V. I. (1968) *Lenin: Selected Works*, Moscow: Progress Publishers.
Löwy, M. (1981) *The Politics of Combined and Uneven Development: The Theory of Permanent Revolution*, London: Verso.
Marx, K. (1973) *Grundrisse*, (tr. M. Nicolaus) Harmondsworth: Penguin.
—— (1977) 'The civil war in France', in D. McLellan (ed.) *Karl Marx: Selected Writings*, Oxford: Oxford University.
Močnik, R. (1993) 'Ideology and fantasy', in E. A. Kaplan and M. Sprinker (eds) *The Althusserian Legacy*, London: Verso.
Mouffe, C. (1979) 'Hegemony and ideology in Gramsci', in C. Mouffe (ed.) *Gramsci and Political Theory*, London: Routledge.
—— (1989) 'Radical democracy: Modern or postmodern?', in A. Ross (ed.) *Universal Abandon? The Politics of Postmodernism*, London: Routledge.
—— (ed.) (1992) *Dimensions of Radical Democracy: Pluralism, Citizenship, Community*, London: Verso.
—— (1993) *The Return of the Political*, London: Verso.
—— (1996) 'Deconstruction, pragmatism and the politics of democracy', in C. Mouffe (ed.) *Deconstruction and Pragmatism*, London: Routledge.
—— (2000) *The Democratic Paradox*, London: Verso.
Mulhall, S. (1996) *Heidegger and Being and Time*, London: Routledge.
Norval, A. J. (1996) *Deconstructing Apartheid Discourse*, London: Verso.
—— (2001) 'Radical democracy', in B. Clarke and J. Foweraker (eds) *Encyclopaedia of Democratic Thought*, London: Routledge.
Olson, M. (1965) *The Logic of Collective Action: Public Goods and the Theory of Groups*, Cambridge: Harvard University Press.
Osborne, P. (1991) 'Radicalism without limit', in P. Osborne (ed.) *Socialism and the Limits of Liberalism*, London: Verso.
Poulantzas, N. (1973) *Political Power and Social Classes*, London: New Left Books.
—— (1978) *State, Power, Socialism*, London: New Left Books.
Rothchild, D. (1986) 'Hegemonial exchange: An alternative model for managing conflict in Middle Africa', in D. L. Thompson and D. Ronen (eds) *Ethnicity, Politics and Development*, Boulder, CO: Lynne Riener Publishers.

Sim, S. (1998) 'Spectres and nostalgia: post-Marxism/post-Marxism', in S. Sim (ed.) *Post-Marxism: A Reader*, Edinburgh: Edinburgh University Press.
Sisk, T. (1995) *Democratization in South Africa: The Elusive Social Contract*, Princeton: Princeton University Press.
Smith, A. M. (1994) *New Right Discourse on Race and Sexuality: Britain 1968–1990*, Cambridge: Cambridge University Press.
—— (1998) *Laclau and Mouffe: The Radical Democratic Imaginary*, London: Routledge.
Sunnemark, F. (2001) *An Inescapable Network of Mutuality: Discursivity and Ideology in the Rhetoric of Martin Luther King, Jr*, Göteborg: Acta Universitas Gothoburgensis.
Thomassen, L. (2001) 'Habermas and the aporias of justification', *Essex Working Papers*, 14.
Torfing, J. (1998) *Politics, Regulation and the Modern Welfare State*, London: Macmillan.
Wittgenstein, L. (1969) *The Blue and Brown Books: Preliminary Studies for the Philosophical Investigations*, Oxford: Blackwell.
Wolf, E. C. (1971) *Peasant Wars of the Twentieth Century*, London: Faber & Faber.
Wood, E. (1986) *The Retreat from Class: A New 'True' Socialism*, London: Verso.
Zerilli, L. M. (1998) 'This universalism which is not one', *Diacritics*, 28(2): 3–20.
Žižek, S. (1989) *The Sublime Object of Ideology*, London: Verso.
—— (1990) 'Beyond discourse-analysis', in E. Laclau, *New Reflections on the Revolution of our Time*, London: Verso.
—— (1991) *For they Know Not What they Do: Enjoyment as a Political Factor*, London: Verso.
—— (ed.) (1994) *Mapping Ideology*, London: Verso.
—— (1999) *The Ticklish Subject*, London: Verso.

Part IV

A REPLY

16

GLIMPSING THE FUTURE

Ernesto Laclau

I am extremely grateful to the editors and contributors to this volume for the many and highly illuminating comments that they have made on my work. They have raised a variety of substantial and pertinent issues and, although in many cases I am not accepting their criticisms, they definitely help to create a dialogical space within which central problems of contemporary theory and politics can be addressed. I will attempt in my reply to introduce, as much as possible, an orderly sequence in the discussion of the theoretical categories – something which, however, will not always be entirely possible given the plurality of intellectual perspectives informing the various interventions. Later, in a concluding section, I will attempt to offer the outlines of a unified problematic which announces itself through the labyrinth of the various discussions.

I will start by referring to the piece by Rodolphe Gasché, because it raises some issues concerning universality which, in different ways, are going to be present in many of the other discussions.

Emptiness and universality

Gasché, in his intervention, after giving a quite accurate description of the main tenets of my theoretical approach, formulates a set of reservations about the way in which my notion of the 'universal' is constructed. Before dealing with his commentaries concerning these matters, let me clarify a first distinction which is crucial for Gasché's discussion and, indeed, for a great deal of the other interventions in this volume. I am referring to the interconnections between 'emptiness' and 'universality'. A first point of clarification is required here: 'emptiness', in the sense in which I am using the category, has nothing to do with the question of formalism. Gasché himself is to a large extent aware of the distinction. Commenting on a previous discussion that I had with Judith Butler, in which she asked herself whether my notion of universality is 'as empty as it is posited to be' and 'whether the truly empty does not carry the trace of the excluded in spectral form as an internal disruption of its own formalism' (Butler 2000: 167), Gasché comments:

> The formulation of Butler's questions shows that she interprets 'emptiness' from a Hegelian perspective as synonymous with 'abstract' and merely formal. Her suspicion is not only that such emptiness is the result of an operation of abstraction, and thus wrought by an exclusion of concrete social and cultural contents, but that such an act of abstraction has its genealogy in equally concrete social practices (28).

Where does Butler's mistaken assimilation lie? In the fact that emptiness – in the sense in which I use the term – is entirely different from the relative poverty of contents resulting from an operation of abstraction. The latter takes place exclusively at the conceptual level and leads to either the a priori transcendental constitution of a certain field or – in an empiricist conception – to the elimination of particular contents through a process of induction/abstraction. But the important point is that this formalism does not lead to emptiness: even the most abstract and formal determinations are still conceptual and, as such, have a certain (although minimal) content. Now, let us compare this with the mystical intuition: God, as far as he is radically ineffable, is an absolutely empty fullness as far as conceptual determinations are concerned. He is beyond *any* conceptual content. So we have an emptiness which is not submitted to any formal rule, and which, as a consequence, does not result from any process of abstraction.

It is this second type of emptiness that I had in mind when elaborating my notion of the 'empty signifiers' as the key elements structuring the socio-political field. Let me briefly recapitulate the main logical steps of my argument: 1) the central category is the notion of discourse (close to that which in other approaches has been called 'practice', consisting in an essential multiplicity governed by some internal rules of structuration); 2) these rules of structuration (which are, of course, immanent rules) are subverted by *constitutive* dislocations. As a result of the latter, something radically irrepresentable within the rules is going to circulate among their constituent elements. This is the moment in which 'emptiness' enters the picture – an emptiness which results, as can be seen, from irrepresentability and not from abstraction; 3) this irrepresentability (these holes in the symbolic order, to use Lacan's terms) acquire a certain form of discursive presence through the production of empty signifiers which, as in the mystical discourse, name an absent fullness – in socio-political analysis, the fullness of the community. For instance: in a situation in which people experience a feeling of being wronged, 'justice' has no content of its own; it is just the positive reverse of a constitutive lack and, as such, it gives discursive presence (it names) something which is at the same time absolutely empty and absolutely full.

With this we reach a non-formalistic notion of 'emptiness'. How do we move from it, however, to 'universality'? The steps of the argument are as follows.[1] 1) The constitutive dislocations of the structure are not concentrated in a unique or 'natural' point within it but affect *all* its constitutive elements, which are submitted to the antagonistic action of the logic of difference (partial fixations within a tendentially structured whole) and the logic of equivalence (articulations between dislocated elements tending to the creation of an internal frontier through an equivalential chain). 2) The representation of the chain as a totality – without which it would have no discursive inscription – can only have as means of representation particular social demands organized around particular points of dislocation. So one demand or group of demands assumes, without entirely giving up its particularity, the added function of representing the series as a whole. (The demands of Solidarnosc, for instance, started as those of a group of workers in Gdansk but, taking place in a society in which many other demands remained unfulfilled, they became the symbols of a total equivalential chain.) This process of one demand assuming the representation of many others is what I call 'hegemony'. 3) Here we finally arrive at the emergence of 'universality': what we have is always a *relative* universality, deriving from equivalential chains constituted around hegemonic nodal points. As can be seen, the possibility of universalization depends on emptiness as a concrete – not abstract – presence.

There are three brief points that I would like to make before moving to Gasché's critical remarks. First, this notion of relative universality presupposes that emptiness is only tendential, and that remainders – in fact more than remainders – of particularity, for essential logical reasons, can never be eliminated. Secondly, the particular is never the factually or empirically *given*, for all particularization necessarily takes place within the organizing parameters of equivalence and difference, which presuppose, in turn, a relational/discursive terrain of emergence. Thirdly, universality, not being either the result of a conceptual abstraction or of a conceptually grounded telos, is simply a concrete historical construction and not an aprioristically determined presupposition of the social as such. The anti-globalization movement, for instance, attempts to construct equivalential chains between many locally based struggles and demands. In that way it breaks with the narrow particularism of the latter and universalizes them by presenting them as part of a wider emancipatory struggle. But this construction of the universal through equivalential inscription is a process of identification which – as all processes of identification – is not purely conceptual but involves a plurality of intellectual, political, and affective dimensions.

Moving now to Gasché's commentaries, a puzzling aspect of them is that, in spite of his clear perception of the shortcomings of Butler's assimilation of the empty to the abstract, his own version remains, in a more nuanced and subtle way, within the very terrain of that assimilation. To start with I am not entirely sure whether, when Gasché refers to the universal, he is speaking about historical constructs or about the categories through which we think about those historical constructs. I do not think that I am distorting his argument if I present it in the following way: universality is – in his interpretation of my approach – a social and political a priori, empty as far as any variety of contents can fill it, and none of these contents can, obviously, be deduced from the form of universality as such. It is for this reason that he stresses that for me universality is not only an empty *signifier* but also an empty *place*, which allows him to underline the relation of pure exteriority that would for me exist between container and content, between universality and particularity. So universality, as a social and political a priori, would play a role of transcendental constitution. If there is thus, in Gasché's version, a reduction of the universal to the transcendental, on the side of the particular the opposite move takes place: here the heterogeneity of the particular *vis-à-vis* the universal is emphasized, insisting in the contingency of the hegemonic construction, in its empirical and pragmatic character, etc. Thus, he asserts:

> In spite of Laclau's statement that universals are always contingent, it is, I believe, fair to say that he does not – to speak in Hobbesian terms – sensualize all concepts, and least of all the concept of the universal. He even speaks of the 'incommensurability' of the universal and the particular, that is, of the impossibility of one particular content ever being adequate to fill the empty place of the universal (31).

And he concludes that the universal, as a philosophical concept, is irreducible. Having, in this way, identified universality as the formal element in a hegemonic construction, Gasché has, obviously, an easy ride in showing that the universal cannot be really empty because, as we have earlier argued, any abstraction has always a minimal content which put limits to the actual particularities which can play a filling role. Although Gasché does not cast his argument in those terms, one can easily imagine a Hegelian jumping into the ring and accusing me of maintaining a Kantian separation between form and content.

The difficulty with this interpretation is that in my approach the universal is *not* a philosophical concept and is not opposed to the particular as the transcendental is opposed to the empirical. On the contrary, both are *in pari materia*. The common terrain within which they constitute themselves as pertinent distinctions is what we call *discourse* which, although it draws its main categories from structural linguistics – especially those elaborated around relations of combination and substitution – is not restricted to any substance – phonic or conceptual – but is synonymous with the general field of objectivity. A series of consequences at the psychoanalytic, rhetorical, and political levels follows from this approach, that I will discuss later in this essay. What is important, however, to stress at this stage of our argument is that particularity and universality are not two ontological orders opposed to each other but possibilities internal to a discursive structure. So to be internal moments of a discursive system, particularities cannot be simply empirical – factually given – but have to be constructed as *differential* identities – i.e. as having always to go beyond themselves. This has been clearly shown in Saussurian linguistics, but also in several other approaches such as Wittgenstein's language games. I have never used the term 'empirical' to refer to particularities. I have spoken, though, of 'pragmatic construction', but what I understand by that is only that structures are never fully closed, that they present wide areas of undecidability and that, as a result, there is an irreducible moment of decision which cannot be referred back to any ground preceding it.

In the same way, I would argue that universality is not a conceptual order under which events should be subsumed, but that it is itself an event: the universalization of a series of particular differences through equivalential inscription. I think that Gasché is right in asserting that there are limits to the particularities which can fill the place of the universal, but not because such 'place' is determined by an irreducible conceptual content through which the universal is constituted, but because of the whole contextual configuration within which the universal is inscribed: chains of equivalence which cannot be broken, differences resisting articulation into those chains, etc. What is the result of a historical construction is not the filling of a transcendentally established place, but the constant production and displacement of the place itself. Gasché himself perceptively points out this mutual subversion between filler and filled, between universality and particularity: speaking about what he calls 'radically secularized and social viable universals', he asserts that 'as the product of operations of the equivalential logic, they themselves have to be progressively voided of all content in order to be capable of occupying the place of the lacking fullness of society' (31). This is undoubtedly true, but precisely for that reason the opposite movement takes place as well: as the absent fullness of society has no content of its own, it permanently borrows such a content from something else that symbolizes it, and this infinite prosopopeia leads to a *sine die* contamination between its two terms. The conclusion is that the social flux cannot be arrested by any conceptual dam. What we can do, however, is to determine the logic of these movements of displacement and contamination, as psychoanalysis does through categories such as overdetermination. I see this as the proper task of social and political theory.[2]

This also explains why the questions that Gasché asks towards the end of his essay cannot be answered, from my perspective, without slightly changing their formulation. Gasché asks himself:

> What is that makes it possible for all particularities to relate to this empty place as the place of the universal, a place with respect to which they themselves come to understand themselves? And conversely, what permits this empty place to make the claim of universality, and to claim the particularities? (32).

My answer is that the 'conversely', which in a syntactico-semantic way attempts to separate both questions, is actually redundant, because the two are actually one and, in addition, one which could not emerge in those terms within my theoretical framework. *The universal is nothing else than an equivalential relation between particularities. And the 'empty place' – which should be better called 'dimension of emptiness' – is just the result of the internal split of all particularities, which cannot fully realize themselves as far as the structure constituting them is inherently decentred.* The difference between Gasché and myself on this point is that, for him, the universal has to have an ultimate content, independent of all particularities, while for me it is only the precipitate of a special articulation between particularities.

This can be seen even more clearly if we move to Gasché's next two questions, which are the next step in his argument:

> Once the empty place is thought of *as* the place of the universal, does it not, as this very place, betoken a content of sorts distinct from whatever contents subsequently come to fill that place? Indeed, how is one to determine that the product of an operation of equivalence is in the position of filling the empty space of the universal, if something, in addition to its tendential emptiness, does not render it recognizable as a contender for this task? (32).

The answer is that the act of *filling* a lack and the act of *recognizing* the actor performing it as a true filler, are one and the same operation. To refer to an example that I have used elsewhere: in a situation of disorder people need that *some* order is restored and, the more generalized disorder is, the more indifferent people will be vis-à-vis the concrete forms that the act of restoration will take. It is the actual bringing about order that is the source of legitimacy of the acts performing that bringing about, not the recognition of some marks a priori inscribed in those acts. So to use Gasché's terms: my analysis is in some way more formalistic than his, for it deprives the universal of that ultimate redoubt of content that Gasché is still prepared to grant it; but, on the other hand, it is less formalistic, as far as it denies that any necessary effect will follow from any aprioristically established form.

One last point requires to be treated, which is the question concerning Husserl. Gasché presents Husserl's universality, linked to the notion of the man of infinite tasks and the centrality of philosophy in shaping the European experience, as one of the directions in which my reflection could possibly move. Thus, he asserts:

> [T]he Husserlian conception of universality is intimately linked with the West; at the same time, it is the idea of humanity itself, that is, an idea that transcends the 'ethnia of the West'. As Laclau has argued, any universal is unavoidably tied to the particular. But for a particularity to be raised to the status of the universal it must also (at least tendentially) be emptied of its particular content. [...] Yet if this is the case, the universal cannot, in principle, be of the order of a fixed, and determinable particular content. Now, the idea of 'Europe' as the idea of universal mankind, that is, of something that, first and foremost, transcends Europe as a geographical and ethnic region, is, at its deepest level, nothing but the idea of a task: the infinite task, precisely, of transcending any particularity (ethnic, racial, cultural and so forth). And which coincides with the idea of humanity itself (32–3).

If the matter is presented in these terms, I think it is clear that the Husserlian perspective fits much better with Gasché's view of universality than with my own. To start with, universality has for Husserl – as for Gasché – a content which transcends all particularities: the achievement of a rational humanity (even if such an achievement amounts to an infinite task). So the universal is far from being empty, in my sense of the term. Secondly, the achievement of universality requires the overcoming of all particularities. As Husserl states in the Vienna lecture:

> They are such [infinite ideals] for the individual man in their nations, such for the nations themselves. But ultimately they are also infinite ideals for the spreading synthesis of nations in which each nation, precisely by pursuing its own ideal task in the spirit of infinity, gives its best to the nations united with it. Through this giving and receiving the supranational whole, with all its social levels, ascends, filled with the exuberant spirit of an infinite task, a task which is divided into various infinite spheres but is still one [...] Within European civilisation, philosophy has to constantly exercise its function as one which is archontic for the civilisation as a whole.
>
> (Husserl 1970: 289)

It could not be clearer. Particularities are not denied, but they are subsumed under increasingly wider rational syntheses which represent their telos. The universal does not confound itself with any particular, but not because it is empty but because it has a content of its own (specified as an infinite task) and a fully determined milieu of emergence (philosophy) whose archontic role vis-à-vis all particularities is clearly asserted.

So I do not think that the minimal preconditions for approaching Husserl's notion of universality to the one I have presented in my work have been really obtained. First, when I identify universality with emptiness, I do not mean, as Husserl, a task specified in its telos, but which, as infinite, cannot be equated to any of its transient stages, but *true* emptiness – i.e. one which does not have a content of its own and can only have discursive presence through a particular, becoming the nodal point of an equivalential chain. Second, particularities are, for me, internally split. They are essentially crossing points for the operation of differential and equivalential logics, not intermediate stages waiting for higher syntheses which will redefine their meaning. Third, the milieu of constitution of the universal is not, for me, primarily conceptual, while for Husserl the discourse of the universal is mainly brought about in order to assert the centrality of philosophy in the European experience.

With this discussion, however, we have not exhausted the dimensions of the notion of emptiness which are crucial to deal with central aspects of our intellectual and political experience. To do so, we have to move to some of the other interventions in this volume.

Ethics and radical investment

Simon Critchley's objections, dealing primarily with ethics, also turn around the question of formalism. He asserts that, for me, the ethical 'is the moment of pure formality that has to be filled, in a particular context, with a normative content' (118). My approach would be ultimately Kantian, in that sense, and exposed to the classical objections addressed to Kantian formalism. So again the reduction of emptiness to abstract formal content. The example of the mystic does, in fact, already answer this objection. As I have shown, the intuition of the divinity as something beyond all determination is anything but the grasping of a formal abstraction. But we should move away from the case of the mystical experience – paradigmatic as it is – to make clear what my argument concerning the ethical is about. It amounts to the following: the root of the ethical is the experience of the fullness of being as that which is essentially lacking. It is, if you want, the experience of the presence of an absence. Let us go back to the example of 'justice' as the name of a fullness which is denied. Justice is an empty term and not a formal conceptual determination because it is the mere positive reverse of a situation lived originally in negative terms: deprivation, dislocation, disorder, etc. This is what creates the distance between what is and what ought to be, which is the root of any ethical experience and reflection. And what I say about justice could be said about other terms such as 'truth', 'faithfulness', 'honesty', 'goodness', etc. What I am arguing is that there is a series of terms whose semantic function consists in pointing to an absent fullness, to an absolutely empty place deprived of any formal conceptual determination. It is in that sense that I have spoken of the 'universal': not as an ultimate content that all things share, but as something that necessarily eludes all of them.

I would argue that without the emptiness associated to certain terms no ethical exchange would be possible. We can discuss whether a fascist society is more or less just than a socialist one, but not whether 'justice' is something that should be looked for. 'Justice' has no ultimate content which is shared by both our fascist and our socialist interlocutors; it can play its role in argument precisely by not being linked to any such content. One can show this is the case by a simple experiment. Let us choose the most abstract and general definition of justice that we want: one can always imagine somebody who does not accept that definition and for whom 'justice', however, is still a meaningful term and a topic for a meaningful discussion.

What about the movement leading from this empty ethical moment (justice, in our example) to the concrete social norms which are associated to it in different contexts? It is clear that, the ethical moment being *essentially* empty, there can be no question of logically deriving, out of it, particular normative contents. But it can neither be the case that – as with Kant's formalism – an imperative dictates the conditions under which particular actions can be considered as ethical. Kant's categorical imperative can be formal, but most definitely it is not empty. It has a content, and it is that content that defines the moral law. In that case, what kind of other link could exist between ethics and normativity? My answer is: *radical investment*, a notion which requires clarification.

I have said that the primary ethical experience is the experience of a lack: it is constituted by the distance between what is and what ought to be. I have also asserted – and that is what approaches the ethical experience to the mystical one – that the object bridging that distance does not have a content of its own because it is just the positive reverse of something lived as negative. Now we can advance one more step in the argument and assert that any positive moral evaluation consists in attributing to a particular content the role of bearer of one of the names of fullness. If I say 'socialism is just' I am not putting together two perfectly defined concepts. What I am doing is identifying 'justice' as one of the names of fullness with a content which cannot be logically derived from that name (because there is no inherent conceptual content associated to that name). Here we have *investment* in an almost literal financial sense: the relevance of the term is greatly increased by making it the embodiment of a fullness totally transcending it. And this investment is *radical* because, justice being an empty term, nothing it in preannounced that socialism *had to* become the body incarnating it.

Radical investment, conceived in this sense, describes the way I see the basic structure of ethical action. This presents, however, the flank to a possible objection. If the investment is truly radical, doesn't that involve that anything goes, that there is no possibility of objective criteria to choose one rather than the other course of action? My answer is that that would indeed be the case if moral choice had as its only starting point the ethical side of the equation – i.e. if we just started from the signifiers of emptiness/fullness and were offered a series of alternative normative orders as possible objects of ethical investment. In that case, as from the empty ethical terms nothing necessarily follows, we would be in the situation described by the existentialists: a sovereign chooser who, precisely because he is sovereign, does not have the ground for any choice. But ethical life is entirely different from that picture. People are installed on both sides of the equation: they are, on the one hand, constructed as positions within a certain symbolic order; on the other hand, however, such an order is always a dislocated structure: it is destabilized by what, using Lacanian terminology, we could call the *real* of the structure. These dislocations show themselves as the distance between the unachievable fullness and what actually exists, and this distance is the source of the ethical experience conceived as the attempt to name the unnameable (which requires, as we have seen, a radical investment). But the ethical subject constituted through this investment is never an unencumbered moral subject; it fully participates in a normative order not all of which is put into question at the same time. That is the reason why moral argument can frequently take the form of showing the consequences that would necessarily derive from some actions and, in this way, appeal to shared values which are presented as grounds for preferring some courses of action rather than others. Not all ethical investments are possible at a given time. So moral choice finds neither its unique source in the ethical nor in the normative, but in the endless negotiation between both. Moral choices would only be equivalent to each other *sub specie aeternitatis*, but moral action takes place in a terrain which is always less than eternity.

Critchley asserts, however, that my reference points in asserting a purely formal criterion for the ethical are not just Kant but also Lacan and Heidegger. However, Critchley's reading of these authors shows the same tendency to inflate the category of formalism which is to be found in his references to my notion of 'emptiness'. He asserts, for instance, that in 'a Lacanian *ethics of the Real*, the latter is the moment of pure formality, a constitutive lack that is filled with normative content when it has become symbolized in relation to a specific content' (118). This seems to suggest that the relationship between the real and the symbolic is equivalent to the relationship form/content, so that the real would be an abstraction and, as a result, conceptual in nature. However, Critchley also goes on to assert, when expressing his agreement with Levinas about the mistake of the philosophical tradition having been the subordination of ethics to ontology:

> In Lacan, the ethical is experienced in relation to the order of the Real insofar as a non-symbolizable *Chose* – *das Ding* in Freud – stands in the place of the Real. This *Chose* is precisely something irreducible to ontological categorization, a permanent excess within discursive symbolization (120).

But Critchley cannot have it both ways: either the real is specified as a formal relation which, as such, is subsumable under the ontological (in the sense that Critchley understands this term), or it exceeds the ontological, in which case it cannot be formal. In fact the Real, in the Lacanian sense, far from being an abstraction which has to be filled by the symbolic, is that which shows – in fact constitutes – itself only through the disruption of the symbolic. Object (a) is a lost object which, in the first place, never was. And the thing – one of the early versions of the object (a) – is, from the very beginning, *hors-signifié*. I cannot enter here into the matter, but both Lacanian theorization and my argument concerning radical investment presuppose the presence of an absence, a lack which, far from being an abstraction, is irreducible to a formal conceptual content which would necessarily belong to the symbolic. As for Levinas, while I am partially prepared to move with him to the otherwise than Being, it should be clear that, given my notion of radical investment, I cannot accept his *derivation* of normative injunctions – such as 'infinite responsibility' – from that 'otherwise'. Although he has advanced more than most authors in his separation of the ethical from the normative he has, in the end, not resisted the temptation of building an aprioristic link between both orders. He, simply, has not been radical enough.

Something similar can be said about Critchley's reading of Heidegger. Critchley assimilates the ontological to the a priori or transcendentally constitutive features, with the implication that the ontic would be the 'concrete' which fills the ontological moulds, so that the distinction between the ontic and the ontological would be established in terms of degrees of abstraction. But this is certainly not Heidegger's conception. From the very beginning of *Being and Time* he asserts:

> 'Being' cannot be derived from higher concepts by definition, nor it can be presented through lower ones [...] Thus we cannot apply to Being the concept of 'definition' as presented in traditional logic, which itself has its foundation in ancient ontology and which, within certain limits, provides a justifiable way of characterizing 'entities'.
>
> (Heidegger 1962: 23)

It is simply not true that the transition from the ontic to the ontological can be conceived in terms of a movement from the empirical to the transcendental. If the reading of Critchley was correct the crucial distinction between *existentials* (applicable to *Dasein*) and categories (applicable to all other entities) would collapse. As for the ontico-ontological privilege of *Dasein*, it does not allude to any de facto unity in *Dasein* of the ontic and the ontological, but to the fact that *Dasein* has an understanding of entities different from itself.

> Dasein also possesses – as constitutive for its understanding of existence – an understanding of the Being of all entities of a character other than its own. Dasein has therefore a third priority as providing the ontico-ontological condition for the possibility of any ontology (ibid. 34).

There are two more aspects of Critchley's critique to which I would like to refer. Critchley sustains that there is a certain asymmetry in my approach, for while I deconstruct the distinction normative/descriptive, I maintain, however, a strict differentiation between the ethical and the normative.

> Thus, for him [myself], the question becomes that of the relationship between the ethical and 'descriptive/normative complexes' [...]. But by virtue of what is this second distinction somehow immune from the kind of deconstruction to which the first distinction was submitted? Logically and methodologically, how can one collapse one distinction only to put in its place another distinction without expecting it also to collapse? (119).

Let us concentrate for a moment on what my actual argument is. In the first place, I do not see why the collapse of one distinction would necessarily involve, 'logically and methodologically', the collapse of all the others as well. The irrelevance of one particular distinction does not mean that any distinction becomes a priori meaningless. What I have asserted – and still maintain – is that the normative/descriptive distinction, which as a strictly dichotomic one is not to be found before Kant, cannot ultimately be accepted, because there are no facts which are not grounded in the elaboration of our practical relationship with the world. It is in that sense that I have spoken about normative/descriptive complexes, pointing to an ontologically primary imbrication between facts and norms. That is the reason why I do not think that I am uncomfortably sitting on the horns of the dilemma that Critchley believes that he is detecting – i.e. either to admit a normative claim in the theory of hegemony, or to give to the latter a purely descriptive status, which 'risks identification and complicity with the dislocatory logic of contemporary capitalist societies' (117). The last part of Critchley's argument is a *non sequitur*: any complete description of the current state of affairs should refer not only to the dominant status quo but also to the forces challenging it. As for the first part, I am happy to concede from the beginning the whole argument: the notion of normative/descriptive complexes involves, precisely, that things could only have been described the way they are from a certain perspective involving a normative dimension and, conversely, that there is no factual reading which will not have some normative consequences. But as far as the ethical/normative distinction is concerned, the situation is entirely different. If the ethical experience is the experience of the unconditioned as lack in an entirely conditioned universe, it can only be so if there is no way of conceptually or logically moving from it to a particular normative order – i.e. if that movement can only be conceived as a 'cathexis' which has no predetermined object. For a Levinasian ethics the ground of the ethical experience is not fullness as *lack* but a *demand* which is the source of an injunction. For me this is a secondary level which presupposes that an ethical investment has already been made.

A last point concerning hegemony and democratic hegemony. Regarding Critchley's question of whether in my discussion on ethics I am doing meta-ethics or normative ethics, my answer is that I am doing primarily the former (except for an aspect to which I will return in a moment) but I fail to see what is banal about it. I think Critchley could only mean one of two things. Either he could be saying (which I doubt) that only a *normative* discourse is non-trivial, in which case any descriptive venture, ethical or otherwise, could be accused of banality – e.g. Heidegger's existential analytic of *Dasein* would be an utterly banal exercise; or he could be saying that what he calls my meta-ethics would just boil down to asserting that ethics exists in all societies – an assertion which, indeed, would not only be banal but also, given my presuppositions, almost tautological. This last conclusion, however, only holds if the ethical is conceived as a purely formal dimension of the normative, which is Critchley's conception but, most definitely, not my own. If, instead, the relation between the ethical and the normative is conceived in terms of radical investment, a set of consequences concerning the structuration of ethical life follows, which could be right or wrong but, certainly, is not trivial.

So what about Critchley's argument concerning the relationship between hegemony and democratic hegemony? Critchley asserts that the alternative to a purely diagnostical meta-ethics is to sustain that the ethical is only part and parcel of democratic societies and concludes:

> I would be inclined to say that democratic political forms are simply *better* than non-democratic ones: more inclusive, more capacious, more just, or whatever. Now, if there is *some* specific content to the ethical, then the distinction between the ethical and the normative cannot be said to hold [...] (121).

Well, I certainly join Critchley in his preferences for democratic political forms, but I reach this result following a far more complex path. For Critchley there is no possible argument here: the content of justice is democracy, and a just democratic society is the only one that gives its content to ethics. This presents various difficulties. First, if the ethical has from the beginning a content necessarily attached to it, all other conceptions have to be rejected offhand as unethical. It is not difficult to realize the authoritarian and ethnocentric consequences which follow potentially from such an approach. But, second, let us suppose that we postulate, as the Habermasians do, not a dogmatism of the contents but of the procedures. Have we advanced a single step with this new solution? No, we are in the same place as before, because only somebody who has already accepted some substantial values will accept also the validity of those procedures. It is only if a set of empty terms – 'justice', 'truth', 'people', etc. – become the names of the ethical, only if they are not necessarily attached to any content but are always given reversible contents through collectively elaborated radical investments, that something like a democratic society becomes possible. This means an endless movement between the ethical and the normative dimensions. And one last point: there is no possibility of *deriving* a normative injunction to keep open the gap between the ethical and the normative, from the *ontological* existence of that gap. Attempts at closing it, at reducing it to a minimum, are always possible forms of alternative radical investments. So the democratic widening of the gap is itself a contingent decision which is not anchored in any necessary grounding.

I would like, finally, to make reference to the essay by Mark Devenney, which is also concerned with ethical matters. Devenney's main point is that there is, implicit in my work, a non fully developed critique of instrumental rationality. This last notion has its ultimate roots, as is well known, in the Kantian ethical discussion on the means/ends relationship, and has been given considerable relevance in Weberian sociology, in the Frankfurt School's thought, and, more contemporarily, in Habermasian theory. Now, the whole notion of instrumental rationality is very alien to my thought. I simply do not think that there is such a thing as a *pure* instrumental rationality, while the whole intellectual effort of a book such as *Dialectic of the Enlightenment* is devoted to showing the latter's increasingly unchallenged autonomy. So I take Devenney's effort as *his* attempt at developing some of my analyses in a new direction. To judge its pertinence I will have to wait until his announced book is published but in the meantime I can point out some areas of tension between my writings and what Devenney makes out of them, as well as indicating the points in which there is a substantial agreement between ourselves.

In the first place, there is Devenney's identification of *nature* with *existence* (see 127) in the existence/reality duality which I have taken from W. T. Stace. The truth is that, in that duality, the only content of 'existence' is 'to be here and now', while 'nature' is already the result of a discursive construction of the object and belongs, as such, to its 'reality'. Second, according to Devenney,

> the empty signifier points to the impossibility of a purely instrumental relation with the other, and thus of a relation in which language is no longer a means to an end, but an opening toward an other which cannot be reduced to the fixed signification of communication which is semantically guaranteed by some appeal to an ideal of communicative rationality (128).

Whatever our ethical evaluation of such a hypothetical opening to the other, it should be clear that it has nothing whatsoever to do with the notion of an empty signifier. The latter takes its place entirely within the signifying process and has nothing to do with 'communication' or with the discourse of intersubjectivity to which the idea of an 'opening to the other' necessarily belongs. Finally, at various points of his argument, Devenney stresses – not necessarily in a critical way – the remnants in my discourse on empty signifiers of an absolutist ethics with religious overtones. Thus, after making reference to Augustine's heavenly realm, he asserts that,

> [t]his makes clear the grip of metaphysics on Laclau's conception of the ethical as well as the failure of all metaphysics to properly address the ethical. It also indicates that we should not too quickly dismiss absolutist versions of the ethical. Indeed they betray an important element of any post-metaphysical ethical theory (132).

And, more explicitly, he sustains that my insistence in calling 'ethical' an impossible object 'maintains a relation to absolutist and religious versions of ethical reflection' (136). This is followed, as a proof, by a long quotation from an article of mine on mystical discourse. Now, it is true that in my work I have used the case of the mystical discourse as a paradigmatic example of an 'emptying' strategy. But this was only the beginning of the analysis. The logic of empty signifiers leads exactly to the opposite of any absolute or religious fixation. What is required in order to attain the latter? Clearly, a command which is beyond any possible appeal. Abraham receives his order and starts his fateful (and faithful) trip. But what such a command makes absolute through an authority which consists in a radical beyond – which is thus unfathomable – is a precise content whose obvious banality – visible at its highest in rituals – is made sacred only because of the divine command. In other words, it is because God is, ontologically, an absolute beyond that the norms that He makes holy can only be ontic in nature. There is nothing multi-layered in the *ens creatum* as far as its only source is at infinite distance from itself. Far from liberating the human world to the operation of empty signifiers, absolutism – of a religious or of any other kind – leads to the fixity and the commanding role of the order of the signified. In this scheme of things, the only reality to which the category of emptiness – in the sense that we have discussed at the beginning of this piece – applies, is divine reality.

If we consider, however, the role of emptiness in the political sphere, we immediately see that its structural dimensions are radically altered. To go back to my earlier example: 'justice' is only the name of an absent fullness, the positive reverse of a given situation which is negatively lived as 'unjust'. I do not know what a just order would be, but I do know that justice is what is lacking. In that case: 1) 'justice' maintains its full absolutism as one of the names of 'fullness'; 2) as, however, the actual content of justice is not established by divine command, but is open to contestation, a split starts taking shape between the orders of the signifier and the signified: the absolutism of the former is not necessarily attached to any determinate content specified by the latter; 3) emptiness is no longer located in a radical *beyond*, but it is inherent to this world as one of its dimensions, which shows itself in the unbridgeable gap opened between signifier and signified. To put it in a nutshell: while the location of emptiness in a transcendent beyond could only translate its effects into worldly reality through the fixation of the signifier within the space of a fully fledged signified, the bringing of emptiness to *this* world will express itself through the autonomization of the signifier vis-à-vis the signified. In other words, secularization does not proceed through the 'liberation' of a largely unaltered worldly sphere from the metaphysical prison to which it was previously confined, but through the alteration of the structural features of that sphere. This alteration consists of the inscription within it of an emptiness which religious thought had only attributed to the 'absolute beyond'. This beyond could not be an empty signifier, simply because its emptiness transcends any possible relation to the structure of the sign. So, far from being the case, as Devenney hints, that to speak of empty signifiers is to remain within metaphysical or religious thought, the becoming–signifier of emptiness is the first step in any supersession of that thought. It is, as with Pascal's zero analysed by Paul de Man, that, by being named, it ceases to be entirely heterogeneous regarding the numerical order, and becomes a *one*. Secularization is nothing else than this process that I have described elsewhere as a deification of man and a mundanization of God. The autonomization of the signifier is the mechanism through which this process takes place.

Let me now move for a moment to the whole discussion on necessity and contingency, which occupies a rather central place in Devenney's argument. He links his discussion to his very laudable attempt at exorcising the bad spirits of 'performative self-contradiction'. I must say, to start with, that I have never been impressed by the argument of performative contradiction. As Heidegger once said, arguments against assertions such as 'I am lying', in Devenney's example, could be logically irrefutable, but what is the consequence of accepting them? Certainly not to prove the rightness of absolute truth, but a general scepticism about knowledge. In actual fact, performative self-contradiction only obtains the terrain of its doubtful validity on the basis of a highly restrictive hypothesis. We have to accept a logical terrain in which necessity and contingency are the only and mutually exclusive alternatives for the performative self-contradiction argument to be valid. But by introducing a 'universal contingency' by hypothesis we could be performing operations very different from postulating a terrain dominated by those stark logical alternatives. First, in order to show that the postulate of universal contingency is self-contradictory, I have to smuggle in the additional principle that the logical terrain within which that postulate is formulated has universal validity – with the result that contingency is defeated before starting. So the argument is perfectly circular. What are the alternatives to this postulate? The first, and most obvious, would be structured around the following points. 1) By contingency we do not understand the *other* of necessity – the terrain of an uncontrollable variation – but the internal limit of any process of self-grounding: the being of an entity depends on conditions which are not definable out of that very being. (What is rejected is Hegel's true infinity.) 2) What this involves is that necessity is internal to contingency, in the sense that it is only in the space of an 'as if' – circumscribing a non-saturated space – which can always be challenged, that some kind of *actual* necessity can operate. 3) What, however, about contingency as a universal horizon? Does this not involve attributing to necessity – even if it is the necessity of contingency – an ultimate mastery (with the result that performative self-contradiction would again raise its ugly head)? This would happen only if our additional assumption of a saturated logical space is brought back into the argument. If it is not, universal contingency does not mean the other of necessity but simply the contingency of the very terrain within which the opposition contingency/necessity makes sense. This means that the term 'contingency' plays two different roles within theoretical discourse: as an alternative within a horizon, and as the name of the horizon as such. It is only the first of these roles which is accepted by the argument of performative self-contradiction, with the result that, with an implacable logic, the other pole of the alternative – necessity – has to be invested with the dignity of providing a horizon.

I imagine that we could be confronted with a last trench of defence by our 'performative contradiction' theoreticians. Does not the transfer of contingency to its role as horizon still involve attributing 'necessity' to that horizon? Only if we endowed that horizon with a 'superhard' transcendentality. But this would be betraying the very notion of contingency. We can, without contradiction, assert 'contingency' as *a limit of thinking* within a theoretical situation without attributing to that limit a necessary character – i.e. admitting that new ways of thought could emerge that would question the very necessity/contingency alternative as the only possible one. It is, indeed, the whole argument of performative self-contradiction which incurs in a performative contradiction in not realizing that the contradiction involved in asserting the necessity of contingency is repeated in the case of the only available alternative within that logical space, which is to assert the contingency of necessity. The only way out of this blind alley is to establish the distinction between horizons and differentiations within those horizons.

These distinctions allow us, I think, to deal in a slightly different way with some of the central questions addressed by Devenney. First, there is the question of whether to defend an ethics based on 'radical investment' does not exclude other theoretical ethical approaches such as the one Devenney calls 'absolutism' and the others that he also mentions. It does, indeed, exclude them, but the truth of this claim is rather trivial. It is obvious that I cannot assert that ethical 'absolutism' is right and wrong at the same time. A different question, however, is whether 'radical investment' is an accurate description of what is involved in moral action. For what one would have to show, if the claims of 'radical investment' are going to be accepted, is that even people – such as the fascist, in Devenney's example – who identify with an absolutist ethics, cannot do so without a radical investment of sorts – i.e. we have to detect the traces of contingency within the very discourse of necessity.

And a last point concerning Devenney's argument about the relationship between ethics and radical democracy. To start with: in what sense would *radical* democracy differ from democracy *tout court*? For Devenney, such a radicalization is related to the institutionalization of uncertainty. I do not disagree with that formulation, providing that one specifies where the uncertainty lies. If it is conceived as an uncertainty concerning the decisions taken by *given* historical actors, the assertion can only lead to political scepticism or relativism, and to all the ambiguities and contradictions that a purely procedural conception of democracy involves. But it can also mean something entirely different: the incorporation into democratic deliberation of actors who had been, so far, excluded from the process of decision-making. Democracy is only radical if it involves an effort to give a political voice to the underdog. And as the constituencies of a potential democratic deliberation are constantly transformed and expanded, the institutional framework which makes that deliberation possible will also be variable. *Radical* democracy cannot be attached to any a priori fixed institutional formula. In Latin America, during the 1930s and 1940s, the nationalist military regimes which incorporated the masses to the public sphere were far more democratic than the corrupt and clientelistically-based parliamentary regimes that preceded them, although the latter respected the formal liberal rules. In that case, however, democracy itself requires to be specified beyond any normative-institutional content. This is the route through which the emptiness of the ethical moment and the emptiness of democracy can start establishing some bridges. This is the point where my argument dovetails with Devenney's: I agree with him that any possible democracy presupposes the break with absolutism and the necessary institutionalization of contingency; I would add, however, that this is not enough for democracy to be radical: what is also necessary is to bring to the historical arena social actors who had been excluded from it. And this is not possible without some kind of 'permanent revolution' in the democratic institutional arrangements. Which is a way of speaking, once again, about contingency.

Radical democracy

I want next to comment on the very interesting piece by Aletta Norval where she locates our concept of radical democracy within the general contemporary discussions on democratic theory. I agree very much with her criticisms to the Habermasian model, with the difficulties implicit in combining a strong element of dialogical rationality with the supplements needed to reach actual consensus, and with the general presentation that she makes of my own argument. So I will concentrate my reply on the two shortcomings that she finds in my argument – an argument with which, on the whole, she agrees.

Norval's two objections are presented as interrelated. An emphasis on disagreement as constitutive of social life in general and of democracy in particular (i.e. an ontological consideration) with a concomitant lack of attention to institutional democratic arrangements operating at the ontic level. Against this unilateralization of the moment of disagreement and its unavoidable consequence – institutional nihilism – Norval advocates some kind of democratic practice which would supersede the false dichotomy consensus/contestation and would combine a weakened version of deliberative democracy with the post-structuralist insights concerning antagonism and social disharmony. She says remarkably little about what these arrangements should, in her view, be; but what she asserts concerning the general question of democratic practice is enough for me to indicate the points where I part company with her approach.

One aspect that immediately catches my attention is the extent to which Norval has implicitly – and sometimes explicitly – accepted the terrain in which the Habermasians have posed the question of democracy. And when I am speaking about the 'Habermasians' I am not only referring to those of strict observance but also to those who, in different degrees, are guilty of apostasy. Norval describes quite well all these nuances in the first part of her essay. The Habermasian terrain is governed by two defining assumptions: 1) democracy is something which has essentially to do with equal conditions of the participants in a process of deliberation – that is, it is intrinsically related to the process of decision-making; 2) the task of democratic theory is to stipulate the institutional arrangements – the procedures – which will ensure that such an equality is guaranteed. The first striking thing about this way of approaching the problem is that the postulated rules will not work unless one presupposes a high degree of social homogeneity. Participants in a Habermasian deliberation have to be at least potentially equal if the question concerning the transformation of potentiality into actuality is going to be merely procedural. It does not take too much time, however, to realize that social inequalities in the present world are deeper than anything that mere procedural agreements could supersede. For three-quarters of the world population the question of democracy starts with the need for access to basic goods, to education, to health, etc. – i.e. with creating the elementary preconditions for participating in the public life of the community. These preconditions are established many times through means which would be considered highly heterodox from the viewpoint of Habermasian proceduralism. Some of these difficulties have been perceived within the Habermasian camp itself, and the results have been the various attempts that Norval describes at amending the original model. But even these amended versions fail to see the problem in its true universality.

According to Norval, who is approvingly quoting W. E. Connolly, democratic politics should be conceived as the 'site of a tension or productive ambiguity between governance and disturbance of naturalized identities. It thrives only while this tension is kept alive' (160). Well, with a statement of such generality I also, obviously, agree. Everything turns, however, around how this tension or ambiguity is going to be conceived. 'Tension' is not a perspicuous theoretical category. For me, the source of this tension is to be found in the way in which the democratic space has been historically constituted. I see it as resulting from bringing together two different logics which can only be contingently articulated and, quite often, cannot be articulated at all – one is forced to choose between them or, at least, to establish between them only a weak form of articulation which clearly privileges one over the other. One is related to the equality of the citizens in a homogeneous public sphere; the other consists in bringing the underdog – those excluded from the process of representation – into the historical arena. Now this second dimension, without which democracy would be merely farcical, requires tampering many times with the basic principles of the first. To give a simple contemporary example: without positive discrimination, in many cases, democracy would be reduced to a set of procedural rules, empty of democratic content, for they would not take into account how social agents are actually constituted. As a South African, Norval knows very well the tension existing between these two logics in the attempt to build up a democratic society in a context of deep inequality. This tension leads to many complex articulations in which apparently contradictory formulae like 'democratic dictatorship' become possible. There is no doubt that Jacobinism was a democratic movement, although it violated all the procedural rules that Habermasians postulate.

I have asserted, in an essay of mine dealing with these matters,[3] that representation takes place only because there is an essential unevenness between social agents, who belong always to particular groups within society, and the community conceived as a whole. The latter only exists as far as a particular group assumes, for a time, the representation of that communitarian universality. This is what hegemony is about. This is what differentiates my position from the Habermasians – for whom universality can be directly expressed once it has been reached through dialogical convergence – but also from extreme particularists like Lyotard, for whom the uncommunicable nature of language games does not leave room for any hegemonic universalization. As I argued in that essay, the process of political representation consists in a double movement: one, by which those represented transmit their will to the representative; the other, by which the representative interpellates those he represents and, in that way, endows them with a new political identity which makes possible their incorporation into the political sphere. The first of these two dimensions is the only one taken into account by the

Habermasians. The second, has been particularly emphasized in radical movements like Jacobinism, but also in a great deal of Third World theorization dealing with the emergence of an anti-colonialist consciousness – let us just think about the way Frantz Fanon describes, in *The Wretched of the Earth*, the development of an anticolonialist identity. It is clear that the tension between these two dimensions cannot be solved by any aprioristic theoretical formula. Everything depends on the historical context and on the options which are available within it. The only thing we can say is that an exclusive emphasis on the incorporation of the underdog, to the point of leaving aside entirely the question of a wider communitarian deliberation, can easily lead to the bureaucratic and ultimately antidemocratic *langues de bois* to which many new African elites, following the process of decolonization, fell prey; while the exclusive insistence on abstract deliberative rules outside any consideration of specificities can result, under the cover of universalism, in Western ethnocentrism. The latter is an entirely possible outcome to which the Habermasians are dangerously close.

I am now in a position to answer Norval's charge that, in my analysis, I have neglected the question of democratic institutional arrangements, and that this results from my exclusive emphasis on the ontological side of the question and my concomitant lack of consideration of the ontic aspects. My answer is that a general theory of democracy can only specify its constituent dimensions, but has to be very cautious about their institutional articulation. Precisely because this articulation is a contingent historical matter, it cannot be determined at the level of a general theory of democracy. To try to proceed to that determination within general theory would lead to results which are the opposite of what Norval tries to achieve – i.e. to transform a particular ontic arrangement into an ontological category. This is the best prescription to end in ethnocentrism and sociological essentialism.

Let me now say a few words about the essay in which W. E. Connolly describes the main lines of his theoretical approach. I agree with him that our theoretical approaches intersect in several crucial respects. Both of us are interested in the question of how to combine the particularism of a plurality of beliefs with the attachment to more universal communitarian values. In the case of Connolly this double source of ethical commitments takes the form of a tension between partisan orientation and an 'ethics of cultivation', and the interaction between the different sources of morality is conceived in terms of rhizomatic movements. In my case, the interaction is conceived in terms of equivalential logics while the moment of universality is linked to the construction of tendentially empty signifiers. So our respective approaches are at least comparable and some of our political conclusions are similar. This cannot, however, conceal the fact that our theoretical allegiances are different, and that those differences produce effects at a variety of levels. I would be most interested to discuss Connolly's theoretical model, but this essay of mine is hardly the place to do so, devoted as it is to answering the criticisms and commentaries on my work which have been raised in this volume.

Discourse and *jouissance*

There are two main reasons why I find myself in a slightly awkward position in answering Glynos and Stavrakakis's very friendly criticisms of my work. The first is that I do not disagree with practically anything they say concerning *jouissance* and its relation to the symbolic; the second, that what they claim is a dimension absent from my work I see, on the contrary, as very much present in it – although admittedly, sometimes in a rather sketchy and inchoate way. I think, however, that this misunderstanding (if there is one) proceeds from what I see as a slightly narrow reading, on their part, of some of my categories – particularly 'discourse'. Going through their piece I get the impression that they have located it within a dualism which can only distort its meaning.

For Glynos and Stavrakakis, a right approach to the socio-political field has to proceed from a double source: the order of the signifier and discourse (the symbolic) and the order of *jouissance* (the real). While Lacan, in his early semi-structuralist phase, would have put the main emphasis on the symbolic, his later work would have involved an increasing shift towards privileging the moment of the real – and, as a result, to giving a clear centrality to affect (conceived as *jouissance*) in explaining any process of identification. Although they accept that my approach to signification – grounded, as it is, in the category of 'empty signifier' – cannot easily be assimilated to any recognizable structuralist paradigm, they maintain nonetheless that only the 'signification' side of the equation is really present in my work, while the notion of 'jouissance' plays no visible role in it.

Let us see. Let us take just one of the examples that they give concerning the structure of enjoyment: the one concerning the advertising universe. They assert:

> within the advertising universe, every experience of lack is projected to the lack of the product which is being advertised [...] Advertising fantasies reduce the constitutive lack in the subject to the lack of the product that it simultaneously offers as an *objet petit a*, as a promise for the final elimination of this lack.

And they add:

> The harmony, however, promised by fantasy cannot be realized; the *objet petit a* can function as the object-cause of desire only insofar as it is lacking. As soon as we buy the product we find out that the enjoyment that we get is partial, that it has nothing to do with what we have been promised: '"That's not it!" is the very cry by which the *jouissance* obtained is distinguished from the *jouissance* expected' [Lacan] .
>
> (210)

Now: which of the moments of this theoretical sequence is absent from my analysis? I think none of them. My theory of hegemony asserts: 1) that there is a constitutive dislocation in any structural arrangement which ultimately makes impossible any kind of full symbolic identification; 2) that the object able to fill that structural lack, being both necessary and impossible, can only be a *particular* object which assumes the role of bringing about a fullness incommensurable with itself (this is the hegemonic link); 3) that, this link being essentially contingent, there is no logical connection between representative and what it represents – there is no 'natural' passage from one to the other (this is why a 'radical investment' is required, the latter involving an *affective* link between two objects); 4) that, as a result, there is no permanent attachment between the signifier of fullness and the various objects incarnating it (in Lacan's terms: there is always going to be a gap between the *jouissance* expected and the *jouissance* obtained).

This homology between the theory of hegemony and Lacanian psychoanalysis can be extended to other aspects mentioned by Glynos and Stavrakakis both in the essay on which I am commenting and in other works. The idea of a 'theft of enjoyment' finds its parallel in the notion of 'antagonism'; the relationship between lack of *jouissance* and fantasy, in the cathecting of particular images which universalizes them by transforming them into tendentially empty signifiers; the relation between *jouissance* and repression, in the notion of 'social symptom'. Even the affective investment explaining, according to Stavrakakis, the long-term attachment to some symbols, finds its parallel in my work in something on which I have insisted, namely that when some particular contents succeed in becoming the signifiers of the fullness, a partial fixity – of an essentially affective nature – results (in Gramscian terms: when hegemony has been won, it has been won for a whole historical period).

In that case, if there is such a considerable common terrain between both approaches, what could have led Glynos and Stavrakakis to think that I have left aside the whole side of affect in Lacanian theory? I think that the explanation is to be found in the fact that, for them, signification and *jouissance*, although closely interconnected in their operation, are conceptually distinguishable dimensions – or, at least, distinguishable to a larger extent than I am prepared to accept. For instance, after discussing the role of the real in both approaches, Glynos and Stavrakakis speak of,

> the 'non-encounter' between Laclau and Lacanian theorists at the level of *jouissance*. To our knowledge there is no reference in Laclau's work to the concept of *jouissance*. Perhaps, however, this is due to the overall mode of Laclau's embrace of the Lacanian real – an embrace framed in formal, structural terms rather than substantive terms (209).

In some other of their writings the sharp distinction between the two sides of the identification process is even more clearly underlined. Thus, Stavrakakis:

> What drives, for example, the endless repetition of identification acts? Is it only imaginary fullness and symbolic coherence? Is identity

> construction merely a semiotic play? Is the transformation taking place in a subject during identification of an exclusively cognitive nature? And, most crucially, what accounts for the pervasive character, the long-term fixity of certain identifications? (2004 [forthcoming]).

Against this one-sidedness Stavrakakis insists on the role of affect in identification and moves to the 'affective libidinal bonds' as described in *Group Psychology*.

What I want to question is the idea that here we are really dealing with two sides. Of course Glynos and Stavrakakis would rightly deny that they are exactly claiming the latter. Have not they themselves asserted that 'it is the real which can never be adequately represented, which can only show itself through the disruption of any attempt (symbolic or imaginary) to represent it' (206)? This is true, but I want to suggest that the link between the two sides is somehow more intimate than they allow for. Let us consider the matter from both sides. Signification, in the first place: what would be required for signification to be grasped as entirely separated from affect? The terms used by Stavrakakis to depict this side of the equation give us a clue: 'imaginary fullness', 'symbolic coherence', 'mere semiotic play', and – most revealing – 'exclusively cognitive nature'. What these denominations have in common is that *they all belong to the order of the signified*, not because they do away with the signifier but because they establish a one-to-one correlation between the two orders. So in the Saussurean distinction between *signification* and *value* it is the former that it is privileged. Saussure had moved away from the notion of language as a nomenclature, in which the real object was the anchoring point of signification (what Wittgenstein, at the beginning of the *Philosopical Investigations*, called the Augustinian theory of language) and had tried, instead, to find such anchoring point within language itself, in the sign, which presupposes an essential isomorphism between the orders of the signifier and the signified. It was perceived however very quickly that such isomorphism requires a strict distinction between phonic and conceptual substances, which is incompatible with linguistic formalism. The result was that, in the Prague and especially in the Copenhagen school, there was a radicalization of the principle of formalism which avoided any *substantial* distinction between the two orders[4] so that the dimension of value had to necessarily prevail over that of signification.

This has a decisive importance for psychoanalytic theory, for the implication is that between associations taking place at the level of the signified and those which proceed through what Freud called verbal bridges (i.e. through associations of signifiers) there is no separating barrier. We have global complexes involving both types of linkage. So meaning in the purely intellectualist sense is secondary and rather superficial. To give just one example: in seminar XI Lacan discusses a clinical case brought forward by Serge Leclair. The word 'Poordjeli', an entirely senseless sequence of sounds, is however, in its absence of meaning, the site of a cathectic investment. It is in this reduction of 'meaning' to a meaningless but nonetheless highly cathected articulation of signifiers where unconscious desire and identification ultimately meet.[5] In an extremely perceptive and well argued essay Glynos (1998) has shown how signifiers, signifieds, and signs all function ultimately as signifiers, as far as it is only this differential articulation – i.e. their value links – which is the meaningless ground of meaning, not a signification which would reduce the interplay of signifiers to the transparent medium through which a fully fledged signified would express itself. In that case, however, radical investment operates exclusively at the level of the signifier, and the link between the signifying elements can only be conceived in terms of a differential cathexis: that is, it can only be of an affective nature. Add just the detachment that affect and representation experience in repression and the affective investment on the substitutive representation that takes place in the symptom, and you will have the blending of satisfaction and dissatisfaction to be found in *jouissance*. If this is so, however, the only possible conclusion is that the dimension of affect is not something to be added to a process of signification but something without which signification, in the first place, would not take place. Once the latter cannot be anchored either in an external referent or in a sign as the locus of a perfect one-to-one overlapping between signifier and signified, the only possible anchoring is to be found in the production of meaning through the differential cathexis of a meaningless substance (it should be clear why this differential cathexis, in political terms, is necessary involved in any hegemonic operation).

What about the other side? Is affect something that we could conceive as independent from the signifying side of the equation? Language, according to Saussure, should be understood in terms of relations of both combination (syntagms) and substitution (paradigms, to which Saussure referred as the associative pole of language). Now the pole of substitutions – which, not surprisingly, has been played down in its linguistic effects by structuralists of strict observance – is governed by the principle of analogy, whose consequence is to introduce rhetoric within the very structure of linguistic functioning. Once the logic of analogy has a constitutive linguistic role to play, we can easily see that it cannot be controlled by any kind of aprioristic syntagmatic limit. Substitution and combination are not only complementary logics, but are also subversive of each other. A term can be seen as having, in the paradigmatic pole, an 'analogic irradiation' which is limited by the dominant syntagmatic differentiations. But these limits are not stable. We can see the components of the associative pole as encroaching upon established syntagmatic combinations – as psychoanalysis has shown, new associations can constantly displace the established parameters of discourse. So we have in language an essential unevenness: each term, as an analogical centre, will have a higher or lower degree of irradiation. Or, to say the same thing with other words, it will be more or less overdetermined. As this means that it will be more or less cathected, the clear consequence is that its centrality will not be simply structural or merely semiotic – let alone cognitive – but it will be essentially affective. Two complementary conclusions follow: given the impossibility of mastering the associative pole of language by any a priori structural differentiation, there is no signification without affect; but, at the same time, there is no affect which is not constituted through its operation within a signifying chain.

Let us return at this point to the main criticism of Glynos and Stavrakakis, which concerns the unilateral emphasis that I would supposedly have given to the discursive at the expense of enjoyment. My answer is that by discourse I do not understand something restricted to the linguistic conceived in its narrow sense, but a relational complex of which enjoyment is a constitutive element. Let us think for a moment about the symptom. We have in the process of its formation a dimension of repression by which affect is withdrawn from a representation and attached to a substitutive representation. *Jouissance* results from the experience of satisfaction/dissatisfaction which crystallizes in the symptom. It is clear that linguistic representation is not an 'other' vis-à-vis *jouissance*, but an internal component of *jouissance* itself. And things are not changed by the fact that – as Glynos and Stavrakakis point out, quoting J. A. Miller – *jouissance* presupposes the body, because the body itself is not a biological datum opaque to language but it is written with signifiers. Conversely, for the reasons that I have indicated above, language itself cannot function without cathexis (i.e. affective unevenness). It is this sequence of structural/relational moments which includes both linguistic and affective components that I call *discourse*. It is worth stressing that, since *Hegemony and Socialist Strategy*, we have always criticized the distinction between the discursive and the extra-discursive as an untenable dualism. Discourse involves both words and the actions to which those words are linked, as in Wittgenstein language games. It would obviously be absurd to criticize the dualism words/actions but to exclude such affects from those relational complexes. Moreover some of the categories that I employ, such as 'radical investment', would be unintelligible without the notion of *jouissance*.[6]

In conclusion: I do not think that my views are ultimately that distant from those presented by Glynos and Stavrakakis. The nuance separating us is to be found in the fact that, while the three of us agree that there is a constitutive relational moment linking the linguistic and the affective, they have concentrated on the *duality* as such, while my attention has been mostly directed to the *relation* which makes that duality possible. That is why I have extracted some categories – such as discourse – from any regional connotation and I have attempted to give to them a more primary ontological role. The complexes that I call 'discursive' include both affective and linguistic dimensions, and, *ergo*, they cannot be either affective or linguistic. This is an intellectual strategy that I am prepared to defend. The dangers of proceeding otherwise are mainly two. First, if affect is seen as a foreign intrusion within the linguistic, the latter will be seen as capable of a closure of its own if that interruption did not take place – however inevitable the interruption is. That is the best road to lead to a purely essentialist/structuralist conception of language. But, conversely, there is the parallel danger of essentializing the operations of the unconscious, making of the latter a fully fledged agency. As Bruce Fink has written:

> Freud at one stage makes the unconscious into a fully-fledged agency (*Instanz*), an agency seemingly endowed with its own intentions and will – a sort of second consciousness built, in some ways, on the model of the first. While Lacan certainly presents the unconscious as that which interrupts the normal flow of events, he never makes an agency of the unconscious; it remains a discourse divorced from consciousness and subjective involvement – the Other's discourse – even as it interrupts the ego's discourse that is based on a false sense of self.
>
> (Fink 1995: 42)

So, the crucial task is to think the specificity of discursive formations in such terms that the interaction between the various instances and registers loses its purely casual and external character and becomes constitutive of the instances themselves. This clearly requires a new ontology. I see the psychoanalytic revolution as an immense widening of the field of objectivity, bringing to consideration kinds of relations between entities which cannot be grasped with the conceptual arsenal of classical ontology. I see as our main intellectual task to rethink philosophy in the light of this project.[7]

Logic and rhetoric

The discussion concerning the role of affect in psychoanalysis is a good introduction to the questions of logic and rhetoric, which are the main topics dealt with by J. Hillis Miller in his intervention. He asserts:

> the one of the three branches of the trivium (grammar, rhetoric, and logic) that dominates in Laclau's work is logic. The opacities or irrationalities of tropes, however subtly and flexibly Laclau treats them, tend to get reassimilated by him to logic (220).

And later on:

> the co-presence of possibility and impossibility is defined by Laclau from the perspective of more or less traditional logical assumptions [...]. The madness of decision is accurately described as a 'blind spot' because the predominantly logical thinking of Laclau's argumentation cannot command those moments of decision, rationalize them, or illuminate them with the light of reason (220).

The result can only be that the traditional category of the subject has necessarily to be reintroduced: 'Laclau recuperates, however carefully and prudently, a notion of the deciding and acting autonomous subject' (223). Again: 'political decision for Laclau is made by a somewhat coolly calculating or rationally logical "I" that sees its chance to intervene in the historical process and takes it' (224). The political consequences of such a logicism are easy to draw: 'Laclau's theory of political change for the better cannot do without the recuperation of the subject or "I" that decides arbitrarily and without justification, but nevertheless rationally and logically' (224).

I am sorry to have been so utterly misunderstood by my friend and respected colleague Hillis Miller, but it is clear from his essay that his analysis and conclusions are based in an initial misreading which permeates his whole argument. Let me put it bluntly: when I am speaking of 'hegemonic logic' I am not referring in the least to formal logic in the usual sense. The two other members of the trivium – grammar and rhetoric – are also 'logics' in the sense in which I use the term. That use, moreover, has nothing of the idiosyncratic. When the Lacanians speak of the 'logic of the signifier' or Deleuze of the *Logique du sens* they are not even remotely referring to the rules of inference of formal logic. In the discussion with Judith Butler that I evoked before, I have written:

> it [my text] dismisses the very idea of a general logic which would establish the foundation of any possible language and insists, on the contrary, that logics are context-dependent – the market, kinship, and so on, depending on the language game in which one is engaged [...] I understand by 'grammar' the set of rules governing a particular 'language game' (the sets of rules defining what chess-playing is, in Wittgenstein's example). By 'logic', on the contrary, I understand the type of relations between entities that makes possible the actual operation of that system of rules. While the grammar merely enounces what the rules of a particular language game are, the logic answers to a different type of question: how entities have to be to make those rules possible? Psychoanalytic categories such as 'projection' or 'introjection', for instance, presuppose processes whose logic is different from those that operate in the physical or biological word. When François Jacob, in his writings on theoretical biology speaks of *la logique du vivant*, he is using the term 'logic' in the exact sense that I am attributing to it. To put it in another way: while 'grammar' is always ontic, 'logic' is 'ontological'.
>
> (2000b: 283–4)

If logics (in the plural) are understood in this sense, I do not see how I could be suspected of being a closet rationalist. It would be tantamount to saying that there is a Freudian rationalism based in the isolation of the logics of condensation and displacement, or a deconstructive rationalism grounding objectivity in logics such as supplementarity, iteration, re-mark, etc. A logic is nothing else than a rarefied system of objects governed by a cluster of rules which makes some combinations and substitutions possible, and excludes others. There is a point, however, which requires further consideration. In distinguishing between grammars and logics (leaving rhetoric, for the moment, aside) am I not reintroducing Hillis Miller's trivium distinction into the discussion and, in that way, undermining my own argument? I do not think so. At the ontic level, classical formal logic and grammar are differentiated systems of rules, and each has logics (rules of object-constitution) which are also differentiated. The idea that grammar and (ontic) logic would overlap at the level of the same (ontological) logic was simply the rationalist illusion of the school of Port-Royal.

What about the third component of the trivium – namely rhetoric? I definitely assert its crucial importance because, if discourse is the terrain of constitution of all objectivity, rhetorical movements are constitutive of discursivity. Let us start by considering catachresis, to which Hillis Miller makes reference in his essay. I do not really understand his objections to my use of this rhetorical category. Anyway, what I have asserted is the following: 1) catachresis is the use of a figural term when there is no literal term that can replace it (e.g. when we speak of a leg of a chair); 2) catachresis is not, strictly speaking, a figure, for any kind of rhetorical figure *sensu stricto* can become catachrestical as far as there is no corresponding literal term – that is the reason why Fontanier, in his systematization of rhetoric in the early nineteenth century could speak of catachreses of metaphor, of metonymy, of synechdoc, etc; 3) as any rhetorical figure adds some meaning which could not be transmitted by the direct use of a literal term, all figures are, to some extent, catachrestical. Catachresis is not, in that sense, a particular figure, but a dimension of rhetoricity as such (Parker 1990: 60–73).

So the centrality of rhetoric depends on whether discursive structures can be conceived as closed in their own literality (so that rhetorical devices would be – as for classical rhetoric – adornments of language which would not tamper with linguistic functioning) or whether the latter requires rhetoric for its very process of constitution. In several essays I have tried to show that the second is the real alternative. In my piece on 'Why do empty signifiers matter to politics?' (in *E*), I have shown that the realization of language as a system of differences requires the construction of the system of signification on the basis of exclusions; that the latter submits all signifying identities to the contradictory logics of equivalence and difference; and that, as a result, no structural arrangement can be closed without one of its component elements assuming the representation of an incommensurable (impossible) totality. Now, this representation is strictly catachrestical in its function, as far as it gives a name to an impossible object – i.e. an object which can only exist through the act of naming it. In another essay (Laclau 2001) I have tried to show that a similar argument is to be found in Paul de Man's analysis of Pascal's attempt at making the zero the starting point of the numerical series (de Man 1998).[8]

But it is not only the internal logic of any structural closure that requires the intervention of a rhetorical mediation: the very presence of relations of substitution along with the paradigmatic pole of language already involves the need for rhetorical analogies and displacements.[9] Analogy operates at very different levels – e.g. at the level of semantic structure and not only at those of syntaxis and phonology, to which Saussure mainly refers – and the kind of associations that psychoanalysis explores operate, as we have seen, both at the level of the signifieds and at that of the verbal bridges. Rhetoric, as a result, is constitutive of discourse. It is interesting to note that this primary role of rhetoric in structuring discourse is an integral part of the Italian humanist tradition of the Renaissance. Summarizing the main theses of that tradition, Ernesto Grassi asserts:

> we claim that we know something when we are able to prove it. To prove [*apo-deiknumis*] means to show something to be something on the basis of something. It is clear that the first *archai* of any proof and hence of knowledge cannot be proved themselves because they cannot be the objects of apodictic, demonstrative, logical speech [...] The indicative [*semeinen*] speech provides the framework within which the proof can come into existence. Such speech is immediately a 'showing' – and for this reason 'figurative' or 'imaginative' and thus in the original sense 'theoretical' [*theorein* – i.e. to see]. It is metaphorical, i.e., it shows something which has a sense, and this means that to the figure, to that which is shown, the speech transfers [*metapherein*] a signification: in this way the speech which realizes the showing 'leads before the eyes' [*phainesthai*] a significance [...] Thus the term 'rhetoric' assumes a fundamental new significance: 'rhetoric' is not, nor can it be, the art of the technique of an external persuasion: it is rather the speech which is the basis of the rational thought.
>
> (Grassi 1980: 64–5)

And it is clear that the affective components of discourse which, as we have seen in our discussion of psychoanalysis, are an integral part of the signifying process, also play an essential role in rhetorical movements.

Given this centrality attributed to affect and rhetoric, it should be clear that my approach is incompatible with any kind of privileging of inferential logic, with any notion of the decision as exclusively grounded in rational calculation, or with a crypto-Cartesian, essentialist, notion of the subject. What I have asserted is exactly the opposite: that the decision is not grounded in any rationality external to itself; that this 'itself', however, should not be conceived in terms of any self-transparency, but as a complex situation whose mechanisms – largely unconscious – escape the 'subject' of the decision; and that this subject does not precede the decision but is rather the product of the latter.

These themes – subject, decision, rhetorical movements – touch, however, issues that relate to some other interventions, and it is to these that I will move now.

On the ontological difference

I want to refer next to Fred Dallmayr's criticisms and to the answer to the main core of them to be found in the essay by Oliver Marchart. Dallmayr starts his piece by offering a very clear and insightful presentation of the main theses of

Hegemony and Socialist Strategy. He has, however, a set of reservations concerning the book, which can be summarized as follows:

1 Assimilating – I think too quickly – our position to the spontaneism of Rosa Luxemburg and the voluntarism of Sorel, he sustains that it leads us to a constructionism 'obfuscating the distinction between praxis (or practical conduct) and technical-instrumental behaviour' (47). This confluence of meaning would not allow us to properly differentiate hegemony from instrumentalism. The result would be a reversal of necessity into contingency, although Dallmayr recognizes that the notion of 'subversion' of one pole into the other to be found in our work cannot be easily equated with any simple reversal and has more to do with Heidegger's *Zwiefalt* and with Derrida's *différance*.
2 Flirtation with the notion of negativity would have led us to some kind of Sartrean opposition between being and nothingness, with the implication of an access to a beyond the differences, while the complex web of relations involved in the notion of hegemony would be better conceived in terms of a Heideggerian 'non-objective type of matrix in which positivity and negativity, ground and abyss (*Abgrund*) are peculiarly intertwined' (49). In the same way, our conception of antagonism as limit would oscillate between the latter being conceived as either internal or external to the social.
3 Finally, this unresolvable tension between interiority and exteriority would have led us, according to Dallmayr, to present an equally ambiguous notion of democracy. The latter would be, on the one hand, the specific logic of the democratic revolution, which transforms the logic of equivalence into the fundamental instrument in the production of the social; while the ideal of a 'plural democracy' as a viable social arrangement would involve not only a 'strategy of opposition' but also – using our own words – the 'strategy of construction of a new order'. Dallmayr looks for historical precedents of a balance between these two dimensions and finds them in the Aristotelian notion of 'friendship' and in Hegel's *Sittlichkeit*.

Let us successively consider these criticisms.

The first objection by Dallmayr is easy to deal with. Although he speaks about cancelling out the distinction between praxis and technical-instrumental behaviour, the way he constructs his argument makes clear that, in his view, we have somehow reduced the former to the latter. To answer his point: first, I do not think that that reduction is *ever* possible; I do not think there is anything that is a *pure* instrumental reason. But, second, the notion of hegemony as we have developed it is also incompatible with a pure instrumentalism. The latter presupposes an identity entirely external to the instrumental action, operating as its source, while the condition to call an action hegemonic is that the identity of the agent is constructed through his hegemonic intervention. It is true that we have insisted that power is inherent to any hegemonic operation, but as power is, for us, also inherent in social relations *tout court*, its presence is hardly a criterion for distinguishing between praxis and instrumental behaviour.

As for the criticism concerning negativity, I think it raises a set of important issues which have been dealt with by Marchart in his reply to Dallmayr – a reply I agree with, almost point by point. 1) Marchart asserts that, in my approach, the relation necessity/contingency is not one of exteriority between two domains, but one of mutual subversion: contingency exists *within* necessity, preventing the consolidation of the latter but, precisely because of that, contingency is also absolutely necessary (this would be the moment of hybridity). 2) However, and in spite of that, the dimension of *outside* has also to be a *radical* one. This is not, nevertheless, the outside of two perfectly delimited ontic territories. It is an outside that can only be approached in terms of a reformulated version of Heidegger's ontological difference. Dallmayr would have erroneously assimilated the ontological nothingness to the ontic one – thus his complaint that we would have been flirting with Sartreanism. But, as Marchart points out quite accurately, Being and Nothingness cannot be conceived in terms of an antithesis. In his words:

> if we restrict our view to the ontological level, it may even be said that Being (= complete closure of the system) and Nothingness (= complete openness of the system) amount to one and the same thing. The real gap – which some might call the gap of the real – consists in the radical separation between the ontological and the ontic level which does not allow for the level of nothingness – the radical outside – to be reached as such. The latter can only show itself in form of failure or dislocation within the ontic order of beings (65).

I fully agree with Marchart's remarks and would like only to add two short commentaries. The first is that it is precisely that inherent dislocation in the ontic order of beings and the relation of antagonism conceived as ontological difference in the sense specified by Marchart, that makes it possible to distinguish my approach from some others which also try to think a moment of radical cut in the structural continuity, but do so in terms of a dualist ontology which in this case, yes, can be traced back to the Sartrean opposition between Being and Nothingness. I am thinking of the distinction *être/événement* as formulated in the work of Alain Badiou. A theory of hegemony such as the one we have formulated requires an entirely different ontological grounding: one, precisely, that starts from the ontological difference as specified by Marchart's argument.

My second remark is that, for me, something which can only show itself as 'failure, or dislocation within the ontic order of beings' means something very precise: tropological displacements. I have earlier hinted at that. Now its meaning can be made more precise: because the ontological difference is absolutely constitutive of the order of being, the latter can only be the terrain of a generalized rhetoric.

As for Dallmayr's reservations concerning what he sees as our ambiguous notion of democracy, I can hardly see them as involving a criticism. It is entirely true that we have distinguished between a democratic logic which transforms the logic of equivalents into the fundamental instrument in the production of the social and the strategy of construction of a new social order. This is because I do not see democracy as a political regime – I do not restrict it, for instance, to *liberal* democracy in the Western sense of the term – but a dimension of politics which, as such, can be present in regimes which widely differ from each other. In our terminology, while the democratic logic finds its constitutive terrain in the equivalential logic (which, of course, does not mean that any equivalence is per se democratic), institutional specificity is constructed through what we have called logic of difference. A hegemonic formation is the result of the articulation/tension between both logics. I can easily agree with Dallmayr that if one searches for comparative locations for such a notion of hegemonic formation one has to refer to intellectual constructs such as Hegel's *Sittlichkeit*, providing, of course, that one specifies not only the structural homologies but also the difference between the various conceptions.

I want to refer, before leaving this point, to the conceptual couples particular/universal and singular/absolute discussed by Marchart. I think that the introduction of the singular/absolute doublet that he makes is a very valuable contribution to the theory of hegemony. He restricts the use of the particular/universal distinction to the cases (and in fact there are no different cases) in which the two dimensions contaminate each other, and proposes the singular/absolute as the limit concepts referring to the (impossible) situation in which either pure universality or pure particularity would obtain. He describes very accurately the nature of this gap:

> What we discover at the bottom of the dialectical play between the universal and the particular – with its relative degrees of universalization and particularization of certain demands – is a more radical difference. What we encounter is that very difference *as difference*: the radical gap (which at the same time is a necessary intertwining) between the 'possible' dialectics between universality and particularity on the one hand and the spectre of their impossible limit cases: the absolute and the singular, on the other. This radical difference is named by Laclau in a variety of ways: contingency, freedom, dislocation, radical historicity, etc. (67).

I also agree very much with Marchart in his assertion that when we identify with the causes of the underdog (he quotes the homeless as an example) we do not identify with them as pure singularities but as '*exemplary species* of the oppressed and of oppression in general' (67). This establishes in relation to any specific social struggle, a complex dialectic between particularity and universality through which a hegemonic construction takes place. This makes it possible to take distances from those discourses which try to ground ethical responsibility in the respect of the different (the singular in Marchart's words) as different – that is the case of Levinas – but also from vociferous universalist discourses such as Žižek's which negate any dialectic between universality and particularity and see in the latter only a betrayal of the former.[10] The only point in which I cannot follow Marchart is when he asserts that '[e]ven a "relatively" universalized content would still remain at the ontic level' (66). I think this goes against the basic trend of Marchart's thought. Following his argument (and mine) one should rather say that the ontic/ontological distinction is constitutive of any actual entity.

Still the universal

The question of the discursive status of the universal is also very much at the root of the interventions of Rado Riha, Linda Zerilli, and Jelica Šumič. Let us go through them.

Rado Riha, in a very insightful and multi-layered paper tries to isolate a conceptual triangle in my work whose vertices would be the universal, the singular and the subject. Summarizing his argument he asserts:

> the universal can only exist by being supplemented by an irreducible singularity; this supplementation in turn requires, as a condition of its possibility, the advent of the subject, which is but a precarious, finite support for the encounter between radical contingency, or irreducible singularity, and the universal. In saying that the subject is ultimately what makes the universal possible, I wish to indicate that the components of the knot do not precede their knotting; rather, they are only constituted after the fact, i.e. in the process of subjectivation. My central claim at this point is that the knot of the universal, the singular, and the subject sheds light not only on Laclau's conception of the universal but also on the relationship between politics and philosophy, and which can be conceived in terms of the *universalization as subjectivation* (74).

I find what Riha has to say in his essay most convincing, and also that he throws light on some crucial aspects of my argument that I had not explored myself. I will concentrate on one particular aspect of Riha's essay to which I would like to add a few considerations. I will refer to the relationship between universality and singularity in Kant's reflexive judgement. Riha's argument runs approximately as follows: 1) in the reflexive judgement there is no universal norm or rule on which the judgement can be grounded, but the mediation of judgement is its own ground; 2) there is no relation of succession between the universal and the particular – as, for instance, in a deductive sequence: both are given simultaneously; 3) universality, not preceding singularity in any aprioristic logical space, can only exist within singularity, which thus becomes groundless yet unconditional; 4) the subject of enunciation, as empty place, devoid of any positionality within the statement, is the only support of this inextricable fusion between universality and singularity. So it is irretrievable within any enouncing structure. As Riha puts it:

> it can only exist in the act of judging that something is a case of the rule or that a particular is a case of the universal. In this sense we cannot say that the act of judgement prescribes a norm of its being to a given reality; nor can a reflexive judgement be considered a result of the decision of the subject pre-existing the act of judgement (84).

It is at this point that I want to add something to Riha's argument – an argument with which, as I said, I entirely agree. The singular universal, in the terms he defines it, the moment of politics as the real of philosophy, defines the parameters of a logical possibility/impossibility without, however, making entirely explicit how the results of that presence/absence game have access to the field of representation. The means of representation of the product of the reflexive judgement have to be necessarily different from those of the determinative judgement, where direct subsumption of the case under the norm makes of representation a straightforward affair. In the same way, in the analysis of the articulation between the singular and the absolute, that we have discussed à propos of Marchart's text, we can understand how the presence of an absence becomes possible within the discursive field, but that is not enough to see how that presence *shows* itself. This is the point at which I want to join Riha's argument: I think that something which cannot be conceptually apprehended (which cannot be directly subsumed under a concept) can still be named. I see naming as an essential component of the reflexive judgement – and, a fortiori, of any hegemonic operation. This argument can be developed in a variety of directions. Let me mention just a few.

1 If in the reflexive judgement there is no straight subordination of the case to the rule but a simultaneity of both, their unity can be provided only by the name – i.e. it is not a conceptual unity. This relates somehow these distinctions to those which have been seen at the heart of the debate between descriptivists and anti-descriptivists in contemporary analytic philosophy. Kripke's notion of a primal baptism makes, precisely, an allusion to a nominal grounding which does not find its formulation in any a priori conceptual determination. Slavoj Žižek (1989: 89–98) has lately probed into this theoretical problematic by asking the highly relevant question of what is the x that supports the process of naming. His Lacanian answer, that the x is a retroactive effect of the process of naming, stresses even more the emancipation of the name from the concept.
2 This emancipation opens the way to something which is central to my theoretical approach and which has been present at several points of this discussion: the constitutive role of the rhetorical in the production of social relations. If every case could be subsumed in a direct and unproblematic way under a rule, there would be no room for rhetorical displacements; but if the case creates its own rule, the role of the name becomes more autonomous – in Lacanian terms: the signified permanently slides under the signifier – no

conceptual or denotative anchorage can be permanent and the space for the primacy of tropological movements is opened.

3 We can see, from this perspective, the history of Marxism as a progressive transition of its categories from the determinative to the reflexive judgement. At the beginning we have a total subordination of the particular cases to the conceptual rules: class, State, stage of development, etc. have a univocal meaning and the political analysis consists in subsuming empirical material under a pre-given system of categories. ('Of what social class is this politics an expression?' 'At what stage of capitalist development is this country located?' etc.). Later on the picture is progressively complicated by the eruption of a 'real' which dislocates the conceptual framework. The phenomena of what was called combined and uneven development, for instance, associate historical features in ways which were unrepresentable within the classical theoretical frameworks. These assemblages of features could be *named*, but they clearly constitute their own rule and were not cases subsumable under a rule preceding them. When we reach Gramsci and his notions of collective wills and hegemonic formations, we have clearly shifted from the primacy of determinative judgement to that of the reflexive one.

The question of the universal is also very much at the centre of Linda Zerilli's piece. She arrives at conclusions remarkably similar to those of Riha concerning reflexive judgement, although her starting point is Hannah Arendt. Zerilli asserts:

> In this [political] idiom the potential moments of intersubjective agreement are anticipated in the context of plurality rather than derived from some notion of an essential commonality or the injunction to reach consensus. For Arendt (following Kant), this idiom is called critical judging: the practice, conducted in the public space of appearances, of assessing particulars without subsuming them under a pregiven universal or rule. For Laclau [...] this idiom is called hegemony, the reinscription (not the sublation) of particulars into chains of equivalence through reference to the universal as an empty place (92–3).

She quotes extensively from Arendt concerning her reading of Kant, links it to the Wittgensteinian notion of language game, and convincingly shows its similitude with my notion of hegemonic practices. The point where she thinks that I part company with Arendt is, however, in our respective ways of conceiving the universal: there would not be, in Arendt, a theory of empty signifiers. In her words:

> But if Laclau (like Arendt) refutes the false universality of abstract rationality or common identity, he by no means rejects universalism 'as an old-fashioned totalitarian dream' [...] Playing a different language

> game with the universal, however, Laclau does not come home to a universalism which is One. Rather, he reinterprets universality as a site of multiple significations which concerns not the singular truths of classical philosophy but the irreducibly plural standpoints of democratic politics (93).

She proceeds later with a very clear and rigorous presentation of my argument concerning empty signifiers and its differences from contemporary versions of universalism and radical particularism and closes her piece with a highly interesting discussion of the possible relevance of my approach for debates concerning feminism and sexual difference.

I find myself in complete agreement with most of Zerilli's analysis. The only point on which I have to establish a difference between our approaches is the one concerning the status of psychoanalytic categories. The question of psychoanalysis is raised by Zerilli in connection with Žižek's reading of our notion of antagonism as formulated in *Hegemony and Socialist Strategy*. According to Zerilli, while Žižek anchors his notion of antagonism in the original *Spaltung* of the subject, our own notion (the one I have formulated together with Chantal Mouffe) goes far beyond the psychic reductionism that the projection of the *Spaltung* to the whole social field would presuppose. So Žižek would be misappropriating our notion when he assimilates it to his own and Zerilli finds it puzzling that I seem to accept such an assimilation:

> Laclau's reception of Žižek's reading is somewhat puzzling insofar as he repeatedly insists [...] that 'in our conception of antagonism [...] denial [of identity] does not originate from the "inside" of identity itself but, in its most radical sense from outside' [...] Although this assertion is aimed at showing the 'limits of objectivity', as we saw above, it is politically significant that Laclau's (and Mouffe's) notion of antagonism precisely does not reduce itself to the original *Spaltung* of the subject but maintains a crucial reference to a remainder which is always historical and contextual, and which gives to antagonism its specifically political dimension (98–9).

And responding to Žižek assertion that, according to Freud, the *Verdrängung* is not just an internalization of external repression (*Unterdrückung*), Zerilli writes:

> that is correct – but it is likewise the case that a psychoanalytically informed political analysis (especially a democratic theory concerned with plurality) has also to argue the reverse: the *Unterdrückung* cannot be reduced to the *Verdrängung*. The original division of the subject no more produces the specific form that social antagonisms take than the latter determine the original *Spaltung* through which the unconscious is constituted (99).

Now, in one sense, Zerilli is, of course, absolutely right. If the socio-political field consists, grosso modo, in what the Lacanians call the symbolic order, it is clear that there can be many different symbolic orders with their own principles of structuration (what we have called hegemonic formations) which have to be studied in their specificity without trying to derive their features from a priori given psychoanalytic categories. If the latter are going to be fruitful for social analysis they have necessarily to enter into an intertextuality with other discourses coming from different fields and traditions. It is this intertextual effort that is absent from Žižek's analysis. He does not make political analysis but simply illustrates psychoanalytic categories with political examples. We would look in vain for a theory of politics in Žižek's work.[11] The most we have in Žižek's work is the *ad hoc* introduction, from time to time, as a *Deus ex machina*, of some very primitive Marxist categories – the 'fundamental class antagonism, etc.'.

I cannot, however, go all the way with Zerilli for the following reason. I think that if she has underlined so much the centrality of the alternative internal/external in her discussion of antagonism, it is because it has to do, in her mind, with another distinction which is crucial for her argument: that between what she calls the *psychic* and the *social*. But if the matter is presented in those terms psychoanalysis is simply a *regional* discipline, dealing with the *individual* mind. Now, I strongly disagree with that view. First, I do not think that psychoanalysis deals with something specifically individual as opposed to 'the social'. At the beginning of *Group Psychology* Freud insists that psychoanalysis is a social discipline, if for no other reason, because all its main categories depend on a social institution which is the family. The whole distinction individual/society which is presupposed by the one between the psychic and the social is for me very suspicious. Now, if this distinction is questioned the whole question of the alternative internal/external in relation to antagonisms loses much of its relevance. In the passage from my work that Zerilli quotes, when I spoke about denial of identity originating from outside and not from inside identity, I was not speaking about the *Spaltung* of the subject before subjectivation, but about the clash between two social forces – i.e. about subjects having achieved, through identification, a symbolic inscription, and the exteriority referred to the impossibility of establishing, within the symbolic order, a stable articulation of their differences.

In the second place, I do not think that the status of psychoanalytic categories is regional (ontic) but ontological. I have argued elsewhere that any change in knowledge involves two moments: on the one hand, a new region of objects becomes available to scientific enquiry; on the other, philosophical reflection develops the ontological implications of this widening of horizons by transforming the new terrain into a new paradigm of objectivity. Let us think, for instance, about what Platonic philosophy did with the ontological possibilities opened by Greek mathematics. In the same way, I think that the psychoanalytic discovery of the unconscious is one of these epoch-making events whose ontological dimensions we are only starting to glimpse. So I do not think that the *object petit a* or the subject of lack are ontic categories limited to a particular region of human reality. When one realizes their full ontological implications they transform *any* field, the political field included. So slightly changing the formulation of Zerilli's argument I think the latter is perfectly legitimate as far as it is seen as a warning about not simplifying the tasks of theoretical reformulation. It is one thing to deconstruct the discourse of political theory by showing how its categories have to be recast once psychoanalytic theory becomes the main form of apprehension of human reality; another – and this is my optimistic reading of what Zerilli is warning us against – would be to conceive this incorporation of psychoanalysis as an exercise of *recognition* by which we think that nothing more is needed once we can identify the psychoanalytic category to which some social event can be ascribed. To do the latter would be the same as to think that because we can recognize the presence of an Indoeuropean abstract paradigm of verbal construction in French, Spanish, and Italian, we are exempted from describing the actual functioning of verbs in those three languages.

Let me, finally, deal with the criticisms of Jelica Šumič, which are clearly inspired by the work of her mentor, Alain Badiou. I have dealt in another work with Badiou's theoretical approach (Laclau 2004) so I will not go back to it and will instead concentrate on the way it is recast in Šumič's criticisms. The main points are the following:

1 Although Šumič has correctly stressed the importance of empty signifiers for my theoretical approach to hegemony, I think she misreads what is involved in that category, at least in the way I conceive of it. According to her, the hegemonic operation would depend for me on the remainders of signifieds which are the residue of the operation of emptying. Now, what I am saying is exactly the opposite: that the division signifier/signified conceived in terms of substance is a residue of essentialism in Saussurean theory which is incompatible with the principle of form as postulated by structural linguistics; that, as a result, there are *only* signifiers – i.e. any change has to be conceived as a displacement in the relation between signifiers and does not pass through any remainder of conceptual *substance* (I have made my main argument and given the example of Freud's Rat Man in another work, Laclau 2000a: 68–71); that by materiality of the signifier I understand a purely formal and relational principle devoid of any substantial determination – on the contrary, Šumič's view of the materiality of the signifier as essentially attached to the phonic substance cannot avoid dealing, at some stage or the other, with the conceptual substance conceived as a signified; finally, that there is nothing more alien to my view of hegemony than conceiving of the hegemonic operation as being anchored in a conceptual substance which persists – though partially deformed – through its various signifying articulations.
2 The reason for this misreading is that, as clearly results from her text, Šumič wants to present my vision of hegemonic logics as incompatible with the Badiouian notion of the event as a cut without any continuity with the situation preceding it. In order to do so it is obviously necessary to present

the 'situation' as a totality without *visible* holes and the event as something essentially not representable within that self-contained totality.

This is perfectly visible in the way Šumič describes the situation: for her 'dislocation' is not visible within the situation and becomes apparently only retroactively; it is only an event incommensurable with the situation which is a possible source of dislocation. 'Dislocation is what is unsituable from any stable assignation of place; it thereby calls into question the prevailing distributive regime of places and functions as a whole' (186). With this kind of logic one should conclude that Hitler invented the crisis of the Weimar Republic; the Jacobins invented the crisis of the Ancien Regime; and St Paul invented the crisis of paganism. It simply does not make sense to think that every situation is a successful and fully fledged distributive regime of places until it is interrupted, out of the blue, by something entirely strange to it. The point is that dislocation and the 'event' capable of suturing it have to be conceptually distinguished. There is still a radical discontinuity between the event and the situation preceding it because we cannot *deduce* the nature of the event from the situation preceding it; but without a previous dislocation in the situation there could not be an event either (at least not a successful one).

3 I am far more happy with the way Šumič describes the relation between hegemony and deconstruction and the way in which, at some crucial points, spectrality and hegemony diverge from each other. I want however to discuss, in this connection, what I see as the most thought-provoking aspect of her piece: what she calls the two functions of the empty signifier. The first is the function of master signifier and presents few problems. It is here that she sees the possible area of confluence between hegemony and deconstruction. The second is a more complex one and there Šumič sees the ground for a de-totalizing function from which a discourse linking hegemony and emancipation could emerge. In her words:

> This particular thus transformed [by filling the void of the absent universal] represents that dimension which de-particularizes all particularities, transcends the horizon of the particularities by making their differences indifferent. [...] On this account, such a signifier signals that the universal comes to exist as a 'universal singular', peculiar to but unlimited by the contents of the situation in which it takes effect, thus allowing the singular universal to escape its specification exclusively in terms of a given situation through a kind of subtraction from the particularities of that situation. Only as such, i.e. deprived of an established place, the singular universal can then be open, non-exclusionary, i.e. 'offered to all' (194).

I think there is something in this argument, but also that the case is overdrawn. It is undoubtedly true that some signifiers come to represent, although only for fleeting moments, something open and 'offered to all'. I have seen several times, after the fall of an oppressive regime, the most disparate social and political movements entering a process of mobilization, living for a short period in the illusion that, because an oppressive regime had fallen, what had actually fallen was oppression as such. And I also agree with Šumič that that 'expansive' dimension, although not totally separated from the function of providing a master signifier, should be analytically separated in the consideration of emptiness. But I cannot follow her in the idea of an absolute subtraction from all particularities of the situation (a notion thinkable in a Badiouian perspective but not in mine) or in what she calls the two dislocations of the universal. There is not, on the one hand, a purely empty signifier and, on the other, an incorporated one. The two of them are exactly the same. And this not because there are always remainders of signifieds, as Šumič says, but because the empty signifier, in spite of being empty, is still part of a system of signification: it signifies the void of the structure, the limits of a signifying system, which is always a concrete one. No operation of radical subtraction is possible here. As the Arab proverb says: nobody can jump outside his own shadow. In order to find what she is searching for Šumič should abandon the notion of empty signifier and the field of signifying practices altogether and move to an entirely different theoretical paradigm – set theory, for instance.

4 I can go briefly through the rest of Šumič's questions. Concerning the notion of 'fidelity' she should put the question to Badiou rather than to myself because fidelity is a category of his theoretical system, not mine. Concerning hegemonic relations being a neutral descriptive expression not necessarily linked to an emancipatory politics, I have already dealt with this point in my reply to Critchley. As for emancipation – in the singular – it should be clear that for me there is nothing corresponding to it but only emancipations – in the plural. This does not necessarily mean political gradualism; a series of social and political demands can overdetermine themselves – condense themselves – in a point of revolutionary rupture, but even those ruptures do not amount to an emancipation conceived as the advent of a transparent society. Šumič, being a Lacanian, I am sure will not find this last assertion entirely unfamiliar.

On the workings of hegemonic logics

Let us finally move to those essays concerning the workings of hegemonic logics – i.e. what is specific to the construction of the political. Urs Stäheli, in his essay, tackles a central issue in the theory of hegemony: the construction of limits – an issue which has also been crucial in my recent reflection. The conclusions at which I have arrived are remarkably similar to those of Stäheli. Let me start by summarizing how my view on this matter has evolved.

In *Hegemony and Socialist Strategy* the notion of limit is more or less synonymous with antagonistic frontier. Objectivity is only constituted through a radical exclusion. Later on I came to realize that this assimilation presented two flaws. The first, that antagonism is *already* a form of discursive inscription – i.e. of mastery – of something more primary which, from *New Reflections on the Revolution of our Time* onwards, I started calling 'dislocation'. Not all dislocation needs to be constructed in an antagonistic way. The second flaw is that antagonism is not equivalent to radical exclusion. What it does is to dichotomize the social space, but *both* sides of the antagonistic relation are necessary in order to create a single space of representation. That is why dialectical contradictions can hardly be seen as showing the limits of objectivity. This new step, however, is not the final one. For although with dislocation we have moved from the total representation inherent in the antagonistic relation to a general crisis of the space of representation, there are other types of exclusion which do not involve such a crisis and which, however, cannot be assimilated to the inclusive exclusion of antagonism either. For instance: the ambition of Hegel's *Philosophy of History* is to draw a picture in which all essential connections in human development are fully represented, and yet this representability is not total. It has to exclude something which Hegel calls the 'peoples without history'. In the same way, Marx's ambition of drawing a 'total history' unified by the development of the productive forces has to exclude from itself the *Lumpenproletariat*, which has no history and exists in the interstices of all social formations. If compared to this kind of radical non-representability, both dislocation and antagonism can be seen as successive stages in the access to full representation. In the distinction discussed by Stäheli at the beginning of his essay between those who are entitled to the benefits of the welfare state and those who are not, the crucial question is to determine the status of the distinction as such: is the distinction *internal* to the space of representation, or is the latter constituted on the basis of excluding from representation the second pole of the distinction? The way I see matters at the moment is that the limits of a discursive formation are not homogeneous but are constituted by the unstable articulation of the three dimensions that I have described and the moving of one into the other. This, of course, means that dislocation is inherent in any hegemonic formation.

I leave aside Stäheli's criticisms of Foucault because my view entirely coincides with his. What I think is especially valid in his essay is his rapprochement between various theoretical moments of discourse theory and of Luhmann's system theory. From what I have said earlier it should become clear that I am in full agreement with his thesis that the notions of limit and of antagonistic limit do not overlap. As he has pointed out very well, the specificity of antagonisms is the crucial point in elaborating a theory of the Political:

> Since there are no natural antagonisms, it is the very construction of antagonism which becomes the potential site of the Political. Instead of presupposing that there is a pre-'existing' antagonism, which has to be analyzed, it becomes necessary to show the discursive strategies constructing a particular antagonism (239).

The distinction between 'marked' and 'unmarked' roughly coincides with the distinction I have established between space of representation and the unrepresented; on the basis of that distinction I can only accept that the *Negativkorrelat* does not necessarily imply an antagonistic relation; finally, I also see the need to separate the idea of a constitutive outside from that of antagonism. The way in which he sees the difference between the Luhmannian approach and mine about the possibility/impossibility of a proper marking ('in contrast to Luhmann, this necessity of unmarking always already implies the impossibility of a proper marking. The mark is always already dislocated' (237)) I also find particularly convincing.

So I think that Stäheli's and my theoretical explorations are moving in a very similar direction. One word of warning: in spite of the homologies that one can detect between systems and discourse theory, one should not lose sight of the fact that they start from different theoretical premises which involve different theoretical requirements. What could be unproblematic to one of them could however create problems of concept-formation to the other. In his n. 5 Stäheli says:

> Such a re-figuring of discourses creates theoretical costs of its own. One might call this the semiotic bias of Laclau's discourse theory. Whereas Foucault is able – at least with the concept of dispositif – to integrate practices of a very different nature, Laclau and Mouffe use the deconstructed model of the sign as their point of departure.

Let me say that the highly formalized logic of the sign to be found in our work has little to do with semiotics (at least in the usual sense of the term) and also that it is overoptimistic to speak about 'integration' in relation to Foucault's overlapping of social practices, but I think it is entirely true that starting from where we start imposes intellectual requirements of a particular kind. But I do not think of those requirements as 'costs'.

Torben Dyrberg, in his intervention, deals extensively with the same subjects treated by Stäheli, namely limits, antagonism, dislocation, equivalence, and difference, although without the reference to Luhmann. So much of what I said in my answer to Stäheli applies also to my answer to Dyrberg. There is, however, one aspect of central importance in Dyrberg's argument which I would like to pick up because it has been at the centre of a great deal of misunderstandings: it is the one related to the notion of 'self-referentiality'. I think that there are several crucial distinctions to be introduced in the process of its conceptual determination. First, and most important, self-reference has to be distinguished from self-determination. The latter, as is well known, is the conceptual content of Hegelian true infinitude. That is, it is the self-constitution of a totality which does not leave anything outside itself. Self-referentiality, however, involves something radically different: self-constitution through naming. I have already said something about naming and what I will add now dovetails with my previous remarks. The difference between a totality which constitutes itself through purely conceptual means (providing this is possible) and one whose constitution entirely proceeds from a name is that the latter includes a possibility that the former axiomatically excludes: that what the name refers to is something which it is not and which acquires a ghostly positive being only through the very process of naming. In that case, self-reference has a performative dimension that is entirely absent from self-determination. In self-determination the totality precedes the moment of its 'for-itself'; in self-reference, the totalization is always retroactive.

This has various capital consequences. First, that the relation between partial moments and totalisation is essentially contingent. Second, that totalization itself becomes essentially contingent and vulnerable (hegemonically constructed, in our terms). Third, that self-referentiality cannot be a ground, because it is essentially contestable and, as a result, the 'self' of self-reference can never be taken for granted. Fourth, it is the tension between 'self' and 'reference' that permanently displaces the locus of their articulation: 'self-reference' becomes an always receding horizon. The autonomy of naming is thus the precondition of any hegemonic approach to politics. I think that all the dimensions discussed by Dyrberg in his essay could be differently illuminated if one starts from making explicit this basic distinction. I think that he has, implicitly, been faithful to it, although in some passages he seems to be dangerously close to some assertions of American system theories.

David Howarth, in his essay, does an excellent job in locating my work within the context of Anglo-American debate, as well as in dispelling the most obvious misreadings of it. I will not touch these aspects and I will not deal either with the whole question of the descriptive and the normative which I have already discussed *in extenso*. I will, instead, concentrate on Howarth's criticisms.

The first and main criticism is that I have concentrated on the ontological dimension of social theory rather than on ontical research. Now, this is a charge to which I plead happily guilty, except that I do not see it as a criticism at all. I have located my theoretical intervention at the theoretical and philosophical level and it is at that level that it has to be judged. Howarth discerns three areas in which my work should be extended to 'middle range' theories that could establish a bridge between the ontological and the ontic, and I wholly agree with Howarth that that bridge should be established, although not necessarily – or not only – by me. Let me briefly go to those three areas. In relation to the concept of articulatory practice, Howarth sustains that stressing their articulatory and discursive character is not enough to explain why people bought 'Free Nelson Mandela' shirts at rock concerts during the 1980s, and that considerations about the South African context have to be introduced to explain that particular practice. With this I can only concur, but it has to be done by a South Africanist, not by somebody working in the field of social ontology. The same applies to the distinction between 'elements' and 'moments', although here Howarth thinks to detect a conceptual hesitation which is, of course, *conceptually* relevant. As for the third area, Howarth thinks that there is an *ontological* theoretical imprecision concerning the relation between 'nodal point' and 'empty signifier'. Are they synonymous, the latter being a refinement of the former, or do they refer to different dimensions of social reality? To this I can answer without hesitation. They have exactly the same referent and the distinction is that 'nodal points' makes allusion to the articulating function, while its empty character points in the direction of its universal signification. This is the distinction that Jelica Šumič had in mind and on the basis of which she attempted – wrongly, in my view – to establish a drastic chasm between both. Finally, I disagree with Howarth that these alleged shortcomings of my approach at the ontic level (and the shortcomings that he indicates are not all ontical), result 'in a significant under-theorization of "hegemony as form"' (269). I think, on the contrary, that hegemony as form – that is, as an ontological category – is perfectly theorized in my work. All that Howarth can do to prove his case is to quote types of hegemony (liberal democratic, authoritarian, authoritarian populist, totalitarian, etc.). It is true that I have not provided such a typology, and that a more empirically oriented theoretician than myself could elaborate it, but this does not show in the least that hegemony as form is theoretically undeveloped.

Let me go to some of the other criticisms from Howarth. I have never posited 'an unconditional subjectivity that is literally able to "create" meaningful structures' (264). Howarth should know that such reintroduction of an unconditional subjectivity could only be tantamount to reintroducing the transcendental subject, something that militates against the very foundations of my theoretical approach. Howarth recognizes – quoting from a text of mine of 1996 – that the subject is partially determined by its structural position. This is true, but let me add that I did not wait until 1996 to know that: it is the main leitmotiv of *New Reflections* of 1990 and is a conviction which has accompanied my whole intellectual trajectory. For that reason, I cannot accept either Howarth's distinction between decisions taken *within* a structure and those taken *about* the structure. All decision is taken within a certain structural context. In order to be valid the distinction would have to schizophrenically put together an existentialist notion of freedom and a structuralist notion of determination ('the structures speak through me').

As for the question of whether 'hegemony' is a category which belongs to the general theory of society – i.e. that it functions as some kind of 'social a priori' – or, on the contrary, describes a specifically modern articulation of the political, let me say the following. Any society constitutes its own 'transcendental' framework out of a particular experience which, in spite of its particularity, illuminates general aspects of social functioning which cannot be reduced to the temporality of that experience. Marx asserts in the *Grundrisse* that the notion of labour in general, beyond all particular forms, could only emerge in capitalist society, when the circulation of unskilled labour force between different branches of production, makes possible the notion of *abstract labour*. Once this notion acquires currency in various forms of economic calculation, it can be projected into the past and questions such as, for instance, how *labour* (without qualification) was distributed in ancient or medieval societies, can be posed. These questions could not have been formulated in those terms in antiquity or the Middle Ages, because the notion of abstract labour, as unspecified use of labour power, had not emerged; but once it *did* emerge, there is no reason why its range of operation should be restricted to those societies which made possible the initial emergence of the categories. And let us be clear: there is no anachronism in this projection. I am not saying that abstract labour was always a sociological – albeit not recognized – reality; what I am saying is that only in societies in which abstract labour becomes a sociological reality does the category of labour as such, without qualifications, become thinkable and can, in that sense, function as a transcendental horizon. Otherwise we would have to establish a strict overlapping between terrains of emergence and terrains of application of social categories, and this would beg the whole question because, obviously, we cannot discriminate between different and successive temporal terrains without some kind of metahistorical theory establishing the basis and limits of historical periodicity. The same happens with 'hegemony': it could only have emerged out of the historical terrain of modernity, but its theoretical projections transcend by far those temporal boundaries.

Finally, let me say that I have never established an 'analogy' between language and society, so I do not think it is really a pertinent question such as '*how far* we can extend Laclau's resultant analogy between language and society' (265–6). What I have said, which is entirely different, is that social practices – language included – are structured by logics of equivalence and difference; that the discursive model is not a linguistic one which should be opposed to a certain 'social' constituted through a different paradigm; and that the task of any 'middle ranging theorization' which starts from a discursive ontology has, as a main task, to redescribe the ontical level in terms of the distinctions brought about by that ontology. Howarth himself, quite correctly, distinguishes between a political theorist interested in describing and classifying different types of political institution and a political ontologist putting into question the very concept of political institution. Now, what would be the use of the second task if it could not transmit its effects to the first? Howarth himself has got involved in this task in, for instance, his excellent studies on the black movement in South Africa.

Howarth raises a last important issue concerning the relationship between what he calls the ontological dimension of dislocation, which would be akin to Heidegger's *Geworfenheit* (being thrown into the world of signification) and the historicist one, 'more like an "event of Being" in which the contingency of this world is disclosed, and other options and choices become possible' (268). My answer is that this double dimension is very much present and that between both of them there is a close interconnection. It is precisely because 'thrownness' is an irreducible ontological condition that contingency shows itself, and that something such as an 'event of Being' becomes possible. In Lacanian terms: it is the lack in the Other involved in *separation* that makes possible the emergence of the subject as the overlapping of two lacks and prepares the way to the further separation involved in the *traversée du phantasme* which is at the root of freedom (*Wo Es war, soll Ich werden*). Or, in Kantian terms: there is more than pathological determination because, even if I surrender to my inclinations, I cannot do so without *me* incorporating them into my maxim. This is a decisive point on which I have very much insisted in my work: thrownness does not only show what there is, the givenness of a situation, but also the constitutive *fractures* of that givenness. We can refer to these fractures – or dislocations – as the *traces* of contingency within the necessary. It is because these traces are not something 'added' but are constitutive of thrownness as such that an 'event of Being' is at all possible.

Conclusions: sketching a possible agenda

I hope that I have answered all the main critical points raised by the various contributors to this volume. I would like to close this essay by sketching, in a more orderly fashion, the succession of those themes which have punctuated my various replies.

There is a first theoretical option where one finds, in my view, the basic watershed in contemporary philosophy: either negativity (a non-dialectical negativity, of course) is seen as constitutive and grounding, or it is seen as the 'superstructural' effect of a deeper movement to be conceived in terms of pure immanence. If this second approach is adopted, history and society have to be seen as dominated by objectivity and necessity. In that view, which has been the dominant one in the Western tradition in a genealogy leading from John Scotus Eriugena to Hegel, passing through moments such as Northern mysticism, Nicholas Cusanus, and Spinoza, negativity is mere appearance and there is no place for a theory of the subject. The latter is only possible within the first approach, centred as it is in the notion of contingency (not conceived as mere accidentality but as the attribute of an entity whose essence does not involve its existence). Dialectics is, from this viewpoint, essentially objectivist and reductive, as it subsumes any negative moment under an underlying movement that both explains and supersedes it – think, for instance, about Hegel's cunning of reason. We can find in contemporary thought several attempts at grasping a negativity which is not dialectical for, far from being subsumable under a deeper objectivity, it is the point where *all* objectivity finds its absolute limit. Let us think, as an example, about the Lacanian notions of the real and of the subject as the subject of lack. It is within this radically anti-objectivist tradition of thought that my intellectual and political project is located.

After this first theoretical option some other options have to be taken – they are, strictly speaking, new options, because they do not logically flow from the original one. What these new options are that I am talking about can be better understood if one compares my theoretical approach to that of Alain Badiou, who shares with me some assumptions. Giving the grounding role that I attribute to negativity I cannot, obviously, assert the unicity of Being. This is also (although for different reasons) the starting point of Badiou: the One is not. But – this is his option – in that case what is is, for him, the multiple. This is the basis for his mathematical approach to ontology and for the grounding ontological role that he attributes to set theory.

For me the starting point – once accepted that what is is not the One – is not multiplicity but *failed unicity*. This means that the ontological task for me is different than for Badiou: it consists in finding in every identity the traces of its contingency – i.e. the presence (in a way to be specified) of something different from itself. This means that while the notion of relation does not play any role in Badiou's ontology – he is even very critical of it – it is absolutely central in my theoretical approach. We are dealing, however, with a peculiar type of relation, one whose defining features are: 1) that the identities do not pre-exist the relations but result from them – i.e. they are strictly differential; 2) that if these identities are, on the one hand, differential, and on the other contingent, this contingency has to be reflected in the identities themselves as something undermining them, and this undermining can only be the subversion of the principle of differentiality. It is easy to see how one can move from here to the logic of equivalence and to the notion of empty signifier, which I have discussed at length in this essay. The two questions that I want to raise at this point are, however, the following: first, how do relations between objects have to be for this complex dialectic between differentiality and contingency to be possible? This is, strictly speaking, a transcendental question. The second is: is there a discipline postulating a type of relation between its defining elements which could provide the basic ontology required to answer the first question? The answer is that this discipline exists and it is linguistics. This thesis has, however, to be accompanied by two complementary ones, without which it would be entirely meaningless. The first is that obviously I am not saying that language considered as substance (speech and writing) determines social life but – and this is an entirely different assertion – that the relations between elements that linguistic analysis explores (combinations and substitutions) are not regional ones but, on the contrary, the most universal relations that a fundamental ontology has to unveil. As I have argued earlier on, the formalization of linguistic categories which takes place in the Copenhagen and Prague schools – which does away with the remainders of Saussurean substantialism – makes it possible to extract from the linguistic categories their true ontological potential.

But a second complementary thesis is necessary at this point. I have argued in my work that the totalization of a differential system (what I have called the 'One') is a logical need of that system, without which no difference could become actual. Such a totalization, however – even at the logical level – is impossible. This is the moment of failed unicity to which I referred earlier. Thus, the problem is how an object which is both necessary and impossible can be socially produced. The first step in solving it is, as we know, that a particular difference within the system assumes the representation of a totality with which it is incommensurable. This is the hegemonic link. But this link presupposes a displacement in signification which is tropological in nature. This is what gives rhetoric its central role in the structuration of any signifying totality. If the social is synonymous with its discursive production, the discursive itself is structured by rhetorical movements. 'Rhetoric' is inherent to 'grammar' and 'logic' and not a different discipline, as in the classical trivium. It has a true ontological import.

But this is not enough. A second step needs to be taken. For what rhetoric can explain is the *form* that an overdetermining investment takes, but not the *force* that explains the investment as such and its perdurability. Here something else has to be brought into the picture. Any overdetermination requires not only metaphorical condensations but also cathectic investments. That is, something belonging to the order of *affect* has a primary role in discursively constructing the social. Freud already knew it: the social link is a libidinal link. And affect, as I pointed out earlier in this essay, is not something *added* to signification, but something consubstantial with it. So if I see rhetoric as ontologically primary in explaining the operations inhering in and the forms taken by the hegemonic construction of society, I see psychoanalysis as the only valid road to explain the drives behind such construction – I see it, indeed, as the most fruitful approach to the understanding of human reality.

This libidinal dimension is crucial in keeping society together, as well as in explaining the moments of its radical disruption. To just go back to one previous example: in discussing democracy I referred to two dimensions which, from a logical point of view, cannot easily be articulated. I also made allusion, as a possible terrain of articulation, to some kind of pragmatic balance or combination between them. However, if we consider social links as libidinal links, we have a far more precise and powerful explanation of how that balance/combination operates. Balance and combination would not just be the names of circumstantial operations where the intervening forces retain their separate identities, but rather the names of the points of symbolic identification where those separate forces supersede their unstable balance and make of that identification point the name of a higher unity. No *conceptual* transition is involved here – there is nothing Hegelian in it. But something of the order of hegemony and rhetoric takes place which could not be explained without the mediating role of affect. Rhetoric, psychoanalysis, and politics (conceived as hegemony): in this triad I see the future of social and political thought.

Notes

1 See *HSS*, ch. 3; and the various pieces of my *Emancipation(s)*.

2 Gasché is critical of my assertion that today we are at the end of philosophy and at the beginning of politics, pointing out that a deconstructed philosophy still has a theoretical content and thus continues to be philosophy. My assertion, which clearly alluded to Heidegger's 'The end of philosophy and the task of thinking', only referred to philosophy as the tradition of Western thought grounded in the metaphysics of presence. Today, however, given all the confused and confusing dispute about the opposition between philosophy and anti-philosophy I tend to be more cautious in my expression and so I am closer to the spirit of Gasché's remark.

3 See 'Power and representation', in *E* 84–105.

4 I have discussed this issue in Laclau 2000a.

5 See the discussion of this point in Fink 1995: 21–2.

6 The internal necessary connection between *jouissance* and radical investment was pointed out to me, in the first place, by Ewa Plonowska Ziarek.

7 Once again, the role of affect in the widening of this relational logic is crucial. I refer, in this respect, to the current work of my colleague Joan Copjec.

8 Hillis Miller disagrees with my interpretation of this essay, but he does not elaborate enough the reasons for his disagreement to make possible a reply. I cannot follow him, however, in his assertion that de Man had some kind of fully fledged political position. I simply fail to see where such political views are expressed. The essay on Rousseau, quoted by Hillis Miller, can hardly be conceived as the expression of a comprehensive view of Politics – let alone a political position.

9 See, on this subject, Normand 1976.

10 See, for instance:

> with the rise of the anti-globalisation movement, the era of the multitude of particular struggles that one should strive to link in a 'chain of equivalences' is over. This struggle (the only serious opposition movement today) – whatever one's critical apprehensions towards it – is clearly focused on capitalism as a global system, and perceives all other struggles (for democracy, ecology, feminism, anti-racism, and so on) as subordinate (2003: 135).

What does not even cross Žižek's mind is the fact that, in a globalized world, capitalism creates throughout a multitude of antagonisms and points of rupture and that the very possibility of an anti-capitalist struggle depends on making them equivalent. Moreover, if Žižek had devoted five minutes of his time to learning what the anti-globalization movement is about instead of pontificating about it, he would have known better. In the various meetings of the Porto Alegre Forum you find a multitude of groups from all over the world speaking about their particular experiences and trying, however, to elaborate a common discourse opposing globalization.

11 Not even, in actual fact, for a coherent argument. He recently wrote: 'Whatever one wants to do with Lacanian theory, there is no way that one can claim that "radical democracy" is its direct implication' (2003: 134). However, in his blurb to the book of Yannis Stavrakakis (1999), written not so long before, he asserts: '*Lacan and the Political* demonstrates that Lacanian psychoanalysis does have precise political consequences: it involves a theory of the political which firmly endorses the stance of radical democracy'. And the reader only needs to go through the introduction of *The Sublime Object of Ideology* to see how he tried to link, in a highly intelligent way, the radicalism of democracy and the Lacanian ethics of the Real. The only commentary that his recent writing on politics deserves is that he could have held his breath. First, he reduces democracy to liberal democracy, second, he reduces liberal democracy to mere proceduralism and when he has constructed that straw-man in which not even a diehard liberal would recognize him/herself, he opposes to it full revolutionary action. It is more or less the case of the village priest referred to by Ortega y Gasset, who in his sermons imagined a stupid Manichean to be able to more easily refute Manicheanism. But not even then is Žižek's task plain sailing, because as he refuses to accept the aims of all contestatory movements in the name of a pure anti-capitalist struggle, one is left wondering: who for him are the agents of a historical transformation? Martians, perhaps?

References

Butler, J. (2000) 'Competing universalities', in J. Butler, E. Laclau and S. Žižek (eds) *Contingency, Hegemony, Universality: Contemporary Dialogues on the Left*, London and New York: Verso.

de Man, P. (1996) 'Pascal's allegory of persuasion', in *Aesthetic Ideology*, Minneapolis and London: University of Minnesota Press.

Fink, B. (1995) *The Lacanian Subject: Between Language and Jouissance*, Princeton: Princeton University Press.

Glynos, J. (1998) 'Of signifiers, signifieds and remainders of particularity: from signifying dissemination to real fixity' (unpublished manuscript).

Grassi, E. (1980) *Rhetoric as Philosophy: The Humanist Tradition*, Carbondale and Edwardsville, IL: Southern Illinois University Press.

Heidegger, M. (1962) *Being and Time*, San Francisco: Harper.

Husserl, E. (1970) 'The Vienna lecture', in *The Crisis of European Sciences and Transcendental Phenomenology*, Evanston, IL: Northwestern University Press.

Laclau, E. (2000a) 'Identity and hegemony: the role of universality in the constitution of political logics', in J. Butler, E. Laclau and S. Žižek (eds) *Contingency, Hegemony, Universality: Contemporary Dialogues on the Left*, London and New York: Verso.

—— (2000b) 'Constructing universality', in J. Butler, E. Laclau and S. Žižek (eds) *Contingency, Hegemony, Universality. Contemporary Dialogues on the Left*, London: Verso.

—— (2001) 'The politics of rhetoric', in T. Cohen, J. H. Miller, A. Warminski and B. Cohen (eds) *Material Events: Paul de Man and the Afterlife of Theory*, Minnesota: Minnesota University Press.

—— (2004) 'An ethics of militant engagement', in P. Hallward (ed.) *Think Again: Alain Badiou and the Future of Philosophy*.

Normand, C. (1976) *Métaphore et concept*, part 1, Brussels: Editions Complexe.

Parker, P. (1990) 'Metaphor and catachresis', in J. Bender and D. E. Wellbery (eds) *The Ends of Rhetoric*, Stanford, CA: Stanford University Press.

Stavrakakis, Y. (1999) *Lacan and the Political*, London: Routledge.

—— (2004) 'Passions of identification: discourse, enjoyment and European identity', in D. Howarth and J. Torfing (eds) *Discourse Theory and European Politics*, London: Palgrave.

Žižek, S. (1989) *The Sublime Object of Ideology*, London: Verso.

—— (2003) '"What some would call ...": a response to Yannis Stavrakakis', *Umbr(a), a Journal of the Unconscious*, 1(8):131–5.

Appendix I
THE USES OF EQUALITY

Judith Butler and Ernesto Laclau

What's the political value, today, of the use of the signifier 'equality'? Considering the poststructuralist elaboration of 'difference' how does 'equality' work today in gender and/or race politics? 'Difference' has been, for more than a decade, the key word for a certain number of programs related to radical democracy. Certainly, 'difference' has given space to the constitution of new types of social solidarity. Recently, however, some reservations on the extension of the term have been published. Chantal Mouffe – in her introduction to *Dimensions of Radical Democracy* – has stated that 'all differences cannot be accepted' in order 'for pluralism to be made compatible with the struggle against inequality'. Mouffe doesn't clarify, in this particular text, the criteria with which to discriminate between 'acceptable' and 'nonacceptable' (or, maybe, 'pertinent' and 'nonpertinent') differences, nor does she give a nonequivocal definition of 'equality'. Both are tasks that seem crucial for the project of a radical democracy. On his part, Alain Badiou has written that 'aujourd'hui, le concept de liberté n'a pas de valeur immédiate de saisie, parce qu'il est captif du liberalisme, de la doctrine des libertés parlamentaires et commerciales', such that 'le vieux mot de l'égalité est aujourd'hui le meilleur' for 'une politique d'émancipation post-marxiste-léniniste'. Would you agree with Badiou's affirmation? I understand, on my part, that 'equality' has received in radical democratic theory, and in recent gay/lesbian and race theory, a treatment much less detailed than 'freedom' or even 'fraternity' (in the form of the problem of the constitution of counterhegemonic types of community). How do you interpret this fact? What sense can we make of 'equality' in the context of progressive politics today?

[Questions posed by Reinaldo Laddaga]

Dear Ernesto,

Sorry to begin this a day late, but too many interruptions happened yesterday. Ernesto, I'm very pleased to be in touch, and hope all is well there (I tried to call you when I was last in England but got a recording from a business that was trying to sell telephones ... struck me as a telephonic *mise en abyme*).

We are asked to begin a conversation on equality, and on the problem of acceptable and unacceptable differences. I hardly know where to begin, and think that you would probably join me in the sense of unease that follows from being asked to decide what kinds of differences ought to be included in an ideal polity, and what kinds of differences undermine the very possibility of polity, perhaps even the very ideality without which no democratic notion of polity can proceed. I am a bit perplexed as well by the question of whether or not the notion of inclusion and exclusion, which I know has occupied your work for some time now, is strictly correlated to the notion of equality. So perhaps I will start by offering a set of distinctions between 'inclusiveness' and 'equality'. It seems to me that inclusiveness is an ideal, an ideal that is impossible to realize, but whose unrealizability nevertheless governs the way in which a radical democratic project proceeds.

I gather that one of the reasons, or the key reason, why inclusiveness is bound to fail is precisely because the various differences that are to be included within the polity are not given in advance. They are, crucially, in the process of being formulated and elaborated, and there is no way to circumscribe in advance the form that an ideal of inclusiveness would take. This openness or incompleteness that constitutes the ideal of inclusion is precisely an effect of the unrealized status of what is or will be the content of what is to be included. In this sense, then, inclusion as an ideal must be constituted by its own impossibility; indeed, it must be committed to its own impossibility in order to proceed along the path of realization.

Equality is, of course, a strange concept when thought of in relation to this model (a model that I take to be derived from your thinking on this issue, as well as Chantal Mouffe's). Equality would not be the equalization of given differences. That formulation suggests that differences are to be understood as tantamount to specificities or particularities. And the point of a futural re-elaboration of the notion of equality would be to hold out the possibility that we do not yet know who or what might make a claim to equality, where and when the doctrine of equality might apply, and that the field of its operation is neither given nor closed. The volatility of the Equal Protection Clause in the US Constitution gives evidence of this in an interesting way. Is it the case that those who are addressed by 'hate speech' are deprived of their abilities to participate equally in the public sphere? Some feminists, such as Catharine MacKinnon, argue that pornography ought to be opposed because it produces an epistemic atmosphere in which women are not entitled to exercise their rights of equal treatment and participation. Although I oppose MacKinnon's view (and her understanding of the performative operation of representation), I do appreciate the way in which the doctrine of equality becomes a site of contestation within recent US constitutional debates. It suggests that we do not yet know when and where the claim to equality might emerge, and it holds out the possibility for a futural articulation of that doctrine.

So, in one sense, then, it seems that the notion of equality would proceed undemocratically if we claim to know in advance who might make use of its claim, and what kinds of issues fall within its purview. And this relates to the ideal of an impossible inclusiveness: who is included among those who might make the claim to equality? What kinds of issues undermine the very possibility of certain groups making such a claim?

But this then raises a different question, namely, are exclusions always to be overcome, and are there certain kinds of exclusions without which no polity can proceed? How might we enumerate such excluded possibilities? Certainly, some kinds of crimes are and ought to be punishable, excluded from the realm of the acceptable, and certainly there are taboos – foreclosures in the Lacanian sense – without which no subject can function as a subject. The 'inclusion' of all excluded possibilities would lead to psychosis, to a radically unlivable life, and to the destruction of polity as we understand it. So if we accept, as I think we both do, that there is no polity, no sociality, no field of the political, without certain kinds of exclusions having already been made – constitutive exclusions that produce a constitutive outside to any ideal of inclusiveness – that does not mean that we accept all sorts of exclusions as legitimate. It would be unwarranted to conclude that just because some exclusions are inevitable all exclusions are justified. But that then gets us into the tricky territory of the problem of justifying exclusions. And here I am compelled to turn the conversation over to you. ...

Dear Judith,

Thank you, Judith. I largely agree with you. Let me complement your analysis with three remarks. The first concerns the relationship between equality and difference. Not only do I think that these two notions are not incompatible but I would even add that the proliferation of differences is the precondition for the expansion of the logic of equality. To say that two things are equal – i.e. equivalent to each other in some respects – presupposes that they are different from each other in some other respects (otherwise there would be no equality but identity). In the political field equality is a type of discourse which tries to deal with differences; it is a way of organizing them, if you want. To assert, for instance, the right of all national minorities to self-determination is to assert that these minorities are equivalent (or equal) to each other. As a general rule I would say that the more fragmented a social identity is, the less it overlaps with the community as a whole, and the more it will have to negotiate its location within that community in terms of rights (i.e. in terms of a discourse of equality which transcends the group in question). That is why I think that a politics of *pure* particularism is self-defeating. On the other hand I think it is necessary to differentiate those situations in which an anti-egalitarian politics takes place through the imposition of a dominant and uniform canon (this is the situation confronted today by multicultural struggles in the Anglo-Saxon world) from those in which the discrimination takes place by violently asserting differences, as in the idea of 'separate developments' which constituted the core of apartheid. This means that, depending on the circumstances, equality can lead to a reinforcement or the weakening of differences.

My second remark concerns the question of exclusion. I agree with you that the ideal of total equality is unreachable and, also, that a society without any kind of exclusion would be a psychotic universe. What I would like to add is that the need for exclusion is inscribed in the structure of all decision making. As I have tried to show elsewhere, a decision, in order to be a decision, has to be taken in a structurally undecidable terrain – otherwise, if the decision was predetermined by the structure it would not be *my* decision. The precondition of a decision is that actual choice is not algorithmically prefigured. But in that case, if the decision is its own ground, the discarded alternatives have been simply put aside, that is, excluded. If we pass from individual to collective decisions this is even more clear, for the excluded alternative could have been preferred by certain groups of people, and so exclusion shows a dimension of repression which was concealed in the individual decision. I would add that a society without exclusions is impossible for more basic reasons than being an empirically unreachable ideal: it is also logically impossible as far as the social is constructed through decisions taken in an undecidable terrain. We can deal as democratically as possible with exclusion (for instance, through the principle of majority, or through the protection of minorities), but this cannot conceal the fact that politics is, to a large extent, a series of negotiations around the principle of exclusion which is always there as the ineradicable terrain of the social. As usual, *determinatio est negatio*.

This leads me to my third remark. We have been asked for a criterion to determine those differences which are acceptable from those which are not. Now, this can be interpreted in various ways. It could involve, for instance, the request for a strict ethical criterion, independent of any context. If it was so, the only possible answer would be that no such criterion could be given. It could also be a question about social ethics – namely, what differences are compatible with the actual workings of a society? This would be a more pertinent question because it makes possible a historicist answer. The gist of my answer would be to say that the very criterion of what is acceptable or not is the locus of a multiplicity of social struggles and that it is wrong to try to give any kind of decontextualized response. Obviously this is not an answer to the question 'how would you draw the frontier between the acceptable and the not acceptable in Western European societies today?', but it allows us to at least discriminate between pertinent and nonpertinent questions.

Ernesto

Dear Ernesto,

Thanks for your response. I would like to concentrate on the last two points you made, one concerning exclusion and its role in any decision making, and the other, concerning how one might decide what kinds of exclusions must be made for equality to remain an active ideal. I think that these two are linked in an interesting way, and the link is suggested to me by your focus on making 'decisions' in both contexts.

I think that you are right in claiming that no decision can be a decision if it is determined in advance by a structure of some kind. For there to be a decision means that there must be some contingency, which is not the same as saying that there must be radical contingency. I take it that the relative determination of structure is what differentiates a position such as yours from a more existentialist or conventionally liberal individualist view on decision making. Indeed, is it not possible to elaborate a notion of 'context' – invoked in your response to the question of how best to decide what ought and ought not to be included in a polity and the inadmissibility of certain 'differences'? It seems clear that a decontextualized answer to the question of what ought not to be included is impossible, and I think that the effort to elaborate principles that are radically context-free, as some 'proceduralists' seek to do, is simply to embed the context in the principle, and then to rarefy the principle so that its embedded context is no longer legible. And yet, this still leaves us with a quandary, since I would imagine that you find the Derridean questions raised in 'Signature, Event, Context' about the 'illimitability' of contexts to be persuasive, as I do. I think that contexts are in some ways produced by decisions, that is, that there is a certain redoubling of decision making in the situation (the context?) in which one is asked to decide what kinds of differences ought not to be included in a given polity. There is first the decision to mark or delimit the context in which such a decision will be made, and then there is the marking off of certain kinds of differences as inadmissible. The first decision is not itself without a context, but it would be subject to the same infinite regression as the second, since there would be no original or defining context that is not at once delimited by a decision of some kind.

I think it is a mistake to think that we might be able to list 'kinds of differences' that are inadmissible, not only because you and I do not have the power to make such decisions, but because the form of the question misreads both what a decision is, and what we might mean by 'differences'. If there is, as you say, no decision without exclusion, without something being foreclosed, and a set of possibilities being framed, brought into relief through that foreclosure, then exclusion, as you say, makes decision-making possible. So perhaps the question is, what kinds of exclusions make decision-making possible, and is making a 'decision' to be valued in such a way that certain kinds of exclusions ought to remain constitutive exclusions? This reminds me of Nietzsche's question: how does man become an animal capable of making promises? How do any of us become (through a certain kind of constitutive foreclosure) the kinds of beings who can and do make decisions? I don't mean to bypass entirely the question posed to us, about the inadmissibility of certain 'differences', but I continue to have a difficult time reading the question. I wonder whether it is a question of 'differences', understood as particular kinds of identities or group formations, or whether what we want to do is to keep the field of differences at play, in contestation, and that what is referred to under the rubric of 'inadmissible differences' is really something which puts a freeze on the play of differences. I look forward to your further thoughts.

Judith

Dear Judith and Ernesto,

Thank you for your comments. One very brief remark. When I mentioned Mouffe's statement it was not my intention to force you to decide which differences would be acceptable (a demand that would be manifestly nonpertinent) but to point to a certain indetermination – an indetermination that could even be considered desirable – in the uses of 'equality' in the context of radical democratic theory. I would prefer my question to be read in this sense: how to freeze the play of differences – to use Judith's terms – and still maintain 'equality' as an 'active ideal'. How do we conceive a political identity which doesn't put a freeze on (which doesn't homogenize) the play of differences internal to itself? And, finally, do we have (and, more fundamentally, do we need) a definition of 'equality' that is not 'conventionally liberal'? You have already begun to answer these questions, I think ...

[Intervention by Reinaldo Laddaga]

Dear Judith,

Let me first answer some of the points raised by Reinaldo Laddaga in his last message, which can serve as an introduction to my reactions to your comments. First, I think that the play of differences is *at the same time* an opening and a freezing of that play. I say this, because I do not think that something such as an unrestricted play of differences can be maintained, not even as an active ideal. I can only open up the terrain of some historical possibilities by closing others. This is equivalent to saying that it is politics, rather than the notion of uncontaminated presence, that organizes social relations. On the other hand, I do not understand what a 'play of differences "internal" to itself' could be. If identity means difference, then the idea of a 'play of differences' internal to difference is something I do not fully grasp. Instead, I think that the play of differences subverts any rigid frontier between the internal and the external. This leads me to a terrain within which I approach the last two questions from Reinaldo. I would locate the notion of equality – from the point of view of the latter's constitutive structuration – within the field of what I have called the 'logic of equivalence'; that is, a process by which the differential nature of all identity is at the same time asserted and subverted. Now, a chain of equivalences is by its very definition constitutively open; there is no way of establishing its boundaries in a decontextualized universe. (Trying to do the latter would be, quoting Quine, something like asking how many points in Ohio are starting points.) Politics is, in this respect, a double operation of breaking and extending chains of equivalence. Any determinate political process in a concrete context is, precisely, an attempt to partially extend equivalences and to partially limit their indefinite expansion. I see liberalism as an attempt to fix the meaning of equality within definite parameters (individualism, and the rigid distinction between public/private, etc.) which are historically limited and in many respects superseded – and not always in a progressive direction – by the experience of contemporary politics. How to deconstruct the basic liberal distinctions while keeping a democratic potential is, as I see it, the task of radical democratic politics.

I come now, Judith, to your reactions to my comments. I am glad to find that we are in agreement on most issues. Let us make, at the start, a point of clarification. I certainly agree with you that 'radical contingency' is an unacceptable notion if we understand by it some kind of abyss which creates a total lack of structuration. What we are speaking of as the course of contingency is, rather, a *failed* structuration. Thus, contingency – if it is properly contextualized – should be reinscribed within the most primary field of the distinction necessary (*contextual* necessity, of course, not logical or causal necessity)/contingent. However, having constructed contingency in this way, I would still say that it is radical in the sense that *within the limits of a partially destructured context* it can only appeal to itself as its own source. Would you buy this?

This leads me to the important issues that you raise, starting with your critique of 'proceduralism' – a critique which I subscribe to. I think that the questions that Derrida poses in 'Signature, Event, Context' (1988) need to be answered and to be very attentive to the double dimension that they open. On the one hand, he is saying that it is not possible to, strictly speaking, attribute closed boundaries to a context. However, as his is not an argument for a return to a Platonic, decontextualized meaning, the very impossibility of delimiting contexts is all we are left with. They have to be defined by their limits, and yet these limits are impossible. Everything here turns around this evanescent object, the 'limit', which is something like the presence of an absence. Or, to put it in Kantian terms, an object which shows itself through the impossibility of an adequate representation. Now, my own view is that if this limit is impossible but also *necessary* – something like Lacan's '*objet petit a*' – it will have to, one way or the other, enter into the field of representation. But as it is necessary yet also *impossible* its representation will be constitutively inadequate. A particular difference *within* the limits will always have to assume the role of limit and, in this way, to fix (to close within itself) a transient context. This relation of fixity/unfixity by which an 'ontic' content assumes the 'ontological' function of constituting a transient context is, as you know, what I call a hegemonic relation. As you see, it involves the Derridean critique of boundaries, but it attempts to prolong it with a notion of the dialectic between impossibility/necessity which makes possible the construction of hegemonic contexts.

This gives me a starting point to begin some sort of response to the questions involved in our exchange. What differences are acceptable or nonacceptable? We both agree that the question cannot be answered outside any context and, also, that the notion of context is far from being an unproblematic one. If contexts, however, are constituted the way I suggest, you have various advantages: (1) you can make compatible the ultimate instability of limits with actual limitations; (2) you have certain rules to decide what will count as a valid inclusion or exclusion, it will depend on the actual hegemonic configuration of a certain community; (3) this hegemonic configuration is not a simple datum but the result of the transient articulation between concrete content and universalization of the community through the construction of a limit which has no necessary link to that content; that hegemonic configuration is always open to contestation and change. In this way we can reach a more democratic view than in the case in which the hegemonic configuration depended on a noncontingent link between context-limiting/constitution function and actual content playing that role of limit; (4) finally, the unevenness that hegemonic games introduce within differential social identities allows us to solve some of the aporias connected to the 'play of differences', and allows us to approach the logic through which those differences are constituted in our actual political world. I wait for your reaction.

Best, Ernesto

Dear Ernesto,

There is much in your last text to think about, and I hope to be able to probe some of the questions raised in what follows.

I very much agree with your formulation of the logic of equivalence, namely, as a 'process by which the differential nature of all identity is at the same time asserted and subverted'. And I wonder whether thinking about equivalence does not significantly alter the kinds of quandaries brought up by the question of equality. It always seemed to me that you and Chantal Mouffe were trying to underscore a structural openness (and, hence, a 'poststructuralism') in the problem of identity that would at once honor the place of identity in contemporary political formations and yet dishonor its foundational or 'ontological' claim. I gather that the point about contingency that you raise in the subsequent paragraph speaks to the question of identity and equivalence as well: to the extent that all identities fail to be fully structured, they are each equally (although not substantively or 'ontically') formed through the same constitutive failure. This 'sameness' is interesting since it is not to be rigorously understood in terms of a given 'content' of identity. On the contrary, it is what guarantees the failure of any given 'content' to successfully lay claim to the status of the ontological or what I call the 'foundational'. I understand that you seek recourse to Lacan to explain this lack or failure, and that is probably where I would differ with you, a difference in emphasis, since I think that the failure of any subject formation is an effect of its iterability, its having to be formed in time, again and again. One might say, via Althusser, that the ritual through which subjects are formed is always subject to a rerouting or a lapse by virtue of this necessity to repeat and reinstall itself.

But I do wonder whether failure, for both of us, does not become a kind of universal condition (and limit) of subject formation; a way in which we still seek to assert a common condition which assumes a transcendental status in relation to particular differences. To the extent that, no matter what our 'difference', we are always only *partially* constituted as ourselves (and this, as a result of our being constituted within a field of differentiations), and to what extent are we also bound together through this 'failure'? How does the limitation on subject constitution become, oddly, a new source of community or collectivity or a presumed condition of universality? I would like to know more about how a contextual necessity is established. Is there a background or context that forms the tenuous yet necessary horizon of what we call 'context'? Would the context that is also partially destructured, that does not yet fully assume the status of the ontological, also have a necessity that, strictly speaking, isn't a logical or causal necessity, but perhaps a historical necessity of some kind? Is it a spatialized historical necessity (Benjamin thought that post-teleology history would have to be read in a landscape)? And what are the conditions under which such a necessity becomes readable to us as such?

I gather that, in your notion of democratic hegemony, there will always be a radical incommensurability between content and universalization, but that the two will also always engender one another in some way. The democratic task would be to keep any given universalization of content from becoming a final one, that is, from shutting down the temporal horizon, the futural horizon of universalization itself. If I understand this correctly, then I agree with it wholeheartedly.

I wonder, then, whether we might conclude our conversation by turning to the question of the 'Americas', a term that figures in the rubric under which our conversation takes place. I ask it because it is so interesting to see, for instance, in 'American Studies', as it takes place in the United States, how the borders of the Americas are drawn. It is often the case that the borders become synonymous with the United States, at which point the border of the epistemological object, 'Americas', encodes and dissimulates a history of colonialism. Or when it is restricted to the continent of North America, excluding South America and the islands in between, there are certain stories one cannot tell about trade, slavery, and colonial expansion. What becomes interesting is how we might think about equality under this rubric, where the 'subject' at hand is not exactly an identity, but a political imaginary, where the very boundaries of what is meant by a pluralized 'Americas' remain importantly uncertain. Clearly the question of equality or, indeed, of equivalence, cannot be asked of an entity, 'the Americas', if the very delimitation of that phenomenon remains to be known. Or is there a way of posing the question of equality without claiming to know, in advance, in what this phenomenon consists? Or even more importantly, is there a way of posing the question of equality that opens up the question of what the 'Americas' are, what they are to become? How does one press the futural possibility wihin the ontic articulation in order to ward off its foreclosure as the ontological?

Best, Judith

Dear Judith,

The problems that you raise in your last text would, indeed, require more thought and space than the limits of this exchange allow me to give. Let me, however, address some of your basic points.

1. You say, concerning my notion of democratic hegemony, that if you understand it correctly, then you agree with it wholeheartedly. As a matter of fact, you have perfectly understood it, so there is no quarrel between us about this central point of my argument.

2. On our difference of emphasis concerning the failure of any given content to lay claim to the status of the 'foundational', let me say the following. I entirely agree with you 'that the failure to which any subject formation yields is an effect of its iterability'. This formulation presents, however, an ambiguity. For it is perfectly possible to think of this iterability as something whose recurrence – or, rather, linearity – cancels the ontological difference, i.e. whose movement is at any stage incomplete (and in that sense a failure), but which as a system does not leave anything outside itself. In that case we would be in the realm of Hegel's Greater Logic: the failure of each single stage cannot be represented as such, because its 'for itself' is a higher stage and, ergo, there is never constitutive failure, no ultimate deadlock. The insistence of Being through its various manifestations is nothing beyond the sequence of the latter. What, however, if the logic of the failure/iteration is not the logic of the *Aufgehoben*, if what insists in iteration is the contingency of the series, the hopelessness of its attempt at an ultimate closure? In that case, this moment of failure, of hopelessness, cannot elude the field of representation. The variety of the insistence, the presence of the absence of the object which sustains any possible iteration has to have some form of discursive presence. The failure of the ontological absorption of all ontic content opens the way to a constitutive 'ontological difference' that makes power, politics, hegemony, and democracy possible. Now, you think that this involves, as far as I'm concerned, taking a Lacanian viewpoint. I am not entirely sure about that. What I am trying to do is to detect the multiplicity of discursive surfaces in which this irreducible 'ontological difference' shows itself in modern and postmodern philosophy and political theory. Lacan's theory is certainly one of those surfaces. But I would not claim that it is the main – let alone the only – one.

3. Finally, 'America'. As you point out, 'America' is some sort of empty ambiguous signifier: it can mean both South and North America, but it can also mean only the latter. This means that (North) American functions as an unmarked term, while the series of suffixes that construct the mark of the South involves, in its succession, a whole history of imperialist domination. America without distinctions was the discourse of subordination of the South to the North: the Monroe doctrine. 'Hispano-America', the name of an older colonialism; 'Ibero-America', the widening of the latter to include Portugal. Finally, 'Latin America' was an invention of French colonialism, at the time of the Maximilian empire in Mexico, to legitimize an intervention which could cut the links with both the Iberic past and a rising (North) American imperialism. The fact that French intervention in the continent had no future made 'Latin-' an innocuous enough prefix for it to function as a political frontier separating the South from the imperialist interventions of the North.

The question, however, which remains to be answered is this: has the signifier 'America' without distinctions, without separation of the South from the North, any positive role to play as far as the Latin American peoples are concerned? My answer is no, I do not think there is any political gain for Latin America in playing around with the possibility of a community of destiny with the Anglo-American peoples. However, what about the Afro-American and the Hispanic minorities in North America: is there, for them, any language game to play around the ambiguities, the floating character of the signifier 'America'? The answer, in this case, has to be different. It would be definitely wrong to think that the signifier 'America' is, for those groups, once and forever fixed to the narrow history represented by the white Anglo-American tradition. Enlargement of the discourse of rights, of pluralist discourses which recognize the demands of ethnic, national, and sexual groups can be presented as a widening of freedoms and rights to equality which were contained in the (North) American political imaginary from its inception, but which were restricted to limited sections of the population. This multicultural and free 'America' will be the locus of much more ambiguous and open significations, but it is this openness and ambiguity which gives its meaning to a democratic political culture.

Best, Ernesto

Further reflections on conversations of our time

Judith Butler

The exchange that Ernesto Laclau and I conducted through email last year at this time begins a conversation that I expect will continue. And I suppose I would like to use this 'supplementary' reflection to think about what makes such a conversation possible, and what possibilities might emerge from such a conversation.

First of all, I think that I was drawn to the work of Laclau and Mouffe when I began to read *Hegemony and Socialist Strategy* and realized that I had found a set of Marxist thinkers for whom discourse was not merely a representation of preexisting social and historical realities, but was also constitutive of the field of the social and of history. The second moment came when I realized that central to the notion of articulation, appropriated from Gramsci, was the notion of *re*articulation. As a temporally dynamic and relatively unpredictable play of forces, hegemony had been cast by both Laclau and Mouffe as an alternative to forms of static structuralism that tend to construe contemporary social forms as timeless totalities. I read in Laclau and Mouffe the political transcription of Derrida's 'Structure, Sign, and Play' (1978): a structure gains its status as a structure, its *structurality*, only through its repeated reinstatement. The dependency of that structure on its reinstatement means that the very possibility of structure depends on a reiteration that is in no sense determined fully in advance, that for structure, and social structure as a result, to become possible, there must first be a contingent repetition at its basis. Moreover, for some social formation to appear as *structured* is for it to have covered over in some way the contingency of its own installation.

The theoretical rearticulation of structure as hegemony marked the work of Laclau and Mouffe as consequentially poststructuralist and offered perhaps the most important link between politics and poststructuralism in recent years (along with the work of Gayatri Chakravorty Spivak). The move from a structuralist account in which capital is understood to structure social relations in relatively homologous ways to a view of hegemony in which power relations are subject to repetition, convergence, and rearticulation brought the question of temporality into the thinking of structure, and marked a shift from a form of Althusserian theory that takes structural totalities as theoretical objects to one in which the insights into the contingent possibility of structure inaugurate a renewed conception of hegemony as bound up with the contingent sites and strategies of the rearticulation of power.

It is, of course, impossible in this context to reconstruct the particular way in which Derrida's work and Foucault's work converge in the reconceptualization of hegemony that Laclau and Mouffe have offered. One of the points, however, that became most salient for me is the reintroduction of temporality and, indeed, of futurity into the thinking of social formations. Among many critical social theorists, the tendency has been to underscore how the systemic character of capital tends to incorporate any instance of opposition in the service of capital's own self-augmentation. I would clearly agree that the incorporative and domesticating possibilities of capital are immense. But I would also argue that any theory that fails to think the possibilities of transformation from within that 'systemic' formation is itself complicit with the idea of the 'eternal' character of capital that capital so readily produces. Hegemony also marks a limit to the totalizing terms within which social formations are to be thought. For what hegemony attends to are the moments of breakage, of rearticulation, convergence, and resistance that are not immediately coopted by social formations in their past and present forms. That no social formation can endure without becoming reinstated, and that every reinstatement puts the 'structure' in question at risk, suggests that the possibility of its own undoing is at once the condition of possibility of structure itself.

Before I knew the work of Laclau and Mouffe very well, I came close to this kind of insight in my work on gender.[1] There I argued that gender is not an inner core or static essence, but a reiterated enactment of norms, ones which produce, retroactively, the appearance of gender as an abiding interior depth. My point as well was that although gender is constituted performatively, through a repetition of acts (which are themselves the encoded action of norms), it is not for that reason determined. Indeed, gender might be remade and restaged through the reiterative necessity by which it is constituted. Here I focused on the transposition of two Derridean insights into gender theory, mirroring what Laclau and Mouffe were doing within the theorization of hegemonic politics: (1) that the term that claims to represent a prior reality produces retroactively that priority as an effect of its own operation and (2) that every determined structure gains its determination by a repetition and, hence, a contingency that puts at risk the determined character of that structure. For feminism, that means that gender does not represent an interior depth, but produces that interiority and depth performatively as an effect of its own operation. And it means that 'patriarchy' or 'systems' of masculine domination are not systemic totalities bound to keep women in positions of oppression, but, rather, hegemonic forms of power that expose their own frailty in the very operation of their iterability. The strategic task for feminism is to exploit those occasions of frailty as they emerge.

But more recently, Laclau has offered another set of insights that converge in interesting ways with my own thinking. The first has to do with his enormously provocative claim that 'the essentially performative character of naming is the precondition for all hegemony and politics' (1989: xiv). What is meant by 'performative' here is of the utmost importance. For names do not merely bring into existence what they name, as divine names do. Names within the sphere of politics produce the possibility of identification, but also foil that possibility. To the extent that they are not descriptive (and, hence, for Laclau, not tied to established contents), they become the sites for a hegemonic rearticulation of subject positions. A name does not fully describe the subject that it nevertheless inaugurates into social space and time. But in what does its productive power consist, and what are the conditions of possibility for such power? Laclau refers to what remains undetermined in the subject through the power of the name, the referential limits of interpellation. What is it that constitutes the limitations of the performative power of naming? What is it, as it were, that holds the name open as a site of hegemonic articulation?

We might say that names function to the extent that they are used within language games in which their functions are already established. Or we might argue that names seek to capture a referent that always eludes the nomination by which that capture is sought. We might say that there is something 'in' the psyche as that which resists interpellation, as Mladen Dolar has argued, and we might call this 'the Real' according to Lacanian protocol. On the other hand, is there perhaps an abyss opened by the name that makes possible the contest over its 'right' and 'proper' function? And if so, how might we begin to approach the thinking of such an abyss? Is the Heideggerian notion of the 'ontological difference' the primary way in which Laclau understands this persistent necessity of *in*determination? Is the indetermination that renders all decision contingent (in the relative sense) the same as that which produces the name as an infinite site of contest (at the level of description)?

These seem to me to be one set of questions that I would hope to pursue as I think about further conversations with Laclau, conversations that we will surely continue. In the spirit of this exercise, then, I leave it open-ended.

Converging on an open quest

Ernesto Laclau

I very much enjoyed the exchange in which Judith Butler and I engaged last year, through an email correspondence between what Borges would have called the 'unlikely geographies' of Berkeley and London. The points of convergence of our respective approaches are clear: as Butler points out, the process of gender formation that she describes and the logic of hegemony as presented in my work (and in that which I wrote in collaboration with Chantal Mouffe) coincide in several of their assumptions. Neither we nor Butler see identities – political in one case, gendered in the other – as the expression of an intemporal mechanism or principle, but as products of the enactment of contingent norms; and both of us deny those norms a transcendental status, an a priori 'hardness' which would reproduce itself unchanged in all historical instances. On the contrary, we see them as submitted to historical variations and as penetrated by a constitutive indetermination and ambiguity.

I have used the word 'transcendental' *ex professo*, because it is the status of the transcendental which is at the root of many of the most crucial problems in contemporary theory. Most people would agree that transcendentalism, in its classical formulations, is today unsustainable, but there is also a generalized agreement that some kind of weak transcendentalism is unavoidable. In the deconstructionist tradition, for instance, the notion of 'quasi-transcendentals' has acquired considerable currency. But most theoretical approaches are haunted by the perplexing question of the precise status of that 'quasi'. The problem touches on, on the one hand, the question of 'metalanguage'; on the other, the status, in theory building, of categories that apparently refer to empirical events but that in practice have a quasi-transcendental status, operating as the a priori conditions of intelligibility of a whole discursive domain. What is the status in psychoanalysis, for instance, of categories such as 'phallus', of the 'castration complex'? Because of the undecided status of the 'quasi', we are confronted with a plurality of alternatives, whose two polar extremes would be a total hardening of those categories, which would thus become a priori conditions of all possible human development, and a no less extreme historicism which sees in them only contingent events, products of particular cultural formations. The first extreme is confronted with the whole array of problems emerging from any transcendentalization of empirical conditions; the second, with the difficulties derived from not dealing with those conditions which make possible even a historicist discourse. The logic of the 'quasi' tries to avoid both extremes, but it is extremely unclear in what that logic would consist. These are questions which have not been dealt with enough, in either Butler's approach or in mine; but they are issues to which both of us will have to return – perhaps in future exchanges.

Let me now move to two central points contained in Butler's latest piece, published in this issue of *Diacritics* as an addendum to our original exchange. They relate to the relationship between hegemony and iteration, and to the role of names in fixing meaning. I think that iteration belongs to the structure of any hegemonic operation, but that the latter stresses a double dimension of both repetition and displacement of meaning. To understand how these two dimensions interact with each other is crucial in order to grasp the logic of the political. (I understand hegemony to be the central category in political analysis.) As Derrida has shown, iterability (the possibility of repetition in a plurality of instances) is something which belongs to the essence of the sign. What would something be which occurs in only one instance? It would simply not be a sign. But if the sign has to be the same, it also has to be different each time – and in that case the instance of its differential use has to be as part of its internal structure as the dimension of sameness. Now, in that case, it can only remain the same by becoming something constantly different from itself. This is the point where the usefulness of this analysis for a theory of the hegemonic becomes visible: for hegemony involves both a relation of power in which something different is assimilated by the same, and a movement in the opposite direction, by which the differential instance, as it is part of a series of equivalent instances, can reproduce the same only by progressively emptying the meaning of the latter. The only logical requirements for this to be thinkable are that: (1) we conceive iteration as an additive process and not merely as a discrete series; and (2) that the dimension of equivalence between the different instances is underlined to the point that the emptying effect over the hegemonic term can operate freely. These two requirements can easily be met without causing violence to the structure of the iterating process. As in Wittgenstein's argument about following a rule: the instance of the application has to be part of the rule itself. In terms of hegemony what we have is a construction of the progressive emptiness of what puts the iterative series together on the basis of an additive pluralization of the instances. That is why hegemony is a dangerous operation: on the one hand its success depends on absorbing within itself larger and larger systems of contextual differences; but precisely because of its very success, the link of the hegemonic principle with the differences which constituted its original identity becomes more tenuous all the time.

Finally, names. Butler asks: 'What is it that constitutes the limitations of the performative power of naming? What is it, as it were, that holds the name open as a site of hegemonic articulation?' My argument here runs parallel to that concerning iteration. My original commentary on this matter – to which Butler refers – was in connection with the analysis made by Slavoj Žižek of the polemic between descriptivists and antidescriptivists on how names refer to reality. Žižek sides – as I do – with the anti-descriptivists (with Kripke's notion of a primal baptism) but adds the crucial remark that the *x* which supports the process of nomination is nothing belonging to the object but a retroactive effect of the process of nomination itself. To this I commented as follows:

> if the unity of the object is the retroactive effect of naming itself, then naming is not just the pure nominalistic game of attributing an empty name to a preconstituted subject. It is the discursive construction of the object itself. The consequences of this argument for a theory of hegemony or politics are easy to see. If the descriptivist approach were correct, then the meaning of the name and the descriptive features of the objects would be given beforehand, thus discounting the possibility of any discursive hegemonic variation that would open the space for a political

> construction of social identities. But if the process of naming the objects amounts to the very act of their constitution, then their descriptive features will be fundamentally unstable and open to all kinds of hegemonic rearticulations.

What is the condition for names to function that way? Clearly, it is that between descriptive features and names a gap should exist, so that the name cannot be *permanently* attached to particular objects. But this requires that the name should be partially or tendentially empty and that its partial fixation is essentially vulnerable. Through naming and renaming, the object is constructed and reconstructed. As we see, this is the same case as with iteration. Names are natural places for hegemonic rearticulations because their contents are constantly being negotiated. If the emptiness of names is partially limited by transient stabilizations, any stabilization, in time, is threatened by the emptiness inherent in the structure of naming.

These are just some themes – which are far from being exhausted – and whose recurrence in present political and theoretical discussion is certainly assured. I hope that the exchange between Judith Butler and myself can act as a modest stimulus for others to join and contribute to an enterprise whose success can be assured only if it becomes a truly collective one.

20 November 1996

Note

This exchange was previously published in *Diacritics*, 27(1) (1997): 3–15.

1 The work of Anna-Marie Smith helped me to understand more clearly the links between our positions.

References

Derrida, J. (1978) 'Structure, sign, and play in the discourse of the human sciences', in *Writing and Difference*, tr. Alan Bass, Chicago: University of Chicago Press.

—— (1988) 'Signature, Event, Context', in *Limited Inc.*, tr. Samuel Weber, Evanston, IL: Northwestern University Press.

Laclau, E (1989) Preface, in S. Žižek, *The Sublime Object of Ideology*, London: Verso.

Mouffe, Chantal, (ed.) (1992) *Dimensions of Radical Democracy: Pluralism, Citizenship, Community*. London: Verso.

Appendix II
BIBLIOGRAPHY OF ERNESTO LACLAU'S WORK

Books

1977 *Politics and Ideology in Marxist Theory: Capitalism. Fascism. Populism*, London: NLB (4th reprint 1987); translated into German, Spanish, Greek, and Portuguese.

1985 (with Chantal Mouffe) *Hegemony and Socialist Strategy. Towards a Radical Democratic Politics*, London: Verso (3rd reprint 1989); translated into Spanish, German, Japanese, Slovenian, Chinese, and Turkish.

1990 *New Reflections on the Revolution of our Time*, London: Verso.

1994 (Editor and contributor) *The Making of Political Identities*, London: Verso.

1996 *Emancipation(s)*, London: Verso.

2000 (with Judith Butler and Slavoj Žižek) *Contingency, Hegemony, Universality: Contemporary Dialogues on the Left*, London: Verso.

Books in preparation

2004 *The Populist Reason*, London: Verso (forthcoming).

2005 *Elusive Universality*, London: Routledge (forthcoming).

Articles

1960 'Un impacto en la lucha de clases: el proceso immigratorio argentino', *Situacion* (Buenos Aires).

1963 'Nota sobre la historia de mentalidades', *Desarrollo Economico* (Buenos Aires) 2.

1969 'Modos de produccion, sistemas economicos y poblacion excedente: approximacion historica a los casos argentino y chileno', *Revista Latinoamericano de Sociologia* (Buenos Aires), 2.

1970 'Argentine: strategie imperialiste et crise mai 1968', *Les Temps Modernes* (October); translated into English and Italian.

1971 'Feudalism and Capitalism in Latin America', *New Left Review*, 62, 19–55, translated into Italian, German, Dutch, Spanish, and Portuguese.

1973 'Peronism and Revolution', *Latin American Review of Books* (London).

1975 'The specificity of the political: around the Poulantzas/Miliband debate', *Economy and Society*, 5(1), 87–110; translated into German, Swedish, Spanish, Italian, and Turkish.

1980 'Populist rupture and discourse', *Screen Education*, 34 (Spring): 87–93; translated into German and Greek.

1980 'Democratic antagonisms and the capitalist state', in M. Freeman and D. Robertson (eds) *The Frontiers of Political Theory*, Brighton: Palgrave Macmillan.

1980 'Togliatti and politics', *Politics and Power*, 2 (London, October).

1981 'Teorias marxistas des Estado: debates y perspectivas', in N. Lechner (ed.) *Estado y politica en America Latina* (Mexico), 21.

1981 'La politique comme construction de l'impensable' in B. Conein *et al.* (eds) *Materialités discursives*, Lille: Presses Universitaires de Lille; translated into German.

1981 (with Chantal Mouffe), 'Socialist strategy: what next?', *Marxism Today* (January); translated into Spanish.

1982 'Diskurs, Hegemonie und Politik: Betrachtungen über die Krise des Marxismus' in W. F. Haug and W. Elfferding (eds) *Neue soziale Bewegungen und Marxismus*, Berlin: Argument.

1982 'Foreword' to Jacques Chevallier, *Civilization and the Stolen Gift*, Toronto: Toronto University Press.

1983 'Transformations of advanced industrial societies and the theory of the subject', in S. Hänninen and L. Paldan (eds) *Rethinking Ideology*, Berlin: Argument.

1983 'Socialisme et transformation des logiques hegemoniques', in Ch. Buci-Gluksmann (ed.) *La gauche, le pouvoir, le socialisme*, Paris: Presses Universitaires de France.

1983 'The impossibility of society', *Canadian Journal of Political and Social Theory*, 7(1–2) (Spring), 21–7.

1984 'The controversy over materialism', in S. Hänninen and L. Paldan (eds) *Rethinking Marx*, Berlin: Argument.

1985 'The hegemonic form of the political: a thesis', in Ch. Abel and C. Lewis (eds) *Latin America: Economic Imperialism and the State*, London: University of London, Institute of Latin American Studies Monographs; translated into Spanish.

1985 'New social movements and the plurality of the social', in D. Slater (ed.) *New Social Movements and the State in Latin America*, Amsterdam: CEDLA.

1986 'Psychoanalysis and Marxism', *Critical Inquiry*, 13(2) (Winter): 330–3.

1987 'Class war and after', *Marxism Today* (April): 20–33.

1987 (with Chantal Mouffe), 'Post Marxism without apologies', *New Left Review*, 166 (November/December): 79–106.

1987 'Populismo y transformacion del imaginario politico en America Latina', *Boletin de Estudios Latinoamericanos y del Caribe*, 42 (Amsterdam, June).

1988 'Metaphor and social antagonisms', in C. Nelson and L. Grossberg (eds) *Marxism and the Interpretation of Culture*, Urbana, IL: University of Illinois Press.

1988 'Politics and the limits of modernity', in A. Ross (ed.) *Universal Abandon?* Minneapolis: University of Minnesota Press.

1990 'Totalitarianism and moral indignation', *Diacritics*, 20(3) (Fall): 88–95.

1991 'Community and its paradoxes: Richard Rorty's "Liberal Utopia"', in Miami Theory Collective (ed.) *Community at Loose Ends*, Minneapolis: University of Minnesota Press.

1992 'Universalism, particularism and the question of identity', *October*, 61 (Summer): 83–90.

1992 'Beyond emancipation', in J. Nederveen Pieterse (ed.) *Emancipations, Modern and Post-Modern*, London: Sage.

1993 'The signifiers of democracy', in H. Carens (ed.) *Democracy and Possessive Individualism*, New York: State University of New York Press.

1993 'Power and representation' in M. Poster (ed.) *Politics, Theory and Contemporary Culture*, New York: Columbia University Press.

1993 'Discourse', in R. A. Goodin and P. Pettit (eds) *A Companion to Contemporary Political Philosophy*, Oxford: Basil Blackwell.

1994 'Why do empty signifiers matter to politics', in J. Weeks (ed.) *The Lesser Evil and the Greater Good*, London: Rivers Oram Press.

1995 'Universalism, particularism and the question of identity', in J. Rajchman (ed.) *The Identity in Question*, New York: Routledge.

1995 'Subject of politics politics of the Subject', *differences*: A Journal of Feminist Cultural Studies 7(1), eds N. Schor and E. Weed, 146–64.

1995 'The time is out of joint', *Diacritics*, 25(2) (Summer): 86–97.

1996 'Deconstruction, pragmatism, hegemony', in Ch. Mouffe (ed.) *Deconstruction and Pragmatism*, London: Routledge (this book consists of the expanded version of the intervention by Simon Critchley, Jacques Derrida, Ernesto Laclau, and Richard Rorty in a workshop held at the Collège International de Philosophie, Paris, 1994).

1996 'The death and resurrection of the theory of ideology', *Journal of Political Ideologies*, 1(3) 201–20.

1997 'The uses of equality' (a discussion between Judith Butler and Ernesto Laclau), *Diacritics*, 27(1) 3–12.

1997 'Converging on an open quest', *Diacritics*, 27(1) 17–19.

1997 'On the names of God', in S. Golding (ed.) *The 8 Technologies of Otherness*, London: Routledge.

1997 'Inklusion, Exklusion und die Logik der Äquivalenz', in P. Weibel and S. Žižek (eds) *Inklusion: Exklusion Probleme des Postkolonialismus und der globalen Migration*, Vienna: Passagen Verlag.

2001 'The politics of rhetoric', in T. Cohen, J. H. Miller, A. Warminski and B. Cohen (eds) *Material Events: Paul de Man and the Afterlife of Theory*, Minneapolis: University of Minnesota Press.

2001 'Democracy and the question of power', in *Constellations*, 8(1) (March): 1–12.

2002 'Democracy between autonomy and heteronomy' in O. Enwezor *et al.* (eds) *Democracy Unrealized*, Ostfildern: Cantz.

2003 'Can immanence explain social struggles', in J. Dean and P. Passavant (eds) *Empire's New Clothes: Reading Hardt and Negri*, New York: Routledge.

(forthcoming) 'On imagined communities', in J. Culler (ed.).

(forthcoming) 'An ethics of militant engagement', in P. Hallward (ed.) *Think Again: Alain Badiou and the Future of Philosophy*, Athlone.

INDEX

absolutism 129, 293, 295; singular-absolute 65–8, 310–11
abstract labour 322–3
actuality, and potentiality 63, 247
Adorno, Theodor and Horkheimer, Max, *Dialectic of Enlightenment* 123
advertising discourse 210, 299
affect 301, 302, 303–4, 326
agonistic respect 9, 176–7, 179
agreement 145–6, 160; disagreement 151–4, 160
Althusser, Louis 38, 258
America 337, 338–9; Equal Protection Clause (US Constitution) 330
anachronism of emancipation 188–97
Anderson, Perry 257
antagonism 4, 39, 40, 43–5, 48–50, 314; and discursive limits 226, 227, 232–9, 318–19; and dislocation 234–9, 245–8, 319; and exclusion 234; fundamental, and the politics of becoming 179; and identity 245–8, 249; and radical contingency 58–60; and social antagonism 97, 98, 99, 100, 266–7; system, and hegemony 249–52; and systemizing differences 248–9; and systems theory 234–6, 251–2; theory of 259–60; universalism and identity 97–100
antagonistic limits 226, 227, 232–4
anti-colonialism 298
approximation 148–9
archaeological discourse analysis 231
Archaeology of Knowledge (Foucault) 227, 229, 231, 232, 238
'archaeology of silence' 230
Arendt, Hannah 92–3, 99, 313
argumentation, democratic 150–1, 159–61
Aristotle 209
articulation 39, 48, 244, 267, 321; and rearticulation 339
assemblages 167, 168
Augustine: City of God and City of Man 124–5, 130, 132, 135–9; *Confessions* 137; ethical life 175
Austin, J.L. 90, 224
Axelrod, Pavel 37

Badiou, Alain 183, 184, 316, 324–5, 329
Balibar, Etienne 38, 184
Bang, H.P. 249, 253
bargaining 146–8
Bataille, Georges 230
Beauvoir, Simone de 103
becoming, politics of 9, 175–9
being 174, 289; discursive 204; and nothingness 309
Being and Time (Heidegger) 289
beliefs *see* faiths
Benhabib, S. 143, 151
Benjamin, Walter, 'Zur Kritik der Gewalt' (essay) 221
Bernstein, Eduard 37
Between Facts and Norms (Habermas) 145–8
binary oppositions (dualisms) 47–9, 258
Bohman, J. 147
Butler, Judith 22, 28, 88, 105, 279–80, 305, 339–44; *Contingency, Hegemony, Universality* (Butler, Laclau and Žižek) 6, 21, 27–8; on equality and difference (correspondence with Laclau)

329–31, 332–3, 336–7, 339–41; and Žižek 6, 9–10, 57, 117, 202–3
capitalism/capital 167–8, 340
catachresis 217, 225, 265, 306
'chains of equivalence' 167, 281, 334, *see also* collective assemblages
Chambers, S., *Reasonable Democracy* 142–3, 144, 145, 148–50, 151, 157
change, political 217–25
Christian concepts of universality 18–19
City of God and City of Man (Augustine) 124–5, 130, 132, 135–9
class 2, 36, 37, 257–8, 258–9, *see also* New Social Movements
classicism: concepts of universality 18, 89–90; and moral philosophy 124–5
collective assemblages 167, 168
community 21, 25–6; absent fullness of 25–6, 58, 96, 100, 280; 'for all' 195, 197; universality of 21, 131, *see also* society
compromise 146–8
'compromise formations' 157
Confessions (Augustine) 137
Connolly, William, E. 129, 138, 160, 178, 298; and the ethos of democratization 9, 167–80
consensus *see* rational consensus
constitutive dislocations 280–1
Contemporary Political Philosophy (Kymlicka) 124
content and form 118, 195
context 335, 336–7
contingency: and determinism 47; and differentiality 325; and fidelity 183; radical contingency 58–62, 335
contingency-necessity 47–8, 60, 62, 242, 293–5, 309; articulations of 155, 158; difference and equality 335
Contingency, Hegemony, Universality (Butler, Laclau and Žižek) 6, 21, 27–8
Critchley, Simon 8, 113–22, 221, 269–70, 286–91; *The Ethics of Deconstruction* 113
critical judging 92–3, 313
critical responsiveness 177–8, 179

Dallmayr, Fred 8, 35–53, 61–2, 64, 307–9, 310
Dasein 119–20, 289, 290
de Man, Paul 217, 219, 222–3, 224–5; the Pascalian zero 219, 293, 306
decisions/decision-making: decision rules and ongoing processes 148–51; democratizing and non-democratizing 116; and exclusion 332–3; hegemonic approach accepted 135; madness of decision 220, 222, 223–4; and political change 217–25; and radical democracy 140, 141; of the subject 223–4; and subjectivity 264–5
deconstruction: of determinism 126; and emancipation 182, 188, 189; and hegemonic theory 5, 113, 115–16, 117; and hegemony 189–90, 195–6, 317; relevance for political theory 42, 155; of socialism 35–6
'Deconstruction, pragmatism, hegemony' (Laclau) (essay) 218, 222, 223
deliberation 150–1
deliberative democracy 8, 140, 141, 142–5; criticisms of 143–4; decision rules and ongoing processes 148–51; democratic agreement and generizable interests 145–6; democratic argumentation 150–1, 159–61; rational consensus, bargaining and compromise 146–8; and universality 144–5, 155–6
democracy: and antagonism 49–50, 99–100; 'democratic deficit' 157–8; the ethical, and decision to accept hegemonic approach 135; and the liberal 137–8, 138–9; politics and hegemony 40, 113–15, 116, 156; radical and plural 4, 41, 42–3, 55; and the universal 105, 154–9, *see also* politics and the political; radical democracy
democracy theory 2, 253
democratic argumentation 150–1, 159–61
democratic hegemony 116, 121, 290–1, 337
democratic struggles 40, 46
democratizing and non-democratizing decisions 116
Derrida, J. 31, 115–16, 125, 126; concept of *différance* 62; deconstruction and emancipation 182; *Force de loi* 221, 222; logic of iterability 269; logic of spectrality 190; 'Signature, event, context' (essay) 335; *Spectres of Marx* 117; 'Structure, sign and play' (essay) 339

Descartes, René, Cartesian discourse theory 230–1, 232
descriptive/normative 115–17, 269–70, 289–90, 290; and the ethical 117–21, 288–9, 291
desire 207, 210
determinative and reflexive judgement 313
determinism: and contingency 47; deconstruction of 126; materialist determinism 220–1
Devenney, Mark 8, 123–39, 291–5
Diacritics (journal) 342
Dialectic of Enlightenment (Adorno and Horkheimer) 123
difference: and differential 249; and equality 329, 329–44; and identity 57, 60, 97, 250; systematizing of, and antagonism 248–9
difference and equivalence *see* equivalence and difference
difference-as-difference 56, 58, 62–5, 67
differential particularism 25–6
differentiality and contingency 325
differentiation, discursive, and antagonism 236–7
Dimensions of Radical Democracy (Mouffe) 329
disagreement 151–4, 160, 296; and agreement 145–6, 160
discourse 4, 39, 48; concept of, and social reality 265; and deliberative democracy 142–3, 146, 147; and *jouissance* 299–304; limits of 203–6, 226–40; and rhetoric 306–7; as system of differences 248
discourse analysis 2, 228, 229; politics and political in 241–54
discourse theory 123–5; Cartesian 230–1, 232; dispersion of discursive statements 227–9; ethics and instrumental rationality 135–9; ethics and politics 129–35; and language 230, 231–2, 302–3; post-Marxism and instrumental rationality 125–9
discursive: formations 227–8; limits 226, 227, 232–9, 236, 318–19; transgression 227, 229–32, *see also* discourse
dislocation 6, 59, 186, 187, 268, 317; and antagonism 234–9, 245–8, 319; constitutive dislocations 280–1; and hegemonic concept 261; negative indices of the real 203–6; ontological dimension of 323–4; positive indices of the real 207; and the universal 193–4
dispersion 227–9
dualisms/duality 47–9, 258
Dyrberg, Torben 9, 241–54, 320–1; and Bang 249; on populism 246

Easton, D. 252
École Freudienne 206
economism 43; capitalism 167–8
ego, or 'I' 224
elements 39, 48, 268, 321
Elster, J. 150
emancipations: anachronism of emancipation 188–97; and deconstruction 182, 188, 189; emancipatory politics 186–7; and fidelity to signifier 182–8, 197; and political change 220–1
Emancipation(s) (Laclau) 6; anachronism of emancipation 188–9, 189–90, 191, 192, 193; antagonism and exclusion 234; elements 268; the empty signifier 207, 233, 261–2; Lacan's influence on 201, 202; the limits of particularism 93–5; the limits of signification 205–6; and ontological difference 57, 59, 60, 64; on political change 218; structure and agency 264; the universal as an empty place 95, 97, 100, 101, 102; the universal and sexual difference 104, 105; the universal-particular 96, 101–2, 155–6; 'Universalism, particularism and the question of Identity'(essay) 73–87; on universality 18–19, 21, 22–30, 89–90, 93
emptiness: and the ethical 132, 286, 287, 292–3; and universality 20, 27–33, 95–102, 243, 279–85
empty signifier 28, 97, 100–2, 105, 125, 156; and anachronism of emancipation 193, 194–5; and conceptualization of hegemony 261–2, 316–18; Devenney on 292; and discursivity 233, 238; the limits of signification 205–6; and nodal points 268–9, 322; as positive indices of the real 207–8; and the universal 281–2, 283
'end of politics' 252–3

enjoyment *see* jouissance
Enlightenment: and ethics 123; and universality 19, 20
environment, and system 235, 236
Epicurus 175, 177
Equal Protection Clause (US Constitution) 330
equality: and difference 329, 329–44; and logic of equivalence 23–5, 26, 39–40, 334, 336
equivalence: 'chains of equivalence' 167, 281, 334; and limits of signifying system 250–1; logic of 23–5, 26, 39–40, 44–5, 190, 334, 336; and radical contingency 59; and signification 24, 25, 59
equivalence and difference 25, 44, 93–4, 101, 105, 190; and social antagonism 266–7; and tropology 219
essentialism, Marxist 36–8
the ethical: and decision to accept hegemonic approach 133–5; and deconstruction 113, 115–16; and emptiness 132, 286, 287, 292–3; ethics of fidelity 187; and ethos of democratization 9, 167–80; meanings of 131–2, 286; and the normative 117–21, 288–9, 290, 291; and political change 221; and politics in discourse theory 123–39; and radical investment 286–95; sources of ethical orientation 170–5
ethical-political discourse 146
The Ethics of Deconstruction (Critchley) 113
ethos: of democratization 9, 167–80; meaning of ethos 123
Eurocentricism: and universality 19, 23, 32–3, 75–6, 95; Western universalism 75, 76, 77
Evans, D. 211
exclusion: and antagonism 234; and decision-making 332–3; inclusion and equality 330–1, 331–2
existence and nature 126–7, 292
existential gratitude 174–5
exteriority/interiority 49
extra-discursive existence 204
eye, concepts of 230–1

failed unicity 325
failure 336, 338
faiths 172–3, 176–7, 177–8, 298, *see also* fidelity; God
Fanon, Frantz, *The Wretched of theEarth* 298
fantasy 207, 208–13
feminism 102–5, 340–1
fidelity: and contingency 183; to emancipation as signifier 182–8, 197
Fink, Bruce 205, 303–4
Force de loi (Derrida) 221, 222
form and content 118, 195
Foucault, Michel 226–32, 245, 247, 251; *Archaeology of Knowledge* 227, 229, 231, 232, 238; *Madness and Civilization* 231
foundationalism *see* non-foundationalism; post-foundationalism
freedom 116–17, 245, 253
French Revolution 40, 50
Freud, Sigmund 205; *Group Psychology* 301, 315
friendship 50
fundamentalization 176, 178–9

Gamble, Andrew 259
Gasché, Rodolphe 7–8, 17–34; Laclau's critique of 279–85
gender 340–1
gender-neutral/gender specific 103–6
generizable interests 145–6, 156
generosity 175, 177; of Laclau 217
Die Gesellschaft der Gesellschaft (Luhmann) 235
Glynos, Jason 212, 302; and Stavrakakis, Yannis 9, 299–303
God 20, 124–5, 136, 222, 224, 292–3, *see also* faiths
grammar 305–6
Gramsci, Antonio: conception of hegemony 155, 156, 257–8, 269; importance for Laclau 55, 258; Laclau on 2, 3, 38; war of position 46, 258
Grassi, Ernesto 307
gratitude, existential 174–5
Griggs, S. and Howarth, David 262
'Ground' 6–7, 8, 30, 55; absence of/non-ground 56, 58, 61
Group Psychology (Freud) 301, 315
Grundrisse (Marx) 322

Habermas, Jürgen 140, 141, 142, 145, 157, 158; *Between Facts and Norms* 145–8; Habermasian democracy 296–7

Hall, Stuart 259
Hegel, Georg/Hegelianism: concrete abstract or universal 29; and Laclau's hegemony 46, 47; *Phenomenology of the Spirit* 118; *Philosophy of History* 319; totality and hegemony 43
hegemonic logics 243–5, 304–7, 318–24
hegemonic relationships 244, 262, 335
'hegemonic suture' 219
hegemonic universality 114
hegemony: act of hegemony 220; conception of 263–71; and conception of the political 241, 243–5; and deconstruction 189–90, 195–6, 317; deconstruction and hegemonic theory 5, 113, 115–16, 117; definitions and meanings of 69, 93, 96, 101, 113–14, 118; democracy and politics 40, 113–15, 116, 156; democratic hegemony 116, 121, 290–1, 337; descriptive and normative dimensions 115–17, 269–70, 289–90; ethical decision on hegemonic approach 133–5; Gramsci's conception of 155, 156, 257–8; and iteration 342–3; Laclau's conception evaluated 262–3; Laclau's definitions of 281; Laclau's reformulation of 7, 26–7, 29–30, 38–41, 54–5, 218, 258–63, 270; and Marxism 3, 36–8, 39, 155, 255, 257–8; and post-structuralism 339–40; a strategic approach 56; system and antagonism 249–52; three models of 258–62; and the universal 114, 156–8; the universal and emancipation 190–1, 194–6; and universality 26–7, 93
Hegemony and Socialist Strategy (Laclau and Mouffe) 2, 3–5, 35–51; on articulation 267; critical comments on 46–51, 113, 116, 339; the decision in radical democracy 140, 141; the deconstruction of determinism 126; ethical decision to accept hegemonic approach 134–5; hegemonic models in 259–60; hegemony, and the political 241, 244, 245, 246, 251; interpretations of 42–6, 97, 98, 99; Lacan's influence on 201–2; the limits of discourse 204, 205, 228, 232, 233, 234, 236, 318–19; positivity/negativity 63–4; on post-structuralism and deconstruction 35–6, 42; and radical contingency 58–9, 62; on radical democracy 154, 155, 270; social antagonism 97, 266–7; synopsis of 36–41; on system 248; on the universal 17–18, 20–1, 22
Heidegger, Martin: *Being and Time* 289; on difference 49, 56; influence on Laclau 6; on 'nothingness' 63; ontological difference 118, 119–20, 266, 288–9
'historical blocs' 38
Hobbes, Thomas 57, 262
Howarth, David 9, 256–76, 321–3
Husserl, Edmund 32, 263, 284–5

'I', or ego 224
the ideal, and the real in democracy 148–51
identification 224, 300–1
identity: and antagonism 245–8, 249; and difference 57, 60, 97, 250; and dislocation 245–8; and equivalence 24–5, 336; and failed unicity 325; and faith 173; group identity and particularism 93–5; Laclau's view of 342; multiple identities 74–5, 80; and overdetermination 45; and the subject 5–6, *see also* New Social Movements
ideology 212–13
Ideology and Discourse (research programme) 212
imaginary, social and political 261, 337
impossible/possible 219, 220
inclusion/exclusion, and equality 330–1, 331–2
indifference 63, 238
individualism 45
inside/outside 61–2
instrumental rationality 125–9, 135–9, 291
interiority/exteriority 49
'intertwining' 61, 62
invisibility 230
Irigary, Luce 103–4
iteration: and hegemony 342–3; logic of iterability 269

jouissance 202, 206, 209–13, 299–304
judging/judgement: critical judging 92–3, 313; reflexive judgement 83–4, 311–13
justice 286–7, 293

Kant, Immanuel 118, 170–2, 174; *Third Critique* 79–80
Kantian reflexive judgement 83–4, 311–13
Kautsky, Karl 36
knowledge 127–8
Kuhn, Thomas 205
Kymlicka, Will 124; *Contemporary Political Philosophy* 124;

labour, abstract 322–3
Lacan, Jacques/Lacanians 97, 98, 120, 218; and the École Freudienne 206; ethics of the Real 288; influence on Laclau 201–15, 261; on *jouissance* 210, 211, 299; subjectivity, theory of 260; *Television* 211
Laclau, Ernesto: 'Deconstruction, pragmatism, hegemony' (essay) 218, 222, 223; on equality and difference (correspondence with Butler) 331–2, 334–6, 337–9, 341–4; intellectual biography of 1–2, 54–5, 217–18; Lacan's influence on 201–15; *The Making of Political Identities* 204; and Mouffe, on discursive limits 226, 227, 232–4, 236, 237, 238; 'The politics of rhetoric' (essay) 218, 219, 223, 224; 'Why do empty signifiers matter to politics?' (essay) 218; and Zac 20, 28, 62–3, 98, *see also Contingency, Hegemony, Universality*; *Emancipations*; *Hegemony and Socialist Strategy*; *New Reflections*; *Politics and Ideology in Marxist Theory*
Laddaga, Reinaldo 329, 334
language: anachronistic 191–2; and discourse theory 230, 231–2, 302–3; instrumentalizing of 128–9; and the political 218, 222; and society 266–7, *see also* linguistics
language games 90–2, 105, 305
Lefort, Claude 69, 115, 152, 154
Leninism 37, 257, 270
Levinas, Emmanuel 113, 118, 120, 174, 221, 288
Lewis, David, 'New Age Travellers' (PhD project) 212
the liberal: and agonistic respect 176–7; difference and equality 334; and the radical democrat 137–8, 138–9
libidinal link 326
limits: articulation of 249–50; of discourse 203–6, 226–40; notion of 318–19; of particularism 93–5; and representation 335; of signification 203, 205–6, 250; of systems 250–1
linguistics 54, 325, *see also* language
logic: of equivalence 23–5, 26, 39–40, 44–5, 190, 266–7, 334, 336; hegemonic logics 220, 243–5, 304–6, 318–24; of iterability 269; of spectrality 190
Lucha Obrera (journal) 2
Luhmann, Niklas 227, 235, 237; *Die Gesellschaft der Gesellschaft* 235
Lumpenproletariat 68, 319
Luxemburg, Rosa 36, 308

MacKinnon, Catherine 330
McLelland, S. 125
Madness and Civilization (Foucault) 231
madness of decision 220, 222, 223–4
Marchart, Oliver 8, 54–70, 68, 309, 310–11
Marx, Karl/Marxism: and deliberative democracy 152; determinative and reflexive judgement 313; ethical and scientific claims 125–6; *Grundrisse* 322; and hegemony 3, 36–8, 39, 155, 257–8; on history 319; the ontical level 267; and political change 220–1; and the *subaltern* 68; and universality 18, 19, *see also* post-Marxism; socialism
master signifier 208, 317
materialist determinism 220–1
materiality of the signifier 191, 192–3
metaphor/metonymy 219
metaphysics 292
metonymy/metaphor 219
militarization 45–6
Miller, David 143
Miller, J. Hillis 9, 217–25, 304
Miller, Jacques-Alain 209, 211
'Minding the gap' (Zac) (essay) 20
Močnik, R. 264
moments 39, 48, 321
moral choice/action 287–8
moral discourse 146
moral philosophy 124–5
moral universalism 129–30
morality 171–3, *see also* the ethical; ethics

Mouffe, Chantal 152–3, 154, 156, 244, 253; *Dimensions of Radical Democracy* 329; and Laclau, on discursive limits 226, 227, 232–4, 236, 237, 238, *see also Hegemony and Socialist Strategy*; Laclau, Ernesto
Mulhall, S. 266
multiculturalism 89, 93, 94–5
multiple identities 74–5, 80
myth 261

name/naming 312, 320–1, 341, 342–4
Nammour, J. 90
nationalism 211–12, 246
nature and existence 126–7, 292
necessity-contingency *see* contingency-necessity
negativity 324
negativity/positivity 48–9, 61, 63–5; and antagonism 246; and identity 247; limits of 249; and ontological difference 309; of the real 203–13
Negitavkorrelat 235, 320
'New Age Travellers' (Lewis) (PhD project) 212
New Reflections (Laclau) 5–7; on antagonism 98–9, 234; conception of society 266; critical comments on 116–17; on 'democratic deficit' 157–8; on dislocation 59, 187, 206, 207, 234, 238, 268, 319; on elements 268; fidelity to emancipation as signifier 182, 184, 185, 187; hegemonic concept in 260–1, 263, 264; Lacan's influence on 201, 202, 261; Laclau's Argentinian experiences 2, 54–5; on the limits of signification 205; on ontological difference 61–2, 64; on politics of emancipation 197; on rules of language games 91–2; on theory of the subject 223; and universality 30, 32, 96
New Social Movements 3–4, 40, 54
Nietzsche, Friedrich 6, 174
nodal points 210–12, 259, 268–9, 322
nominalism/realism 90
non-foundationalism 156
'normative deficit' 269–70
normative/descriptive 115–17, 269–70, 289–90; and the ethical 117–21, 288–9, 291
Norval, Aletta 8, 140–66, 236–7, 296–8
nothingness 62–5; and being 309

objectivism 130
objet petit a 207, 208, 210, 213
ontological difference 56–8, 62–5, 66, 266–8, 307–11; and dislocation 323–4; the ethical and the normative 118, 119–20, 288–9; and social theory 321
order, nature of 207–8
Osborne, P. 264
the Other 206, 211–12
ousia 209
outside/inside 61–2
overdetermination 45

Parker, P. 306
particularism: differential 25–6; limits of 93–5, *see also* universal-particular
partisan ethical sources 173, 174–5, 179
Pascalian zero 219, 293, 306
peasant uprisings 260
performative contradiction 293–4
Phenomenology of the Spirit (Hegel) 118
Philosophical Investigations (Wittgenstein) 90–2
philosophy: moral philosophy 124–5; philosophical dimensions of Laclau's work 6, 54–8, 65–8, 69; philosophy/politics relationships and the universal 73, 74–80, 85; politicization of 81–4; politics as the real of philosophy 73–87; subjectivation of 79; and universality 30–1
Philosophy of History (Hegel) 319
Plato, *The Republic* 129
Plekhanov, Georgii 37
plural and radical democracy 4, 41, 42–3, 55
pluralism/plurality 45, 75, 76, 92, 99–100; and fundamentalization 176, 178–9; plural identities 80
polarization 45–6
political change 217–25
Politics and Ideology in Marxist Theory (Laclau) 2, 258, 268
politics and the political: and antagonism 319; and conception of hegemony 263–71; in discourse analysis 241–54; emancipation and the universal 190–1, 194–6; the 'end of politics' 252–3; ethical decision to accept hegemonic approach 134–5; and ethics in discourse theory 123–39; the ethos of democratization

9, 167–80; hegemony and democracy 40, 113–15, 116, 156; of identity 95; Laclau's Argentinian experiences 2, 54–5; and language 218, 222; political theory in *HSS* 42, 49–50; politics of becoming 9, 175–9; politics of emancipation 183–8; politics of production 43; as the real of philosophy 73–87; 'singularity' and the *subaltern* 68, *see also* democracy
'The politics of rhetoric' (Laclau) (essay) 218, 219, 223, 224
popular struggles 40, 46
populism 246
positivity *see* negativity
possible/impossible 219, 220
post-foundationalism 55, 58, 69; and antagonism 99
post-Marxism 125–9, 138
post-structuralism 5, 35–6, 42, 97–8, 339–40; conceptions of democracy 151–61
potentiality/actuality 63, 247
practical reason 171
pragmatic discourse 146
praxis, and technical-instrumental behaviour 47, 308–9
production, politics of 43
psychic division/psychic reality 99, 100
psychoanalysis/psychoanalytic theory 213, 301, 304, 314–16, 326

quasi-transcendentals 342

racism 211, 246
radical contingency 58–62, 335
radical democracy 116, 135, 137–9, 270–1, 295, 296–8; and decision-making 140, 141; and plural democracy 4, 41, 42–3, 55; and politics of emancipation 183–4; poststructuralist conceptions of 151–9; and theory of emancipation 196
radical investment 287–95
Rancière, Jacques 152, 153–4, 184
rational consensus 146–8; and approximation 148–9
rationalism: and concepts of universality 18–19; of Hegel 43; instrumental rationality 125–9, 135–9, 291
reactivation/sedimentation 185, 197, 263
the real/reality: and the ethical 288; and the ideal in democracy 148–51; negative dimensions of 203–6; of politics 80–4; positive dimensions of 206–13
realism/nominalism 90
rearticulation 339
Reasonable Democracy (Chambers) 142–3, 144, 145, 148–50, 157
Reflexions sur la violence (Sorel) 221
reflexive judgement 83–4, 311–13
Rehg, William 148
relative universality 281
religion *see* faiths
representation 297–8, 320, 335
The Republic (Plato) 129
revisionism 37
revolution, anachronistic language of 191
revolutionary conservatism 183
revolutionary general strike 221, 222
rhetoric 306–7, 326
rhetorical theory 218, 219, 221
Riha, Rado 8, 73–86, 311–13
Rousseau, J.J., *Social Contract* 222
rule/rules: decision rules and ongoing processes 148–51; of discourse 142–3, 147, 148–51; in language 90–2

Sameness 85
Sanders, Lynn M. 143, 144, 150, 151, 154
Saussure, Ferdinand de 54, 59, 219, 301, 302
Schor, Naomi 95, 101, 103, 106
Schürmann, Reiner 62–3
Scott, Joan 103
secularism: and the ethical 293; and universality 19–20, 29–30
sedimentation: and reactivation 185, 197, 263; social 116, 269
self-determination 321
self-reference 231, 232, 320–1
sexual difference 103–6
'Signature, event, context' (Derrida) (essay) 335
signification: and equivalence 24, 25, 59; and *jouissance* 299–304; limits of 203, 205–6, 250; and radical contingency 62; signs 343; and the universal 27, 33

signifier: emancipation as 185–8; materiality of 191, 192–3; and the signified 293, 302, *see also* empty signifier
signs 343
singular/absolute 65–8, 310–11
singular/universal 77–8, 79, 194, 311, 317
singularity 67–8, 74, 84–5
Smith, Anne Marie 263
the social: and logic of equivalence 23, 39–40, 266–7; and politics of emancipation 185–6; politics and the political 242
social antagonism *see* antagonism
Social Contract (Rousseau) 222
social imaginary 261
social plurality 99
social practice 267
social sedimentation 116, 269
social structures 265–9
socialism: deconstruction of 35–6; and universality 19–20, *see also* Marx
society 265–9; hegemony, politics and democracy 114–15; instrumentalizing of 128; and language 266–7; social link as libidinal link 326, *see also* community
sociology 42
Sorel, Georges 37, 46–7; *Reflexions sur la violence* 221
Spaltung 99, 260, 314
spectrality, logic of 190
Stace, W.T. 292
Stäheli, Urs 9, 226–40, 236, 318–20
statements: discursive 227–9; Foucault's definition of 228–9
Staten, Henry 91, 92
Stavrakakis, Yannis 206; and Glynos, Jason 9, 299–303
strategy/strategic thought 55–6
structure 339; and agency 264–5; social structures 265–9; and subjectivity 322
'Structure, sign and play' (Derrida) (essay) 339
struggles, popular and democratic 40, 46
subaltern 68
the subject: and decision-making 223–4; and discourse 39; and the ethical decision 133; and identity 5–6; instrumentalizing of 127; as lack 5; Laclau's theory of 223–4; location of, and dislocation 187; and philosophy/politics relationships 73, 74–80, 84
subjectivity: and decision-making 264–5; and ethics/morality 130; political, and hegemonic practices 263–5; and structure 322; theories of 259, 260
The Sublime Object of Ideology (Žižek) 212
subversion 47–8, 59, 62
Šumič, Jelica 9, 182–97, 316–18, 322
supplementarity 141, 147, 223
the symbolic: emptiness, and the ethical 132; and jouissance 206, 209, 299; the Real and reality 205, 206; symbolic order 315
system: and discourse theory 320; of dispersion 227, 228; and environment 235, 236; hegemony and antagonism 249–52; systematicity of 229–30; systematizing differences 248–9
systems theory, and antagonism 234–6, 251–2

Tarrying with the Negative (Žižek) 211
Television (Lacan) 211
tempo 178–9, 261
temporality 194, 340
theism/nontheism 174–5
Togliatti, P. 218–19
the transcendental/quasi-transcendentals 342
transgression 227, 229–32
tropology 218, 220, 309, 313
Tully, James 143

the universal: and democracy 105, 154–9; and discursivity 311–18; and dislocation 193–4; and emptiness 20, 27–33, 95–102, 243, 279–85; and empty signifier 281–2, 283; and hegemony 114, 156–8; hegemony and emancipation 190–1, 194–6; and philosophy/politics relationships 73, 74–80, 85; politics and emancipation 190–1, 194–6; problem of 89–93; 'return to', and a 'new' universal 88–9; and signification 27, 33; true and false universal 96, *see also* universality
universal-particular 6–7, 18–19, 25–6, 27, 31–2, 282–3; and language games 92–3; limits of particularism 93–5;

and politics as the real of philosophy 73–4, 85–6; relation between, and 'universals' 89–93; and sexual difference 103–6; and singular-absolute 65–8, 310–11, *see also* universality
'Universalism, particularism and the question of Identity' (Laclau) (essay): Riha's commentary on 73–80; Riha's interpretation of 80–6
universality 17–34; abandonment of 20–1; and deliberative democracy 144–5, 155–6; and the ethical 132; hegemonic universality 114; and hegemony 26–7, 93; indispensibility of 21, 22; meanings of 282–3; moral universalism 129–30; and particularism 6–7, 18–19, 25–6, 27, 31–2, 282–3; reformulation of 22–4, 93; universalism, democracy and hegemony 154–9; Western universalism 75, 76, 77, *see also* the universal; universal-particular
'universalization principle' 145
US Constitution, Equal Protection Clause 330
utilitarianism 130

violence 221

Western universalism 75, 76, 77; Eurocentricism 19, 23, 32–3, 75–6, 95
White, S.K 145, 146
'Why do empty signifiers matter to politics?' (Laclau) (essay) 218
Wittgenstein, Ludwig: *Philosophical Investigations* 90–2, 120; *Tractatus* 120
Wolf, Eric 260
The Wretched of the Earth (Fanon) 298

Young, Iris Marion 143, 144

Zac, Lilian: and Laclau 28, 62–3, 98; 'Minding the gap' (essay) 20
Zarathustra 175
Zerilli, Linda 8, 88–108, 313–16
Žižek, Slavoj 5, 211, 259, 312, 343; on antagonism 97, 98, 99, 100, 206, 237, 239, 245–6, 314; and Butler 6, 9–10, 57, 117, 202–3; *Contingency, Hegemony, Universality* (Butler, Laclau and Žižek) 6, 21, 27–8; on democracy 152, 155; on the empty universal 243; on *Hegemony and Socialist Strategy* 259–60; on *jouissance* 210, 212, 213; on the master signifier 208; on name/naming 312, 343; and politics 315; on subjectivity 264; *Tarrying with the Negative* 211–12; *The Sublime Object of Ideology* 212
'Zur Kritik der Gewalt' (Benjamin) (essay) 221